THE
GREEN MOUNTAIN

WOOD PELLET GRILL

COOKBOOK FOR
BEGINNERS

FOR REAL MASTERS. 600 DELICIOUS RECIPES AND TECHNIQUES TO SMOKE MEATS, FISH, AND VEGETABLES LIKE A PRO

JAMES LOEFFLER

CONTENTS

SEAFOOD RECIPES 47

APPETIZERS AND SNACKS **74**

COCKTAILS RECIPES..**82**

PORK RECIPES 96

POULTRY RECIPES...127

7

VEGETABLES RECIPES

BEEL LAMB AND GAME RECIPES

RECIPE INDEX

INTRODUCTION

How the Green Mountain Wood Pellet Grill Works

Because pellet grills can perform so many cooking functions and require little to no monitoring, you might expect them to operate using complicated technology. In reality, wood pellet smokers are simple, straightforward cooking tools that are easy and safe to operate.

The following parts of a pellet grill work together to help you achieve a delicious, evenly cooked meal:

1. **Wood Pellets:** Pellets are small cylindrical food-grade wood that act as fuel for a pellet grill. Some wood pellets come from flavored woods, like apple or hickory, which add layers of flavor to food.

2. **Hopper:** The hopper is the vessel that holds the pellets, keeping them dry until they are ready for use.

3. **Auger:** Once you start the grill, the auger moves wood pellets from the hopper onto the firepot.

4. **Firepot:** The firepot is exactly what you expect — the place where the fire ignites, using the wood pellets for fuel.

5. **Induction fan:** The induction fan keeps the fire going and circulates the heat and smoke throughout your pellet grill and into your food.

6. **Controller:** The controller is on the outside of the pellet grill, and it is where you set and monitor the cooking temperature and pellet grill heating. Every smoker is different, so keep in mind some models may offer more precise control than others.

7. **Drip tray:** You'll find the drip tray between the cooking grates and the grill's inner workings. This tray collects any grease or food drippings, so they don't fall into the fire, and keeps food safe from direct heat.

To use a pellet grill, you fill the hopper with wood pellets marked safe for pellet grills. Follow manufacturer guidelines and be careful not to overfill or underfill your smoker. Once the pellets are in the hopper, use the digital controller to set your desired temperature. The induction fan will keep the fire going while your pellets move through the auger into the firepot. As the wood pellets ignite, the hot smoke circulates back through the grill to create a flavorful cooking chamber.

The Benefits of Choosing the Green Mountain Wood Pellet Grill

1. Amazing Versatility

One of the best features of having a pellet grill is its versatility.

A traditional charcoal grill or gas grill simply doesn't compare when cooking with pellets, as with this grill you are also able to smoke, braise, bake, roast, and sear your food.

This means you can have the chance to cook a lot more varieties of food and try out different recipes and cooking styles, including smoked meat which totally eliminates the need for a separate smoker.

The temperature is also a benefit of using a pellet grill as they mostly feature precision temperature control systems which can range from around 180 degrees to 500 degrees.

2. ADDS GREAT FLAVOR

If you haven't already heard, one of the main benefits of having a pellet grill is the quality and flavor food that you can prepare when using it.

Sometimes, when using more traditional grills, they can tend to leave quite a smoky or chemical taste on the meat after it's been smoked. With pellet grills, however, the addition of smoking with pellets can make a big difference to the final flavor.

This is because the wood pellets used really help to flavor the meat, a whole lot better than when cooking over gas and charcoal.

Wood pellets also come in various different flavors, such as apple, peach, mesquite, pecan, oak, cherry, maple and hickory, which can all really make a difference to your meals.

These pellets can also be mixed and matched as you like, allowing you to discover the perfect flavor for your taste buds.

In fact, many professional chefs opt for wood when cooking as it provides the best flavor possible. Therefore, if it is top flavor you are after, a pellet grill is your best option.

3. EASY TO USE

When it comes to cooking with a pellet grill, there are more advantages yet again.

Although some people may at first seem intimidated by their versatile design, they are actually not difficult to operate at all and in fact very easy to use.

Quite a few of the more recent grill styles have integrated one button start up controls, which means they will be super easy to get working.

As previously mentioned, the temperature control systems on a pellet grill is a lot better than more traditional ones.

These grills will be able to control the temperature throughout the entire cooking process, meaning all you will have to do is place the meat down and let the grill do its job.

They work similar to a convection oven, in that you won't need to fear your food ever being cooked uneven. This definitely helps to give the BBQ chef complete peace of mind!

Most pellet grills also feature flare prevention, which can stop any troubling flare-ups from occurring.

Hints on Using Your Green Mountain Wood Pellet Grill

1. Allow yourself some time to get acquainted with your new grill/smoker.

Allow yourself some time to get acquainted with your new grill/smoker. We know you'll be anxious to try it out, but don't be overly ambitious. Instead of a whole brisket, which could take 15 hours or more, or a budget-busting prime rib roast, start with chicken (parts, such as breasts or wings, or a whole bird), pork loin tenderloin, or blade (shoulder) steaks, Cornish hens, salmon steaks or fillets, or other relatively inexpensive cuts that can be completed in 2 hours or less.

2. Identify any hot spots—most grills have them.

Identify any hot spots—most grills have them. Preheat your grill to medium-high as directed by the owner's manual, then lay slices of cheap white bread shoulder to shoulder across the grate. Watch carefully, then flip after a few minutes. Take a photo of the results. The darkest bread will indicate where the temperature might be hotter. (Print the photo out and add it to your owner's manual for reference.)

3. Don't let your meat come to room temperature before cooking.

Whatever meat you select, put it on the preheated grill/smoker straight from the refrigerator. Do not, as many recipes suggest, allow it to come to room temperature before cooking.

As Steven often notes, high-end steak houses do not leave their meats out at room temperature. (The danger area is 40 to 140 degrees.) The heat of the grill is sufficient to raise the internal temperature of the meat by those few degrees.

4. Invest in a good meat thermometer.

A laser-type thermometer such as this one will give you a more accurate temperature reading at grill level than a built-in dome thermometer. Determine the temperature range of your grill model from lowest to highest (180 degrees to 500+, for example).

5. Take advantage of your pellet grill's searing capabilities.

Many pellet grills feature searing capabilities, meaning they can reach temperatures over 500 degrees. Again, check your owner's manual for information

Cleaning Methods for the Green Mountain Wood Pellet Grill

A clean grill is a safe appliance that makes delicious food as a bonus. Before you begin your search for kitchen items to clean your grill, you should know some general grill cleaning tips.

1. Clean and scrape grates while they're still warm: Warm residue is easier to clean than dry, stuck-on grease. If you go with this method, be extra careful while handling your grill grates. Use protective gloves and be sure the DIY grill cleaner you're using isn't flammable if you're working with a warm grill.

2. Give it a quick clean after every use: You don't need to do a deep clean every time you grill out. But a once-over scrub after using it can save you from painstaking scraping later.

3. Do deep cleans depending on your usage: In general, you should do a deep clean every couple of months. If you use your grill more often, consider a deep clean once a month. If you hardly use your grill — but let's be real, we're using it all the time — every few months will suffice.

4. Deep clean a cool grill: If you have to get deep into your grill to clean it, make sure it's had a chance to cool. If you're cleaning up charcoal or pellet ash, be sure the material isn't still warm before taking a shop vacuum to it.

Along with those grill cleaning tips, some preventive measures can save you from dealing with a gunked-up grill. Be sure to:
➢ Cover surfaces with aluminum foil.
➢ Use a grill pan or basket.
➢ Use cooking oil, either on the grates or the food itself.
➢ Clean out ashes from pellets or charcoal.
➢ Use a grill cover when you aren't cooking.

BAKING RECIPES

Double Chocolate Chip Brownie Pie

Servings: 8-12
Cooking Time: 45 Minutes

Ingredients:
- 1/2 Cup Semisweet Chocolate Chips
- 1 Cup butter
- 1 Cup brown sugar
- 1 Cup sugar
- 4 Whole eggs
- 2 Teaspoon vanilla extract
- 2 Cup all-purpose flour
- 333/500 Cup Cocoa Powder, Unsweetened
- 1 Teaspoon baking soda
- 1 Teaspoon salt
- 1 Cup Semisweet Chocolate Chips
- 3/4 Cup White Chocolate Chips
- 3/4 Cup Nuts (optional)
- 1 Whole Hot Fudge Sauce, 8oz
- 2 Tablespoon Guinness Beer

Directions:
1. Coat the inside of a 10-inch (25 cm) pie plate with non-stick cooking spray.
2. When ready to cook, set the grill temperature to 350°F (180 C)and preheat, lid closed for 15 minutes.
3. Melt 1/2 cup (100 g) of the semi sweet chocolate chips in the microwave. Cream together butter, brown sugar and granulated sugar. Beat in the eggs, adding one at a time and mixing after each egg, and the vanilla. Add in the melted chocolate chips.
4. On a large piece of wax paper, sift together the cocoa powder, flour, baking soda and salt. Lift up the corners of the paper and pour slowly into the butter mixture.
5. Beat until the dry ingredients are just incorporated. Stir in the remaining semi sweet chocolate chips, white chocolate chips, and the nuts. Press the dough into the prepared pie pan.
6. Place the brownie pie on the grill and bake for 45-50 minutes or until the pie is set in the middle. Rotate the pan halfway through cooking. If the top or edges begin to brown, cover the top with a piece of aluminum foil.
7. In a microwave-safe measuring cup, heat the fudge sauce in the microwave. Stir in the Guinness.
8. Once the brownie pie is done, allow to sit for 20 minutes. Slice into wedges and top with the fudge sauce. Enjoy.

Chocolate Almond Cake

Servings: 8

Cooking Time: 50 Minutes

Ingredients:
- 7 oz good quality dark chocolate; melted
- 5 eggs; separated
- Pinch salt
- 6.5 oz caster sugar
- 7 oz butter; cubed at room temperature
- 7 oz ground almonds
- 1 oz cocoa powder
- 1 tsp. baking powder
- Icing sugar; for dusting

Directions:
1. Supply your smoker with wood pellets and follow the start-up procedure. Preheat the grill, with the lid closed, to 347 °F.
2. Beat together the butter and sugar until light and fluffy. Then beat in the yolks, one at a time.
3. Gently fold in the almonds.
4. Add the melted chocolate and mix well.
5. Beat the egg whites with a pinch of salt in a separate bowl until stiff.
6. Sift the baking powder and cocoa powder into the cake mix and fold in gently, then fold in the egg whites.
7. Pour the mix into an 8.5" round spring form cake tin (greased and lined), smooth over, and bake in the center of the grill for about 50 minutes. If the top starts to dry out after 25-30 minutes, cover with foil.

Onion Cheese Nachos

Servings: 6
Cooking Time: 10 Minutes

Ingredients:
- 1 Pound Beef, Ground
- 3 Cups Cheddar Cheese, Shredded
- 1 Green Bell Pepper, Diced
- 1/2 Cup Green Onion
- 1/2 Cup Red Onion, Diced
- 1 Large Bag Tortilla Chip

Directions:
1. Supply your smoker with wood pellets and follow the start-up procedure. Preheat the grill, with the lid closed, to 350° F.
2. While you're waiting, empty a large bag of nacho chips evenly onto a cast iron pan. Start loading up with toppings - cooked ground beef, red onion, red pepper, cheese, green onions. These are just the toppings we had on hand, so feel free to add anything you like! Make sure you do a couple layers of chips so everyone

gets a good serving of nachos. And don't be skimpy with the cheese - lay it on heavy!

3. Place your loaded nachos on the grill and let the hot smoke melt your toppings into one cheesy creation. Heat at 350°F for 10 minutes or until the cheese has fully melted. Remove and serve with sour-cream and salsa.

Grilled Beer Cheese Dip

Servings: 6
Cooking Time: 20 Minutes

Ingredients:
- 6 Oz Beer, Can
- 8 Oz Cream Cheese
- 1 Tsp Onion Powder
- ½ Tsp Pepper
- ½ Tsp Salt
- 2 Cups Shredded Cheese

Directions:
1. Supply your smoker with wood pellets and follow the start-up procedure. Preheat the grill, with the lid closed, to 350° F. If you're using a gas or charcoal grill, set it up for medium high heat. Preheat with lid closed for 10-15 minutes.
2. In the cast iron pan add cream cheese, shredded cheese, beer, onion powder, salt and pepper. Once grill is at 350°F place cast iron skillet onto the grill and cook for about 10 minutes, stir and cook for another 5-10 minutes.
3. Top with more shredded cheese and fresh parsley. Serve with fresh baked pretzels as well.

Sourdough Pizza

Servings: 4
Cooking Time: 12 Minutes

Ingredients:
- 1 1/2 Cup Fresh Sourdough Starter
- 1 Tablespoon olive oil
- 1 Teaspoon Jacobsen Salt Co. Pure Kosher Sea Salt
- 1 1/4 Cup all-purpose flour

Directions:
1. Supply your smoker with wood pellets and follow the start-up procedure. Preheat the grill, with the lid closed, to 450° F.
2. Mix together the fresh sourdough starter, one tablespoon of oil, Jacobsen salt and 1-1/4 cups of flour. Add more flour, a little at a time, as needed to form a pizza dough consistency.
3. Allow the dough to rest for 30 minutes, to allow for easier rolling. Roll the dough out into a circle, using a small amount of flour to prevent sticking.
4. Place on a pizza stone. Bake the crust for approximately 7 minutes Grill: 450 °F

5. Remove the crust from the grill; brush on remaining oil to prevent toppings from soaking into the crust. Add the desired toppings and return pizza to grill; bake until the crust browns and the cheese melts.

Rosemary Cranberry Apple Sage Stuffing

Servings: 7
Cooking Time: 45 Minutes

Ingredients:
- 10 Cups Day Old Diced Bread, Sliced Loaf
- 2 1/2 Cups Broth, Chicken
- 1 Cup Butter, Unsalted
- 1 Cup Diced Celery, Cut
- 1 1/2 Cups Fresh Cranberries
- 1 Beaten Egg
- 1 Medium Granny Smith Apple, Peel, Core And Dice
- 2 Tbsp Minced Parsley, Fresh
- 1 Tbsp Minced Rosemary, Fresh
- 2 Tbsp Roughly Chopped Sage
- Salt And Pepper
- 1 Tbsp Minced Thyme
- 2 Cups Diced Yellow Onion, Sliced

Directions:
1. Supply your smoker with wood pellets and follow the start-up procedure. Preheat the grill, with the lid closed, to 350° F.
2. Melt butter over medium heat. Add onions then celery and cook until onions start to become translucent.
3. In a large bowl, mix together bread, apples, cranberries, cooked onion and celery mixture, and fresh herbs.
4. Add half of the chicken broth to the mixture and stir.
5. Beat together eggs and the rest of the chicken broth in a small bowl. Pour into the bread mixture and stir until completely combined.
6. Add salt and pepper to taste.
7. Pour stuffing into a cast iron pan or baking dish. Cover with foil and bake on the grill for 30 minutes. Remove the foil and cook for an additional 15 minutes.
8. Serve immediately and enjoy!

Baked Peach Cobbler Cupcakes

Servings: 8
Cooking Time: 30 Minutes

Ingredients:
- 2 Large Peaches, fresh
- 3/4 Cup sugar
- 2 Teaspoon lemon juice
- 1/2 Teaspoon ground cinnamon
- Yellow Cake Mix, Boxed

- 1 Can vanilla icing

Directions:

1. Bring a pot of water to a boil. Turn peaches upside down and cut a small shallow X across the bottom. Put peaches in boiling water and boil for 1 minute to help loosen the skin.
2. Drain the peaches into a colander and rinse off with cold water. Peel skin off peaches.
3. Filling: Dice peaches and place into a large pan. Cook peaches over medium heat. As it starts to sizzle, add sugar, lemon and cinnamon. Cook mixture on medium heat for 10-15 minutes until a majority of the juice from the peaches evaporates leaving a thick syrup.
4. Transfer to a bowl to cool.
5. Supply your smoker with wood pellets and follow the start-up procedure. Preheat the grill, with the lid closed, to 350° F.
6. Cupcakes: Follow the directions on box cake mix and put the mixture into cupcake pan with liners.
7. When grill has preheated, bake cupcakes for 13-16 minutes, until a light golden brown. Grill: 350 °F
8. When cupcakes have cooled, use a piping bag to pipe the peach cobbler mixture into the middle of the cupcake.
9. Ice with your favorite vanilla icing. Enjoy!

Dark Chocolate Brownies With Bacon-salted Caramel

Servings: 8
Cooking Time: 40 Minutes

Ingredients:

- 8 Strips bacon
- 1/2 Cup kosher salt
- 1 Whole Brownie Mix
- 1 Jar caramel sauce

Directions:

1. For the bacon salt: Cook a few strips of bacon (6 to 8) until very crisp: 350 degrees for about 25 minutes should do it. Let cool, then pulse in a food processor until finely chopped. Mix with 1/2 cup kosher salt. Store in the refrigerator until ready to use.
2. Supply your smoker with wood pellets and follow the start-up procedure. Preheat the grill, with the lid closed, to 350° F.
3. Mix the brownies according to package directions and pour into a greased pan. Drizzle approximately 2 tablespoons of the caramel sauce over the brownie batter. Sprinkle with approximately 1 teaspoon of the bacon salt. Place directly on the grill grate of your preheated Traeger.
4. Bake the brownies for 20-25 minutes, until the batter has started to set up. Remove from the grill and drizzle with 2 more tablespoons of caramel sauce and sprinkle with more bacon salt.

Return to the grill for 20-25 more minutes, or until a toothpick inserted in the middle of the brownies comes out clean.
5. If you like extra caramel, drizzle another layer of caramel on the hot brownies and sprinkle with a final bit of bacon salt. Allow the brownies to cool completely before cutting them into squares. Clean your knife in between each slice to prevent the brownies from sticking to the knife. Enjoy!

Smoker Wheat Bread

Servings: 6
Cooking Time: 60 Minutes

Ingredients:

- As Needed extra-virgin olive oil
- 2 Cup all-purpose flour
- 1 Cup whole wheat flour
- 1 1/4 Ounce Packet, Active Dry Yeast
- 1 1/4 Teaspoon salt
- 1 1/2 Cup water
- As Needed Cornmeal

Directions:

1. Oil a large mixing bowl and set aside. In a second mixing bowl, combine the flours, yeast, and salt.
2. Push your sleeve up to your elbow and form your fingers into a claw. Mix the dry ingredients until well-combined.
3. Add the water and mix until blended. The dough will be wet, shaggy, and somewhat stringy.
4. Tip the dough into the oiled mixing bowl and cover with plastic wrap.
5. Allow the dough to rise at room temperature-- about 70 degrees-- for 2 hours, or until the surface is bubbled.
6. Turn the dough out onto a lightly floured work surface and lightly flour the top. With floured hands, fold the dough over on itself twice. Cover loosely with plastic wrap and allow the dough to rest for 15 minutes.
7. Dust a clean lint-free cotton towel with cornmeal, wheat bran, or flour. With floured hands, gently form the dough into a ball and place it, seam side down, on the towel.
8. Dust the top of the ball with cornmeal, wheat bran, or flour, and cover the dough with a second towel. Let the dough rise until doubled in size; the dough will not spring back when poked with a finger.
9. In the meantime, start the smoker grill and set temperature to 450 F. Preheat, lid closed, for 10-15 minutes.
10. Put a lidded 6- to 8-quart cast iron Dutch oven - preferably one coated with enamel, on the grill grate.
11. When the dough has risen, remove the top towel, slide your hand under the bottom towel to support the dough, then carefully tip the dough, seam side up, into the preheated pot.

12. Remove the towel. Shake the pot a couple of times if the dough looks lopsided: It will straighten out as it bakes.

13. Cover the pot with the lid and bake the bread for 30 minutes. Remove the lid and continue to bake the bread for 15 to 30 minutes more, or until it is nicely browned and sounds hollow when rapped with your knuckles.

14. Turn onto a wire rack to cool. Slice with a serrated knife. Enjoy!

Delicious Pellet Grill Cornbread

Servings: 6
Cooking Time: 35 Minutes

Ingredients:

- 1 cup flour
- 1 cup cornmeal
- 2 teaspoons baking powder
- 2 teaspoons salt
- 3/4 cup sugar
- 2 tablespoons honey
- 1/2 cup butter
- 1 cup sour cream
- 3 eggs
- 1 cup milk

Directions:

1. Supply your smoker with wood pellets and follow the start-up procedure. Preheat the grill, with the lid closed, to 350° F.
2. Grease a 12-inch cast iron skillet or an equivalent baking pan.
3. Add flour, cornmeal, baking powder, salt, sugar, honey, butter, sour cream, eggs, and milk into a mixing bowl.
4. Mix well then pour into pan and bake on the grill for 30-35 minutes or until the cornbread is baked through in the center.

Blueberry Pancakes

Servings: 4
Cooking Time: 10 Minutes

Ingredients:

- 2 Cups Blueberries, Fresh
- 1 Cup Pancake Mix
- 1/2 Cup Sugar
- 3/4 Cup Water, Warm

Directions:

1. Supply your smoker with wood pellets and follow the start-up procedure. Preheat the grill, with the lid closed, to 350° F.
2. Place the cast iron griddle on the grates of your grill.
3. In a large bowl, pour water, pancake mix and 1/2 cup of the blueberries and mix until combined.
4. Pour the batter onto the griddle in 4 equal parts. Cook with the lid closed for about 6 minutes, or until the edges of the

pancakes are slightly cooked. Flip each pancake and continue cooking for another 4 minutes.

5. Pour the hot blueberry sauce over your freshly cooked pancakes and enjoy!

Grilled Apple Pie

Servings: 4
Cooking Time: 40 Minutes

Ingredients:

- 5 Whole Apples
- 1/4 Cup sugar
- 1 Tablespoon cornstarch
- 1 Whole refrigerated pie crust
- 1/4 Cup Peach, preserves

Directions:

1. Supply your smoker with wood pellets and follow the start-up procedure. Preheat the grill, with the lid closed, to 375° F. In a medium bowl, mix the apples, sugar, and cornstarch; set aside.
2. Unroll pie crust. Place in ungreased pie pan. With the back of a spoon, spread preserves evenly on crust. Arrange the apple slices in an even layer in the pie pan. Slightly fold crust over filling.
3. Place a baking sheet upside down on the grill grate to make an elevated surface. Put the pan with pie on top so it is elevated off grill. (This will help prevent the bottom from overcooking.) Cook the pie for 30 to 40 minutes or until crust is golden brown, the filling is bubbly. Grill: 375 ˚F
4. Remove from grill; cool 10 minutes before serving. Enjoy!
*Cook times will vary depending on set and ambient temperatures.

Garlic Lemon Pepper Chicken Wings

Servings: 4
Cooking Time: 30 Minutes

Ingredients:

- 1/4 Cup Black Peppercorns, Ground
- 4 Pounds Chicken, Wing
- 2 Tsp Coriander, Ground
- 2 Tsp Garlic Powder
- 2-3 Tbsp Lemon, Zest
- 1 Tsp Salt, Kosher
- 3 Tsp Dried Thyme, Fresh Sprigs

Directions:

1. Supply your smoker with wood pellets and follow the start-up procedure. Preheat the grill, with the lid closed, to 400° F.
2. In a bowl, begin to mix the ground pepper and zest of the lemon together, then add the rest of the ingredients.
3. Place the wings in a bowl and toss with a little olive oil, add a few tablespoons of the seasoning, toss with your hands, then repeat until the wings are well seasoned to your liking.

4. Place the wings on the grill, and cook them for about 15 minutes, then flip and grill for another 15 minutes.

5. Continue to flip the wings, until they are done and crispy. Remove the wings from the grill, and serve.

Basil Margherita Pizza

Servings: 6
Cooking Time: 25 Minutes

Ingredients:
- Basil, Chopped
- 2 Cups Flour, All-Purpose
- Mozzarella Cheese, Sliced Rounds
- 1 Cup Pizza Sauce
- 1 Teaspoon Salt
- 1 Teaspoon Sugar
- 1 Tomato, Sliced
- 1 Cup Water, Warm
- 1 Teaspoon Yeast, Instant

Directions:

1. Combine the water, yeast, and sugar in a small bowl and let sit for about 5 minutes.

2. In a large bowl, stir together the flour and salt. Pour in the yeast mixture and mix until a soft dough forms. Knead for about 2 minutes. Place in an oiled bowl and cover with a cloth. Let the dough sit and rise for about 45 minutes or until the dough has doubled in size.

3. Roll out on a flat, floured surface (or on a pizza stone) until you"ve reached your desired shape and thickness.

4. Supply your smoker with wood pellets and follow the start-up procedure. Preheat the grill, with the lid closed, to 350° F.

5. On the rolled out dough, pour on the pizza sauce, cheese, and then tomatoes and basil. Place in your Grill and bake for about 25 minutes, or until the cheese is melted and slightly golden brown.

Cherry Ice Cream Cobbler

Servings: 8
Cooking Time: 45 Minutes

Ingredients:
- 1 Tsp Baking Powder
- 3 Tbsp Butter, Melted
- 1 Cup Flour
- Ice Cream, Prepared
- 1/4 Tsp Salt
- 3/4 Cup Sugar
- 1/2 Cup Milk

Directions:

1. Supply your smoker with wood pellets and follow the start-up procedure. Preheat the grill, with the lid closed, to 350° F.

2. In a bowl, combine flour, sugar, baking powder, salt and mix to incorporate. Stir in butter and milk and mix until combined. In a cast iron pan, dump in cherry pie filling and pile on the prepared topping to cover.

3. Place in your Grill and bake for about 45 minutes, or until the topping is golden brown.

4. Let cool for a couple minutes and serve with ice cream.

Irish Soda Bread

Servings: 8-12
Cooking Time: 45 Minutes

Ingredients:
- As Needed Cornmeal
- 3 1/2 Cup all-purpose flour
- 1 1/2 Teaspoon sugar
- 1 1/4 Teaspoon baking soda
- 1 Teaspoon salt
- 1 Cup buttermilk
- To Taste butter

Directions:

1. When ready to cook, set the temperature to 400F (205 C) and preheat, lid closed, for 10 to 15 minutes.

2. Lightly dust the bottom of an 8-inch (20-cm) round cake pan with cornmeal and set aside.

3. Tear off a large sheet of wax paper and lay it on your work surface.

4. Combine the flour, sugar, soda, and salt in a large sifter and sift onto the wax paper. Carefully lift up the sides of the wax paper and tip the flour mixture back into the sifter. Re-sift into a large mixing bowl.

5. Lightly flour your work surface. Make a well in the middle of the flour mixture in the bowl and pour in 1 cup (240 mL) of buttermilk. Stir with a wooden spoon. Work quickly and gently as the carbon dioxide bubbles formed when the buttermilk hits the dry ingredients will deflate, the dough will look somewhat shaggy. If the dough seems dryish, add a little more buttermilk.

6. Turn out onto the floured surface, and with floured hands, knead gently for 10 to 20 seconds - just long enough to bring the dough bits together. (It will look more like biscuit dough than bread dough.)

7. Form into a flattish round and transfer to the prepared pan. Flour a sharp knife, and deeply cut a cross in the top of the loaf all the way to the edge of the bread. Quickly get it in to bake, if it sits too long, it will deflate.

8. Bake the bread for 45 to 50 minutes, or until it is browned and the bottom of the loaf sounds hollow when rapped with your knuckles.

9. Remove the bread from the baking pan and cool on a cooling rack. Just be-fore serving, cut the loaf in half and then slice each half into thin slices.

10. Serve with butter. Wrap leftovers tightly in plastic wrap or foil. This bread makes great toast. Enjoy!

Baked Parker House Rolls

Servings: 8
Cooking Time: 15 Minutes

Ingredients:
- 1/2 Ounce (2 packets) active dry yeast
- 6 Tablespoon plus 1 teaspoon cane sugar
- 1 Cup warm water (110°F to 115°F)
- 5 Cup all-purpose flour, plus more as needed
- 2 Teaspoon salt
- 1 Cup warm milk (110°-115°F)
- 1 Large eggs
- oil
- 4 Tablespoon melted butter, divided
- 1 Tablespoon Maldon Sea Salt Flakes
- 2 Tablespoon poppy seeds
- 2 Tablespoon white sesame seeds
- 1 Tablespoon garlic flakes

Directions:
1. Place the yeast, 1 teaspoon of cane sugar and warm water in a mixing bowl or the base of a stand mixer. Stir to combine. Allow the yeast to proof for 5 minutes- it should start to bubble a bit, showing that the yeast is alive.

2. Sprinkle the flour, salt and remaining 6 tablespoons of sugar over the yeast mixture. Using a dough hook or a wooden spoon, stir for 30 seconds. Pour in the warm milk and egg.

3. Knead again on the medium-low setting, or on a floured work surface by hand until the dough is very soft, adding up to one more cup of flour so the dough is soft and smooth and has lost its sticky quality.

4. Coat the bowl with a small film of oil and place the dough in the bowl, turning to coat dough evenly with the oil. Cover the bowl with a clean cloth, place in a warm spot in the kitchen and allow to proof about 45 minutes. The dough will almost double in size.

5. Punch down the dough and place on a floured work surface. Divide the dough in half, then divide each half into 12 equal pieces.

6. Using your hands, tuck in the seams of each piece of dough then place the dough on a lightly floured surface.

7. Place your fingers around the piece of dough, and roll it in a circular motion to create a smooth, even ball. Alternately, roll the dough between your two hands to create a round ball shape. Repeat with the remaining 23 pieces.

8. Butter a 9x13 inch baking pan with a tablespoon of the melted butter. Place the dough balls evenly in the pan, creating rows of 4 pieces of dough across and 6 down. Cover again with a clean towel and allow the dough to rise in a warm spot, about 30 minutes longer.

9. While the dough is proofing, supply your smoker with wood pellets and follow the start-up procedure. Preheat the grill, with the lid closed, to 325° F. Brush the remaining 3 tablespoons of butter on the bread and sprinkle with the flake salt, seeds and garlic flakes.

10. Place the pan on the grill, cover and bake about 15 to 20 minutes, or until rolls are lightly browned on top and cooked through. When done, you should be able to pull apart two pieces and see that the dough is cooked and the bottoms are lightly browned. Grill: 325 °F

Strawberry Basil Daiquiri

Servings: 2
Cooking Time: 20 Minutes

Ingredients:
- 4 strawberries, stemmed
- 6 Tablespoon granulated sugar, divided
- 6 basil leaves
- 3 Ounce white rum
- 2 Ounce lime juice
- 1 Ounce Smoked Simple Syrup
- 2 fresh basil leaves, for garnish
- 2 lime slice, for garnish

Directions:
1. Supply your smoker with wood pellets and follow the start-up procedure. Preheat the grill, with the lid closed, to 375° F.

2. Cut strawberries in half and coat in 2 tablespoons granulated sugar. Place directly on grill grate and cook for 15 to 20 minutes. Remove from heat and cool. Grill: 375 °F

3. Add 1 tablespoon granulated sugar and basil leaves to shaking tin and lightly muddle. Add strawberries and muddle again.

4. Pour in white rum, lime juice and Smoked Simple Syrup. Shake with ice.

5. Strain contents into a chilled glass and garnish with large fresh basil leaf and sliced lime. Enjoy!

Baked Green Chile Mac & Cheese By Doug Scheiding

Servings: 8
Cooking Time: 120 Minutes

Ingredients:
- 24 Ounce shredded cheddar cheese, divided
- 8 Ounce mozzarella cheese, shredded

- 6 Tablespoon unsalted butter
- 16 Ounce large dry elbow macaroni noodles
- 2 1/2 Cup half-and-half
- 2 Cup heavy whipping cream
- 8 Ounce cream cheese
- 16 Ounce 505 Southwestern Hatch Valley Flame Roasted Green Chile
- 2 Tablespoon Prime Rib Rub

Directions:

1. Supply your smoker with wood pellets and follow the start-up procedure. Preheat the grill, with the lid closed, to 165° F.

2. Place 16 ounces of the shredded cheddar and the 8 ounces of shredded mozzarella cheese into a shallow pan or cookie sheet and place the pan directly on the grill grate. Smoke for 30 to 40 minutes. Remove from grill and set aside. Grill: 165 °F

3. Increase the grill temperature to 300°F and place a large disposable aluminum half pan in the Traeger with the butter. Remove the pan from the grill after the butter has fully melted. Grill: 300 °F

4. Add the noodles to the pan, along with half-and-half, heavy whipping cream, 16 ounces of the cold smoked cheddar, all of the smoked mozzarella cheese and cream cheese broken into small pieces. Add the green chiles to taste (12 ounces for mild and 16 ounces for spicy) and stir to combine.

5. Place the pan in the grill and bake for 2 hours, stirring every 20 minutes. If macaroni and cheese looks like it is getting dry, add a little more half-and-half and stir to combine. Grill: 300 °F

6. During the last 20 minutes of cooking, sprinkle the remaining (unsmoked) cheddar cheese on top and add a light dusting of Traeger Prime Rib Rub. Serve hot. Enjoy!

Baked Bourbon Monkey Bread

Servings: 6
Cooking Time: 40 Minutes

Ingredients:
- 3 Can Pillsbury Grands Buttermilk Biscuits
- 1 Cup sugar
- 3 Teaspoon ground cinnamon
- 1 Cup Butter, unsalted
- 1 Cup dark brown sugar
- Tablespoon bourbon

Directions:

1. Supply your smoker with wood pellets and follow the start-up procedure. Preheat the grill, with the lid closed, to 350° F.

2. Cut each biscuit into quarters. In a Ziploc bag, combine sugar and cinnamon and add quartered biscuits. Toss to coat in cinnamon sugar.

3. Dump coated biscuit dough into a bundt pan coated with non-stick spray.

4. In a small saucepan, combine the brown sugar, butter, and bourbon. Cook over medium heat until the sugar has dissolved.

5. Pour the butter mixture over the biscuits in the bundt pan.

6. Place in the center of the grill and cook for 40 minutes or until dark golden brown.

7. Let cool on the counter for 5-10 minutes, then flip out onto a serving plate. Enjoy!

Cornbread Chicken Stuffing

Servings: 6 - 8
Cooking Time: 95 Minutes

Ingredients:
- 2 Tbsp Butter
- 1 Cup Chicken Stock
- 6 Cups Cornbread, Cubed
- ½ Cup Dried Cranberries
- 1 Egg
- ½ Cup Heavy Whipping Cream
- 1 Lb. Italian Sausage
- 1 Diced Onion
- 1 ½ Tsp Pulled Pork Rub
- 2 Tbsp Sage, Fresh
- ½ Tsp Fresh Thyme

Directions:

1. Supply your smoker with wood pellets and follow the start-up procedure. Preheat the grill, with the lid closed, to 250° F. If using a gas or charcoal grill, set the temp to low heat.

2. Portion sausage into quarter-size pieces and place on mesh grate. Place grate on the grill and cook for 1 hour. Sausage pieces will have a smoky deep brown color. Move the mesh tray of sausage to the side of the grill with indirect heat.

3. Open the Flame Broiler Plate and increase the temperature to 350°F. Place a large cast iron skillet on the grill, over direct flame. Add butter and onions and cook until the onions caramelize lightly, stirring often. Add the sage and thyme and stir to combine.

4. Gently fold in the dried cranberries and cubed cornbread, then add sausage directly from mesh grate.

5. In a small mixing bowl, whisk together the heavy cream, chicken stock, egg, and Pulled Pork Rub. Pour mixture over the cornbread stuffing mix.

6. Cover grill and cook 30 minutes or until heated through and crispy on top.

Savory Cheesecake With Bourbon Pecan Topping

Servings: 6
Cooking Time: 75 Minutes

Ingredients:

- Crust
- 12 ounce Oreos
- 6 ounce melted butter
- Filling
- 24 ounces cream cheese - room temperature
- 1 cup granulated sugar
- 3 tbs cornstarch
- 2 large eggs
- 2/3 cup heavy cream
- 1 tbs vanilla
- 1 1/2 tbs bourbon
- Topping
- 3 large eggs beaten
- 1/3 cup granulated sugar
- 1/3 cup brown sugar
- 8 tbsp corn syrup dark corn syrup recommended
- 2 tbsp bourbon
- 1/2 tbsp vanilla
- 1/8 tbsp salt
- 3/4 cup rough chopped pecans (smoked pecans recommended)

Directions:

1. Supply your smoker with wood pellets and follow the start-up procedure. Preheat the grill, with the lid closed, to 350 °F.
2. Wrap foil on the bottom and up the sides of a 9" spring-form pan (outside of pan).
3. Butter the bottom & insides of the pan.
4. Crust
5. Throw ingredients in a food processor until they are finely ground.
6. Spread in 9" cheesecake pan on bottom & about ½ way upsides.
7. Filling
8. Place 8 oz of cream cheese in mixer bowl with 1/3 of sugar & cornstarch.Mix until smooth andcreamy.
9. Add another 8 oz cream cheese andbeat until smooth, then add remaining cream cheese,beating until smooth.
10. Then mix in the rest of the sugar, bourbon & vanilla.
11. Add eggs one at a time beating well after each one.
12. Add the heavy cream and mix just until smooth. Reminder: Do not over mix.
13. Pour batter into the prepared crust.
14. Topping
15. Mix all together except pecans.
16. Sprinkle pecans on top of cheesecake batter.
17. Pour topping over cheesecake batter.
18. Place in a pan big enough to hold a spring-form pan. Pour boiling water in the roasting pan to come up about ½ way up the spring-form pan.
19. Bake at 350 °F for 75 minutes until the top just barely jiggles. Carefully take the pan out of water-bath and put on cooling rack.
20. Let cool for 2 hours in pan. After 2 hours put in fridge until totally chilled then serve.

Eyeball Cookies

Servings: 20
Cooking Time: 35 Minutes

Ingredients:

- 2 Packages Candy Eyeballs
- Green, Blue And Purple Food Coloring
- 1 Box Of Yellow Gluten Free Cake Mix
- 1/2 Cup (Optional) Granulated Sugar
- 2 Large Eggs
- 1/3 Cup Powdered Sugar
- 1 Teaspoon Pure Vanilla Extract
- 6 Tablespoon Melted Vegan Butter (Unsalted)

Directions:

1. Supply your smoker with wood pellets and follow the start-up procedure. Preheat the grill, with the lid closed, to 350° F.
2. Line two large baking sheets with parchment paper. In a large bowl, combine cake mix, melted butter, eggs (or egg substitute), powdered sugar, sugar (optional), and vanilla and stir until combined. (substitute 2 flax eggs for Vegan – 1 tbsp flax seed meal and 5 tbsp water per egg).
3. Divide dough between 3 bowls and dye each bowl a different color.(We used green, blue and purple).
4. Roll dough into tablespoon-sized balls.
5. Place about 2" apart on the baking sheet and grill until tops have cracked and the tops look set, 8 to 10 minutes. – Turn half way through baking, after 4-5 minutes.
6. Immediately, while the cookies are still warm, stick candy eyeballs all over the cookies.
7. Let cool completely before serving.

Chocolate Lava Cake With Smoked Whipped Cream

Servings: 4
Cooking Time: 45 Minutes

Ingredients:
- 1 Pint heavy whipping cream
- 9 Tablespoon Butter
- 220 G Semisweet Chocolate
- 1 1/4 Cup powdered sugar
- 2 Large eggs
- 2 egg yolk
- 6 Tablespoon flour
- 1 Tablespoon Bourbon Vanilla
- Powdered Sugar
- cocoa powder

Directions:
1. Supply your smoker with wood pellets and follow the start-up procedure. Preheat the grill, with the lid closed, to 180° F.
2. For the Smoked Whipped Cream: Add cream to a shallow, aluminum baking pan. Place the pan on the grill and smoke for 30 minutes.
3. Pour the smoked cream into a large mixing bowl and refrigerate for later use. Grill: 180 °F
4. Increase the grill temperature to 375°F and preheat. Grill: 375 °F
5. Brush 4 small soufflé cups with 1 tablespoon melted butter.
6. Melt the chocolate and remaining butter in a heatproof bowl over simmering water, stir until smooth.
7. Stir in powdered sugar. Add eggs and egg yolks, stirring continuously. Whisk in flour until blended completely.
8. Pour batter into the prepared soufflé cups. Place them on the Traeger and bake for 13-14 minutes, or until the sides are set. Grill: 375 °F
9. For the Whipped Cream: Remove the chilled smoked cream from the refrigerator, add the bourbon vanilla and whip until airy.
10. Add confectioners sugar and continue whipping until whipped cream forms stiff peaks.
11. Dust lava cakes with confectioners sugar and cocoa, top with a dollop of smoke-infused whipped cream. Enjoy!

Cake With Smoked Berry Sauce

Servings: 12
Cooking Time: 90 Minutes

Ingredients:
- 12 Oz Blackberries
- 18 Oz Blueberries, Fresh
- 1/4 Cup Brown Sugar
- 2 Tsp Cinnamon, Ground
- 4 Eggs
- 2 Tbsp Flour
- 1 3/4 Cup Granulated Sugar
- 1 Lemon, Juice & Zest
- 1/2 Cup Unsalted Butter
- 3.4 Ounce Box Vanilla Instant Pudding Mix
- 3/4 Cup Vegetable Oil
- 3/4 Cup Water
- 1 Cup White Wine
- 1 Box Yellow Cake Mix

Directions:
1. Fire up your Grill and set to Smoke mode. If using a gas or charcoal grill, set it up for low, indirect heat. Supply your smoker with wood pellets and follow the start-up procedure. Preheat the grill, with the lid closed, to 450° F.
2. Place blueberries and blackberries on a sheet tray, then transfer to upper shelf of smoking cabinet. Make sure that the sear slide and side dampers are open, then preheat the grill, with the lid closed, to 375° F, to ensure the cabinet maintains temperature between 225° F and 250° F. Smoke for 30 to 45 minutes.
3. Place cast iron skillet on grill grate. Add sugar, lemon juice and zest, and wine to skillet. Stir with a wooden spoon until sugar dissolves, then add berries from smoking cabinet.
4. Simmer berries for 15 minutes, then remove sauce from grill to cool.
5. While berries are smoking, prepare cake pans and batter. Grease and flour 2 - 9-inch round cake pans. Set aside.
6. In a large mixing bowl, combine cake mix, brown sugar, granulated sugar, pudding mix, cinnamon, eggs, water, oil, and white wine. Using a hand mixer, mix on low speed for 1 minute, then slowly increase mixing speed to high, and beat an additional 2 to 3 minutes, or until batter is smooth.
7. Evenly distribute batter among cake pans, then place pans on grill shelf and bake at 350° F, for 25 to 30 minutes, or until a toothpick inserted comes out clean. Remove from grill and set aside to cool slightly.
8. While cake is cooling, prepare glaze. Melt butter with sugar in a sauce pot on the grill. Stir for 3 minutes, then add wine. Remove from grill and set aside.
9. Turn out cake onto a sheet tray lined with parchment. Use a toothpick to poke holes in the cake, then slowly pour hot glaze over cake.
10. Spread half of smoked berry sauce on top of one layer, then place second cake layer on top. Pour additional sauce on top of cake and dust with powdered sugar, if desired. Serve warm, or room temperature.

Baked Pear Tarte Tatin

Servings: 6
Cooking Time: 45 Minutes

Ingredients:

- 2 1/2 Cup all-purpose flour
- 2 Tablespoon sugar
- butter chilled
- 8 Tablespoon cold water
- 1/4 Cup granulated sugar
- 1/4 Cup butter
- 8 Whole Bartlett Pear

Directions:

1. Supply your smoker with wood pellets and follow the start-up procedure. Preheat the grill, with the lid closed, to 350° F.
2. For the crust: Place flour and sugar in a food processor and pulse to mix. Add butter a little at a time while pulsing. Once it starts to looks like cornmeal, add the water until dough start to come together.
3. Form a round with the dough, wrap in plastic and let it cool in the refrigerator.
4. While dough cools, make the caramel sauce. In a sauce pan, add 1/4 cup granulated sugar and 1/4 cup butter. Cook butter and sugar until it becomes a dark caramel, a couple minutes.
5. Pour caramel in the bottom of 10 inch deep cake pan. While the caramel is still hot, arrange pear wedges in a fan formation covering the caramel.
6. Roll the chilled pie dough into a circle big enough to cover the pan. Prick the pie dough with a fork and cover the pan with the pie dough. Trim the crust leaving room for shrinkage.
7. Place on the grill and bake for 45 minutes or until pears are soft. The pears will be soft and most of the juice will evaporate and thicken.
8. Let sit for 3 minutes. While pan is still hot, place a plate over pie and flip over. Slowly lift the plate.
9. Serve warm, topped with vanilla ice cream or whipped cream. Enjoy!

Baked Molten Chocolate Cake

Servings: 4
Cooking Time: 20 Minutes

Ingredients:

- all-purpose flour
- butter
- 4 Ounce butter
- 6 Ounce Chocolate, Bittersweet
- 2 eggs
- 2 egg yolk
- 1/2 Cup sugar

- 1 Pinch salt

Directions:

1. Supply your smoker with wood pellets and follow the start-up procedure. Preheat the grill, with the lid closed, to 450° F.
2. Butter and flour four (6oz) ramekins. Tap out excess flour. Place ramekins on a baking sheet and reserve.
3. Melt butter and chocolate in a double boiler over simmering water. In a medium bowl, beat eggs and yolks with sugar and salt on high until thick and pale.
4. Whisk in chocolate until smooth and quickly fold into the egg mixture along with flour.
5. Spoon the batter into prepared ramekins and bake for 20 minutes or until sides are firm but centers are soft. Grill: 450 °F
6. Let cool for 1 minute, then cover each with an inverted dessert plate. Carefully turn each over, let stand 10 seconds, then unmold.
7. Serve immediately with Maple Ice Cream with Candied Bacon. Enjoy!

Skillet Buttermilk Cornbread

Servings: 6
Cooking Time: 25 Minutes

Ingredients:

- 1 Cup Cornmeal
- 1 Cup all-purpose flour
- 1/3 Cup granulated sugar
- 1 Teaspoon salt
- 1 Teaspoon baking powder
- 1 1/2 Cup buttermilk
- 2 Whole eggs
- 8 Tablespoon butter, melted

Directions:

1. Grease a cast iron skillet or 9-inch square baking pan with bacon fat. Put a 10-inch well-seasoned cast iron skillet on the grill grate. If using a regular baking pan, do not preheat.
2. Supply your smoker with wood pellets and follow the start-up procedure. Preheat the grill, with the lid closed, to 400° F.
3. In a large mixing bowl, combine the cornmeal, flour, sugar, salt, and baking powder and whisk to mix thoroughly. Make a well in the center of the dry ingredients.
4. In a separate mixing bowl, whisk together the buttermilk and eggs until well-combined. Add the melted butter. Pour into the dry ingredients and mix until the batter is fairly smooth. Do not overmix.
5. Carefully pour the batter into the preheated skillet. Bake for 20 to 25 minutes, or until the top is firm and a tester inserted in the center of the cornbread comes out clean. Be careful when removing the skillet from the grill as it will be very hot. Let the cornbread cool slightly on a trivet or cooling rack before slicing into wedges or squares.

Smoked Lemon Cheesecake

Servings: 16
Cooking Time: 130 Minutes

Ingredients:

- For the crust
- Vegetable oil, for oiling the pan
- 12 ounces gingersnaps (about 36) or chocolate icebox cookies (about 36)
- 3 tablespoons light brown sugar
- 8 tablespoons (1 stick) unsalted butter, melted
- For the filling
- 4 packages (8 ounces each) cream cheese, at room temperature
- 1 cup firmly packed light brown sugar
- 2 teaspoons pure vanilla extract
- 2 teaspoons finely grated lemon zest
- 1 tablespoon fresh lemon juice
- 2 tablespoons (1/4 stick) unsalted butter, melted
- 5 large eggs
- Burnt Sugar Sauce (recipes follows, optional)

Directions:

1. Supply your smoker with wood pellets and follow the start-up procedure. Preheat the grill, with the lid closed, to 400° F. Lightly oil the springform pan with vegetable oil and wrap a sheet of aluminum foil around the outside.
2. Make the crust: Break the cookies into pieces and grind with the brown sugar to a fine powder in a food processor. You'll want about 1 3/4 cups of crumbs. Add the melted butter and run the processor in short bursts to obtain a crumbly dough. Press the mixture evenly across the bottom and halfway up the sides of the springform pan. Indirect-grill or bake the crust until lightly browned, 5 to 8 minutes. Transfer the pan to a wire rack and let cool.
3. Make the filling: Wipe out the food processor bowl. Add the cream cheese, brown sugar, vanilla, lemon zest, lemon juice, and butter, and process until smooth. Work in the eggs one by one, processing until smooth after each addition. (You can also use a stand mixer, beating the cream cheese mixture until smooth and beating in the eggs one at a time.) Pour the filling into the crust. Gently tap the pan on the countertop a few times to knock out any air bubbles.
4. Supply your smoker with wood pellets and follow the start-up procedure. Preheat the grill, with the lid closed, to 225 °F-250 °F.
5. Place the cheesecake in the smoker. Smoke until the top is bronzed with smoke and the filling is set, 1 1/2 to 2 hours. To test for doneness, gently poke the side of the pan—the filling will jiggle, not ripple. Alternatively, insert a slender metal skewer in the center of the cake; it should come out clean.
6. Transfer the cheesecake in its pan to a wire rack to cool to room temperature. Refrigerate until serving; the cheesecake can be made up to 8 hours ahead. Run a slender knife around the inside of the springform pan. Unclasp and remove the ring. (You'll serve the cheesecake off the bottom of the pan.) Let the cheesecake warm slightly at room temperature before serving.
7. If serving with the sauce, pour some of it over the cheesecake and the rest into a pitcher. Cut into wedges and pass the remaining sauce.

Baked Pumpkin Pie

Servings: 6
Cooking Time: 50 Minutes

Ingredients:

- 4 Ounce cream cheese
- 15 Ounce pumpkin puree
- 1/3 Cup Cream, whipping
- 1/2 Cup brown sugar
- 1 Teaspoon pumpkin pie spice
- 3 Large eggs
- 1 frozen pie crust, thawed

Directions:

1. Supply your smoker with wood pellets and follow the start-up procedure. Preheat the grill, with the lid closed, to 325° F.
2. Mix cream cheese, puree, milk, sugar, and spice. One at a time, incorporate an egg to the mixture. Pour mixture into pie shell.
3. Bake for 50 minutes, edges should be golden and pie should be firm around edges with slight movement in middle. Let cool before whip cream is applied. Serve and enjoy! Grill: 325 °F

Vanilla Chocolate Bacon Cupcakes

Servings: 12
Cooking Time: 120 Minutes

Ingredients:

- 1 Lb Bacon
- 1 1/2 Tsp Baking Powder
- 1 1/2 Tsp Baking Soda
- 1 Cup Cocoa, Powder
- 2 Egg
- 1 3/4 Cups Flour
- 1 Cup Milk, Whole
- 1/2 Cup Oil
- 1 Tsp Salt
- 2 Cups Sugar
- 2 Tsp Vanilla

Directions:

1. Supply your smoker with wood pellets and follow the start-up procedure. Preheat the grill, with the lid closed, to 250° F.

2. Once your grill is preheated, place bacon strips on the grates. Smoke for 1hr-1 ½ hours or until desired crispiness is achieved.

3. Remove the bacon from the grill and set aside.

4. Increase set the temperature to 350°F and preheat.

5. Mix the rest of the ingredients in a bowl with an electric mixer until it is nice and smooth.

6. Pour the mixture into a cupcake tin.

7. Transfer the tin to your grill and bake for about 20 - 25 minutes.

8. Allow the cupcakes to cool on a wire rack. Once cooled, top with your favorite premade icing and a half of strip of the bacon. Serve and enjoy!

Savory Beaver Tails

Servings: 8
Cooking Time: 2 Minutes

Ingredients:
- 2 Tbsp Butter, Melted
- 1 Tbsp Cinnamon, Ground
- 1 Egg
- 2 1/2 Cups Flour, All-Purpose
- 1/2 Cup Milk, Warm
- 1/2 Tsp Salt
- 1 Tsp Sugar
- 1/2 Tsp Vanilla
- 1 L Vegetable Oil
- 1/4 Cup Water, Warm
- 2 1/2 Tsp Active Yeast, Instant

Directions:
1. In a small bowl, combine water, milk, yeast, and sugar. Let it sit for about 10 minutes or until frothy.

2. In another bowl, pour in the flour and make a well in the middle. Pour in butter, sugar, salt, vanilla and egg. Mix everything together until the dough is smooth. Knead for about 5 minutes and set the dough in a greased bowl. Cover with a towel and set aside for about an hour, or until the dough has doubled in size.

3. After one hour, supply your smoker with wood pellets and follow the start-up procedure. Preheat the grill, with the lid open, to 450° F.Pour 1L of vegetable oil into a cast iron pan and place on the grates of your Grill. Keep your flame broiler closed so as to prevent grease flareups. Preheat the oil so that it is 350 degrees F.

4. While you"re waiting for the oil to heat up, punch down the dough and separate into 8 small balls. Shape each piece of dough into a flat circle. Fry the dough in the preheated oil for about 1 minute per side, or until the dough is golden brown.

5. Sprinkle with cinnamon sugar immediately, or top with your desired toppings. Enjoy!

Pumpkin Bread

Servings: 6
Cooking Time: 60 Minutes

Ingredients:
- 1 Cup Pumpkin, canned
- 2 eggs
- 2/3 Cup vegetable oil
- 1/2 Cup sour cream
- 1 Teaspoon vanilla extract
- 2 1/2 Cup flour
- 1 1/2 Teaspoon baking soda
- 1 Teaspoon salt
- 1/2 Teaspoon ground cinnamon
- 1/4 Teaspoon ground nutmeg
- 1/4 Teaspoon ground cloves
- 1/4 Teaspoon ground ginger
- As Needed butter

Directions:
1. In a large mixing bowl, combine the pumpkin, eggs, vegetable oil, sour cream, and vanilla and whisk to blend.

2. In a separate bowl, combine the flour, baking soda, salt, cinnamon, nutmeg, cloves, and ginger. Add the dry ingredients to the wet ingredients and stir to combine. Do not overmix.

3. If desired, stir in one or more of the optional ingredients (walnuts, dried cranberries, raisins, or chocolate chips). Butter the interiors of two loaf pans.

4. Sprinkle with flour to coat the buttered surfaces, and tap out any excess. Divide the batter evenly between the two pans.

5. When ready to cook, set the smoker to 350°F and preheat, lid closed for 15 minutes.

6. Arrange the loaf pans directly on the grill grate. Bake for 45 to 50 minutes, or until a skewer or toothpick inserted in the center comes out clean. Also, the top of the loaf should spring back when pressed gently with a finger.

7. Transfer the loaf pans to a cooling rack and let cool for 10 minutes before carefully turning out the pumpkin bread. Let the loaves cool thoroughly before slicing. Wrap in aluminum foil or plastic wrap if not eating right away. Serve and enjoy!

Sweet Cheese Muffins

Servings: 3
Cooking Time: 15 Minutes

Ingredients:
- 1 package butter cake mix
- 1 package Jiffy Corn Muffin Mix
- 1 cup self-rising or cake flour
- 12 tablespoons (1½ sticks) unsalted butter, softened, plus 8 tablespoons (1 stick) melted

- 3½ cups shredded Cheddar cheese
- 2 eggs, beaten, at room temperature
- 2¼ cups buttermilk
- Nonstick cooking spray or butter, for greasing
- ¼ cup packed brown sugar

Directions:

1. Supply your smoker with wood pellets and follow the start-up procedure. Preheat, with the lid closed, to 375°F.

2. In a large mixing bowl, combine the cake mix, corn muffin mix, and flour.

3. Slice the 1½ sticks of softened butter into pieces and cut into the dry ingredients. Add the cheese and mix thoroughly.

4. In a medium bowl, combine the eggs and buttermilk, then add to the dry ingredients, stirring until well blended.

5. Coat three 12-cup mini muffin pans with cooking spray and spoon ¼ cup of batter into each cup.

6. Transfer the pans to the grill, close the lid, and smoke, monitoring closely, for 12 to 15 minutes, or until the muffins are lightly browned.

7. While the muffins are cooking, make the topping: In a small bowl, stir together the remaining 1 stick of melted butter and the brown sugar until well combined.

8. Remove the muffins from the grill. Brush the tops with the sweet butter and serve warm.

Eggs Ham Benedict

Servings: 6
Cooking Time: 15 Minutes

Ingredients:

- 1 Biscuit Dough, Tube
- 6 Egg
- 16 Ham, Sliced
- 1 Packet Hollandaise Sauce, Package

Directions:

1. Supply your smoker with wood pellets and follow the start-up procedure. Preheat the grill, with the lid closed, to 350° F.

2. Grease a muffin tin and crack an egg in each cup. Place on the grate of the for about 10 minutes or until the whites are fully cooked.

3. At the same time, place your biscuit dough on a greased pan. Follow the directions on the packaging but bake on the . Place 2 slices of ham per biscuit on the pan as well.

4. While the ham, eggs, and biscuits are cooking, prepare the Hollandaise Sauce according to the directions on the packet.

5. When everything is fully cooked, cut a biscuit in half, and stack one or two slices of ham, 1 egg and a dollop of Hollandaise sauce. Repeat for each half biscuit. Serve with fresh fruit.

Chicken Pot Pie

Servings: 6
Cooking Time: 60 Minutes

Ingredients:

- 2 Chicken, Boneless/Skinless
- 1 Cream Of Chicken Soup, Can
- 1 Tsp Curry Powder
- 1/2 Cup Mayo
- 1 1/2 Cups Mixed Frozen Vegetables
- 1 Onion, Sliced
- 2 Frozen Pie Shell, Deep
- 1/2 Cup Sour Cream

Directions:

1. Supply your smoker with wood pellets and follow the start-up procedure. Preheat the grill, with the lid closed, to 425° F.

2. Cut the onion in half and place on the grates of the grill. If you"re using fresh chicken breasts, barbecue the chicken at the same time as the onions. The chicken is fully cooked when the internal temperature reached 170F. While the onion and chicken are cooking, prepare the pie crust by putting one crust in a pie plate. When the chicken and onions are done, shred chicken and chop onion into small pieces and place in the prepared pie plate along with the mixed vegetables.

3. Combine cream of chicken soup, mayo, sour cream, and curry powder in a bowl. Pour into the pie crust with the chicken and mix to combine. Wet the sides of the bottom crust with a small amount of water and top with the second pie crust. Push gently along the sides of the crust to seal the two pie crusts together.

4. Place in the and bake for 40 minutes, or until the crust is golden brown. Serve hot.

The Dan Patrick Show Pull-apart Pesto Bread

Servings: 8
Cooking Time: 25 Minutes

Ingredients:

- 1 Sourdough Bread, loaf
- 1/2 Cup butter, melted
- 1 Cup Pesto Sauce
- 1 1/2 Cup Italian Cheese Blend

Directions:

1. Supply your smoker with wood pellets and follow the start-up procedure. Preheat the grill, with the lid closed, to 350° F.

2. Using a serrated knife, make 1" diagonal cuts through the bread leaving the bottom crust intact. Turn the bread and make diagonal cuts in the opposite direction, creating diamonds.

3. Place the bread on a sheet of foil large enough to wrap around the entire loaf. Pour the melted butter into the cracks in the bread. Using a spoon spread the pesto into the cracks then follow with the cheese stuffing it down into each crack.

4. Fold up the edges of the foil to wrap up the loaf and transfer to a baking sheet. Place the baking sheet directly on the grill grate.

5. Bake for 15 minutes then unwrap the foil and cook for an additional 10 minutes. Remove from the grill and serve. Enjoy! Grill: 350 °F

6. Follow along as we give you a recipe each day this week from The Dan Patrick Show Game Day Recipes eBook.

Quick Baked Dinner Rolls

Servings: 8
Cooking Time: 30 Minutes

Ingredients:
- 2 Tablespoon quick-rise yeast
- 1 Teaspoon salt
- 1/4 Cup sugar
- 3 1/3 Cup flour
- 1/4 Cup unsalted butter, softened
- 1 egg
- cooking spray
- 1 egg, for egg wash

Directions:
1. Combine yeast and warm water in a small bowl to activate the yeast. Let sit until foamy, about 5-10 minutes.

2. Combine salt, sugar, and flour in the bowl of a stand mixer fitted with the dough hook. Pour water and yeast into the dry ingredients with the machine running on low.

3. Add butter and egg and mix for 10 minutes gradually increasing the speed from low to high.

4. Form the dough into a ball and place in a buttered bowl. Cover with a cloth and let the dough rise for approximately 40 minutes.

5. Transfer the risen dough to a lightly floured surface and divide into 8 pieces forming a ball with each.

6. Lightly spray a cast iron pan with cooking spray and arrange balls in the pan. Cover with a cloth and let rise 20 minutes.

7. Supply your smoker with wood pellets and follow the start-up procedure. Preheat the grill, with the lid closed, to 375° F.

8. Brush rolls with egg wash and then bake for 30 minutes until lightly browned. Serve hot. Enjoy! Grill: 375 °F

Baked Brie

Servings: 6
Cooking Time: 8 Minutes

Ingredients:

- 16 Ounce (16 oz) brie wheel
- 1/3 Cup honey
- 1/4 Cup pecans
- Crackers
- apple, sliced

Directions:
1. Supply your smoker with wood pellets and follow the start-up procedure. Preheat the grill, with the lid closed, to 350° F.

2. Line a rimmed baking sheet with a piece of parchment or aluminum foil. Using a sharp serrated knife, slice top—the white rind—off the brie. (Le the ave the rind on the sides and bottom intact.)

3. Put the brie, cut side up, on the prepared baking sheet and drizzle with the honey. Sprinkle nuts on top.

4. Bake the brie until it is soft and oozing, but not melting, 8 to 10 minutes. Let it cool for a couple of minutes and transfer to a serving plate. Grill: 350 °F

5. Serve with crackers and sliced apple wedges. Drizzle with more honey, if desired. Enjoy!

Double Vanilla Chocolate Cake

Servings: 12
Cooking Time: 40 Minutes

Ingredients:
- 1 1/2 Tsp Baking Soda
- 1/2 Cup Butter, Melted
- 1 Cup Buttermilk, Low Fat
- 1 Jar Chocolate Icing, Prepared
- 3/4 Cup Cocoa, Powder
- 1 Cup Coffee, Hot
- 2 Large Egg
- 1 3/4 Cups Flour, All-Purpose
- 3/4 Tsp Salt
- 2 Cups Sugar
- 1 Tbsp Vanilla

Directions:
1. Supply your smoker with wood pellets and follow the start-up procedure. Preheat the grill, with the lid closed, to 350° F.

2. Stir together flour, sugar, cocoa, baking soda and salt in a large bowl. Combine eggs, buttermilk, butter and coffee and mix until smooth. Add in hot coffee and stir until combined and the dough is runny.

3. Pour the batter into two prepared baking pans and bake on the top rack of your for 40 minutes, turning the pans 180 degrees halfway through.

4. Allow to cool and then frost with chocolate icing.

Green Bean Casserole Circa 1955

Servings: 6
Cooking Time: 30 Minutes

Ingredients:

- 1 1/2 Pound Green Beans, fresh
- 1 Can cream of mushroom soup
- 1/2 Cup milk
- 2 Teaspoon soy sauce
- 1/2 Teaspoon Worcestershire sauce
- 1/2 Teaspoon black pepper
- 1.334 Cup French's Original Crispy Fried Onions
- 1/4 Cup red bell pepper, diced

Directions:

1. In a mixing bowl, combine the beans (trimmed and cooked until tender, or may use 2 16 oz. cans), soup, milk, soy sauce, Worcestershire sauce, black pepper, 2/3 cup of the onion rings, and red pepper, if using. Transfer to a 1-1/2 quart casserole dish.
2. Supply your smoker with wood pellets and follow the start-up procedure. Preheat the grill, with the lid closed, to 375° F.
3. Cook the casserole until the filling is hot and bubbling, 25 to 30 minutes. Top with the remaining onions and cook for 5 to 10 minutes more, or until the onions are crisp and beginning to brown. Grill: 375 °F

Delicious Peanut Butter Cookies

Servings: 24
Cooking Time: 15 Minutes

Ingredients:

- 1 Egg
- 1 Cup Peanut Butter
- 1 Cup Sugar

Directions:

1. Supply your smoker with wood pellets and follow the start-up procedure. Preheat the grill, with the lid closed, to High heat.
2. Combine all ingredients in a bowl. Drop tablespoon amounts of dough on a prepared baking sheet and bake in your Grill for 15-20 minutes. Allow cookies to cool for 5 minutes on the baking sheet before you enjoy!

Spiced Carrot Cake

Servings: 10
Cooking Time: 35 Minutes

Ingredients:

- 1/2 Cup Apple Sauce, Unsweetened
- 2 Tsp Baking Powder
- 1 Tsp Baking Soda
- 1 1/2 Cups Brown Sugar
- 1/2 Cup Butter, Room Temp
- 3/4 Cup Canola Oil
- 3 Cups Carrot, Grated
- 1 1/2 Tsp Cinnamon, Ground
- 2 (8-Ounce) Packages Cream Cheese, Room Temperature
- 4 Egg
- 2 Cups Flour, All-Purpose
- 1/2 Tsp Ginger, Ground
- 1/4 Tsp Nutmeg, Ground
- 1/2 Tsp Salt
- 1/2 Cup Sugar
- 3 Cups Sugar, Icing

Directions:

1. Supply your smoker with wood pellets and follow the start-up procedure. Preheat the grill, with the lid closed, to 350° F.
2. Line the bottom of 2 9-inch cake pans with parchment paper and spray the sides with cooking spray. Set aside.
3. In a large bowl, combine flour, baking powder and soda, spices and salt.
4. In a smaller bowl, combine oil, eggs, sugars, and applesauce and whisk together. Add carrots and stir until well combined.
5. Pour the wet ingredients into the dry. Stir until combined but take care not to over mix. Pour the batter evenly between the two cake pans. Bake for about 35 minutes in your Grill, rotating the cake pans halfway between the cook. Remove once a toothpick is inserted in the middle of the cake and comes out clean.
6. While the cake is cooling, prepare the frosting. Beat the cream cheese until smooth with a hand mixer. Add the butter and icing sugar and mix until fully combined.
7. On a clean plate or cake stand, place one half of the cake and top with a good layer of cream cheese frosting. Place the second half on top and cover with the remaining frosting. Icing tip: try not to lift your knife while icing. Instead make long, smooth strokes. Lifting the knife often make cause crumbs to get into your icing. Top with pecans if desired.

Vanilla Chocolate Chip Cookies

Servings: 12
Cooking Time: 20 Minutes

Ingredients:

- 3/4 cup brown sugar
- 3/4 cup white sugar
- 1 stick butter, room temp
- 2 eggs
- 1 tsp vanilla
- 2 1/2 cups flour
- 1/2 tsp salt
- 1 tsp baking soda
- 1 cup Chocolate Chips

Directions:

1. Cream your butter and sugar together in a mixing bowl using a hand mixer or stand mixer on medium speed for about 4-5 minutes.
2. Once the butter is creamed, add the eggs and vanilla. Continue mixing for an additional minute.
3. Put flour, salt, and baking soda in a sifter. Sift it into your creamed butter mixture.
4. Scrape the sides of your mixing bowl with a rubber spatula, and then turn your mixer on to low speed.
5. Let it mix a little, and then scrape the sides again. Stop mixing when there are one or two streaks of flour left in the cookie dough.
6. Scrape the sides of your bowl and pour in a cup of chocolate chips, and turn the mixer to low again to mix the chocolate. It should take just a few turns for the chocolate pieces to be well incorporated.
7. Line a large baking sheet with parchment paper. Using a medium cookie scoop (about 1.5 tbsp), drop evenly spaced dollops of cookie dough onto the cookie sheet.
8. Supply your smoker with wood pellets and follow the start-up procedure. Preheat the grill, with the lid closed, to 350° F. Place the cookie sheet in your smoker, and let them cook for about 12 minutes.
9. Let them sit on a cooling rack while you continue to cook the additional cookies.
10. Cool for a few minutes to let cookies set.
11. Enjoy!

Baked Irish Creme Cake

Servings: 4
Cooking Time: 60 Minutes

Ingredients:

- 1 Cup Pecans, pieces
- 1 Yellow Cake Mix, Boxed
- 1 Vanilla Pudding Mix, Instant Package (3.4oz)
- 4 Large eggs
- 1/2 Cup water
- 1/2 Cup vegetable oil
- 1 Cup Irish Cream Liquor
- 1/2 Cup butter
- 1 Cup sugar

Directions:

1. Grease and flour a 10" (25 cm) Bundt pan. Sprinkle pecans along the bottom.
2. In a large bowl, with a mixer, combine yellow cake mix, pudding mix, eggs, water, oil, and Irish Cream liquor. Pour batter over nuts in the pan.

3. Supply your smoker with wood pellets and follow the start-up procedure. Preheat the grill, with the lid closed, to 325° F.
4. Place Bundt pan on the Traeger and bake for 1 hour, or until a toothpick comes out clean. Remove from heat, cool for 10 minutes. Grill: 325 °F
5. While the cake is cooling, combine the butter, water and sugar and bring to a boil. Boil for 5 minutes, stirring constantly. Remove from heat and add Irish cream liquor.
6. Use a bamboo skewer to poke holes in the cooled cake. Spoon glaze over the cake. Allow cake to absorb the glaze. Enjoy!

Lemon Strawberry Rhubarb Pie

Servings: 8
Cooking Time: 30 Minutes

Ingredients:

- 1/3 Cup Flour
- 1 Tbsp Lemon, Zest
- 1 Prepard Pie Shell, Deep
- 3 Stalks Rhubarb
- 2 1/2 Cups Strawberry
- 1 Cup Sugar

Directions:

1. Summer baking never has to stop when you can use your Wood Pellet Grill to bake anything from cookies to pie! In this recipe, we will show you how to bake a delicious barbecued strawberry rhubarb pie without turning your kitchen into an oven.
2. Supply your smoker with wood pellets and follow the start-up procedure. Preheat the grill, with the lid closed, to 400° F.
3. Slice rhubarb and strawberries into bite sized pieces. Combine sugar, flour and lemon zest with rhubarb and strawberries. Pour into prepared pie crust. Cover with top crust.
4. Bake in Grill for 1 hour or until crust is crispy.
5. Serve hot.

Cast Iron Pineapple Upside Down Cake

Servings: 6
Cooking Time: 40 Minutes

Ingredients:

- 1/4 Cup butter, melted
- 1 Cup brown sugar
- 20 Ounce Pineapple, sliced
- 6 Ounce maraschino cherries
- 1 Whole Yellow Cake Mix, Boxed
- vegetable oil
- eggs

Directions:

1. Supply your smoker with wood pellets and follow the start-up procedure. Preheat the grill, with the lid closed, to 350° F.

2.   Pour melted butter into a 12-inch cast iron pan. Sprinkle brown sugar on top of the butter. Arrange pineapple slices on brown sugar, squeezing in as many slices as possible. Place a cherry in center of each pineapple slice; press gently into brown sugar.

3.   Make cake batter as directed on box, substituting pineapple juice mixture for as much of the water as possible, and adding in required oil and eggs. Pour batter into cast iron dish, over pineapple and cherries.

4.   Place the cast iron pan on the grill grate and cook for 20 minutes. Rotate the pan a half turn to ensure it cooks evenly. Cook for an additional 20 minutes, or until toothpick inserted in center comes out clean.

5.   Immediately run knife around side of pan to loosen cake. Place heatproof serving plate upside down onto pan; turn plate and pan over.

6.   Leave pan over cake 5 minutes so brown sugar topping can drizzle over cake. Cool 30 minutes. Enjoy!

Baked Potatoes & Celery Root Au Gratin

Servings: 2
Cooking Time: 60 Minutes

Ingredients:
- 5 Tablespoon butter, softened
- 2 Large leeks, white parts only, cleaned and sliced into half moons
- kosher salt
- freshly ground black pepper
- 5 Small Yukon Gold potatoes, sliced 1/4 inch thick
- 2 Whole celery root, peeled and sliced 1/4 inch thick
- 2 Cup cream
- 1 Tablespoon minced sage
- 1 Cup shredded Gruyere or other hearty Swiss cheese, divided

Directions:
1.   Supply your smoker with wood pellets and follow the start-up procedure. Preheat the grill, with the lid closed, to 400° F.

2.   Butter a 9x13 baking dish with 1 tablespoon of the softened butter. In a medium frying pan over medium heat, melt the remaining butter. Add the leeks and a generous pinch of salt and pepper and cook, stirring often until softened, about 5 minutes.

3.   Remove from the heat and allow to cool. Place the potato and celery root slices into a large mixing bowl. Add the cream, leek mixture, minced sage, 1 teaspoon salt, 1/2 teaspoon pepper and 1 cup cheese. Stir gently to coat.

4.   Arrange a layer of potato and celery root slices so they're slightly overlapping in the prepared baking dish. Repeat two more times so there are three layers of potatoes. Pour remaining cream from the bowl over the gratin, then sprinkle the top with the remaining cup of cheese.

5.   Cover the dish loosely with foil and bake on the grill for 45 minutes. Remove the foil and continue baking until the top is golden and bubbly and the potatoes are tender when pierced, about 30 to 45 minutes longer. Let stand for 10 minutes before serving. Enjoy!

Baked Wood-fired Pizza

Servings: 6
Cooking Time: 12 Minutes

Ingredients:
- 2/3 Cup warm water (110°F to 115°F)
- 2 1/2 Teaspoon active dry yeast
- 1/2 Teaspoon granulated sugar
- 1 Teaspoon kosher salt
- 1 Tablespoon oil
- 2 Cup all-purpose flour
- 1/4 Cup fine cornmeal
- 1 Large grilled portobello mushroom, sliced
- 1 Jar pickled artichoke hearts, drained and chopped
- 1 Cup shredded fontina cheese
- 1/2 Cup shaved Parmigiano-Reggiano cheese, divided
- To Taste Roasted Garlic, minced
- 1/4 Cup extra-virgin olive oil
- To Taste banana peppers

Directions:
1.   In a glass bowl, stir together the warm water, yeast and sugar. Let stand until the mixture starts to foam, about 10 minutes. In a mixer, combine 1-3/4 cup flour, sugar and salt. Stir oil into the yeast mixture. Slowly add the liquid to the dry ingredients while slowly increasing the mixers speed until fully combined. The dough should be smooth and not sticky.

2.   Knead the dough on a floured surface, gradually adding the remaining flour as needed to prevent the dough from sticking, until smooth, about 5 to 10 minutes.

3.   Form the dough into a ball. Apply a thin layer of olive oil to a large bowl. Place the dough into the bowl and coat the dough ball with a small amount of olive oil. Cover and let rise in a warm place for about 1 hour or until doubled in size.

4.   When ready to cook, set smoker temperature to 450°F and preheat, lid closed for 15 minutes.

5.   Place a pizza stone in the grill while it preheats.

6.   Punch the dough down and roll it out into a 12-inch circle on a floured surface.

7.   Spread the cornmeal evenly on the pizza peel. Place the dough on the pizza peel and assemble the toppings evenly in the following order: olive oil, roasted garlic, fontina, portobello, artichoke hearts, Parmigiano-Reggiano and banana peppers.

8.   Carefully slide the assembled pizza from the pizza peel to the preheated pizza stone and bake until the crust is golden brown, about 10 to 12 minutes. Enjoy!

Grilled Bourbon Pecan Pie

Servings: 6
Cooking Time: 45 Minutes

Ingredients:

- 2 Tbsp Bourbon
- 1/2 Cup Brown Sugar
- 1/3 Cup Unsalted Butter, Melted
- 1/2 Cup Light, 1/2 Cup Dark Corn Syrup
- 3 Egg
- 1/4 Tsp Hickory Honey Smoked Salt
- Decoration Pecan
- 1 1/4 Cup Chopped Pecans, Coarsely Broken
- 1 Prepared Or Homemade Pie Shell, Deep
- 1/2 Cup Sugar
- 1 Tsp Vanilla Extract

Directions:

1. Supply your smoker with wood pellets and follow the start-up procedure. Preheat the grill, with the lid closed, to 375° F. Meanwhile, prepare your pie crust in a 9 cast iron skillet or heat proof pie plate.
2. In a large bowl, beat the eggs until smooth. Add the brown sugar and white sugar and mix until smooth. Add the light corn syrup, dark corn syrup, vanilla, bourbon, melted butter, and Hickory Honey Salt. Mix until smooth. Stir in your chopped pecans and pour into the pie crust. Top with the whole pecans, if desired.
3. Grill covered for 35-45 minutes, until the pie is just set around the edges but still has a slight jiggle in the center.
4. Allow the pie to cool completely before slicing. Enjoy!

Baked Buttermilk Biscuits

Servings: 4
Cooking Time: 15 Minutes

Ingredients:

- 2 Cup all-purpose flour
- 1/4 Cup butter
- 3/4 Cup buttermilk

Directions:

1. Supply your smoker with wood pellets and follow the start-up procedure. Preheat the grill, with the lid closed, to High heat. Spoon the flour into a measuring cup and level with a knife.
2. Put the flour into a mixing bowl. Using a pastry blender, cut the butter into the flour until the mixture resembles coarse crumbs.
3. With a fork, gently stir in just enough of the buttermilk so the dough leaves the sides of the bowl. (You may not need all the buttermilk.) For the most tender biscuits, do not overmix.
4. Lightly flour a work surface as well as your hands. Tip the dough onto the floured surface and gently bring together using your fingertips. (Re-flour your hands or the board if the dough is too sticky.) Knead two or three times, just to bring the dough together.
5. With a floured rolling pin, lightly and quickly roll the dough out to a thickness of about 1/2". Using a 1-1/2" floured cutter, cut out as many biscuits as you can. (Do not twist the cutter; push it straight down.) You can reroll the scraps if desired, but the "second string" biscuits will be tougher.
6. Transfer the biscuits to an ungreased baking sheet. Using a pastry brush, brush the tops with melted butter. Bake until golden brown, 10 to 15 minutes. Enjoy! Grill: 500 °F

Mexican Black Bean Cornbread Casserole

Servings: 6
Cooking Time: 30 Minutes

Ingredients:

- 1 Lb Beef, Ground
- 1 15Oz Drained Black Beans, Can
- 1 Box Corn Muffin Mix
- 1 15Oz Enchilada Sauce, Can
- 1 Onion, Chopped
- 1 15Oz Drained Pinto Beans, Can

Directions:

1. Supply your smoker with wood pellets and follow the start-up procedure. Preheat the grill, with the lid closed, to 300° F.
2. Mix corn muffin mix according to directions.
3. Place cast iron skillet over flame broiler and heat for a few minutes, leaving Grill lid open.
4. Add onion and ground beef/sausage to skillet and break up
5. Cook until meat is done about 5 to 10 minutes.
6. Add both cans of beans, and enchilada sauce, stir to combine.
7. Bring mixture to a simmer.
8. Carefully close flame broiler and turn Grill up to 400 degrees.
9. Spread prepared corn muffin mix over top of meat and bean mixture and bake for 15 minutes until cornbread mixture is lightly browned.
10. Let sit 15 minutes before serving.

Chili Cheese Fries

Servings: 6
Cooking Time: 10 Minutes

Ingredients:

- 1 Cup Cheddar Cheese, Shredded
- 1 Cup Chili Con Carne, Prepared
- 1 Bag French Fries
- 1 Tablespoon Olive Oil
- 1 Tablespoon Sweet Heat Rub

Directions:

1. Supply your smoker with wood pellets and follow the start-up procedure. Preheat the grill, with the lid closed, to 350° F. If you're using charcoal or gas, set it up for medium high heat.
2. Bake the fries according to manufacturer's instructions. Once the fries are done, place them in a large bowl and add the olive oil and Sweet Heat Rub. Toss the fries to coat. Once everything is well coated with the oil and seasoning, spread the fries on a baking sheet.
3. Top the fries with the chili and the shredded cheddar cheese. Place the baking sheet on the grill and grill for 7-10 minutes, or until the cheese is melted and bubbly, and the chili is warm all the way through.
4. Remove the baking sheet from the grill and serve the fries immediately.

Bacon Chocolate Chip Cookies

Servings: 2
Cooking Time: 10-12 Minutes

Ingredients:

- 2¾ cups all-purpose flour
- 1½ teaspoons baking soda
- ½ teaspoon salt
- 12 tablespoons (1½ sticks) unsalted butter, softened
- 1 cup light brown sugar
- 1 cup granulated sugar
- 2 eggs, at room temperature
- 2½ teaspoons apple cider vinegar
- 1 teaspoon vanilla extract
- 2 cups semisweet chocolate chips
- 8 slices bacon, cooked and crumbled

Directions:

1. In a large bowl, combine the flour, baking soda, and salt, and mix well.
2. In a separate large bowl, using an electric mixer on medium speed, cream the butter and sugars. Reduce the speed to low and mix in the eggs, vinegar, and vanilla.
3. With the mixer speed still on low, slowly incorporate the dry ingredients, chocolate chips, and bacon pieces.
4. Supply your smoker with wood pellets and follow the start-up procedure. Preheat, with the lid closed, to 375°F.
5. Line a large baking sheet with parchment paper.
6. Drop rounded teaspoonfuls of cookie batter onto the prepared baking sheet and place on the grill grate. Close the lid and smoke for 10 to 12 minutes, or until the cookies are browned around the edges.

Crème Brûlée

Servings: 2

Cooking Time: 45minutes

Ingredients:

- 1 Quart heavy whipping cream
- 1 Pieces Vanilla Bean, split and scraped
- 6 Large egg yolk
- 1 Cup sugar

Directions:

1. Supply your smoker with wood pellets and follow the start-up procedure. Preheat the grill, with the lid closed, to 325° F.
2. Pour the cream into a saucepan over medium-high heat, add the vanilla bean and the scraped seeds. Bring to a boil. Remove from the heat and allow to steep (about 15 minutes). Remove the vanilla bean from saucepan and discard.
3. In a bowl, whisk together egg yolks and 1/2 cup (100 g) of the sugar until the mix starts to lighten in color. Add the cream a little at a time, stirring continually.
4. Pour the mixture into 6 (8 oz) ramekins and place the ramekins into a large roasting pan. Pour hot water into the pan so that it comes halfway up the sides of the ramekins.
5. Place water bath pan on the grill and bake until the Crème Brûlées still jiggle in the center, about 40 to 45 minutes. Grill: 325 °F
6. Remove the ramekins from the roasting pan and refrigerate for at least 2 hours and up to 2 days.
7. To serve, let the Crème Brûlée come to temperature (about 20 minutes) before torching the tops.
8. Sprinkle the remaining 1/2 cup (100 g) sugar equally on top of each ramekin. Using a torch in a circular motion, melt the sugar until it caramelizes and forms a crispy top.
9. Allow the Crème Brûlée to sit for a few minutes before serving. Enjoy!

Chocolate Peanut Cookies

Servings: 4
Cooking Time: 12 Minutes

Ingredients:

- 1/2 Tsp Baking Soda
- 1/2 Cup Brown Sugar
- 1/2 Cup + 1 Tbsp Butter, Unsalted
- 1/3 Cup Cocoa Powder, Dark And Unsweetened
- 2 Eggs, Beaten
- 1 1/2 Cups Flour, All-Purpose
- 1/3 Cup Miniature Chocolate Chips
- 2 Cups Peanut Butter Chips, Divided
- 1/4 Tsp Sea Salt
- 1/2 Cup Sugar, Granulated
- 1 Tsp Vanilla Extract

Directions:

1. Supply your smoker with wood pellets and follow the start-up procedure. Preheat the grill, with the lid closed, to medium-low heat. If using a gas or charcoal grill, preheat a cast iron skillet.

2. In a mixing bowl, whisk together the flour, cocoa powder, baking soda, and salt. Set aside.

3. Set a metal saucepan on the griddle, then add ½ cup of butter to melt. Whisk in the sugars and vanilla extract and cook for 2 minutes. Remove the pan from the griddle, and transfer contents to a large mixing bowl.

4. Slowly pour the beaten eggs into the sugar mixture, whisking constantly to temper the eggs.

5. Add the dry mixture to the wet ingredients until just combined. Fold in 1 cup of peanut butter chips and chocolate chips. Refrigerate mixture for 15 to 30 minutes.

6. Remove the dough from the refrigerator, then add an additional cup of peanut butter chips.

7. Portion dough into 16 to 18 cookie balls.

8. Melt 1 tablespoon of butter on the griddle, then transfer the cookie balls to the griddle. Press down gently on the cookies, then cook for 10 to 12 minutes, flipping halfway.

9. Transfer cookies to a cooling rack for 5 minutes before enjoying.

Lemon Chicken, Broccoli, String Beans Foil Packs

Servings: 4
Cooking Time: 20 Minutes

Ingredients:
- 2 Cups Broccoli
- 3 Tbsp Butter, Melted
- 4 Chicken, Boneless/Skinless
- 1 Garlic, Minced
- 1 1/2 Tsp Italian Seasoning, Dried
- 1 Lemon, Sliced
- Pepper
- Salt
- 1 Cup String Beans

Directions:
1. Supply your smoker with wood pellets and follow the start-up procedure. Preheat the grill, with the lid closed, to 450° F.

2. Lay four 12 x 12 inch pieces of foil out on a flat surface, then place one chicken breast in the middle of each foil.

3. Divide the broccoli and string beans between the four foil packs. Thinly slice the lemon, split them between each foil pack, and place the slices on, in and around the chicken and vegetables.

4. Mix the butter, garlic, juice of the remaining lemon, and Italian seasoning together, and then brush over the chicken and vegetables. Sprinkle with salt and pepper to taste.

5. Fold the foil over the chicken and vegetables to close the pack, and pinch the ends together so the pack will remain closed.

6. Grill for 7-9 minutes on each side. Turn off grill, remove the foil packets, and serve immediately.

Chicken Pizza On The Grill

Servings: 4
Cooking Time: 10 Minutes

Ingredients:
- 3 Boneless, Skinless Chicken Breast
- 5 Cups Flour, Strong
- 3 Cups Georgia Style Bbq Sauce
- 3 Cups Mozzarella Cheese, Shredded
- 1 Tsp Olive Oil
- 3 Cups Georgia Style BBQ Sauce
- 1 1/2 Cups Red Bell Peppers, Diced
- 1 1/2 Cups Red Onion, Diced
- 1 Tsp Sugar
- 1/2 Cup Water, Hot
- 1 1/4 Cup Water, Warm
- 2 Tsb Active Yeast, Instant

Directions:
1. Roll your pizza dough so it forms a base about a 1/2 inch thick. To impress your friends and family, you'll want to aim for a nice, pizza like shape. HINT: use a sprinkle of cornmeal on the countertop to aid in moving the dough.

2. Now for the toppings! Start by spreading 1 cup of Georgia Style BBQ sauce onto each base. Make sure to leave a small portion for the crust! Next, load up with sliced, cooked chicken breasts, diced red onions and red bell peppers before finishing off with a two cups of shredded mozzarella cheese.

3. Supply your smoker with wood pellets and follow the start-up procedure. Preheat the grill, with the lid closed, to 500° F. Place the pizza stone in your grill. Pick up your pizza using a flat surface like a chopping board and slide the pizza carefully onto the hot stone. Close the lid and let your homemade wood-fired pizza bake for 10 - 12 minutes. Remove once your pizza has a golden crust and the cheese is bubbling. Cut and serve for pizza you'll hardly want to share.

Sweet And Spicy Baked Pork Beans

Servings: 20
Cooking Time: 120 Minutes

Ingredients:

- 1 - 21 Oz Apple Pie Filling, Can
- 1 Gallon Baked Beans
- 1 Tbs Chilli, Powder
- 1 Green Bell Pepper, Diced
- 1 10 Oz Drained Jalapeno, Can Diced
- 1 Cup Maple Syrup
- 1 Onion, Diced
- 1 Lb Pork, Pulled

Directions:

1. Supply your smoker with wood pellets and follow the start-up procedure. Preheat the grill, with the lid closed, to 350° F.
2. Place all ingredients in mixing bowl and mix well.
3. Pour bean mixture into foil pans.
4. Bake in grill till bubbling throughout – about 2 hours.
5. Rest at least 15 minutes before serving.

Butternut Squash Macaroni And Cheese

Servings: 2
Cooking Time: 50 Minutes

Ingredients:

- 1 Medium butternut squash
- 2 Cup macaroni, uncooked
- 1 Small yellow onion
- 1/2 Cup chicken broth
- 1 Cup milk
- salt
- pepper
- 1 Cup cheese, grated

Directions:

1. Supply your smoker with wood pellets and follow the start-up procedure. Preheat the grill, with the lid closed, to 225° F.
2. Puncture butternut squash with a fork several times and place on grill grate. Cook until tender, about 40 minutes to an hour. When cooked, scoop out meat and discard seeds. Grill: 225 °F
3. Cook elbow macaroni according to package instructions. Drain and set aside.
4. In a medium skillet, sauté chopped onion until fragrant and golden. Add broth, milk, salt, onions and butternut squash to a food processor. Puree until smooth and creamy. Add salt and pepper to taste.
5. Pour pureed sauce over cooked noodles and add the shredded cheese. Stir to melt the cheese and add milk to reach desired consistency. Serve warm. Enjoy!

Delicious Smoked Candied Pecan Pie

Servings: 4
Cooking Time: 55 Minutes

Ingredients:

- 1 cup brown sugar
- 1/4 cup granulated sugar
- 1 1/2 teaspoon vanilla
- 1/2 teaspoon corn starch
- 1/2 teaspoon orange zest
- 1/2 teaspoon salt
- 3/4 cup light corn syrup
- 1/2 cup butter (aka- 1 stick), melted
- 3 eggs, beaten
- 1 1/2 cups smoked candied pecans
- 1 pie crust

Directions:

1. Supply your smoker with wood pellets and follow the start-up procedure. Preheat the grill, with the lid closed, to 350° F.
2. Put brown sugar, granulated sugar, vanilla, corn starch, orange zest, salt, light corn syrup, melted butter, and three eggs in a medium mixing bowl. Stir ingredients together.
3. Lightly grease a pie pan and put your rolled out pie crust in. Make sure pie crust conforms to the pie tin. Sprinkle half of your pecans onto pie crust in pie pan. Pour ingredients from mixing bowl into pie pan, then evenly top with the remaining pecans.
4. Cover pie in foil and put on the grill. After 30 minutes, remove foil and cook for another 25 minutes.
5. Remove the pecan pie from grill and let it cool to room temperature before serving.

Bananas Rum Foster

Servings: 4
Cooking Time: 10 Minutes

Ingredients:

- 1/3 Cup Banana Nectar
- 4 Bananas, Quartered
- 3/4 Cup Brown Sugar
- 1/4 Cup Butter
- 1/2 Tsp Cinnamon, Ground
- 1/3 Cup Dark Rum
- Vanilla Ice Cream

Directions:

1. Supply your smoker with wood pellets and follow the start-up procedure. Preheat the grill, with the lid closed, to medium heat. If using a gas or charcoal grill, preheat a cast iron skillet.
2. Place a large skillet on the griddle, then melt butter in the skillet. Whisk in brown sugar and cinnamon, stirring until sugar dissolves.

3. Add the banana nectar and bananas. Stir to coat
4. Once the bananas begin to soften and turn brown, add the rum. Stir, then ignite the sauce with a stick lighter. After the flames subside, simmer the sauce for 2 minutes.
5. Divide the bananas among 4 scoops/bowls of vanilla ice cream, then spoon the warm sauce over the top of the ice cream. Serve immediately.

Pound Cake

Servings: 8
Cooking Time: 60 Minutes

Ingredients:
- 1 1/2 Cup butter
- 8 Ounce cream cheese
- 3 Cup sugar
- 6 eggs
- 3 Teaspoon Bourbon Vanilla
- 1 Tablespoon lemon zest
- fresh strawberries
- whipped cream

Directions:
1. In a large bowl, cream the butter, cream cheese, and sugar. Add eggs one at a time, whipping in between. Add vanilla and lemon zest, whip.
2. Pour batter into greased loaf pans, about halfway full to allow cake to rise.
3. Supply your smoker with wood pellets and follow the start-up procedure. Preheat the grill, with the lid closed, to 325° F.
4. Place loaf pans on grill and cook for 1 hour - 1 hour and 15 minutes. Check the cake at 45 minutes, if golden brown, cover loosely with foil and continue to cook until a toothpick inserted comes out clean. Grill: 325 °F
5. Cool loaf in pan for 10 minutes before removing to a wire rack.
6. Cut into 1 inch slices and serve with fresh sliced strawberries, top with smoked whip cream.

Zucchini Bread

Servings: 6
Cooking Time: 50 Minutes

Ingredients:
- 1 Cup Walnuts, Chopped
- 2 Large zucchini
- 1 Teaspoon salt
- 1 Teaspoon ground cinnamon
- 1/4 Teaspoon ground cloves
- 1/4 Teaspoon baking powder
- 3 Cup all-purpose flour

- 1 eggs
- 2 Cup sugar
- 1/2 Cup vegetable oil
- 1/2 Cup Yogurt
- 1 1/2 Teaspoon vanilla extract

Directions:
1. Grease and flour two 9- by 5-inch bread pans, preferably nonstick.
2. When ready to cook, set the temperature to 350°F and preheat, lid closed for 15 minutes.
3. Spread the walnuts on a pie plate and toast for 10 minutes, stirring once. Let cool, then coarsely chop. Set aside.
4. Trim the ends off the zucchini, then coarsely grate into a colander set over the sink on a box grater (or use the shredding disk on a food processor). You'll need 2 cups.
5. Sprinkle with the salt and let drain for 30 minutes. Press on the zucchini with paper towels to expel excess water.
6. Sift the flour, baking powder, cinnamon, and cloves in a mixing bowl or on a large sheet of parchment or wax paper.
7. Combine the eggs, sugar, oil, yogurt, and vanilla in a large mixing bowl and mix on medium speed. (You can mix the batter by hand, if desired.) Add half the dry ingredients and mix on low speed; add the remaining dry ingredients and mix until just combined.
8. Stir in the walnuts and zucchini by hand.
9. Divide the batter between the prepared baking pans.
10. Arrange the pans directly on the grill grate and bake for 50 minutes, or until a bamboo skewer inserted in the center of the breads comes out clean.
11. Transfer to a wire rack and let cool for 10 minutes, then remove the breads from the pans. For best results, let the breads cool completely before slicing.

Carrot Cake

Servings: 4-6
Cooking Time: 60 Minutes

Ingredients:
- 8 carrots, peeled and grated
- 4 eggs, at room temperature
- 1 cup vegetable oil
- ½ cup milk
- 1 teaspoon vanilla extract
- 2 cups sugar
- 2 cups self-rising or cake flour
- 2 teaspoons baking soda
- 1 teaspoon salt
- 1 cup finely chopped pecans
- Nonstick cooking spray or butter, for greasing
- 8 ounces cream cheese

- 1 cup confectioners' sugar
- 8 tablespoons (1 stick) unsalted butter, at room temperature
- 1 teaspoon vanilla extract
- ½ teaspoon salt
- 2 tablespoons to ¼ cup milk

Directions:

1. For the cake:
2. Supply your smoker with wood pellets and follow the start-up procedure. Preheat, with the lid closed, to 350°F.
3. In a food processor or blender, combine the grated carrots, eggs, oil, milk, and vanilla, and process until the carrots are finely minced.
4. In a large mixing bowl, combine the sugar, flour, baking soda, and salt.
5. Add the carrot mixture to the flour mixture and stir until well incorporated. Fold in the chopped pecans.
6. Coat a 9-by-13-inch baking pan with cooking spray.
7. Pour the batter into prepared pan and place on the grill grate. Close the lid and smoke for about 1 hour, or until a toothpick inserted in the center comes out clean.
8. Remove the cake from the grill and let cool completely.
9. For the frosting:
10. Using an electric mixer on low speed, beat the cream cheese, confectioners' sugar, butter, vanilla, and salt, adding 2 tablespoons to ¼ cup of milk to thin the frosting as needed.
11. Frost the cooled cake and slice to serve.

Mint Butter Chocolate Chip Cookies

Servings: 24
Cooking Time: 12 Minutes

Ingredients:

- 1/2 Cup Butter, Melted
- 1 Package Chocolate Chip Cookie Mix
- 8-10 Drop Food Coloring
- 1/2 Tsp Mint, Extract

Directions:

1. Supply your smoker with wood pellets and follow the start-up procedure. Preheat the grill, with the lid closed, to 350° F.
2. Follow the directions on the back of the Chocolate Chip Cookie mix and also add the mint extract and green food coloring. Mix until combined.
3. On a baking sheet lined with parchment paper, drop balls of dough about 2 tbsp in size onto the pan.
4. Place in your Grill and bake for 10-12 minutes. Let cool for a couple minutes before removing from the pan. Enjoy!

Spiced Lemon Cherry Pie

Servings: 6-8

Cooking Time: 60 Minutes

Ingredients:

- 1/2 Teaspoon Cinnamon, Ground
- 1/2 Teaspoon Cloves, Ground
- 1/2 Cup Cornstarch
- 1 Pound Frozen Sweet Dark Cherries, Thawed
- 1 Teaspoon Water (Beaten With Egg) 1 Egg
- 1 Lemon, Juice
- 1 Lemon, Zest
- 2 Prepared Store Bought Or Homemade Pie Crust
- 1 Teaspoon Hickory Honey Sea Salt Seasoning
- 1 Cup Sugar, Granulated
- 1 Teaspoon Vanilla Extract

Directions:

1. In a large bowl, mix together the thawed cherries and their juices, sugar, cornstarch, lemon zest, lemon juice, cinnamon, clove, vanilla extract and Hickory Honey Sea Salt. Allow to sit for 30 minutes.
2. Flour a work surface and roll out one of the prepared pie crusts so that it fits a 9 inch pie tin. Fill with the cherry pie filling and refrigerate. When the pie is chilled, roll out the second pie crust, brush the edge of the first pie crust with the egg mixture, top with the second pie crust, crimp the edge with a fork, and chill. Alternatively, cut the second pie crust into strips and form a lattice pattern, attaching the strips with the egg mixture. Chill the pie for 15-30 minutes, or until the dough is very cold and firm. Brush the top of the pie with the remaining egg mixture.
3. Supply your smoker with wood pellets and follow the start-up procedure. Preheat the grill, with the lid closed, to 350° F and grill for 45 minutes to 1 hour, or until the pie crust is golden and firm and the filling is bubbly. Remove from the grill and allow to cool at room temperature for at least 4 hours to set the filling, then serve and enjoy!

Caramel Bourbon Bacon Brownies

Servings: 16
Cooking Time: 60 Minutes

Ingredients:

- 2 Cup All-Purpose Flour
- 1/4 Cup Bourbon
- 1 Cup Brown Sugar
- 1 Cup Canola Oil
- Caramel Sauce
- 1.5 Cup Cocoa Powder
- 1 Tablespoon Hickory Honey Sea Salt
- 2 Tablespoon Instant Coffee
- 6 Large Eggs
- 1/2 Teaspoon Smoked Infused Hickory Honey Sea Salt
- 1 Cup Powdered Sugar

- 6 Slices Bacon, Raw
- 4 Tablespoons Water
- 3 Cups White Sugar

Directions:

1. Supply your smoker with wood pellets and follow the start-up procedure. Preheat the grill, with the lid closed, to 400° F.
2. In a large mixing bowl, whisk together the cocoa, powdered sugar, white sugar, instant coffee and flour.
3. To the flour mixture, add the eggs, oil and water until just combined.
4. Spray the 9 x 13 pan well with cooking spray.
5. Pour half the batter in the pan, drizzle with caramel.
6. Pour other half of batter on top and drizzle with caramel again and add candied bacon to the top.
7. Bake the brownies in the smoker for 1 hour, or until a toothpick inserted in the center of the pan comes out clean.
8. Remove from the smoker and allow to cool before slicing.

Baked Chocolate Brownie Cookies With Egg Nog

Servings: 6
Cooking Time: 12 Minutes

Ingredients:

- 16 Ounce Bar bittersweet chocolate, finely chopped
- 4 Tablespoon unsalted butter, room temperature
- 4 eggs
- 1 1/3 Cup granulated sugar
- 1 Teaspoon vanilla extract
- 1 1/2 Cup all-purpose flour
- 1/2 Teaspoon baking powder
- 1 Cup semisweet chocolate chips

Directions:

1. Supply your smoker with wood pellets and follow the start-up procedure. Preheat the grill, with the lid closed, to 350° F.
2. Line two baking sheets with parchment paper.
3. Put the finely chopped chocolate and butter in a heatproof bowl and set over a saucepan of barely simmering water; stir occasionally until chocolate is completely melted and smooth. Set aside and allow to cool to room temperature.
4. Whisk together eggs, sugar and vanilla extract in a medium bowl. Set aside.
5. Sift together the flour and baking powder in a small bowl. Add the melted chocolate mixture to the egg mixture and stir with a rubber spatula until completely combined.
6. Add the flour mixture in three batches, folding gently into the batter with a spatula. Once all of the flour has been incorporated, stir in the chocolate chips.

7. Scoop 1-1/2 tablespoons of dough onto prepared baking sheets. Bake for 10 to 12 minutes or until they are firm on the outside. Do not over bake. Grill:350° F
8. Leave to cool completely on the baking sheets. Enjoy!

Cheese Mac

Servings: 6 - 10
Cooking Time: 60 Minutes

Ingredients:

- 5 Tbsp All-Purpose Flour
- 4 Strips Bacon
- Black Pepper
- 2 Cups Breadcrumbs
- 4 Oz Brie
- 4 Oz Brie Cheese
- ½ Cup Butter, Melted
- 12 Oz Cheddar Cheese, Grated
- 3 Cloves Garlic, Minced
- 2 Tbsp Extra Virgin Olive Oil
- 1 Tsp Fresh Grated Nutmeg
- 1 Tsp Ground Cayenne
- 8 Oz, Grated Gruyere Cheese
- 1 Cup Heavy Cream
- 1, Minced Jalapeno Pepper
- 4 Oz Mozzarella Cheese, Grated
- 2 Tbsp Parsley, Minced Fresh
- 12 Oz Raclette
- To Taste Salt
- 5 Tbsp Unsalted Butter
- 4 Oz Whole Milk, Warm
- 1 Yellow Onion, Diced

Directions:

1. Supply your smoker with wood pellets and follow the start-up procedure. Preheat the grill, with the lid closed, to 350° F. Bring a large saucepan of water to a boil. Add the pasta and cook according to the package instructions for al dente. Drain.
2. Heat the oil in a large saucepan over medium-high heat.
3. Add the onion and cook for about 5 minutes, stirring often, until lightly colored, then add the garlic and the jalapeño and cook for 2 more minutes.
4. Reduce the heat to medium, add the butter, and stir until melted. Add the flour and cook, stirring often, for 5 minutes to form a light roux.
5. Add the cheeses, the milk, and cream, reduce the heat to medium-low, and cook, stirring often, until the cheese is melted, and a smooth sauce comes together, about 7 minutes.
6. Stir in the cayenne and truffle oil, then add the pasta and stir to fully coat it in the sauce. Season with salt and pepper. Transfer

the mixture to a 12-inch cast-iron skillet and cover with aluminum foil.

7. Place on the grill and bake for 20 minutes. Remove the foil and cover the mac and cheese with the breadcrumbs.

8. Return to the grill and bake for another 15 to 20 minutes, until the cheese is bubbling and the breadcrumbs are golden brown. Serve family style right out of the skillet.

Marbled Brownies With Amaretto & Ricotta

Servings: 4
Cooking Time: 30 Minutes

Ingredients:
- 1 Cup Ricotta Cheese
- 1 eggs
- 1 Tablespoon Amaretto Liqueur
- 1/4 Cup sugar
- 2 Teaspoon cornstarch
- 1/2 Teaspoon vanilla extract
- 1 Brownie Mix

Directions:
1. Coat a 9- by 13-inch nonstick baking pan with cooking spray or softened butter and set aside. (If you do not have a nonstick pan, line a regular one with buttered foil or parchment paper.)

2. In a medium bowl, combine the ricotta, egg, amaretto, sugar, cornstarch, and vanilla and whisk together thoroughly. Set aside.

3. Prepare the brownie mix according to the package directions. Spread the brownie batter evenly in the prepared pan. Randomly drop dollops of the ricotta mixture over the batter. Run a plastic knife through the ricotta mixture to give the brownies a marbled look. (A plastic knife is less likely to scratch your pan's nonstick surface.)

4. Supply your smoker with wood pellets and follow the start-up procedure. Preheat the grill, with the lid closed, to 350° F.

5. Put the pan with the brownie mixture directly on the grill grate and bake, about 25 to 30 minutes. Insert a bamboo skewer or toothpick in the center of the brownies to determine if they are done: the batter should not be wet. Grill: 350 °F

6. Transfer the brownies to a wire cooling rack to cool completely. Cut into squares.

Smoked, Salted Caramel Apple Pie

Servings: 4
Cooking Time: 60 Minutes

Ingredients:
- 1 Cup cream
- 1 Cup brown sugar
- 3/4 Cup Light Corn Syrup
- 6 Tablespoon butter
- 1 Teaspoon sea salt
- 1 Pastry for Double-Crust Pie
- 6 Granny Smith Apples, Cut Into Wedges

Directions:
1. Supply your smoker with wood pellets and follow the start-up procedure. Preheat the grill, with the lid closed, to 180° F.

2. Fill a large pan with ice and water. Pour the cream into a smaller, shallow pan. Place the pan with the cream in the ice bath and place them both on the Traeger to smoke for 15-20 minutes. Grill: 180 °F

3. To make the caramel, combine the sugar and corn syrup in a saucepan and cook over medium heat, stirring constantly until it coats the back of your spoon and starts to turn a copper color, then stir in butter, salt, and smoked cream.

4. To assemble the pie, gather the pie crust, salted caramel, and apples. Place one of the pie crusts into the pie plate and fill with apple slices. Pour caramel over the apples. Lay the top crust over the filling, then crimp the top and bottom crusts together.

5. Make slits in the top crust to release the steam and finish by brushing with egg or cream. Sprinkle with raw sugar and sea salt.

6. When ready to bake, set the Traeger to 375°F and preheat, lid closed for 15 minutes.

7. Place the pie on the grill and bake for 20 minutes. Grill: 375 °F

8. Reduce heat to 325°F and cook for 25 more minutes. When ready, the crust should be golden brown and the filling, bubbly. Grill: 325 °F

9. Remove the pie from the grill and let cool. Serve with vanilla ice cream. Enjoy!

Beer Bread

Servings: 4
Cooking Time: 60 Minutes

Ingredients:
- 400 g all-purpose flour
- 2 Tablespoon sugar
- 1 Tablespoon baking powder
- 1 Teaspoon salt
- 12 Ounce beer
- 2 Tablespoon honey
- 6 Tablespoon butter, melted

Directions:
1. Supply your smoker with wood pellets and follow the start-up procedure. Preheat the grill, with the lid closed, to 350° F.

2. Spray a loaf pan (9x5x3 inches) (55x12x20 cm) with nonstick cooking spray and set aside.

3. Put the flour, sugar, baking powder, and salt in a large mixing bowl. Whisk with a wire whisk to combine and aerate. Add the

beer and honey and stir with a wooden spoon until the batter is just mixed. (Do not overmix.) If desired, gently stir in one or more of the optional add-ins.

4. Pour half of the melted butter in the prepared loaf pan and spoon in the batter. Pour the remainder of the butter over the top of the loaf.

5. Put the loaf pan directly on the grill grate and bake until a wooden skewer or toothpick inserted in the center of the loaf comes out clean, 50 to 60 minutes, and the bread is golden-brown. (Note: If using a glass loaf pan, the baking time might be shorter.)

6. Let the loaf cool slightly in the pan before removing from the pan. Leftovers make great toast.

7. Optional Add-ins: Bacon, cooked and crumbled, 1 cup (100 g) Grated Cheese, Red Bell Pepper and Onion, diced and sauted in Butter (1/4 cup each), Green Onions, minced, Dried Herbs such as Dill, Rosemary, Mixed Italian Herbs, etc,.Cracked Black Pepper, Your favorite Barbecue Rub, such as Traeger's Pork and Poultry Shake, Ground Cinnamon, Dry Ranch Dressing Mix, Coarse-grained Mustard.

Cinnamon Pull-aparts

Servings: 6
Cooking Time: 20 Minutes

Ingredients:

- 16.3 Ounce Biscuits, Homestyle, Canned
- 1 Cup packed brown sugar
- 1/2 Cup butter
- 1/4 Cup water
- 1 Teaspoon ground cinnamon
- 1/2 Cup Nuts (optional)

Directions:

1. Cut each biscuit into 4 pieces and peel each piece in half; set aside.

2. Combine brown sugar, butter and water in a large saucepan and bring to a boil; reduce heat and simmer for 1 minute. Stir in cinnamon and nuts; add biscuit quarters and mix to coat. Pour into greased 13 by 9 inch casserole dish and spread evenly in the dish.

3. Supply your smoker with wood pellets and follow the start-up procedure. Preheat the grill, with the lid closed, to 350° F.

4. Place the casserole dish on the grill; close lid and cook for 20 to 25 minutes or until the biscuits are done. Grill: 350 °F

5. Remove from the grill and transfer to a serving platter making sure to get all the gooey syrup onto the biscuits. Serve warm. Enjoy!

Caramelized Bourbon Baked Pears

Servings: 4
Cooking Time: 30 Minutes

Ingredients:

- 3 Whole Pears, fresh
- 1/4 Cup brown sugar
- 1/4 Cup bourbon
- 2 Tablespoon butter, melted
- 1 Teaspoon vanilla extract
- 1/2 Teaspoon salt

Directions:

1. Supply your smoker with wood pellets and follow the start-up procedure. Preheat the grill, with the lid closed, to 325° F.

2. Peel and core the pears. Arrange them in a buttered baking dish.

3. In a small bowl, combine the brown sugar, bourbon, butter, vanilla, cinnamon and salt. Pour the bourbon mixture over the pears.

4. Place the baking dish on the grill grate, close the lid and bake for 30-35 minutes or until the pears are fork tender. Grill: 325 °F

5. Transfer to a serving plate and spoon the caramelized bourbon mixture over the pears.

6. Serve warm over vanilla ice cream. Enjoy!

Blueberry Sour Cream Muffins

Servings: 8
Cooking Time: 25 Minutes

Ingredients:

- 2 Cup flour
- 1/2 Teaspoon salt
- 1/2 Teaspoon baking soda
- 1/2 Cup butter
- 3/4 Cup sugar, plus more for muffin tops
- 2 Large eggs
- 3/4 Cup sour cream
- 1 1/2 Teaspoon vanilla extract
- 1 1/2 Cup blueberries, fresh or thawed

Directions:

1. In a small mixing bowl, whisk together the flour, salt and baking soda.

2. In another bowl, using a wooden spoon or a mixer, beat the butter and sugar until light-colored and fluffy. Beat in the eggs, one at a time. Stir in sour cream and vanilla.

3. Add the flour mixture gradually and mix just until incorporated. Using a rubber spatula, gently fold in the blueberries.

4. Line a 12-cup muffin tin with the cupcake liners. Using an ice cream scoop or spoon, fill each muffin cup two-thirds full with the batter. Sprinkle sugar evenly over the top of each muffin.

5. Supply your smoker with wood pellets and follow the start-up procedure. Preheat the grill, with the lid closed, to 375° F.

6. Bake the muffins 25 to 30 minutes, or until a toothpick inserted comes out clean. Served warm and with butter. Grill: 375 °F

Traeger Baked Protein Bars

Servings: 6

Cooking Time: 25 Minutes

Ingredients:

- 2 Cup Frozen Sweet Cherries
- 1 Cup Apricots, Frozen
- 1 Scoop Vanilla Protein Powder
- 2 Tablespoon honey
- 1 Teaspoon vanilla extract
- 1 Cup rolled oats

Directions:

1. Supply your smoker with wood pellets and follow the start-up procedure. Preheat the grill, with the lid closed, to 350° F.
2. In the bowl of a food processor, add cherries, apricots (revived in hot water for 5 minutes and drained), vanilla protein powder, honey, and vanilla. Pulse about 10 to 15 times, to break the fruit into smaller pieces and to mix all ingredients.
3. In a separate bowl, fold together oats and fruit mixture. Transfer mixture to a loaf pan or silicone mold and place in grill.
4. Bake for approximately 20 to 25 minutes. Grill: 350 °F
5. Let cool completely and cut into 8 pieces. Enjoy!

Sopapilla Cheesecake By Doug Scheiding

Servings: 8

Cooking Time: 45 Minutes

Ingredients:

- 2 Tablespoon softened butter
- 24 Ounce cream cheese
- 2 Cup granulated sugar, divided
- 2 Teaspoon vanilla
- 2 Can Pillsbury Butter Flake Crescent Rolls
- 1/2 Cup butter, melted
- cinnamon

Directions:

1. Coat a 9x13 inch baking dish with 2 tablespoons softened butter and set aside.
2. Supply your smoker with wood pellets and follow the start-up procedure. Preheat the grill, with the lid closed, to 350° F.
3. In a mixer, combine cream cheese, 1 to 1-1/2 cups of sugar and vanilla. Mix for 60 to 90 seconds on high with paddle attachment.
4. Take crescents out of the refrigerator. Open one can and place into the buttered 9x13 inch rectangular metal pan or glass dish. Make sure to fill in the gaps in this bottom layer of crescents.
5. Put the cream cheese mixture on the top of the crescent layer using a spatula to make it level.

6. Open the second can of crescents and put on top of the cream cheese layer, again filling in the gaps in the crescents to cover middle.
7. Pour 1/2 cup of melted butter on the top of the last layer of crescent. Start on sides first then middle.
8. Then sprinkle 1/4 cup to 1/2 cup of sugar over the entire pan followed by a light, even dusting of cinnamon.
9. Place pan directly on the grill grate and bake for 40 to 50 minutes until top is brown and starting to get crusty. Grill: 350 °F
10. Remove from grill and let cool 5 to 10 minutes. This allows the cheesecake to set which makes portioning easier. This dessert can be served warm or cold. Enjoy!

Italian Herb & Parmesan Scones

Servings: 8

Cooking Time: 20 Minutes

Ingredients:

- 2 1/2 Cup all-purpose flour
- 2 Teaspoon baking powder
- 1 Teaspoon baking soda
- 1/2 Teaspoon garlic salt
- 1 Tablespoon Italian Seasoning
- 1 Cup Parmesan cheese, grated
- 2 Large eggs
- 1 1/2 Cup buttermilk
- 1/4 Cup olive oil

Directions:

1. In a large mixing bowl, combine flour, baking powder, baking powder, soda, garlic salt, Italian seasoning, and 1/2 cup of the cheese. Make a well in the center.
2. In a smaller bowl, whisk together eggs, buttermilk, and olive oil.
3. Pour into the well in the dry ingredients, and stir batter just until it's combined. It will appear lumpy.
4. Oil 12 muffin cups, spray with cooking spray, or line with disposable paper liners.
5. Divide the batter evenly between the cups. Sprinkle the tops of the muffins with the remaining Parmesan cheese.
6. Supply your smoker with wood pellets and follow the start-up procedure. Preheat the grill, with the lid closed, to 400° F.
7. Arrange the muffin tin directly on the grill grate and bake the muffins for 20 to 25 minutes, or until a toothpick inserted in the center of the muffin comes out clean.
8. Cool for several minutes before removing from the muffin tin. Serve warm with butter or olive oil. Enjoy!

Vanilla Cheesecake Skillet Brownie

Servings: 2
Cooking Time: 30 Minutes

Ingredients:

- 1 Box Brownie Mix
- 1 Package Cream Cheese
- 2 Egg
- 1/2 Cup Oil
- 1 Can Pie Filling, Blueberry
- 1/2 Cup Sugar
- 1 Tsp Vanilla
- 1/4 Cup Water, Warm

Directions:

1. Combine all brownie ingredients and mix. In a separate bowl, combine cream cheese, sugar, egg and vanilla and mix until smooth. Grease skillets and pour in brownie batter. Top with cheesecake and cherry pie filling, using a knife to blend to give it that marbled look.
2. Supply your smoker with wood pellets and follow the start-up procedure. Preheat the grill, with the lid closed, to 350°F and bake for about 30 minutes.
3. Let cool for about 10 minutes and enjoy!

Maple Syrup Pancake Casserole

Servings: 6
Cooking Time: 60 Minutes

Ingredients:

- 2 Tbsp Butter
- 1/2 Cup Chocolate Chips
- 4 Egg
- Maple Syrup
- 12 - 14 Pancakes
- Powdered Sugar
- 1/4 Cup Sugar, Granulated
- 1 Tsp Vanilla Extract
- 1 1/2 Cup Whole Milk

Directions:

1. In a mixing bowl, whisk together flour, baking powder, sugar, and salt. Then pour in the milk, egg and melted butter; mix until smooth.
2. Supply your smoker with wood pellets and follow the start-up procedure. Preheat the grill, with the lid closed, to medium-low heat. If using a gas or charcoal grill, preheat a large cast iron skillet over medium-low heat.
3. Lightly oil the griddle, then scoop the batter onto the griddle, using approximately ¼ cup for each pancake. Cook 1 to 2 minutes per side, until golden brown. Set aside to cool for 15 minutes, then assemble the casserole.

Pretzel Rolls

Servings: 6
Cooking Time: 20 Minutes

Ingredients:

- 2 3/4 Cup Bread Flour
- 1 Quick-Rising Yeast, envelope
- 1 Teaspoon salt
- 1 Teaspoon sugar
- 1/2 Teaspoon celery seed
- 1/2 Teaspoon Caraway Seeds
- 1 Cup hot water
- As Needed Cornmeal
- 8 Cup water
- 1/4 Cup baking soda
- 2 Tablespoon sugar
- 1 Whole Egg White
- Coarse salt

Directions:

1. Combine bread flour, 1 envelope yeast, salt, 1 teaspoon sugar, caraway seeds and celery seeds in food processor or standing mixer with dough hook and blend.
2. With machine running, gradually pour hot water, adding enough water to form smooth elastic dough. Process 1 minute to knead. (You could also knead it by hand for a few minutes.)
3. Grease medium bowl. Add dough to bowl, turning to coat. Cover bowl with plastic wrap, then towel; let dough rise in warm draft-free area until doubled in volume, about 35 minutes.
4. Flour a large baking sheet. Punch dough down and knead on lightly floured surface until smooth. Divide into 8 pieces. Form each dough piece into a ball.
5. Place dough balls on prepared sheet, flattening each slightly. Using serrated knife, cut X in top center of each dough ball. Cover with towel and let dough balls rise until almost doubled in volume, about 20 minutes.
6. When ready to cook, start the smoker on Smoke with the lid open until a fire is established (4-5 minutes). Turn temperature to 375 F (190 C) and preheat, lid closed, for 10 to 15 minutes.
7. Grease another baking sheet and sprinkle with cornmeal. Bring water to boil in large saucepan. Add baking soda and sugar (water will foam up). Add 3 rolls (or however many will fit comfortably in the pot) and cook 30 seconds per side.
8. Using slotted spoon, transfer rolls to prepared sheet, arranging X side up. Repeat with remaining rolls. Brush rolls with egg white glaze. Sprinkle rolls generously with coarse salt.
9. Bake rolls until brown, about 20 to 25 minutes. Transfer to racks and cool 10 minutes. Serve rolls warm or at room temperature. Enjoy!

Anzac Coconut Biscuits

Servings: 4
Cooking Time: 30 Minutes

Ingredients:

- This recipe makes a dozen biscuits.
- 1 cup rolled oats
- 3/4 cup raw sugar
- 3/4 cup desiccated coconut
- 1 cup plain flour, sifted
- 125 g butter, melted
- 2 tablespoons Golden Syrup
- 1/2 tsp bicarb soda
- 3 tablespoons boiling water

Directions:

1. Combine and mix thoroughly sifted flour, oats, sugar and coconut in a large bowl.
2. Melt the butter and Golden Syrup over low heat.
3. Add boiling water to the bicarb soda, once dissolved add into the butter/syrup mix, it will bubble/fizz up a bit.
4. Add the liquid into the dry ingredients and mix throughly.
5. Rolls the mix into golf ball size balls and layout on grease proof paper on baking tray and flatten the tops just slightly.
6. Space the balls with about 3 fingers between each ball as they will flatten to about triple the diameter as they cook.
7. Supply your smoker with wood pellets and follow the start-up procedure. Preheat the grill, with the lid closed, to 350° F. Cook for 25-30 minutes until golden brown.
8. Rest on cooling rack until at room temperature then store in air-tight container.

Pineapple Cake

Servings: 4
Cooking Time: 30 Minutes

Ingredients:

- 2/3 cup of vegetable oil (olive oil works great, not virgin)
- 3 eggs
- 1/3 cup brown sugar (not too sweet)
- 3/4 cup self raising plain flour
- 1/4 cup wholemeal self raising flour
- 1/3 cup saltanas
- 1/3 cup diced canned pineapple (drained)
- 1/3 cup diced raw walnuts
- 2 large carrots grated
- Icing Ingredients
- 250 grams cream cheese
- 35 grams icing sugar (not too sweet)
- Whole lemon or orange zest

Directions:

1. Mix all ingredients in a large bowl.
2. Place into 6″ greased baking tray or un-greased silicone tray.
3. Supply your smoker with wood pellets and follow the start-up procedure. Preheat the grill, with the lid closed, to 190 °F. Cook for 25-30min until golden brown and no dough when probed.
4. Let cool on rack (not directly on plate or board) then apply icing.
5. Whip icing ingredients and place in fridge until ready to coat the cake.

Pizza Bites

Servings: 6
Cooking Time: 20 Minutes

Ingredients:

- 4 1/2 Cup Bread Flour
- 1 1/2 Tablespoon sugar
- 2 Teaspoon Instant Yeast
- 2 Teaspoon kosher salt
- 3 Tablespoon extra-virgin olive oil
- 15 Fluid Ounce Water, Lukewarm
- 8 Ounce Pepperoni, sliced
- 1 Cup pizza sauce
- 1 Cup mozzarella cheese
- 1 Whole egg, for egg wash
- 1 As Needed salt

Directions:

1. For the Pizza Dough: Combine flour, sugar, salt, and yeast in food processor. Pulse 3 to 4 times until incorporated evenly. Add olive oil and water. Run food processor until mixture forms ball that rides around the bowl above the blade, about 15 seconds. Continue processing 15 seconds longer.
2. Transfer dough ball to lightly floured surface and knead once or twice by hand until smooth ball is formed. Divide dough into three even parts and place each into a 1 gallon zip top bag. Place in refrigerator and allow to rise at least one day.
3. At least two hours before baking, remove dough from refrigerator and shape into balls by gathering dough towards bottom and pinching shut. Flour well and place each one in a separate medium mixing bowl. Cover tightly with plastic wrap and allow to rise at warm room temperature until roughly doubled in volume.
4. When ready to cook, set the grill temperature to 350°F and preheat, lid closed for 15 minutes.
5. After the first rise remove the dough from the fridge and let come to room temperature. Roll dough on a flat surface. Cut dough into long strips 3" wide by 18" long.
6. Slice pepperoni into strips.
7. In a medium bowl combine the pizza sauce, mozzarella and pepperoni.

8. Spoon 1 TBSP of the pizza filling onto the pizza dough every two inches, about halfway down the length of the dough. Dip a pastry brush into the egg wash and brush around pizza filling. Fold the half side of the dough (without the pizza filling) over the other half that contains the pizza filling.

9. Press down between each pizza bite slightly with your fingers. With a ravioli or pizza cutter, cut around each filling- creating a rectangle shape and sealing the crust in.

10. Transfer each pizza bite onto a parchment lined cookie sheet. Cover with a kitchen towel and let them rise for 30 minutes.

11. When ready to cook, preheat the grill to 350 F with the lid closed for 10-15 minutes.

12. Brush the bites with remaining egg wash, sprinkle with salt and place directly on the sheet tray. Bake 10-15 minutes until the exterior is golden brown.

13. Remove from grill and transfer to a serving dish. Serve with extra pizza sauce for dipping and enjoy!

Smoked Blackberry Pie

Servings: 4-6
Cooking Time: 25 Minutes

Ingredients:

- Nonstick cooking spray or butter, for greasing
- 1 box (2 sheets) refrigerated piecrusts
- 8 tablespoons (1 stick) unsalted butter, melted, plus 8 tablespoons (1 stick) cut into pieces
- ½ cup all-purpose flour
- 2 cups sugar, divided
- 2 pints blackberries
- ½ cup milk
- Vanilla ice cream, for serving

Directions:

1. Supply your smoker with wood pellets and follow the start-up procedure. Preheat, with the lid closed, to 375°F.

2. Coat a cast iron skillet with cooking spray.

3. Unroll 1 refrigerated piecrust and place in the bottom and up the side of the skillet. Using a fork, poke holes in the crust in several places.

4. Set the skillet on the grill grate, close the lid, and smoke for 5 minutes, or until lightly browned. Remove from the grill and set aside.

5. In a large bowl, combine the stick of melted butter with the flour and 1½ cups of sugar.

6. Add the blackberries to the flour-sugar mixture and toss until well coated.

7. Spread the berry mixture evenly in the skillet and sprinkle the milk on top. Scatter half of the cut pieces of butter randomly over the mixture.

8. Unroll the remaining piecrust and place it over the top of skillet or slice the dough into even strips and weave it into a lattice. Scatter the remaining pieces of butter along the top of the crust.

9. Sprinkle the remaining ½ cup of sugar on top of the crust and return the skillet to the smoker.

10. Close the lid and smoke for 15 to 20 minutes, or until bubbly and brown on top. It may be necessary to use some aluminum foil around the edges near the end of the cooking time to prevent the crust from burning.

11. Serve the pie hot with vanilla ice cream.

Smokin' Lemon Bars

Servings: 8-12
Cooking Time: 60 Minutes

Ingredients:

- 3/4 Cup lemon juice
- 1 1/2 Cup sugar
- 2 eggs
- 3 Egg Yolk
- 1 1/2 Teaspoon cornstarch
- Pinch sea salt
- 4 Tablespoon unsalted butter
- 1/4 Cup olive oil
- 1/2 Tablespoon lemon zest
- 1 1/4 Cup flour
- 1/4 Cup granulated sugar
- 3 Tablespoon Confectioner's Sugar
- 1 Teaspoon lemon zest
- 1/4 Teaspoon Sea Salt, Fine
- 10 Tablespoon Unsalted Butter, Cut Into Cubes

Directions:

1. When ready to cook, set grill temperature to 180°F and preheat, lid closed for 15 minutes.

2. In a small mixing bowl, whisk together lemon juice, sugar, eggs and yolks, cornstarch and fine sea salt. Pour into a sheet tray or cake pan and place on grill. Smoke for 30 minutes whisking mixture halfway through smoking. Remove from grill and set aside.

3. Pour mixture into a small saucepan. Place on stove top set to medium heat until boiling. Once boiling, boil for 60 seconds. Remove from heat and strain through a mesh strainer into a bowl. Whisk in cold butter, olive oil, and lemon zest.

4. To make a crust, pulse together the flour, granulated sugar, confectioners' sugar, lemon zest and salt in a food processor. Add butter and pulse until just mixed into a crumbly dough. Press dough into a prepared 9" by 9" baking dish lined with parchment paper that is long enough to hang over 2 of the sides.

5. When ready to cook, set the smoker to 350°F and preheat, lid closed for 15 minutes.

6. Bake until crust is very lightly golden brown, about 30 to 35 minutes.

7. Remove from grill and pour the lemon filling over the crust. Return to grill and continue to bake until filling is just set about 15 to 20 minutes.

8. Allow to cool at room temperature, then refrigerate until chilled before slicing into bars. Sprinkle with confectioners' sugar and flaky sea salt right before serving. Enjoy!

Baked Cast Iron Berry Cobbler

Servings: 6
Cooking Time: 35 Minutes

Ingredients:
- 4 Cup Berries
- 12 Tablespoon sugar
- Cup orange juice
- 2/3 Cup Flour
- 3/4 Teaspoon baking powder
- 1 Pinch salt
- 1/2 Cup butter
- 1 Tablespoon Sugar, raw

Directions:
1. Supply your smoker with wood pellets and follow the start-up procedure. Preheat the grill, with the lid closed, to 350° F.

2. In a 10-inch (25-cm) cast iron or other baking pan, mix together the berries, 4 Tbsp sugar and the orange juice.

3. In a small bowl, mix together the flour, baking powder and salt. Set aside.

4. In a separate bowl, cream together the butter and granulated sugar. Add the egg and vanilla extract and mix to combine. Gradually fold in the flour mixture.

5. Spoon the batter on top of the berries and sprinkle raw sugar on top.

6. Bake the cobbler for approximately 35-45 minutes. Cool slightly and serve with whipped cream. Enjoy! Grill: 350 °F

Smoky Apple Crepes

Servings: 6
Cooking Time: 60 Minutes

Ingredients:
- 1/2 Cup Apple Juice
- 2 Lbs Apples
- 2 Tbsp Brown Sugar
- 5 Tbsp Butter
- 3 Tbsp Butter, Melted
- Tt Caramel
- 3/4 Tsp Cinnamon, Ground
- Tt Cinnamon-Sugar

- 3/4 Tsp Cornstarch
- 2 Eggs
- 1 Cup Flour
- 2 Tsp Lemon Juice
- Tennessee Apple Butter Seasoning
- 1/2 Cup Water
- 3/4 Cup Milk

Directions:
1. Supply your smoker with wood pellets and follow the start-up procedure. Preheat the grill, with the lid closed, to 225° F. If using a gas or charcoal grill, set it up for low, indirect heat.

2. Peel, halve, and core apples.

3. Season apples with Tennessee Apple Butter then place directly on the grill grate, and smoke for 1 hour.

4. Meanwhile, prepare crêpe batter: combine eggs, milk, water, flour, and 3 tbsp of melted butter in a blender, and blend until smooth.

5. Refrigerate for 30 minutes.

6. Remove apples from grill, cool slightly, then slice thin.

7. Place a cast iron skillet on the grill and melt 3 tbsp butter with brown sugar, cinnamon, cornstarch, apple and lemon juices. Cook for 5 minutes until thick.

8. Add apples and cook for another 3 to 5 minutes, stirring to coat apples in sauce.

9. Remove from grill and set aside.

10. Preheat griddle to medium-low. If using a standard grill, preheat a cast iron skillet on medium-low heat.

11. Melt 1 teaspoon of butter on the griddle.

12. Then add ½ cup of batter, and spread with the bottom of a metal spatula, working quickly, as the batter cooks fast.

13. Cook one minute per side, until edges begin to brown. Remove from griddle, set aside, and repeat with remaining batter.

14. Spoon ¼ cup of apple filling into the center of each crêpe, then quarter-fold into a triangle.

15. Serve warm with additional apple filling, drizzle of warm caramel, and a dusting of cinnamon-sugar.

Pull-apart Dinner Rolls

Servings: 8
Cooking Time: 10 Minutes

Ingredients:
- 1/4 Cup warm water (110°F to 115°F)
- 1/3 Cup vegetable oil
- 2 Tablespoon active dry yeast
- 1/4 Cup sugar
- 1/2 Teaspoon salt
- 1 egg
- 3 1/2 Cup all-purpose flour
- cooking spray

Directions:

1. Supply your smoker with wood pellets and follow the start-up procedure. Preheat the grill, with the lid closed, to 400° F.

2. In the bowl of a stand mixer, combine warm water, oil, yeast and sugar. Let mixture rest for 5 to 10 minutes, or until frothy and bubbly.

3. With a dough hook, mix in salt, egg and 2 cups of flour until combined. Add remaining flour 1/2 cup at a time (dough will be sticky).

4. Prepare a cast iron pan with cooking spray and set aside.

5. Spray your hands with cooking spray and shape the dough into 12 balls.

6. After shaped, place in the prepared cast iron pan and let rest for 10 minutes. Bake in Traeger for about 10 to 12 minutes, or until tops are lightly golden. Enjoy! Grill: 400 °F

SEAFOOD RECIPES

Mezcal Shrimp With Salsa De Molcajete

Servings: 4
Cooking Time: 14 Minutes

Ingredients:
- 18 to 24 jumbo shrimp, about 1½lb (680g) total, peeled and deveined
- ⅓ cup mezcal
- juice of ½ lime
- 2 tbsp extra virgin olive oil
- 2 tsp coarse salt
- 1 tsp ground cumin
- lime wedges
- for the salsa
- 2 Roma tomatoes
- 2 tomatillos, husked and washed
- 2 garlic cloves, peeled and impaled on a toothpick
- 1 jalapeño or serrano pepper
- 1 small white onion, halved
- ½ tsp coarse salt, plus more
- juice of ½ lime
- ¼ cup loosely packed fresh cilantro leaves

Directions:
1. Supply your smoker with wood pellets and follow the start-up procedure. Preheat the grill, with the lid closed, to 450° F.
2. In a large bowl, combine the shrimp, mezcal, lime juice, olive oil, salt, and ground cumin. Toss with your hands to mix thoroughly. Set aside for 15 minutes and then toss once more.
3. Begin to make the salsa by placing the tomatoes, tomatillos, garlic, jalapeño, and onion on the grate. Grill until they begin to char, about 3 minutes for the garlic and about 6 to 8 minutes for the other vegetables, turning as needed. Transfer the vegetables to a rimmed sheet pan. Remove the skewers from the garlic. Let everything cool. Coarsely chop the vegetables and leave them in separate piles.
4. Place the garlic in the molcajete and add the salt. Mash the garlic to a purée using the temolote. Add the onion and grind it into the garlic paste. Stir in the jalapeño (deseeded for a milder salsa), tomatoes, and tomatillos. Stir in the lime juice and cilantro leaves. Taste, adding salt. (If you don't own a molcajete or temolote, prepare the salsa using a small food processor.)
5. Drain the shrimp and discard the marinade. Thread the shrimp on wood or bamboo skewers. Place the shrimp on the grate and grill until they're white and opaque, about 4 to 6 minutes, tossing with tongs.
6. Transfer the shrimp to a platter. Serve with the salsa and lime wedges.

Traeger Crab Legs

Servings: 4
Cooking Time: 30 Minutes

Ingredients:
- 3 Pound crab legs, thawed and halved
- 1 Cup butter, melted
- 2 Tablespoon fresh lemon juice
- 2 Clove garlic, minced
- 1 Tablespoon Fin & Feather Rub or Old Bay Seasoning, plus more to taste
- lemon wedges
- Italian Parsley, chopped

Directions:
1. If the crab legs are too long to fit in the roasting pan, break them down at the joints by twisting, or use a heavy knife or cleaver. Split the shells open lengthwise. Transfer to the roasting pan.
2. Combine the butter, lemon juice and garlic; whisk to mix. Pour mixture over the crab legs, turning the legs to coat. Sprinkle the Traeger Fin & Feather Rub or Old Bay Seasoning over the legs.
3. Supply your smoker with wood pellets and follow the start-up procedure. Preheat the grill, with the lid closed, to 350° F.
4. Cook the crab legs, basting once or twice with the butter sauce from the bottom of the pan, for 20 to 30 minutes (depending on the size of the crab legs) or until warmed through. Grill: 350 °F
5. Transfer the crab legs to a large platter and divide the sauce and accumulated juices between 4 dipping bowls. Enjoy!

Grilled Salmon

Servings: 4
Cooking Time: 25 Minutes

Ingredients:
- 1 (2-pound) half salmon fillet
- 3 tablespoons mayonnaise
- 1 batch Dill Seafood Rub

Directions:
1. Supply your smoker with wood pellets and follow the start-up procedure. Preheat the grill, with the lid closed, to 325°F.
2. Using your hands, rub the salmon fillet all over with the mayonnaise and sprinkle it with the rub.
3. Place the salmon directly on the grill grate, skin-side down, and grill until its internal temperature reaches 145°F. Remove the salmon from the grill and serve immediately.

Garlic Blackened Salmon

Servings: 4
Cooking Time: 10 Minutes

Ingredients:
- 1 Tablespoon, Optional Cayenne Pepper
- 2 Cloves Garlic, Minced
- 2 Tablespoons Olive Oil
- 4 Tablespoons Sweet Rib Rub
- 2 Pound Salmon, Fillet, Scaled And Deboned

Directions:
1. Supply your smoker with wood pellets and follow the start-up procedure. Preheat the grill, with the lid closed, to 350° F.
2. Remove the skin from the salmon and discard. Brush the salmon on both sides with olive oil, then rub the salmon fillet with the minced garlic, cayenne pepper and Sweet Rib Rub.
3. Grill the salmon for 5 minutes on one side. Flip the salmon and then grill for another 5 minutes, or until the salmon reaches an internal temperature of 145°F. Remove from the grill and serve.

Coconut Shrimp Jalapeño Poppers

Servings: 6
Cooking Time: 55 Minutes

Ingredients:
- 8 Whole shrimp, peeled and deveined
- 1/2 Teaspoon Chicken Rub, plus more as needed
- olive oil
- 6 Whole jalapeños
- 8 Ounce cream cheese, softened
- 2 Tablespoon fresh chopped cilantro
- 1/2 Cup unsweetened coconut flakes
- 12 Slices bacon

Directions:
1. Supply your smoker with wood pellets and follow the start-up procedure. Preheat the grill, with the lid closed, to 425° F.
2. Rinse and season the shrimp with the Traeger Chicken Rub.
3. Drizzle the shrimp with olive oil and cook on the Traeger for about 5 minutes per side, or until the shrimp is opaque. Grill: 425 °F
4. Remove the shrimp and let cool.
5. Reduce Traeger temperature to 350°F. Grill: 350 °F
6. Meanwhile, get those poppers going. Cut the jalapeños in half then remove the stems and seeds.
7. Chop the shrimp. Mix together the softened cream cheese, chopped shrimp, 1/2 teaspoon Traeger Chicken Rub and 2 tablespoons chopped cilantro.
8. Load a generous amount of the filling in each pepper half. Top with a sprinkle of coconut.

9. Wrap each stuffed pepper with a slice of bacon and place on a foil-lined baking sheet.
10. Cook the peppers on the Traeger for about 45 minutes, or until the bacon fat has rendered and the cream cheese is golden. Enjoy! Grill: 350 °F

Smoked Sugar Halibut

Servings: 8
Cooking Time: 120 Minutes

Ingredients:
- 1/4 cup granulated sugar
- 1/4 cup brown sugar
- 1/2 cup kosher salt
- 1 tsp ground coriander
- 2 lbs fresh halibut

Directions:
1. In a small bowl, mix the sugars, salt, and coriander together. Season the halibut on all sides.
2. Wrap the halibut in plastic wrap, place on a rimmed sheet pan, and brine in the fridge for 3 hours.
3. Remove the plastic wrap and rinse the fish. Pat it dry. Set it on a drying rack over a sheet pan for 1-2 hours in the fridge.
4. Supply your smoker with wood pellets and follow the start-up procedure. Preheat the grill, with the lid closed, to 200° F. Smoke the fish for 2 hours or until its internal temperature reaches 140 °F.
5. Serve your preferred sauce with the fish.

Grilled Lemon Lobster Tails

Servings: 3
Cooking Time: 7 Minutes

Ingredients:
- 6 lobster tails
- 1/4 cup melted butter
- 1/4 cup fresh lemon juice
- 1 tablespoon fresh dill
- 1 teaspoon salt
- 6 lime wedges

Directions:
1. Supply your smoker with wood pellets and follow the start-up procedure. Preheat the grill, with the lid closed, to 375° F.
2. Split the lobster tails in half place then back side down.
3. Cut down through the center to the shell the whole length of each tail.
4. Pull the shell back, exposing the meat.
5. Pat the lobster tails with paper towel to dry.
6. Combine in a small mixing bowl the butter, lemon juice, dill, and salt until the salt has dissolved.
7. Brush the mixture onto the flesh side of each lobster tail.

8. Place the lobster tails onto the grill and cook for 5 to 7 minutes, turning them once during the cooking process. (The shells should turn a bright pink).
9. Remove the heat.
10. Serve with lime wedges!

Barbecued Shrimp

Servings: 4
Cooking Time: 10 Minutes

Ingredients:
- 1 pound peeled and deveined shrimp, with tails on
- 2 tablespoons olive oil
- 1 batch Dill Seafood Rub

Directions:
1. Soak wooden skewers in water for 30 minutes.
2. Supply your smoker with wood pellets and follow the start-up procedure. Preheat the grill, with the lid closed, to 375°F.
3. Thread 4 or 5 shrimp per skewer.
4. Coat the shrimp all over with olive oil and season each side of the skewers with the rub.
5. Place the skewers directly on the grill grate and grill the shrimp for 5 minutes per side. Remove the skewers from the grill and serve immediately.

Seared Bluefin Tuna Steaks

Servings: 2
Cooking Time: 5 Minutes

Ingredients:
- 3 Whole Tuna, steak
- olive oil
- salt and pepper
- soy sauce
- Sriracha

Directions:
1. Lightly baste both sides of tuna steaks in olive oil; sprinkle sea salt and ground pepper on each side.
2. Supply your smoker with wood pellets and follow the start-up procedure. Preheat the grill, with the lid closed, to High heat.
3. Grill tuna steaks on each side for 2 to 2-1/2 minutes.
4. Remove tuna from grill and allow to cool slightly.
5. Cut into 1/2 - 3/4" pieces. Serve with a mixture of Soy Sauce and Sriracha. Enjoy!"

Oysters In The Shell

Servings: 4
Cooking Time: 20 Minutes

Ingredients:

- 8 medium oysters, unopened, in the shell, rinsed and scrubbed
- 1 batch Lemon Butter Mop for Seafood

Directions:
1. Supply your smoker with wood pellets and follow the start-up procedure. Preheat the grill, with the lid closed, to 375°F.
2. Place the unopened oysters directly on the grill grate and grill for about 20 minutes, or until the oysters are done and their shells open.
3. Discard any oysters that do not open. Shuck the remaining oysters, transfer them to a bowl, and add the mop. Serve immediately.

Thai-style Swordfish Steaks With Peanut Sauce

Servings: 4
Cooking Time: 8 Minutes

Ingredients:
- 4 center-cut swordfish steaks, each about 6oz (170g) and 1 inch (2.5cm) thick
- Peanut Sauce
- lime wedges
- for the marinade
- 1/2 cup light Thai-style unsweetened coconut milk
- 2 garlic cloves, peeled and smashed with a chef's knife
- juice and zest of 1 lime
- 1-inch (2.5cm) piece of fresh ginger, peeled and roughly chopped
- 1/2 Thai bird's eye chili pepper or serrano pepper, deseeded and thinly sliced, plus more
- 2 tbsp fresh cilantro leaves, coarsely chopped
- 1 tbsp Asian fish sauce
- 1 tbsp light soy sauce or liquid aminos
- 1 tbsp light brown sugar or low-carb substitute
- 1 tsp ground coriander
- 1/2 tsp ground turmeric

Directions:
1. In a medium bowl, make the marinade by whisking together the ingredients. Whisk until the brown sugar dissolves.
2. Place the swordfish steaks in a single layer in a nonreactive baking dish and pour the marinade over them, turning the steaks to coat thoroughly. Refrigerate for 1 hour.
3. Supply your smoker with wood pellets and follow the start-up procedure. Preheat the grill, with the lid closed, to 450° F.
4. Remove the swordfish from the marinade and scrape off any solids. (Discard the marinade.) Place the steaks on the grate and grill until the fish easily flakes when pressed with a fork, about 3 to 4 minutes per side, turning with a thin-bladed spatula.
5. Transfer the swordfish steaks to a platter. Serve with the peanut sauce and lime wedges.

Baked Whole Fish In Sea Salt

Servings: 4

Cooking Time: 30 Minutes

Ingredients:

- 3 Pound Whole Branzino, (1.5 each)
- 10 Sprig thyme sprigs
- 1 Medium lemon, thinly sliced
- 5 Cup sea salt
- 10 Whole egg white
- olive oil
- 1 Whole lemon juice

Directions:

1. Supply your smoker with wood pellets and follow the start-up procedure. Preheat the grill, with the lid closed, to High heat.
2. Clip the fins and remove the gills from the fish. Stuff cavity with thyme and lemon slices. Whip the egg whites to soft peaks and fold in the sea salt.
3. Place directly on the grill grate and bake for 30 minutes or until a thermometer poked through the salt crust and into the flesh of the fish registers an internal temperature of 135-140 degrees F. Remove fish from the grill and let stand 10 minutes.
4. Using a wooden spoon, strike the crust to crack it open and brush remaining salt from the surface of the fish.
5. Remove the skin and drizzle fish with good olive oil and a squeeze of lemon. Enjoy!

Smoked Salt Cured Lox

Servings: 8

Cooking Time: 30 Minutes

Ingredients:

- 1 Cup kosher salt
- 1 Cup sugar
- 1 Tablespoon cracked black pepper
- 1 Whole lemon zest
- 1 Whole orange zest
- 1 Whole Packaged Dill, roughly chopped including stems
- 2 Pound salmon fillet, skin on

Directions:

1. Mix together salt, sugar, black pepper, lemon zest, orange zest, and dill.
2. Slice salmon in half. Coat all flesh of salmon completely with salt sugar mixture. Sandwich the 2 pieces together, flesh to flesh and completely cover with salt sugar mixture.
3. Wrap tightly with plastic wrap and place into a gallon zip top bag. Squeeze out as much air as possible. Place wrapped salmon into a baking dish and place something heavy on top like a pot filled with water or a brick wrapped in foil. Place into the refrigerator for 10 hours. After 10 hours, flip over and put the weight back on top. Refrigerate for another 10 hours.
4. Remove from refrigerator, unwrap and rinse of remaining salt with cold water. Pat dry and leave on counter for 1 hour.
5. Supply your smoker with wood pellets and follow the start-up procedure. Preheat the grill, with the lid closed, to 180° F.
6. Place salmon onto a baking pan. Fill another baking pan with ice and place baking pan with salmon over ice.
7. Place onto grill and smoke for 30 minutes. Remove from grill and slice thin. Grill: 180 ˚F
8. Serve with bagels, cream cheese, capers, dill, lemon wedges, sliced tomatoes, and red onion. Enjoy!

Smoked Cedar Plank Salmon

Servings: 4

Cooking Time: 20 Minutes

Ingredients:

- 1/4 Cup Brown Sugar
- 1/2 Tablespoon Olive Oil
- Competition Smoked Seasoning
- 4 Salmon Fillets, Skin Off

Directions:

1. Soak the untreated cedar plank in water for 24 hours before grilling. When ready to grill, remove and wipe down.
2. Supply your smoker with wood pellets and follow the start-up procedure. Preheat the grill, with the lid closed, to 350° F.
3. In a small bowl, mix the brown sugar, oil, and Lemon Pepper, Garlic, and Herb seasoning. Rub generously over the salmon fillets.
4. Place the plank over indirect heat, then lay the salmon on the plank and grill for 15-20 minutes, or until the salmon is cooked through and flakes easily with a fork. Remove from the heat and serve immediately.

Delicious Smoked Trout

Servings: 8

Cooking Time: 120 Minutes

Ingredients:

- 6 rainbow trout fillets
- Brine:
- 2 Tablespoons kosher salt
- 2 Tablespoons brown sugar
- 4 cups cool water

Directions:

1. For the brine, dissolve the kosher salt and brown sugar in water.
2. Place the trout fillets in the brine, skin side up, and brine the fillets for 15 minutes.

3. Supply your smoker with wood pellets and follow the start-up procedure. Preheat the grill, with the lid closed, to 180° F.

4. Remove the trout from the brine and transfer it to the grill grates.

5. Smoke the trout for 1.5 to 2 hours with the lid closed, depending on the thickness of your fillets.

6. Smoke until the trout reaches an internal temperature of 145 °F, or until the trout flakes easily.

7. Remove the trout from the smoker and serve warm, or let it cool completely and serve chilled with your favorite accouterments.

Lemon Shrimp Scampi

Servings: 3
Cooking Time: 10 Minutes

Ingredients:
- 2 Tsp Blackened Sriracha Rub Seasoning
- 1/2 Cup Butter, Cubed, Divided
- 1/2 Tsp Chili Pepper Flakes
- 3 Garlic Cloves, Minced
- To Taste, Lemon Wedges, For Serving
- 1 Lemon, Juice & Zest
- Linguine, Cooked
- 3 Tbsp Parsley, Chopped
- 1 1/2 Lbs Shrimp, Peeled & Deveined
- Toasted Baguette, For Serving

Directions:
1. Supply your smoker with wood pellets and follow the start-up procedure. Preheat the grill, with the lid closed, to medium-high heat. If using a gas or charcoal grill, set it up for medium-high heat.

2. Add half of the butter to the griddle, then sauté the garlic, Blackened Sriracha, and chili flakes for 1 minute, until fragrant.

3. Add the shrimp, turning occasionally for 2 minutes, until opaque.

4. Add the remaining butter, parsley, lemon zest and juice. Toss the shrimp to coat in lemon butter, then remove from the griddle, and transfer to a serving bowl.

5. Serve immediately, with fresh lemon wedges, and toasted baguette. Serve over linguine, spaghetti or zucchini noodles, if desired.

Shrimp Cabbage Tacos With Lime Cream

Servings: 4
Cooking Time: 10 Minutes

Ingredients:
- 1/4 Cabbage, Shredded
- 2 Tsp Cilantro, Chopped
- Corn Tortillas
- 1/2 Lime, Wedges
- 1/4 Cup Mayonnaise
- Blackened Sriracha Rub
- 1/4 Red Bell Pepper, Chopped
- 1 Lb Shrimp, Peeled & Deveined
- 1/4 Cup Sour Cream
- 2 Tsp Vegetable Oil
- 1/2 White Onion, Chopped

Directions:
1. Place shrimp In a medium bowl. Season with Blackened Sriracha Rub, then drizzle with vegetable oil. Toss by hand to coat well then set aside.

2. In a small mixing bowl, stir together mayonnaise, sour cream, and fresh lime juice. Season to taste with Blackened Sriracha. Set aside.

3. In a small mixing bowl, combine jalapeño, onion, red bell pepper, and cilantro. Set aside.

4. Supply your smoker with wood pellets and follow the start-up procedure. Preheat the grill, with the lid closed, till over medium heat. If using a grill, preheat a cast iron skillet over medium-heat.

5. Place tortillas on the griddle to warm each side, then turn off the burner below.

6. Transfer shrimp to the hot griddle, and cook for 4 to 6 minutes, tossing occasionally, until opaque. For spicier shrimp, season with additional Blackened Sriracha.

7. Assemble tacos: shredded cabbage, shrimp, pepper mixture, then drizzle with sauce. Serve warm with fresh lime wedges.

Grilled Pepper Lobster Tails

Servings: 3
Cooking Time: 10 Minutes

Ingredients:
- Tt Black Pepper
- 3/4 Stick Butter, Room Temp
- 2 Tablespoons Chives, Chopped
- 1 Clove Garlic, Minced
- Lemon, Sliced
- 3 (7-Ounce) Lobster, Tail
- Tt Salt, Kosher

Directions:
1. Start your Grill on "SMOKE" with the lid open until a fire is established in the burn pot (3-7 minutes).

2. Supply your smoker with wood pellets and follow the start-up procedure. Preheat the grill, with the lid closed, to 350° F.

3. Blend butter, chives, minced garlic, and black pepper in a small bowl. Cover with plastic wrap and set aside.

4. Butterfly the tails down the middle of the softer underside of the shell. Don't cut entirely through the center of the meat. Brush the tails with olive oil and season with salt, to your liking.

5. Grill lobsters cut side down about 5 minutes until the shells are bright red in color. Flip the tails over and top with a generous tablespoon of herb butter. Grill for another 4 minutes, or until the lobster meat is an opaque white color.

6. Remove from the grill and serve with more herb butter and lemon wedges.

Cider Hot-smoked Salmon

Servings: 4
Cooking Time: 60 Minutes

Ingredients:
- 1 1/2 Pound Wild Caught Salmon Fillet, skinned, pin bones removed
- 12 Ounce apple juice or cider
- 4 Pieces juniper berries
- 1 Pieces Star Anise, Broken
- 1 Pieces bay leaf, coarsely crumbled
- 1/2 Cup kosher salt
- 1/4 Cup brown sugar
- 2 Teaspoon Blackened Saskatchewan Rub
- 1 Teaspoon coarse ground black pepper, divided

Directions:
1. Rinse the salmon fillet under cold running water and check for pin bones by running a finger over the fleshy part of the fillet. If you feel a bone, remove it with kitchen tweezers or a needle-nose pliers.

2. In a sturdy resealable plastic bag, combine the cider, crushed juniper berries, star anise, and bay leaf. Add the salmon fillet and put the bag in a bowl or pan in the refrigerator. Let sit for at least 8 hours, or overnight.

3. Remove the salmon from the bag and discard the cider mixture. Dry the salmon well on paper towels. Make the cure: In a small mixing bowl, combine the kosher salt, brown sugar, and Traeger rub.

4. Pour half into a shallow plate, or baking dish. Put the salmon fillet, skin-side down, on top of the cure. Generously sprinkle the top with the remaining cure, cover with plastic wrap, and refrigerate for 1 to 1-1/2 hours. Any longer, and the fish will get too salty.

5. Remove the salmon from the cure and pat dry with paper towels. Sprinkle the black pepper on top of the fillet.

6. Supply your smoker with wood pellets and follow the start-up procedure. Preheat the grill, with the lid closed, to 200° F.

7. Lay the salmon skin-side down on the grill grate. Cook for 1 hour, or until the internal temperature in the thickest part of the fish reaches 150 or the fish flakes easily when pressed with a finger or fork. Grill: 200 °F Probe: 150 °F

8. Let cool slightly. Turn the fillet over and remove the skin; it should come off in one piece.

9. If not serving immediately, let the salmon cool completely, then wrap in plastic wrap and refrigerate for up to 2 days. Transfer to a platter and serve with some or all of the suggested accompaniments. Enjoy!

Hot-smoked Salmon

Servings: 4
Cooking Time: 180minutes

Ingredients:
- 1½lb (680g) skinless center-cut salmon fillet, preferably wild caught
- for the brine
- 1 quart (1 liter) distilled water
- ¼ cup coarse salt
- ¼ cup light brown sugar or low-carb equivalent
- ¼ cup gin (optional)

Directions:
1. In a saucepan on the stovetop over medium-high heat, make the brine by combining the water, salt, brown sugar, and gin (if using). Bring the mixture to a boil. Stir until the salt and sugar dissolve. Remove the pan from the stovetop and let the brine cool to room temperature. Refrigerate until cool.

2. Run your fingers over the salmon fillet, feeling for bones. Remove any with kitchen tweezers or needle-nosed pliers. Rinse the salmon under cold running water. Place the salmon in a resealable plastic bag and pour the brine over it. Refrigerate for 4 to 8 hours.

3. Place a wire rack on a rimmed sheet pan. Remove the salmon from the brine and rinse under cold running water. Pat dry with paper towels and then place the salmon on the wire rack. Place the pan in a cool area with good air circulation (such as near a fan). In 2 to 4 hours, you'll notice the salmon has developed a pellicle—a kind of sticky skin or coating that will help the smoke adhere to the fish. (Don't skip this step.)

4. Supply your smoker with wood pellets and follow the start-up procedure. Preheat the grill, with the lid closed, to 150° F.

5. Place the salmon on the grate and smoke until the fish flakes easily when pressed with a fork and the internal temperature reaches 140°F (60°C), about 3 hours. If albumin (a harmless white protein) appears on top of the fillet as it smokes, gently remove it with a paper towel.

6. Remove the salmon from the grill and let rest for 10 minutes. (You can also transfer the fish to a clean wire rack and let it cool to room temperature. Cover and refrigerate if not using immediately. The salmon will keep for up to 5 days.)

7. Serve the salmon with eggs, on salads, with Mustard Caviar, or with its traditional accompaniments: cream cheese, capers, chopped hard-boiled eggs, diced red onion, and dark bread.

Alder Smoked Scallops With Citrus & Garlic Butter Sauce

Servings: 4
Cooking Time: 35 Minutes

Ingredients:

- 2 Pound large dry sea scallops
- kosher salt
- freshly ground black pepper
- 8 Tablespoon salted butter, melted
- 1 Clove garlic, minced
- 1 Small orange
- 1/4 Teaspoon Worcestershire sauce
- 1 1/2 Teaspoon fresh chopped parsley or tarragon
- flat-leaf parsley, for serving

Directions:

1. Wash the scallops under cold running water and thoroughly pat dry on paper towels. Remove any tags of abductor muscle tissue you find on the sides of the scallops.
2. Arrange the scallops on a baking sheet fitted with a cooling rack, and season with salt and pepper.
3. Supply your smoker with wood pellets and follow the start-up procedure. Preheat the grill, with the lid closed, to 165° F.
4. Place the baking sheet with the scallops on the grill grate and smoke for 20 minutes.
5. While your scallops are smoking, make your sauce. Melt the butter in a small saucepan over medium-low heat. Add a pinch of salt, garlic, Worcestershire sauce, zest and juice from half of the orange, and parsley. Simmer for 5 minutes. Keep warm.
6. Remove the baking sheet with the scallops from the grill and set aside. Increase the temperature to 400°F and preheat, lid closed. Optional: Place an oyster bed or oyster pan in the grill to preheat. These heavy iron pans are a great way to sear the scallops. Grill: 400 °F
7. Return the baking sheet with the scallops to the grill, brush with the butter sauce, reserving some for serving. Roast until just opaque and tender, 10 to 15 minutes. The time will depend on how thick the scallops are. Do not overcook. If you are using an oyster pan, brush each compartment lightly with olive oil to prevent sticking. Spoon butter sauce on each of the scallops, reserving some for serving.
8. Serve the scallops hot with a little more orange zest, fresh parsley and the the warm citrus and garlic butter sauce. Enjoy!

Grilled Crab Legs With Herb Butter

Servings: 2
Cooking Time: 15 Minutes

Ingredients:

- 12 Tablespoon butter
- 3 Tablespoon Fresh Herbs (Parsley, Chives, Tarragon), finely chopped
- 4 Pound King Crab Legs or Dungeness Crab Leg Clusters
- 3 Whole Lemons, cut into wedges

Directions:

1. Supply your smoker with wood pellets and follow the start-up procedure. Preheat the grill, with the lid closed, to 375° F.
2. Place the butter, garlic, herbs, and a pinch of salt into a small cast iron sauce pan. Place on grill for 5 minutes to melt. Remove from grill and stir. Grill: 375 °F
3. If using king crab legs, split down the center and pour herb butter over meat reserving a quarter for serving. If using crab clusters, toss clusters with herb butter in a large mixing bowl reserving a quarter for serving.
4. Place crab legs directly on the grill grate, meat side up. Grill for 5 to 10 minutes or until hot and beginning to develop a little char on the shell. Grill: 375 °F
5. Serve crab legs with lemon wedges and reserved herb butter. Enjoy!

Grilled Maple Syrup Salmon

Servings: 6
Cooking Time: 30 Minutes

Ingredients:

- 1 large salmon fillet (around 3 pounds)
- 1/2 cup salted butter (melted)
- 2 tablespoons soy sauce
- Salt and pepper
- 1/4 cup maple syrup

Directions:

1. Supply your smoker with wood pellets and follow the start-up procedure. Preheat the grill, with the lid closed, to 400° F.
2. Place the salmon fillet in a baking pan lined with parchment paper.
3. Sprinkle the fish with salt and pepper.
4. Add half of the melted butter to the salmon and place the baking pan on the grill.
5. Grill for 15-20 minutes or until fish is roughly 70% cooked. It will feel still gelatinous in the thickest parts of the salmon.
6. Combine the remaining melted butter, soy sauce, and maple syrup and pour over the salmon.It will run off the sides so use a spoon to pour it back over the fish. It's also perfectly fine that some will be left on the sides of the pan.
7. Cook for 5 to 10 additional minutes or until the fish is cooked through. The fish should be firm to the touch but still moist and soft when pressed on,and the ridges will flake or pull apart if pressed on.

Grilled Tuna Steaks With Lemon & Caper Butter

Servings: 4
Cooking Time: 8 Minutes

Ingredients:

- 4 tuna steaks, each about 8oz (225g) and 1 inch (2.5cm) thick
- extra virgin olive oil
- coarse salt
- freshly ground black pepper
- for the butter
- 6 tbsp unsalted butter, chilled, divided
- 1 garlic clove, peeled and minced
- 3 tbsp brined capers, drained and coarsely chopped
- 1 tbsp freshly squeezed lemon juice, plus more
- 1 tsp lemon zest
- 1 tbsp minced fresh chives or flat-leaf parsley

Directions:

1. Supply your smoker with wood pellets and follow the start-up procedure. Preheat the grill, with the lid closed, to 450° F.
2. In a small saucepan on the stovetop over medium-low heat, begin making the butter by melting 1 tablespoon of butter. (Cut the remaining butter into ½-inch (1.25cm) cubes and keep them cold.) Add the garlic and capers. Cook until the garlic is softened, about 3 minutes. Stir in the lemon juice and zest. Remove the saucepan from the heat and set aside.
3. Lightly brush the tuna steaks with olive oil. Season with salt and pepper. Place the steaks on the grate and grill until seared, about 3 to 4 minutes per side. (The tuna will be quite rare in the center, almost like sashimi. If you prefer your tuna more well done, add 4 to 6 minutes to the grilling time.)
4. Transfer the steaks to a platter and let rest for 5 minutes.
5. Reheat the butter and caper mixture over low heat. Whisk in the chilled butter one or two cubes at a time until the sauce has emulsified. Stir in the chives. Ladle the sauce over the tuna. Serve immediately.

Charleston Crab Cakes With Remoulade

Servings: 4
Cooking Time: 45 Minutes

Ingredients:

- 1¼ cups mayonnaise
- ¼ cup yellow mustard
- 2 tablespoons sweet pickle relish, with its juices
- 1 tablespoon smoked paprika
- 2 teaspoons Cajun seasoning
- 2 teaspoons prepared horseradish
- 1 teaspoon hot sauce
- 1 garlic clove, finely minced
- 2 pounds fresh lump crabmeat, picked clean
- 20 butter crackers (such as Ritz brand), crushed
- 2 tablespoons Dijon mustard
- 1 cup mayonnaise
- 2 tablespoons freshly squeezed lemon juice
- 1 tablespoon salted butter, melted
- 1 tablespoon Worcestershire sauce
- 1 tablespoon Old Bay seasoning
- 2 teaspoons chopped fresh parsley
- 1 teaspoon ground mustard
- 2 eggs, beaten
- ¼ cup extra-virgin olive oil, divided

Directions:

1. For the remoulade:
2. In a small bowl, combine the mayonnaise, mustard, pickle relish, paprika, Cajun seasoning, horseradish, hot sauce, and garlic.
3. Refrigerate until ready to serve.
4. For the crab cakes:
5. Supply your smoker with wood pellets and follow the start-up procedure. Preheat, with the lid closed, to 375°F.
6. Spread the crabmeat on a foil-lined baking sheet and place over indirect heat on the grill, with the lid closed, for 30 minutes.
7. Remove from the heat and let cool for 15 minutes.
8. While the crab cools, combine the crushed crackers, Dijon mustard, mayonnaise, lemon juice, melted butter, Worcestershire sauce, Old Bay, parsley, ground mustard, and eggs until well incorporated.
9. Fold in the smoked crabmeat, then shape the mixture into 8 (1-inch-thick) crab cakes.
10. In a large skillet or cast-iron pan on the grill, heat 2 tablespoons of olive oil. Add half of the crab cakes, close the lid, and smoke for 4 to 5 minutes on each side, or until crispy and golden brown.
11. Remove the crab cakes from the pan and transfer to a wire rack to drain. Pat them to remove any excess oil.
12. Repeat steps 6 and 7 with the remaining oil and crab cakes.
13. Serve the crab cakes with the remoulade.

Traeger Jerk Shrimp

Servings: 8
Cooking Time: 10 Minutes

Ingredients:

- 1 Tablespoon brown sugar
- 1 Tablespoon smoked paprika
- 1 Teaspoon garlic powder
- 1/4 Teaspoon Thyme, ground
- 1/4 Teaspoon ground cayenne pepper
- 1 Teaspoon sea salt
- 1 lime zest

- 2 Pound shrimp in shell
- 3 Tablespoon olive oil

Directions:

1. Combine spices, salt, and lime zest in a small bowl and mix. Place shrimp into a large bowl, then drizzle in the olive oil, Add the spice mixture and toss to combine, making sure every shrimp is kissed with deliciousness.

2. Supply your smoker with wood pellets and follow the start-up procedure. Preheat the grill, with the lid closed, to 450° F.

3. Arrange the shrimp on the grill and cook for 2 – 3 minutes per side, until firm, opaque, and cooked through. Grill: 450 °F

4. Serve with lime wedges, fresh cilantro, mint, and Caribbean Hot Pepper Sauce. Enjoy!

Grilled Salmon Gravlax

Servings: 4
Cooking Time: 10 Minutes

Ingredients:

- 1 center-cut salmon fillet, about 2lb (1kg), preferably wild caught, skin on
- ½ cup aquavit or vodka
- 4 whole juniper berries
- ¼ cup finely chopped fresh dill, plus more
- lemon wedges
- for the rub
- 3 tbsp granulated light brown sugar or low-carb substitute
- 2 tbsp coarse salt
- 2 tsp freshly ground black pepper
- 1 tsp freshly ground white pepper
- 1 tsp ground coriander

Directions:

1. Run your fingers over the fillet, feeling for bones. Remove them with kitchen tweezers or needle-nosed pliers. Rinse the salmon under cold running water and pat dry with paper towels.

2. Place the salmon skin side down in a nonreactive baking dish and pour the aquavit over it. Crush the berries with the flat of a chef's knife and add them to the dish. Cover and refrigerate for 1 hour.

3. In a small bowl, make the rub by combining the ingredients.

4. Remove the salmon from the aquavit and pat dry with paper towels. Discard the soaking liquid and juniper berries. Rinse out the baking dish and place the salmon in the dish. Lightly but evenly sprinkle the rub on the flesh side of the fillet and gently distribute it with your fingertips. Scatter the dill over the top. Cover the dish and refrigerate for 4 hours.

5. Supply your smoker with wood pellets and follow the start-up procedure. Preheat the grill, with the lid closed, to 400° F.

6. With a sharp knife, slice the fillet into 4 equal portions. Place the fillets on the grate and grill until the fish is somewhat opaque but still translucent in the center and the internal temperature reaches 125°F (52°C), about 3 to 5 minutes per side.

7. Transfer the fillets to a platter. Scatter more dill over the top. Serve with lemon wedges.

Lime Mahi Mahi Fillets

Servings: 4
Cooking Time: 8 Minutes

Ingredients:

- 3/4 cup extra-virgin olive oil
- 1 clove garlic, minced
- 1/8 teaspoon ground black pepper
- 1/2 teaspoon cayenne pepper
- 2 tablespoons dill weed.
- 1 pinch salt
- 2 tablespoons lime juice
- 1/8 teaspoon grated lime peel
- 2 (4 ounce) mahi mahi fillets

Directions:

1. Supply your smoker with wood pellets and follow the start-up procedure. Preheat the grill, with the lid closed, to 325° F.

2. Lightly oil the grate.

3. Combine in a bowl the extra-virgin olive oil, minced garlic, black pepper, cayenne pepper, salt, lime juice, and grated lime zest.

4. Wisk to prepare the marinade.

5. Place the mahi mahi fillets in the marinade and turn to coat.

6. Allow to marinate at least 15 minutes.

7. Cook on preheated grill until fish flakes easily with a fork and is lightly browned (Typically 3 to 4 minutes per side).

8. Garnish with the twists of lime zest to serve.

Smoked Fish Chowder

Servings: 4
Cooking Time: 60 Minutes

Ingredients:

- 12 Ounce (1-1/2 to 2 lb) skin-on salmon fillet, preferably wild-caught
- Fin & Feather Rub
- 2 Corn Husks
- 3 Slices Bacon, sliced
- 4 Can Cream of Potato Soup, Condensed
- 3 Cup whole milk
- 8 Ounce cream cheese
- 3 green onions, thinly sliced
- 2 Teaspoon hot sauce

Directions:

1. Supply your smoker with wood pellets and follow the start-up procedure. Preheat the grill, with the lid closed, to 180° F.

2. Sprinkle Traeger Fin & Feather rub as needed on salmon. Arrange the salmon skin-side down on the grill grate. Smoke for 30 minutes. Grill: 180 °F

3. Increase the grill temperature to 350°F. Grill: 350 °F

4. Cook the salmon for 30 minutes, or until the fish flakes easily with a fork. (The exact time will depend on the thickness of the fillet.) There is no need to turn the fish. Using a large thin spatula, transfer the salmon to a wire rack to cool. Remove the skin. (The salmon can be made a day ahead, wrapped in plastic wrap and refrigerated.) Break into flakes and set aside.

5. Arrange the corn and bacon strips on the grill grate. (The salmon will be roasting while you do this.) Roast the corn and the bacon until the corn is cooked through and browned in spots, turning as needed, and the bacon is crisp, about 15 minutes.

6. In the meantime, bring the cream of potato soup and the milk to a simmer over medium heat in a large saucepan or Dutch oven on the stovetop. Gradually stir in the cream cheese and whisk to blend. Chop the bacon into bits and slice the corn off the cobs using long strokes of a chef's knife.

7. Add to the soup along with the green onions. Stir in the salmon. Heat gently for 5 to 10 minutes. Add the hot sauce to taste. If the chowder is too thick, add more milk. Serve at once. Enjoy!

Smoked Mango Shrimp

Servings: 4
Cooking Time: 5 Minutes

Ingredients:
- 2 Tablespoon Olive Oil
- 1 Pound Raw Tail-On, Thawed And Deveined Shrimp, Uncooked

Directions:
1. Supply your smoker with wood pellets and follow the start-up procedure. Preheat the grill, with the lid closed, to 425° F. Rinse shrimp off in sink with cold water. Place in bowl and season generously with Mango Magic seasoning and olive oil. Toss well in bowl.

2. Thread several shrimp onto a skewer, so that they are all just touching each other. Repeat with other skewers and remaining shrimp.

3. Grill shrimp for 2 - 3 minutes on each side, or until pink and opaque all the way through. Remove from grill and serve immediately.

Spicy Crab Poppers

Servings: 8
Cooking Time: 30 Minutes

Ingredients:

- 18 Whole jalapeño
- 8 Ounce cream cheese, softened
- 1 Cup Canned Corn, drained
- 1/2 Cup Crab meat, lump
- 1 1/4 Teaspoon Old Bay Seasoning
- 2 Scallions, minced

Directions:
1. Cut each jalapeño in half lengthwise through the stem and remove the ribs and seeds.

2. Filling: In a mixing bowl, combine the cream cheese, corn, crab meat, scallions, and Old Bay Seasoning and stir until blended. Stir in the scallions. Spoon the filling into the jalapeño halves, mounding it slightly.

3. Arrange the poppers on a baking sheet covered with foil or parchment paper.

4. Supply your smoker with wood pellets and follow the start-up procedure. Preheat the grill, with the lid closed, to 350° F.

5. Roast the jalapeños for 25 to 30 minutes, or until the peppers have softened and the filling is hot and bubbling.

6. Let cool slightly before serving. Enjoy!

Smoky Crab Dip

Servings: 6
Cooking Time: 20 Minutes

Ingredients:
- 1/3 Cup mayonnaise
- 3 Ounce sour cream
- 1 Teaspoon smoked paprika
- 1/4 Teaspoon cayenne pepper
- 1 1/2 Pound Crab meat, lump
- salt and pepper
- scallions, chopped
- butter crackers

Directions:
1. Supply your smoker with wood pellets and follow the start-up procedure. Preheat the grill, with the lid closed, to 350° F.

2. Meanwhile, in a large bowl gently stir together all of the ingredients except the crackers, garnish scallions and the crab meat until thoroughly combined. Gently fold in the crab meat, being careful not to break it up too much.

3. Season to taste and transfer to an oven-safe serving dish.

4. Bake for 20 to 25 minutes, until bubbly and golden on top. Grill: 350 °F

5. Garnish with the additional chopped scallions and serve warm with butter crackers. Enjoy!

Prosciutto-wrapped Scallops

Servings: 4

Cooking Time: 10 Minutes

Ingredients:

- 1½lb (680g) jumbo sea or diver scallops (size U-10)
- 8 to 10 thin slices of prosciutto, each halved lengthwise
- coarse salt
- freshly ground black pepper
- for the butter
- 8oz (225g) unsalted butter
- 2 tsp minced fresh curly or flat-leaf parsley
- 1½ tsp finely grated orange zest
- 1 tbsp freshly squeezed orange juice
- 1 tsp finely grated lemon zest
- 1 tsp finely grated lime zest
- ½ tsp coarse salt

Directions:

1. Supply your smoker with wood pellets and follow the start-up procedure. Preheat the grill, with the lid closed, to 450° F.
2. In a small saucepan on the stovetop over medium-low heat, make the citrus butter by melting the butter. Add the remaining ingredients and simmer for 3 to 5 minutes to blend the flavors. Keep warm.
3. Rinse the scallops under cold running water and dry with paper towels. Place each scallop on its side at the end of a piece of prosciutto and wrap the prosciutto around the scallop. Secure with a toothpick. Season the exposed sides of the scallop with salt and pepper.
4. Place the scallops exposed sides down on the grate and grill until the edges of the prosciutto begin to frizzle and the scallop is warm inside, about 3 to 5 minutes per side.
5. Transfer the scallops to a platter. Brush with some of the warm citrus butter before serving. Serve the remaining butter on the side.

Smoked Crab Legs

Servings: 4
Cooking Time: 30 Minutes

Ingredients:

- 4 Whole crab legs
- 4 Tablespoon butter, melted
- 1/2 Cup Texas Spicy BBQ Sauce
- salt and pepper
- 1 Tablespoon Fin & Feather Rub

Directions:

1. Supply your smoker with wood pellets and follow the start-up procedure. Preheat the grill, with the lid closed, to 250° F.
2. Place the crab legs directly on the grill grate and smoke for 20 minutes. Grill: 250 °F

3. While the crab is smoking, make the sauce. In a medium bowl, combine melted butter, Traeger Texas Spicy BBQ sauce, salt, pepper and Traeger Fin & Feather Rub.
4. After 20 minutes of cooking, brush the crab legs with the BBQ sauce mixture. Continue to cook for another 10 minutes reserving the remaining sauce to serve. Remove crab legs from the grill, and serve with melted butter and BBQ sauce mixture. Enjoy!

Grilled Lemon Salmon

Servings: 4
Cooking Time: 60 Minutes

Ingredients:

- Dill, Fresh
- 1 Lemon, Sliced
- 1 1/2 - 2 Lbs Salmon, Fresh

Directions:

1. Supply your smoker with wood pellets and follow the start-up procedure. Preheat the grill, with the lid closed, to 225° F.
2. Place the salmon on a cedar plank. Lay the lemon slices along the top of the salmon. Smoke in your Grill for about 60 minutes.
3. Top with fresh dill and serve.

Tequila & Lime Shrimp With Smoked Tomato Sauce

Servings: 4
Cooking Time: 6 Minutes

Ingredients:

- 24 to 28 jumbo shrimp, about 2lb (1kg) total, peeled and deveined
- 1 lime, quartered
- Smoked Tomato Sauce
- for the marinade
- ½ cup tequila or mezcal
- juice and zest of 1 lime
- 2 garlic cloves, peeled and roughly chopped
- ½ cup freshly squeezed orange juice
- ¼ cup extra virgin olive oil
- 2 tsp agave, light brown sugar, or low-carb substitute
- 2 tsp Mexican hot sauce, plus more
- 1½ tsp coarse salt
- 1 tsp baking soda
- 1 tsp chili powder
- ½ tsp ground cumin

Directions:

1. In a medium bowl, make the marinade by whisking together the ingredients. Whisk until the salt dissolves. Taste for seasoning, adding more hot sauce if desired.

2. Place the shrimp in a resealable plastic bag and pour the marinade over them, turning the bag several times to coat thoroughly. Refrigerate for 30 minutes.

3. Supply your smoker with wood pellets and follow the start-up procedure. Preheat the grill, with the lid closed, to 450° F.

4. Drain the shrimp and discard the marinade. Pat the shrimp dry with paper towels. Thread the shrimp on 4 bamboo skewers (preferably flat ones). Make sure all the shrimp face the same direction. Finish each skewer with a lime wedge.

5. Place the skewers on the grate and grill until the shrimp are white and opaque, about 2 to 3 minutes per side, turning once. (Don't overcook.)

6. Remove the shrimp from the grill. Serve immediately with the warm tomato sauce.

Traeger Baked Rainbow Trout

Servings: 2
Cooking Time: 20 Minutes

Ingredients:

- 2 Tablespoon olive oil, divided
- 2 Whole rainbow trout, gutted and cleaned, heads and tails still on
- 1/2 Teaspoon fresh dill
- 1/2 Teaspoon fresh thyme
- 1 Teaspoon Jacobsen Salt Co. Pure Kosher Sea Salt
- 1/2 Large onion, sliced
- 1 Large lemon, thinly sliced
- 1 Teaspoon freshly ground black pepper

Directions:

1. Supply your smoker with wood pellets and follow the start-up procedure. Preheat the grill, with the lid closed, to 400° F.

2. Grease a 9x13 inch baking dish with 1 tablespoon olive oil.

3. Place trout in the prepared baking dish and coat fish with remaining olive oil. Season the inside and outside of fish with dill, thyme and salt. Stuff each fish with onion and lemon slices then grind pepper over the top. Place 1 lemon slice on each fish.

4. Bake in the Traeger for 10 minutes. Add 2 tablespoons hot water to the baking dish. Continue baking until fish flakes easily with a fork, about 10 more minutes. Enjoy! Grill: 400 °F

Lemon Herb Grilled Salmon

Servings: 4
Cooking Time: 25 Minutes

Ingredients:

- 1 1/2 pounds salmon with skin
- 1/2 tablespoon lemon zest
- 1 tablespoon lemon juice
- 1 tablespoon unsalted butter

- 1/2 teaspoon sea salt
- 1/2 teaspoon ground black pepper
- 2 teaspoons freshly chopped dill
- 1 teaspoon freshly chopped parsley
- lemon slices for the garnish

Directions:

1. Supply your smoker with wood pellets and follow the start-up procedure. Preheat the grill, with the lid closed, to 325° F.

2. In a small bowl, combine the lemon zest, lemon juice, softened unsalted butter, dill, parsley, sea salt, and ground black pepper.

3. Generously slather the top of the salmon fillet with the mixture and top with a slice of lemon. You may allow marinating for about 10 minutes or so to absorb the mixture.

4. Place the salmon fillets on the hot grill grate, skin-side facing down.

5. Cook the salmon for 20 to 25 minutes, until it reaches an internal temperature of 145 °F and flakes easily, or until the salmon is cooked to your preferred taste.

6. Serve with lemon slices. Enjoy!

Spicy Lime Shrimp

Servings: 4
Cooking Time: 10 Minutes

Ingredients:

- 2 Tsp Chili Paste
- 1/2 Tsp Cumin
- 2 Cloves Garlic, Minced
- 1 Large Lime, Juiced
- 1/4 Tsp Paprika, Powder
- 1/4 Tsp Red Flakes Pepper
- 1/2 Tsp Salt

Directions:

1. In a bowl, whisk together the lime juice, olive oil, garlic, chili powder, cumin, paprika, salt, pepper, and red pepper flakes.

2. Then pour it into a resealable bag, add the shrimp, toss the coat, let it marinate for 30 minutes.

3. Supply your smoker with wood pellets and follow the start-up procedure. Preheat the grill, with the lid closed, to 400° F.

4. Next place the shrimp on skewers, place on the grill, and grill each side for about two minutes until it's done. One finished, remove the shrimp from the grill and enjoy!

Grilled Albacore Tuna With Potato-tomato Casserole

Servings: 8
Cooking Time: 20 Minutes

Ingredients:
- 6 Tuna Steaks, 6oz
- 1 Whole lemon zest
- 1 chile de árbol, thinly sliced
- 1 Tablespoon thyme
- 1 Tablespoon fresh parsley

Directions:
1. To make the fish: Season the fish with the lemon zest, chile, thyme, and parsley. Cover and refrigerate at least 4 hours.
2. Remove fish from the refrigerator 30 minutes before cooking to come to room temperature.
3. Season the fish with salt and pepper on both sides. Grill 2-3 minutes per side (next to the cast iron with the casserole) rotating it once or twice. The tuna should be well seared but still rare.

Garlic Blackened Catfish

Servings: 4
Cooking Time: 10 Minutes

Ingredients:
- ½ Cup Cajun Seasoning
- ¼ Tsp Cayenne Pepper
- 1 Tsp Granulated Garlic
- 1 Tsp Ground Thyme
- 1 Tsp Onion Powder
- 1 Tsp Ground Oregano
- 1 Tsp Pepper
- 4 (5-Oz.) Skinless Catfish Fillets
- 1 Tbsp Smoked Paprika
- 1 Stick Unsalted Butter

Directions:
1. In a small bowl, combine the Cajun seasoning, smoked paprika, onion powder, granulated garlic, ground oregano, ground thyme, pepper and cayenne pepper.
2. Sprinkle fish with salt and let rest for 20 minutes.
3. Supply your smoker with wood pellets and follow the start-up procedure. Preheat the grill, with the lid closed, to 450° F. If you're using a gas or charcoal grill, set it up for medium-high heat. Place cast iron skillet on the grill and let it preheat.
4. While grill is preheating, sprinkle catfish fillets with seasoning mixture, pressing gently to adhere. Add half the butter to preheated cast iron skillet and swirl to coat, add more butter if needed. Place fillets in hot skillet and cook 3-5 minutes or until a dark crust has been formed. Flip and cook an additional 3-5 minutes or until the fish flakes apart when pressed gently with your finger.
5. Remove fish from grill and sprinkle evenly with fresh parsley. Serve with lemon wedges and enjoy!

Grilled Garlic Lobster Tails

Servings: 2
Cooking Time: 11 Minutes

Ingredients:
- 4 Lobster Tails (8 oz Each)
- 3 Sticks Unsalted Butter
- 4 Cloves Garlic Minced
- ½ Cup Fresh Parsley Chopped
- Juice of 1 Lemon
- 2 Tablespoons Fresh Lemon Zest
- 2 Teaspoons Crushed Red Pepper
- ¼ Cup Olive Oil
- 1 TBS Kosher Salt
- 1 TBS Cracked Black Pepper

Directions:
1. Supply your smoker with wood pellets and follow the start-up procedure. Preheat the grill, with the lid closed, to 375° F.
2. Split lobster tails in half lengthwise and season with salt, pepper, and olive oil.
3. Place butter in an aluminum pan and put the pan on the hot side of the grill to melt the butter.
4. Add garlic, parsley, lemon zest, lemon juice, and red pepper to butter and simmer for 5 minutes.
5. Place lobster tails meat side down on the grill and cook for 6 minutes. Baste the shell side with the butter mixture.
6. Dunk each tail in the butter mixture and then transfer to the grill, shell side down. Baste meat again with butter mixture.
7. Cook for an additional 5 minutes or until the lobster meat turns opaque and shells are bright pink.
8. Serve with remaining butter mixture, fresh parsley, and lemon wedges.

Baked Tuna Noodle Casserole

Servings: 4
Cooking Time: 45 Minutes

Ingredients:
- 1 Whole Wheat Pasta, Box (13.25oz)
- 2 Cup Yogurt
- 1 Cup almond milk
- 1 Teaspoon ground mustard
- 1/2 Teaspoon celery salt
- 1 Cup Button Mushrooms, Sliced
- 10 Ounce Tuna, Cooked
- 1 Cup Peas, canned
- 1 Cup Cheese, Colby/Cheddar

Directions:

1. Bring a large pot of salted water to a boil over high heat. Add pasta and cook according to manufacturer's directions. Drain and set aside.
2. In a medium bowl mix yogurt, milk, ground mustard, and celery salt. Fold in mushrooms, tuna, peas and cooked pasta. Fold in half the cheese.
3. Transfer the mixture to a greased 13" x 9" baking dish and top with remaining cheese.
4. Supply your smoker with wood pellets and follow the start-up procedure. Preheat the grill, with the lid closed, to 350° F.
5. Place casserole dish directly on grill grate and cook for 45 minutes or until warmed through and cheese is melted. Enjoy! Grill: 350 °F

Grilled Fresh Fish

Servings: 2
Cooking Time: 15 Minutes

Ingredients:
- 1 Whole fillet of firm white fish: sea bass, halibut or cod
- Fin & Feather Rub
- 2 Whole lemons

Directions:
1. Supply your smoker with wood pellets and follow the start-up procedure. Preheat the grill, with the lid closed, to 325° F.
2. Season fish with Traeger Fin & Feather Rub and let sit for 30 minutes. Slice lemons in half.
3. Place the fish and the lemons (cut side down) directly on the grill grates. Cook for 10 to 15 minutes until the fish is flaky and is at least 145°F in the thickest part of fish. Be careful not to over cook.
4. Serve with the grilled lemons. Enjoy!

Grilled Lobster Tails With Smoked Paprika Butter

Servings: 4
Cooking Time: 10-12 Minutes

Ingredients:
- 4 lobster tails, each about 8 to 10oz (225 to 285g), thawed if frozen
- 3 lemons, 1 quartered lengthwise, 2 halved through their equators
- for the butter
- 1¼ cup unsalted butter, at room temperature
- 2 garlic cloves, peeled and finely minced
- 3 tbsp chopped fresh parsley
- 2 tbsp chopped fresh chives
- 1 tbsp freshly squeezed lemon juice
- 2 tsp finely chopped lemon zest

- 2 tsp smoked paprika
- 1 tsp coarse salt

Directions:
1. Supply your smoker with wood pellets and follow the start-up procedure. Preheat the grill, with the lid closed, to 450° F.
2. In a medium bowl, make the paprika butter by combining the ingredients. Beat with a wooden spoon until well blended.
3. Use a sharp, heavy knife or sturdy kitchen shears to cut lengthwise through the top shell of each lobster tail in a straight line toward the tail fin. Gently loosen the meat from the bottom shell and sides. Lift the meat through the slit you just made so the meat sits on top of the shell. Slip a lemon quarter underneath the meat (between the meat and the bottom shell) to keep it elevated. Spread 1 tablespoon of paprika butter on top of each lobster. Melt the remaining butter and keep it warm.
4. Place the lobster tails flesh side up and lemon halves cut sides down on the grate. Grill the lobsters until the flesh is white and opaque and the internal temperature of the lobster meat reaches 135 to 140°F (57 to 60°C), about 10 to 12 minutes, basting at least once with some of the melted butter. (Don't overcook or the lobster will become unpleasantly rubbery.)
5. Transfer the lobsters and the lemon halves to a platter. Divide the remaining melted butter between 4 ramekins before serving.

Mango Rice Wine Thai Shrimp

Servings: 4
Cooking Time: 15 Minutes

Ingredients:
- 2 Tablespoons Brown Sugar
- 2 Tablespoons Mango Magic Seasoning
- 1 Pinch (Optional) Red Pepper Flakes
- 1/2 Tablespoons Rice Wine Vinegar
- 1 Pound Raw Tail-On, Thaw And Deveined Shrimp, Uncooked
- 2 Tablespoons Soy Sauce
- 1 Teaspoon Sriracha Hot Sauce
- 1/2 Cup Sweet Chili Sauce

Directions:
1. Supply your smoker with wood pellets and follow the start-up procedure. Preheat the grill, with the lid closed, to 425° F. Rinse shrimp off in sink with cold water. Place in bowl and put in all of the ingredients listed above. Let marinade for 2 - 4 hours.
2. Thread several shrimp onto a skewer, so that they are all just touching each other. Repeat with other skewers and remaining shrimp.
3. Grill shrimp for 2 - 3 minutes on each side, or until pink and opaque all the way through. Remove from grill and serve immediately.

Mexican Mahi Mahi With Baja Cabbage Slaw

Servings: 4
Cooking Time: 10 Minutes

Ingredients:

- 1½lb (680g) skinless mahi mahi, cod, or other firm white fish fillets
- coarse salt
- freshly ground black pepper
- chili powder
- lime wedges
- for the slaw
- 2 cups finely shredded green cabbage
- 2 cups finely shredded purple cabbage
- 4 tbsp reduced-fat mayo
- 2 tsp hot sauce, plus more
- 2 tsp freshly squeezed lime juice
- ½ tsp coarse salt
- for the marinade
- ¼ cup freshly squeezed orange juice
- ¼ cup freshly squeezed lime juice
- 2 tbsp extra virgin olive oil

Directions:

1. In a medium bowl, make the slaw by combining the ingredients. Stir well. Transfer to a serving bowl. Cover and refrigerate until ready to serve.
2. Place the fish fillets in a baking dish and pour the orange and lime juices and olive oil over them. Turn the fillets to coat thoroughly. Cover and refrigerate for 15 to 20 minutes.
3. Supply your smoker with wood pellets and follow the start-up procedure. Preheat the grill, with the lid closed, to 450° F.
4. Drain the fish and pat dry with paper towels. (Discard the marinade.) Season the fillets on both sides with salt and pepper and chili powder. Place the fillets on the grate and grill until golden brown, about 4 to 5 minutes per side, turning with a thin-bladed spatula.
5. Transfer the fish to a platter. Serve with the slaw and lime wedges.

Smoked Salmon Candy

Servings: 4
Cooking Time: 180 Minutes

Ingredients:

- 2 Cup gin
- 1 Cup dark brown sugar
- 1/2 Cup kosher salt
- 1 Cup maple syrup
- 1 Tablespoon black pepper

- 3 Pound salmon
- vegetable oil
- dark brown sugar

Directions:

1. In a large bowl, combine all ingredients for the cure.
2. Cut the salmon into 2 ounce pieces and place in the cure.
3. Cover and refrigerate overnight.
4. Supply your smoker with wood pellets and follow the start-up procedure. Preheat the grill, with the lid closed, to 180° F.
5. Spray foil with vegetable oil. Place salmon on foil and sprinkle with additional brown sugar.
6. Place foil directly on the grill grate. Close the lid and smoke the salmon for 3 to 4 hours or until fully cooked. Grill: 180 °F
7. Serve hot or chilled. Enjoy!

Spiced Smoked Swordfish

Servings: 4
Cooking Time: 60 Minutes

Ingredients:

- 4 swordfish fillets (about 4 ounces each)
- For the brine:
- 1 gallon water
- ½ cup kosher salt
- ½ cup brown sugar
- For the rub:
- 1 tablespoon olive oil
- 1 tablespoon kosher salt
- 1 tablespoon coarse ground black pepper
- 1 tablespoon garlic powder
- 1 tablespoon onion powder

Directions:

1. Make the brine by mixing the water, salt,and sugar in a large pot and stir. Add swordfish fillets to the bowl and refrigerate overnight in the mixture.
2. Supply your smoker with wood pellets and follow the start-up procedure. Preheat the grill, with the lid closed, to 225° F.
3. Remove the fillets from the brine, rinse,and blot dry.
4. Brush a coat of olive oil on each fillet and mix salt, pepper, garlic powder,and onion powder in a small bowl for the rub. Apply the rub liberally to each fillet.
5. Put the fillets skin-side down on the smoker and cook for about 1 hour or until the internal temperature in the thickest part of the fillets reaches 145 °F.
6. Enjoy.

Grilled Trout With Citrus & Basil

Servings: 4
Cooking Time: 10 Minutes

Ingredients:

- 6 Whole Trout

- 2 Teaspoon Blackened Saskatchewan Rub
- 10 Sprig fresh basil
- 2 Lemons, cut in half
- extra-virgin olive oil

Directions:

1. Supply your smoker with wood pellets and follow the start-up procedure. Preheat the grill, with the lid closed, to 450° F.

2. Season the center cavity of the trout with the Traeger Blackened Saskatchewan. Place two sprigs of Basil in each cavity, then add 4 lemon halves.

3. Next tie the fish closed using the Butchers twine, and then rub with olive oil.

4. Place the trout on the hot grill and cook 5 minutes on each side. Enjoy! Grill: 450 °F

Sweet Smoked Salmon Jerky

Servings: 6
Cooking Time: 300 Minutes

Ingredients:

- 2 Quart water
- 3/4 Cup kosher salt
- 1 Cup Morton Tender Quick Home Meat Cure, optional
- 4 Cup dark brown sugar
- 2 Cup maple syrup, divided
- 1 (2-3 lb) wild caught salmon fillet, skinned and pin bones removed

Directions:

1. In a large nonreactive bowl, combine 2 quarts water, salt, curing salt (if using), brown sugar and 1 cup of the maple syrup. Stir with a long-handled spoon to dissolve the salts and sugar.

2. With a sharp, serrated knife, slice the salmon into 1/2 inch thick slices with the short side parallel to you on the cutting board. In other words, make your cuts from the head end to the tail end. (This is considerably easier if the fish is frozen.) Cut each strip crosswise into 4 or 5 inch lengths.

3. Immerse the strips in the brine, weighing down with a plate or a bag of ice. Cover with plastic wrap and refrigerate for 12 hours.

4. Supply your smoker with wood pellets and follow the start-up procedure. Preheat the grill, with the lid closed, to 180° F.

5. Drain the salmon strips and discard the brine. Arrange the salmon strips in a single layer directly on the grill grate. Smoke for several hours (5 to 6), or until the jerky is dry but not rock-hard. You want it to yield when you bite into it. Halfway through the smoking time, mix the remaining cup of maple syrup with 1/4 cup of warm water and brush the salmon strips on all sides with the mixture. Grill: 180 °F

6. Transfer to a resealable bag while the jerky is still warm. Let the jerky rest for an hour at room temperature. Squeeze any air from the bag, and refrigerate the jerky. Enjoy!

Sweet Mandarin Salmon

Servings: 2
Cooking Time: 10 Minutes

Ingredients:

- 1 Whole lime juice
- 1 Teaspoon sesame oil
- 1 1/2 Cup Mandarin Orange Sauce
- 1 1/2 Tablespoon soy sauce
- 2 Tablespoon cilantro, finely chopped
- Freshly cracked black pepper
- 1 Whole (4 oz) wild salmon fillets

Directions:

1. Supply your smoker with wood pellets and follow the start-up procedure. Preheat the grill, with the lid closed, to 375° F.

2. For the glaze, combine Mandarin orange sauce, lime juice, sesame oil, soy sauce, cilantro and fresh cracked black pepper. Mix together.

3. Cut the salmon into 4 fillets. Brush with glaze and place directly on the grill grate, skin side down.

4. Cook until salmon reaches an internal temperature of 155 degrees F (about 15-20 minutes). Half way through cook time, brush salmon again with the glaze.

5. Remove the salmon from the grill and serve with remaining glaze if desired. Enjoy!

Cajun-blackened Shrimp

Servings: 4
Cooking Time: 20 Minutes

Ingredients:

- 1 pound peeled and deveined shrimp, with tails on
- 1 batch Cajun Rub
- 8 tablespoons (1 stick) butter
- ¼ cup Worcestershire sauce

Directions:

1. Supply your smoker with wood pellets and follow the start-up procedure. Preheat the grill, with the lid closed, to 450°F and place a cast-iron skillet on the grill grate. Wait about 10 minutes after your grill has reached temperature, allowing the skillet to get hot.

2. Meanwhile, season the shrimp all over with the rub.

3. When the skillet is hot, place the butter in it to melt. Once the butter melts, stir in the Worcestershire sauce.

4. Add the shrimp and gently stir to coat. Smoke-braise the shrimp for about 10 minutes per side, until opaque and cooked through. Remove the shrimp from the grill and serve immediately.

Pacific Northwest Salmon

Servings: 4
Cooking Time: 75 Minutes

Ingredients:

- 1 (2-pound) half salmon fillet
- 1 batch Dill Seafood Rub
- 2 tablespoons butter, cut into 3 or 4 slices

Directions:

1. Supply your smoker with wood pellets and follow the start-up procedure. Preheat the grill, with the lid closed, to 180°F.
2. Season the salmon all over with the rub. Using your hands, work the rub into the flesh.
3. Place the salmon directly on the grill grate, skin-side down, and smoke for 1 hour.
4. Place the butter slices on the salmon, equally spaced. Increase the grill's temperature to 300°F and continue to cook until the salmon's internal temperature reaches 145°F. Remove the salmon from the grill and serve immediately.

Bacon Wrapped Scallops

Servings: 8
Cooking Time: 20 Minutes

Ingredients:

- 24 jumbo deep sea diver scallops, dry-packed
- 1/2 Cup butter
- salt
- freshly ground black pepper
- 1 Clove garlic, minced
- 12 Slices thin-cut bacon, cut in half crosswise
- lemon wedges, for serving

Directions:

1. Remove the small, crescent-shaped muscle from the side of each scallop, if still attached. Dry the scallops thoroughly on paper towels, then transfer to a medium bowl.
2. Melt butter in a small saucepan, add garlic and cook for 1 minute. Let cool slightly then pour over the scallops. Season with salt and pepper and gently toss to coat.
3. Wrap a piece of bacon around each scallop and secure with a toothpick.
4. Supply your smoker with wood pellets and follow the start-up procedure. Preheat the grill, with the lid closed, to 400° F.
5. Arrange the scallops directly on the grill grate. Grill for 15 to 20 minutes, or until the scallop is opaque and the bacon has begun to crisp. If desired, you can turn the scallops on their side, bacon-side down, turning occasionally to crisp the bacon. Do not overcook. Grill: 400 °F
6. Transfer the scallops to a platter and serve with lemon wedges.

Garlic Grilled Shrimp Skewers

Servings: 3
Cooking Time: 6 Minutes

Ingredients:

- 1 pound large shrimp
- 1/4 cup olive oil
- 1/4 cup fresh cilantro, finely chopped
- 1/4 cup fresh parsley, finely chopped
- 4 cloves garlic, minced
- 1 tablespoon lemon juice
- 1/2 teaspoon salt
- 1/4 teaspoon black pepper
- Pinch cayenne pepper, adjust to spice preference

Directions:

1. Add the olive oil, herbs, and spices to a small mixing bowl and whisk together.
2. Place the shrimp in a bowl and pour 3/4 of the marinade on top of the shrimp. Mix together gently to coat the shrimp evenly.
3. Cover the bowl and marinate the shrimp for 30 minutes to an hour.
4. Thread the shrimp on the skewers and make sure to get all the good garlic and herbs from the bowl and spread on to the shrimp.
5. Supply your smoker with wood pellets and follow the start-up procedure. Preheat the grill, with the lid closed, to medium high heat.
6. Once the grill is hot, arrange the shrimp skewers on the grill and cook for 2-3 minutes per side, or until they turn pink and opaque.
7. Remove the shrimp skewers to a plate and spoon the remaining marinade on top before serving.

Cold-smoked Salmon Gravlax

Servings: 6
Cooking Time: 30 Minutes

Ingredients:

- 1 Cup kosher salt
- 1 Cup sugar
- 1 Tablespoon freshly ground black pepper
- 2 Pound Sushi-Grad Salmon Fillet, Skin-on, Pin Bones Removed
- 2 Bunch Dill Weed, fresh
- capers, drained

- red onion, sliced
- cream cheese
- lemons

Directions:

1. In a bowl stir together the salt, sugar and black pepper until thoroughly combined. On a work surface, turn salmon skin side up and sprinkle about half of salt mixture all over and rub in.

2. Arrange half the dill on the bottom of a baking dish large enough to hold the salmon. Set salmon skin side down on bed of dill.

3. Rub remaining salt mixture all over top and sides of salmon, then top with remaining dill. Cover with plastic, then top with a weight on a smaller baking dish or a plate with cans of beans on top, then place in refrigerator and allow to cure for 2 days.

4. Remove salmon from refrigerator, rinse under cold water and pat dry with paper towels. Allow to sit at room temperature on the counter for 1 hour

5. Supply your smoker with wood pellets and follow the start-up procedure. Preheat the grill, with the lid closed, to 180° F. Place salmon onto a baking pan. Fill another baking pan with ice and place baking pan with salmon over ice. Place onto grill and smoke for 30 minutes.

6. Remove from grill and slice thin. Serve with capers, red onion, dill, cream cheese, and lemon. Enjoy!

Grilled Salmon Steaks With Dill Sauce

Servings: 4
Cooking Time: 8 Minutes

Ingredients:

- 4 salmon steaks, each about 6 to 8oz (170 to 225g) and 1 inch (2.5cm) thick
- extra virgin olive oil
- coarse salt
- freshly ground rainbow peppercorns or freshly ground black pepper
- lemon wedges
- for the sauce
- 1 cup reduced-fat mayo
- ⅓ cup light sour cream
- ¼ cup chopped fresh dill
- 2 tbsp freshly squeezed lemon juice
- coarse salt
- freshly ground black pepper
- sprigs of fresh dill

Directions:

1. Supply your smoker with wood pellets and follow the start-up procedure. Preheat the grill, with the lid closed, to 450° F.

2. In a small bowl, make the dill sauce by combining the mayo, sour cream, dill, and lemon juice. Mix until smooth. Season with

salt and pepper to taste. Transfer to a serving bowl. Scatter the dill sprigs over the top. Cover and refrigerate until ready to serve.

3. Brush the salmon with olive oil and season with salt and pepper. Place the salmon on the grate at an angle to the bars. Grill until grill marks begin to appear, about 4 minutes. Use a thin-bladed spatula to turn the salmon. Grill until the internal temperature reaches 140°F (60°C), about 4 minutes more.

4. Transfer the salmon to a platter. Serve immediately with the lemon wedges and dill sauce.

Kimi's Simple Grilled Fresh Fish

Servings: 2
Cooking Time: 45 Minutes

Ingredients:

- 1 Cup soy sauce
- 1/3 Cup extra-virgin olive oil
- 1 Tablespoon garlic, minced
- 2 lemons, juiced
- fresh basil
- 4 Pound Fresh Fish, cut into portion-sized pieces

Directions:

1. Mix all ingredients to create sauce and cover fish in marinade for 45 minutes.

2. Supply your smoker with wood pellets and follow the start-up procedure. Preheat the grill, with the lid closed, to 140° F. Grill the marinated fish on the grill until it reaches an internal temperature of 140-145°F. Serve immediately, enjoy! Grill: 350 °F Probe: 145 °F

Roasted Halibut With Spring Vegetables

Servings: 4
Cooking Time: 20 Minutes

Ingredients:

- 4 thick-cut halibut fillets
- 2 Tablespoon Fin & Feather Rub
- Butcher Paper
- 1 Pound Carrots, Peeled and Cut into 3/4" Inch Slices
- 1 Pound asparagus, ends trimmed
- 1/2 Pound Oyster Mushrooms
- 2 Tablespoon butter
- salt and pepper
- 1/2 Cup white wine

Directions:

1. Season the halibut fillets with Traeger Fin and Feather Rub.

2. To build the packets: Start with four sheets of parchment paper about twenty inches long. Fold in half, then open it back up.

3. Divide the carrots, asparagus, and mushrooms between the four pieces of parchment and top each with a little bit of butter.

Season with salt and pepper. Place a halibut fillet on top of the vegetables in each packet.

4. Next, fold the paper over so the two ends meet, enclosing the food. Beginning at either end of the center crease, make small, overlapping diagonal folds around the filling, sealing the packet tight. Before finishing the final fold, pour a little bit of wine in each packet then seal completely.

5. Supply your smoker with wood pellets and follow the start-up procedure. Preheat the grill, with the lid closed, to 500° F.

6. Place all four packets on a sheet tray and place in the grill. Cook for 7-10 minutes or until the internal temperature of the fish reaches 145°F. Remove from the grill and place packet on a serving dish. Grill: 500 °F Probe: 145 °F

7. Using a knife or scissors, cut open each packet and fold the edges back. Finish with a little bit of lemon juice if desired. Enjoy!

Wood-fired Halibut

Servings: 4
Cooking Time: 20 Minutes

Ingredients:
- 1 pound halibut fillet
- 1 batch Dill Seafood Rub

Directions:
1. Supply your smoker with wood pellets and follow the start-up procedure. Preheat the grill, with the lid closed, to 325°F.
2. Sprinkle the halibut fillet on all sides with the rub. Using your hands, work the rub into the meat.
3. Place the halibut directly on the grill grate and grill until its internal temperature reaches 145°F. Remove the halibut from the grill and serve immediately.

Teriyaki Smoked Honey Tilapia

Servings: 4
Cooking Time: 120 Minutes

Ingredients:
- 4 tilapia fillets
- 1 cup teriyaki sauce
- 2/3 cup honey
- 1 tbsp sriracha sauce
- Green onions (optional)

Directions:
1. In a large bowl, make the marinade by mixing together the teriyaki sauce, honey,and sriracha. Make sure honey is dissolved and well blended.
2. Place the tilapia fillets in the marinade. Turn the fillets so they are completely coated. Cover with a plastic wrap and marinate in the fridge for about 2 hours.

3. Supply your smoker with wood pellets and follow the start-up procedure. Preheat the grill, with the lid closed, to 275° F.
4. Remove the tilapia fillets from the marinade and transfer them to the grill. Smoke the fillets until they reach an internal temperature of 145°F, about 2 hours.
5. Sprinkle with green onions if desired.

Baked Steelhead

Servings: 4
Cooking Time: 20 Minutes

Ingredients:
- 1 steelhead fillet
- 16-oz bottle Italian dressing
- 3 Tablespoon unsalted butter
- Blackened Saskatchewan Rub
- 1/2 shallot, minced
- 2 Clove garlic, minced
- 1 lemon

Directions:
1. Supply your smoker with wood pellets and follow the start-up procedure. Preheat the grill, with the lid closed, to 350° F.
2. Put butter in a small cast iron pan and place inside Traeger while preheating to soften. Pour Italian dressing over fillet to evenly coat.
3. Shake Traeger Blackened Saskatchewan rub evenly in a thin layer to cover dressing. Mince shallot and garlic.
4. Remove butter from pre-heated grill, careful as the cast iron will be hot. Stir in shallots and garlic.
5. Spread a nice thick layer of mixture on the top-middle of the fillet. Cut lemon into thin slices and place on top of butter mix.
6. Place steelhead on the grill and cook for 20 to 30 minutes, until fish is flaky, being careful not to over cook.
7. Remove fillet from the grill. Enjoy!

Lemon Lobster Rolls

Servings: 4
Cooking Time: 35 Minutes

Ingredients:
- 1/2 Cup Butter
- 4 Hot Dog Bun(S)
- 1 Lemon, Whole
- 4 Lobster, Tail
- 1/4 Cup Mayo
- Pepper

Directions:
1. Supply your smoker with wood pellets and follow the start-up procedure. Preheat the grill, with the lid closed, to 300° F.

2. Using kitchen shears, cut the shell of the tail and crack in half so that the meat is exposed. Pour in butter and season with pepper. Place the tails meat side up on the grill and cook until the shell has turned red and the meat is white, about 35 minutes.

3. Remove from the grill and separate the shell from the meat. Place the meat in a bowl with mayo, lemon juice and rind and season with pepper. Stir to combine and evenly distribute into the hot dog buns.

Flavour Fire Spiced Shrimp

Servings: 2
Cooking Time: 8 Minutes

Ingredients:

- 1 pound of extra large raw whole wild shrimp
- 1 tablespoon vegetable oil
- 1 tablespoon chili powder
- 1 teaspoon garlic powder
- 1/2 teaspoon onion powder
- 1/2 teaspoon cayenne pepper
- 1/4 teaspoon paprika
- 1/4 teaspoon dried oregano
- Pinch of Kosher salt

Directions:

1. Supply your smoker with wood pellets and follow the start-up procedure. Preheat the grill, with the lid closed, to High heat.

2. While grill is preheating, remove the shrimp shells, leaving the heads.

3. Butterfly shrimp by using a knife to cut each shrimp down the middle, from the head down to the tail.

4. Remove the vein, rinse off the shrimp and lightly dry off with paper towels.

5. Place the shrimp in a large bowl, sprinkle with all the seasonings and the oil.

6. Mix together, ensuring the mixture evenly covers each shrimp.

7. Using a skewer, impale the whole body of a shrimp, from head to tail. (Wrap them in aluminum foil if using wooden skewers).

8. Place the whole shrimp on the grill and cook for 3-4 minutes on each side (Or until shells turns pink and the shrimp is opaque).

9. Serve with your favorite sauce or condiment.

Moules Marinières With Garlic Butter Sauce

Servings: 4
Cooking Time: 12 Minutes

Ingredients:

- 3lb (1.4kg) fresh mussels, scrubbed under cold running water and debearded

- lemon wedges
- crusty bread (optional)
- for the sauce
- 6 tbsp unsalted butter
- 3 garlic cloves, peeled and minced
- 1 cup dry white wine or hard cider
- 1 tbsp freshly squeezed lemon juice
- 2 tsp hot sauce, plus more
- coarse salt
- freshly ground black pepper
- 2 tbsp chopped fresh curly parsley or tarragon

Directions:

1. Supply your smoker with wood pellets and follow the start-up procedure. Preheat the grill, with the lid closed, to 450° F.

2. In a small saucepan on the stovetop over medium-low heat, make the sauce by melting the butter. Add the garlic and sauté for 1 to 2 minutes. Add the wine, lemon juice, and hot sauce. Season with salt and pepper to taste. Simmer for 5 minutes. Remove the saucepan from the heat and stir in the parsley. Keep warm.

3. Discard any mussels that are cracked or don't snap shut when tapped. Place the mussels in a large aluminum foil roasting pan and cover tightly with heavy-duty aluminum foil.

4. Place the pan on the grate and steam the mussels until the shells open, about 10 to 12 minutes. Remove the pan from the grill and use long-handled tongs to remove the foil from the pan. (Be careful of escaping steam.) Use the tongs to discard any mussels that don't open.

5. Pour the reserved garlic butter sauce over the mussels. Serve from the pan or transfer the mussels to a shallow serving bowl. Serve immediately with lemon wedges, additional hot sauce, and crusty bread (if using) to sop up the juices.

Vodka Brined Smoked Wild Salmon

Servings: 4
Cooking Time: 60 Minutes

Ingredients:

- 1 Cup brown sugar
- 1 Tablespoon black pepper
- 1/2 Cup coarse salt
- 1 Cup vodka
- 1 (1-1/2 to 2 lb) wild caught salmon
- 1 lemon wedges
- capers

Directions:

1. In a small bowl, whisk together brown sugar, pepper, salt and vodka.

2. Place the salmon in a large resealable bag. Pour in marinade and massage into the salmon. Refrigerate for 2 to 4 hours.

3. Remove from bag, rinse and dry with paper towels.

4.	Supply your smoker with wood pellets and follow the start-up procedure. Preheat the grill, with the lid closed, to 180° F.

5.	Smoke the salmon, skin-side down for 30 minutes.

6.	Increase grill temperature to 225°F and continue to cook salmon for an additional 45 to 60 minutes or until the internal temperature in the thickest part of the fish reaches 140°F or the fish flakes easily when pressed with a finger or fork. Grill: 225 °F Probe: 140 °F

7.	Serve with lemons and capers. Enjoy!

Summer Paella

Servings: 6
Cooking Time: 45 Minutes

Ingredients:

*	6 tablespoons extra-virgin olive oil, divided, plus more for drizzling

*	2 green or red bell peppers, cored, seeded, and diced

*	2 medium onions, diced

*	2 garlic cloves, slivered

*	1 (29-ounce) can tomato purée

*	1½ pounds chicken thighs

*	Kosher salt

*	1½ pounds tail-on shrimp, peeled and deveined

*	1 cup dried thinly sliced chorizo sausage

*	1 tablespoon smoked paprika

*	1½ teaspoons saffron threads

*	2 quarts chicken broth

*	3½ cups white rice

*	2 (7½-ounce) cans chipotle chiles in adobo sauce

*	1½ pounds fresh clams, soaked in cold water for 15 to 20 minutes2 tablespoons chopped fresh parsley

*	2 lemons, cut into wedges, for serving

Directions:

1.	Make the sofrito: On the stove top, in a saucepan over medium-low heat, combine ¼ cup of olive oil, the bell peppers, onions, and garlic, and cook for 5 minutes, or until the onions are translucent.

2.	Stir in the tomato purée, reduce the heat to low, and simmer, stirring frequently, until most of the liquid has evaporated, about 30 minutes. Set aside. (Note: The sofrito can be made in advance and refrigerated.)

3.	Supply your smoker with wood pellets and follow the start-up procedure. Preheat, with the lid closed, to 450°F.

4.	Heat a large paella pan on the smoker and add the remaining 2 tablespoons of olive oil.

5.	Add the chicken thighs, season lightly with salt, and brown for 6 to 10 minutes, then push to the outer edge of the pan.

6.	Add the shrimp, season with salt, close the lid, and smoke for 3 minutes.

7.	Add the sofrito, chorizo, paprika, and saffron, and stir together.

8.	In a separate bowl, combine the chicken broth, uncooked rice, and 1 tablespoon of salt, stirring until well combined.

9.	Add the broth-rice mixture to the paella pan, spreading it evenly over the other ingredients.

10.	Close the lid and smoke for 5 minutes, then add the chipotle chiles and clams on top of the rice.

11.	Close the lid and continue to smoke the paella for about 30 minutes, or until all of the liquid is absorbed.

12.	Remove the pan from the grill, cover tightly with aluminum foil, and let rest off the heat for 5 minutes.

13.	Drizzle with olive oil, sprinkle with the fresh parsley, and serve with the lemon wedges.

Bacon Wrapped Shrimp

Servings: 6
Cooking Time: 20 Minutes

Ingredients:

*	1 1/2 Pound Jumbo Shrimp, Peeled And Deveined

*	10 Strips Bacon

*	Cheesy Grits, For Serving

*	1/4 Cup extra-virgin olive oil

*	2 Tablespoon lemon juice

*	1 Teaspoon Fresh Chopped Parsley

*	1 Tablespoon lemon zest

*	1 Teaspoon garlic, minced

*	1 Teaspoon salt

*	1/2 Teaspoon black pepper

Directions:

1.	Rinse the shrimp under cold running water and dry thoroughly on paper towels.

2.	Transfer to a re-sealable plastic bag or a bowl.

3.	For the marinade: Combine the olive oil, lemon juice, lemon zest, garlic, salt, pepper, and parsley in a small jar with a tight-fitting lid and shake vigorously until combined.

4.	Pour over the shrimp and refrigerate for 30 minutes to 1 hour.

5.	Supply your smoker with wood pellets and follow the start-up procedure. Preheat the grill, with the lid closed, to 400° F.

6.	Lay the bacon strips diagonally on the grill grate and grill for 10 to 12 minutes, or until the bacon is partially cooked but still very pliable.

7.	Cut each strip in half width-wise. Leave the grill on.

8.	Drain the shrimp, discarding the marinade. Wrap a strip of bacon around the body of each shrimp, securing with a toothpick. Grill for 4 minutes per side, turning once. Enjoy! Grill: 400 °F

9.	Wrap a strip of bacon around the body of each shrimp, securing with a toothpick.

10. Grill for 4 minutes per side, turning once. Serve over cheesy grits, if desired. Enjoy!

Bbq Oysters

Servings: 4
Cooking Time: 6 Minutes

Ingredients:

- 1 Pound unsalted butter, softened
- 1 Tablespoon Meat Church Holy Gospel BBQ Rub
- 1 Bunch green onions, chopped
- 2 Clove garlic, minced
- 12 oysters
- 1/4 Cup seasoned breadcrumbs
- 8 Ounce shredded pepper jack cheese
- Sweet & Heat BBQ Sauce
- 1/2 Bunch green onions, minced

Directions:

1. Supply your smoker with wood pellets and follow the start-up procedure. Preheat the grill, with the lid closed, to 375° F.
2. For the compound butter: Combine butter, garlic, onion and Meat Church Rub thoroughly.
3. Lay the butter on parchment paper or plastic wrap. Roll it up to form a log and tie each end with butcher's twine. Place in the freezer for an hour to solidify. You can use this butter on any grilled meat to enhance the flavor. You can also use a high-quality butter to replace the compound butter.
4. Shuck the oysters, keeping all of the juice in the shell. Sprinkle the oysters with breadcrumbs and place directly on the Traeger. Cook them for 5 minutes. You will be looking for the edge of the oyster to start to curl slightly.
5. After 5 minutes, place a spoonful of compound butter in the oysters. After the butter melts, add a pinch of pepper jack cheese.
6. Remove the oysters after 6 minutes on the grill total. Top oysters with a squirt of Traeger Sweet & Heat BBQ Sauce and a few chopped onions. Allow to cool for 5 minutes, then enjoy!

Grilled Mussels With Lemon Butter

Servings: 4
Cooking Time: 15 Minutes

Ingredients:

- 2 Pound Mussels, debearded, washed
- 5 Quart water
- 1/3 Cup salt
- 2 Clove garlic, minced
- 1/3 Cup white wine
- 1 Whole lemon juice
- 3 Tablespoon parsley, chopped
- 1 loaf French country bread

Directions:

1. Supply your smoker with wood pellets and follow the start-up procedure. Preheat the grill, with the lid closed, to 375° F.
2. Scrub mussels well in running water making sure to remove all dirt and barnacles.
3. Place clean mussels in a large bowl with 5 quarts (5 L) water and 1/3 cup (91 g) of salt for about 15 minutes.
4. Drain, rinse and repeat soaking method two more times to purge and remove all sand.
5. Melt butter in a saute pan over medium high heat. Add garlic and cook for 1 minute until fragrant. Add wine and bring to a simmer. Add mussels and lemon juice to the pan and toss to coat.
6. Cover with a tight fitting lid and transfer to the grill. Let the mussels steam 8-10 minutes. Remove from the grill and discard any unopened mussels.
7. Sprinkle with chopped parsley and transfer to a serving dish. Serve with sliced bread. Enjoy!

Whole Vermillion Red Snapper

Servings: 6
Cooking Time: 20 Minutes

Ingredients:

- 1 Whole Vermillion Red Snapper, scaled & gutted
- 4 Clove garlic, chopped
- 1 Whole lemon, thinly sliced
- 2 Sprig rosemary sprigs
- sea salt and freshly ground black pepper

Directions:

1. Supply your smoker with wood pellets and follow the start-up procedure. Preheat the grill, with the lid closed, to High heat.
2. Stuff the cavity of the fish with chopped garlic. Sprinkle the fish with sea salt, pepper, rosemary, and lemon.
3. Grill fish directly on the grill grate. Cook for 20-25 minutes. Serve. Enjoy!

Grilled Whole Steelhead Fillet

Servings: 6
Cooking Time: 30 Minutes

Ingredients:

- (2-1/2 to 3 lb) steelhead or salmon fillet, skin-on
- 2 Tablespoon Montana Mex Sweet Seasoning
- 1 Teaspoon Montana Mex Jalapeño Seasoning Blend
- 1 Teaspoon Montana Mex Mild Chile Seasoning Blend
- 2 Tablespoon Montana Mex Avocado Oil
- 2 Tablespoon freshly grated ginger
- 1 lemon, thinly sliced

Directions:

1. Coat fillet evenly with all three dry seasonings, avocado oil, grated ginger and thinly sliced lemon.
2. Supply your smoker with wood pellets and follow the start-up procedure. Preheat the grill, with the lid closed, to 380° F.
3. Place the fish skin-side down on the grill grate and cook for 20 minutes. Grill: 380 °F
4. Remove fillet from grill and let rest for 5 minutes. Enjoy!

Honey Balsamic Salmon

Servings: 2
Cooking Time: 25 Minutes

Ingredients:

- 1 Medium salmon fillet
- Fin & Feather Rub
- 1/2 Cup balsamic vinegar
- 1 Tablespoon minced garlic
- 2 Tablespoon honey

Directions:

1. Season the fillet with the Traeger Fin & Feather Rub.
2. Make the glaze: Combine the vinegar, garlic and honey in a small saucepan. Simmer over medium heat until reduced by half. Usually 10 to 15 minutes. The glaze will be properly reduced when it coats the back of a spoon. Using a basting brush, coat the fillet with the glaze.
3. Supply your smoker with wood pellets and follow the start-up procedure. Preheat the grill, with the lid closed, to 350° F.
4. Arrange the salmon fillet on the grill grate. Grill for 25 to 30 minutes, or until the salmon is opaque and flakes easily with a fork. Grill: 350 °F
5. Transfer to a platter or plates and serve immediately. If desired, heat any remaining glaze to a boil and drizzle over top of the salmon. Enjoy!

Florentine Shrimp Al Cartoccio

Servings: 4

Cooking Time: 13 Minutes

Ingredients:

- 6 tbsp unsalted butter, melted
- ½ cup heavy whipping cream
- ½ cup grated Parmesan cheese
- 2 garlic cloves, peeled and minced
- 1 cup thinly sliced button mushrooms, cleaned and destemmed
- 1 cup baby spinach leaves
- 2 tbsp chopped sun-dried, oil-packed tomatoes
- ½ tsp dried oregano
- ½ tsp dried basil
- ½ tsp crushed red pepper flakes, plus more
- ½ tsp coarse salt
- ½ tsp freshly ground black pepper
- 20 to 24 jumbo shrimp, about 1lb (450g) total, peeled and deveined
- sprigs of fresh rosemary, basil, thyme, or oregano

Directions:

1. Supply your smoker with wood pellets and follow the start-up procedure. Preheat the grill, with the lid closed, to 400° F.
2. In a large bowl, combine the butter and whipping cream. Stir in the Parmesan, garlic, mushrooms, spinach, tomatoes, oregano, basil, red pepper flakes, and salt and pepper. Add the shrimp and stir gently to coat.
3. Place four 12-inch (30.5cm) sheets of wide heavy-duty aluminum foil on a workspace and pull up the sides. Divide the shrimp mixture evenly between the sheets of foil. Roll and crimp the top and sides of the foil to create sealed packages.
4. Place the packets seam side up on the grate and grill until the shrimp are cooked through, about 10 to 13 minutes. (You can carefully open one package to check on the shrimp.)
5. Transfer the packets to plates. Carefully open the packets to avoid any steam. Scatter fresh herbs over the shrimp before serving.

Cured Cold-smoked Lox

Servings: 6
Cooking Time: 360 Minutes

Ingredients:

- ¼ cup salt
- ¼ cup sugar
- 1 tablespoon freshly ground black pepper
- 1 bunch dill, chopped
- 1 pound sashimi-grade salmon, skin removed
- 1 avocado, sliced
- 8 bagels
- 4 ounces cream cheese
- 1 bunch alfalfa sprouts
- 1 (3.5-ounce) jar capers

Directions:

1. In a small bowl, combine the salt, sugar, pepper, and fresh dill to make the curing mixture. Set aside.
2. On a smooth surface, lay out a large piece of plastic wrap and spread half of the curing salt mixture in the middle, spreading it out to about the size of the salmon.
3. Place the salmon on top of the curing salt.
4. Top the fish with the remaining curing salt, covering it completely. Wrap the salmon, leaving the ends open to drain.
5. Place the wrapped fish in a rimmed baking pan or dish lined with paper towels to soak up liquid.
6. Place a weight on the salmon evenly, such as a pan with a couple of heavy jars of pickles on top.
7. Put the salmon pan with weights in the refrigerator. Place something (a dishtowel, for example) under the back of the pan in order to slightly tip it down so the liquid drains away from the fish.
8. Leave the salmon to cure in the refrigerator for 24 hours.
9. Place the wood pellets in the smoker, but do not follow the start-up procedure and do not preheat.
10. Remove the salmon from the refrigerator, unwrap it, rinse it off, and pat dry.
11. Put the salmon in the smoker while still cold from the refrigerator to slow down the cooking process. You'll need to use a cold-smoker attachment or enlist the help of a smoker tube to hold the temperature at 80°F and maintain that for 6 hours to absorb smoke and complete the cold-smoking process.
12. Remove the salmon from the smoker, place it in a sealed plastic bag, and refrigerate for 24 hours. The salmon will be translucent all the way through.
13. Thinly slice the lox and serve with sliced avocado, bagels, cream cheese, alfalfa sprouts, and capers.

Spicy Shrimp Skewers

Servings: 4
Cooking Time: 6 Minutes

Ingredients:

- 2 Pound shrimp, peeled and deveined
- 6 Thai chiles
- 6 Clove garlic
- 2 Tablespoon Winemaker's Napa Valley Rub
- 1 1/2 Teaspoon sugar
- 1 1/2 Tablespoon white vinegar
- 3 Tablespoon olive oil

Directions:

1. If using bamboo skewers, place them in cold water to soak for 1 hour before grilling.
2. Place shrimp in a bowl and set aside. Combine all remaining ingredients in a blender and blend until a coarse-textured paste is reached. Note: if a milder flavor is preferred, feel free to adjust amount of chiles to taste.

3. Add chile-garlic mixture to the shrimp and place in fridge to marinate for at least 30 minutes.
4. Remove from fridge and thread shrimp onto bamboo or metal skewers.
5. Supply your smoker with wood pellets and follow the start-up procedure. Preheat the grill, with the lid closed, to 450° F.
6. Place shrimp on grill and cook for 2 to 3 minutes per side or until shrimp are pink and firm to touch. Enjoy! Grill: 450 °F

Smoked Trout

Servings: 6
Cooking Time: 120 Minutes

Ingredients:

- 8 rainbow trout fillets
- 1 Gallon water
- 1/4 Cup salt
- 1/2 Cup brown sugar
- 1 Tablespoon black pepper
- 2 Tablespoon soy sauce

Directions:

1. Clean the fresh fish and butterfly them.
2. For the Brine: Combine one gallon water, brown sugar, soy sauce, salt and pepper and stir until salt and sugar are dissolved. Brine the trout in the refrigerator for 60 minutes.
3. Supply your smoker with wood pellets and follow the start-up procedure. Preheat the grill, with the lid closed, to 225° F.
4. Remove the fish from the brine and pat dry. Place fish directly on grill grate for 1-1/2 to 2 hours, depending on the thickness of the trout. Fish is done when it turns opaque and starts to flake. Serve hot or cold. Enjoy! Grill: 225 °F
5. Fish is done when it turns opaque and starts to flake. Serve hot or cold. Enjoy!

Cajun Catfish

Servings: 6
Cooking Time: 15 Minutes

Ingredients:

- 2½ pounds catfish fillets
- 2 tablespoons olive oil
- 1 batch Cajun Rub

Directions:

1. Supply your smoker with wood pellets and follow the start-up procedure. Preheat the grill, with the lid closed, to 300°F.
2. Coat the catfish fillets all over with olive oil and season with the rub. Using your hands, work the rub into the flesh.
3. Place the fillets directly on the grill grate and smoke until their internal temperature reaches 145°F. Remove the catfish from the grill and serve immediately

Peper Fish Tacos

Servings: 12
Cooking Time: 10 Minutes

Ingredients:

- 1 Tsp Black Pepper
- 1/4 Tsp Cayenne Pepper
- 1 1/2 Lbs Cod Fish
- 1/2 Tsp Cumin
- 1 Tsp Garlic Powder
- 1 Tsp Oregano
- 1 1/2 Tsp Paprika, Smoked
- 1/2 Tsp Salt

Directions:

1. Supply your smoker with wood pellets and follow the start-up procedure. Preheat the grill, with the lid closed, to 350° F.

2. Mix together paprika, garlic powder, oregano, cumin, cayenne, salt and pepper. Sprinkle over cod.

3. Place the cod on your preheated for about 5 minutes per side. Toast tortillas over heat, if desired.

4. Break the cod into pieces, smash the avocado, slice the tomatoes in half and place evenly among the tortillas. Top with red onion, lettuce, jalapenos, sour cream, and cilantro. Spritz with lime juice and enjoy!

Seared Ahi Tuna Steak With Soy Sauce

Servings: 2
Cooking Time: 60 Minutes

Ingredients:

- 1/2 Cup Gluten Free Soy Sauce
- 1 Large Sushi Grade Ahi Tuna Steak, Patted Dry
- 1/4 Cup Lime Juice
- 2 Tablespoons Rice Wine Vinegar
- 2 Tablespoons Sesame Oil, Divided
- 2 Tablespoons Sriracha Sauce
- 4 Tablespoons Sweet Heat Rub
- 2 Cups Water

Directions:

1. Supply your smoker with wood pellets and follow the start-up procedure. Preheat the grill, with the lid closed, to 400° F. If using gas or charcoal, set it up for high heat over direct heat.

2. In the glass baking dish, pour in the water, soy sauce, lime juice, rice wine vinegar, 1 tablespoon sesame oil, sriracha sauce, and mirin. Whisk the marinade together with the whisk until everything is well combine. Place the ahi steak into the marinade and place the glass baking dish with the ahi steak in the refrigerator for 30 minutes. After 30 minutes, flip the ahi steak over so that the ahi has the chance to fully marinate on all sides, and allow to marinate for 30 more minutes.

3. After the tuna steak has finished marinating, drain off the marinade and pat the steak dry with paper towels on all sides. Pour the Sweet Heat Rub onto the plate and rub the remaining tablespoon of sesame oil generously on all sides of the tuna steak, and then gently place the tuna steak into the seasoning on the plate, turning on all sides to coat evenly.

4. Insert a temperature probe into the thickest part of the ahi steak and place the steak on the hottest part of the grill. Grill the ahi tuna steak for 45 seconds on each side, or just until the outside is opaque and has grill marks. Flip the steak and allow it to grill for another 45 seconds until the outside is just cooked through. The ahi tuna steak's internal temperature should be just at 115°F.

5. Remove the steak from the grill once it reaches 115°F, and immediately slice and serve. The inside of the steak should still be cool and ruby pink.

Cedar Smoked Garlic Salmon

Servings: 6
Cooking Time: 60 Minutes

Ingredients:

- 1 Tsp Black Pepper
- 3 Cedar Plank, Untreated
- 1 Tsp Garlic, Minced
- 1/3 Cup Olive Oil
- 1 Tsp Onion, Salt
- 1 Tsp Parsley, Minced Fresh
- 1 1/2 Tbsp Rice Vinegar
- 2 Salmon, Fillets (Skin Removed)
- 1 Tsp Sesame Oil
- 1/3 Cup Soy Sauce

Directions:

1. Soak the cedar planks in warm water for an hour or more.

2. In a bowl, mix together the olive oil, rice vinegar, sesame oil, soy sauce, and minced garlic.

3. Add in the salmon and let it marinate for about 30 minutes.

4. Start your grill on smoke with the lid open until a fire is established in the burn pot (3-7 minutes).

5. Supply your smoker with wood pellets and follow the start-up procedure. Preheat the grill, with the lid closed, to 225° F.

6. Place the planks on the grate. Once the boards start to smoke and crackle a little, it's ready for the fish.

7. Remove the fish from the marinade, season it with the onion powder, parsley and black pepper, then discard the marinade.

8. Place the salmon on the planks and grill until it reaches 140°F internal temperature (start checking temp after the salmon has been on the grill for 30 minutes).

9. Remove from the grill, let it rest for 10 minutes, then serve.

Smoke-roasted Halibut With Mixed Herb Vinaigrette

Servings: 4
Cooking Time: 12 Minutes

Ingredients:

- 4 halibut fillets, each about 6 to 8oz (170 to 225g)
- for the vinaigrette
- 2 tbsp white wine vinegar or sherry vinegar, plus more
- ¼ tsp coarse salt, plus more
- ¼ tsp freshly ground black pepper, plus more
- ½ cup extra virgin olive oil
- 2 tbsp minced fresh herbs, such as dill, flat-leaf parsley, or oregano
- for serving
- 4 cups loosely packed baby arugula, spinach, or other mixed greens
- 1 lemon, cut lengthwise into 4 wedges

Directions:

1. Supply your smoker with wood pellets and follow the start-up procedure. Preheat the grill, with the lid closed, to 400° F.
2. In a small bowl, make the vinaigrette by whisking together the vinegar, and salt and pepper. Whisk until the salt dissolves. Continue to whisk while slowly adding the olive oil. Whisk until the vinaigrette is emulsified. Stir in the herbs. Taste, adding vinegar or salt and pepper to taste. Pour 1/3 of the vinaigrette into a separate container. Reserve the remainder.
3. Place the fillets on a rimmed sheet pan. Lightly brush both sides with the smaller portion of vinaigrette. (Dividing the vinaigrette into two containers prevents cross-contamination.) Lightly season with salt and pepper.
4. Place the fillets on the grate at an angle to the bars. Grill until the edges begin to look opaque, about 4 to 6 minutes. Gently turn and grill until the fish is cooked through, about 4 to 6 minutes more. (A fillet will break into clean flakes when pressed with a fork when it's done.)
5. Remove the fish from the grill. Place the greens in a large bowl and toss them with 2 to 3 tablespoons of the reserved vinaigrette (you want the greens lightly coated) and divide between 4 plates. Place a fillet on the greens on each plate. Drizzle a bit more of the vinaigrette over the top. Serve with lemon wedges.

Grilled Blackened Saskatchewan Salmon

Servings: 4
Cooking Time: 30 Minutes

Ingredients:

- 1 salmon fillets
- zesty Italian dressing
- Blackened Saskatchewan Rub
- lemon wedges

Directions:

1. Brush salmon with Italian dressing and season with Traeger Blackened Saskatchewan Rub.
2. Supply your smoker with wood pellets and follow the start-up procedure. Preheat the grill, with the lid closed, to 325° F.
3. Place salmon on the grill and cook for 20 to 30 minutes, until it reaches an internal temperature of 145°F and flakes easily. Remove salmon from grill. Serve with lemon wedges. Enjoy! Grill: 325 °F Probe: 145 °F

Swordfish With Sicilian Olive Oil Sauce

Servings: 4
Cooking Time: 10 Minutes

Ingredients:

- 1/2 Cup extra-virgin olive oil, plus 2 tablespoons for oiling the fish
- 1 Whole lemon, juiced
- 2 Clove garlic, minced
- 3 Tablespoon finely chopped fresh parsley
- 1 Tablespoon finely chopped fresh oregano or 1 teaspoon dried oregano
- 1 Tablespoon brined capers, drained (optional)
- 4 (6 to 8 oz) swordfish, halibut, tuna or salmon steaks, 1 inch thick
- salt and pepper

Directions:

1. Put 1/2 cup of olive oil in a small saucepan and warm over low heat.
2. Whisk in lemon juice and 2 tablespoons hot water. Stir in garlic, parsley, oregano, capers (if using), and salt and pepper to taste (go easy on the salt if you're using capers). Keep warm.
3. Supply your smoker with wood pellets and follow the start up procedure. Preheat the grill, with the lid closed, to 400° F.
4. Brush the fish steaks with 2 tablespoons of olive oil and season with salt and pepper. Grill: 400 °F
5. Arrange on the grill grate and grill until the fish is opaque and flakes easily when pressed with a fork, about 18 minutes. (If you prefer your tuna or salmon on the rare side, cook them for less time.) Grill: 400 °F
6. Transfer the fish steaks to a platter or plates and drizzle with the warm olive oil sauce.
7. Serve the remaining sauce on the side. Enjoy!

Lobster Tail

Servings: 2
Cooking Time: 25 Minutes

Ingredients:

- 2 lobster tails
- Salt
- Freshly ground black pepper
- 1 batch Lemon Butter Mop for Seafood

Directions:

1. Supply your smoker with wood pellets and follow the start-up procedure. Preheat the grill, with the lid closed, to 375°F.
2. Using kitchen shears, slit the top of the lobster shells, through the center, nearly to the tail. Once cut, expose as much meat as you can through the cut shell.
3. Season the lobster tails all over with salt and pepper.
4. Place the tails directly on the grill grate and grill until their internal temperature reaches 145°F. Remove the lobster from the grill and serve with the mop on the side for dipping.

Grilled Lemon Shrimp Scampi

Servings: 4
Cooking Time: 6 Minutes

Ingredients:

- 1 ½ pounds medium shrimp, peeled and deveined
- ¼ cup olive oil
- ¼ cup lemon juice
- 3 tablespoons chopped fresh parsley
- 1 tablespoon minced garlic
- ground black pepper to taste
- ¼ teaspoon crushed red pepper flakes to taste

Directions:

1. In a large, non-reactive bowl, stir together the olive oil, lemon juice, parsley, garlic, and black pepper. Season with crushed red pepper, if desired. Add shrimp, and toss to coat. Marinate in the refrigerator for 30 minutes.
2. Supply your smoker with wood pellets and follow the start-up procedure. Preheat the grill, with the lid closed, to high heat.
3. Thread shrimp onto skewers, piercing once near the tail and once near the head. Discard any remaining marinade.
4. Lightly oil grill grate. Place the shrimp skewers on the grill grates.
5. Grill for 2 to 3 minutes per side, or until opaque.

Barbecued Scallops

Servings: 4
Cooking Time: 10 Minutes

Ingredients:

- 1 pound large scallops
- 2 tablespoons olive oil
- 1 batch Dill Seafood Rub

Directions:

1. Supply your smoker with wood pellets and follow the start-up procedure. Preheat the grill, with the lid closed, to 375°F.
2. Coat the scallops all over with olive oil and season all sides with the rub.
3. Place the scallops directly on the grill grate and grill for 5 minutes per side. Remove the scallops from the grill and serve immediately.

Honey-soy Garlic Salmon

Servings: 4
Cooking Time: 6 Minutes

Ingredients:

- 1 Tsp Chili Paste
- Chives, Chopped
- 2 Grate Garlic, Cloves
- 2 Tbsp Minced Ginger, Fresh
- 1 Tsp Honey
- 2 Tbsp Lemon, Juice
- 4 Salmon, Fillets (Skin Removed)
- 1 Tsp Sesame Oil
- 2 Tbsp Soy Sauce, Low Sodium

Directions:

1. Supply your smoker with wood pellets and follow the start-up procedure. Preheat the grill, with the lid closed, to 400° F.
2. Take the salmon and place it in a large resealable plastic bag, and then top with all remaining ingredients, except the chives. Seal the plastic bag and toss evenly to coat the salmon. Marinade in the refrigerator for 20 minutes.
3. After the salmon has been marinading for 20 minutes, place salmon on a flat pan or right on the grates and grill for about 3 minutes, and then flip and grill on the second side for about 3 minutes. Turn off the Grill, remove the pan from grill, plate, garnish with chives, and enjoy!

APPETIZERS AND SNACKS

Chicken Wings With Teriyaki Glaze

Servings: 4
Cooking Time: 50 Minutes

Ingredients:

- 16 large chicken wings, about 3lb (1.4kg) total
- 1 to 1½ tbsp toasted sesame oil
- for the glaze
- ½ cup light soy sauce or tamari
- ¼ cup sake or sugar-free dark-colored soda
- ¼ cup light brown sugar or low-carb substitute
- 2 tbsp mirin or 1 tbsp honey
- 1 garlic clove, peeled, minced or grated
- 2 tsp minced fresh ginger
- 1 tsp cornstarch mixed with 1 tbsp distilled water (optional)
- for serving
- 1 tbsp toasted sesame seeds
- 2 scallions, trimmed, white and green parts sliced sharply diagonally

Directions:

1. Supply your smoker with wood pellets and follow the start-up procedure. Preheat the grill, with the lid closed, to 350° F.
2. Place the chicken wings in a large bowl, add the sesame oil, and turn the wings to coat thoroughly.
3. Place the wings on the grate at an angle to the bars. Grill for 20 minutes and then turn. Continue to cook until the wings are nicely browned and the meat is no longer pink at the bone, about 20 minutes more.
4. To make the glaze, in a saucepan on the stovetop over medium-high heat, combine the ingredients and bring the mixture to a boil. Reduce the glaze by 1/3, about 6 to 8 minutes. If you prefer your glaze to be glossy and thick, add the cornstarch and water mixture to the glaze and cook until it coats the back of a spoon, about 1 to 2 minutes more.
5. Transfer the wings to an aluminum foil roasting pan. Pour the glaze over them, turning to coat thoroughly. Place the pan on the grate and cook the wings until the glaze sets, about 5 to 10 minutes.
6. Transfer the wings to a platter. Scatter the sesame seeds and scallions over the top. Serve with plenty of napkins.

Bacon-wrapped Jalapeño Poppers

Servings: 12
Cooking Time: 30 Minutes

Ingredients:

- 8 ounces cream cheese, softened
- ½ cup shredded Cheddar cheese
- ¼ cup chopped scallions
- 1 teaspoon chipotle chile powder or regular chili powder
- 1 teaspoon garlic powder
- 1 teaspoon salt
- 18 large jalapeño peppers, stemmed, seeded, and halved lengthwise
- 1 pound bacon (precooked works well)

Directions:

1. Supply your smoker with wood pellets and follow the start-up procedure. Preheat, with the lid closed, to 350°F. Line a baking sheet with aluminum foil.
2. In a small bowl, combine the cream cheese, Cheddar cheese, scallions, chipotle powder, garlic powder, and salt.
3. Stuff the jalapeño halves with the cheese mixture.
4. Cut the bacon into pieces big enough to wrap around the stuffed pepper halves.
5. Wrap the bacon around the peppers and place on the prepared baking sheet.
6. Put the baking sheet on the grill grate, close the lid, and smoke the peppers for 30 minutes, or until the cheese is melted and the bacon is cooked through and crisp.
7. Let the jalapeño poppers cool for 3 to 5 minutes. Serve warm.

Bacon Pork Pinwheels (kansas Lollipops)

Servings: 4-6
Cooking Time: 20 Minutes

Ingredients:

- 1 Whole Pork Loin, boneless
- To Taste salt and pepper
- To Taste Greek Seasoning
- 4 Slices bacon
- To Taste The Ultimate BBQ Sauce

Directions:

1. When ready to cook, start the smoker and set temperature to 500F. Preheat, lid closed, for 10 to 15 minutes.
2. Trim pork loin of any unwanted silver skin or fat. Using a sharp knife, cut pork loin length wise, into 4 long strips.
3. Lay pork flat, then season with salt, pepper and Cavender's Greek Seasoning.
4. Flip the pork strips over and layer bacon on unseasoned side. Begin tightly rolling the pork strips, with bacon being rolled up on the inside.
5. Secure a skewer all the way through each pork roll to secure it in place. Set the pork rolls down on grill and cook for 15 minutes.
6. Brush BBQ Sauce over the pork. Turn each skewer over, then coat the other side. Let pork cook for another 5-10 minutes, depending on thickness of your pork. Enjoy!

Bayou Wings With Cajun Rémoulade

Servings: 8
Cooking Time: 40 Minutes

Ingredients:

- 16 large whole chicken wings or 32 drumettes and flats, about 3lb (1.4kg) total
- for the rub
- 1 tbsp kosher salt
- 1 tsp freshly ground black pepper
- 1 tsp paprika
- ½ tsp ground cayenne, plus more
- ½ tsp garlic powder
- ½ tsp celery salt
- ½ tsp dried thyme
- 2 tbsp vegetable oil
- for the rémoulade
- 1¼ cups reduced-fat mayo
- ¼ cup Creole-style or whole grain mustard
- 2 tbsp horseradish
- 2 tbsp pickle relish
- 1 tbsp freshly squeezed lemon juice
- 1 tsp paprika, plus more
- 1 tsp hot sauce, plus more
- 1 tsp Worcestershire sauce
- coarse salt
- for serving
- lemon wedges
- pickled okra (optional)

Directions:

1. Supply your smoker with wood pellets and follow the start-up procedure. Preheat the grill, with the lid closed, to 350° F.
2. If using whole wings, cut through the two joints, separating them into drumettes, flats, and wing tips. (Discard the wing tips or save them for chicken stock.) Alternatively, leave the wings whole. Place the chicken in a resealable plastic bag.
3. In a small bowl, make the rub by combining the ingredients. Mix well. Pour the rub over the wings and toss them to thoroughly coat. Refrigerate for 2 hours.
4. In a small bowl, make the Cajun rémoulade by whisking together the mayo, mustard, horseradish, pickle relish, lemon juice, paprika, hot sauce, and Worcestershire. Season with salt to taste. The mixture should be highly seasoned. Transfer to a serving bowl and lightly dust with paprika. Cover and refrigerate until ready to serve.
5. Remove the wings from the refrigerator and allow the excess marinade to drip off. Place the wings on the grate at an angle to the bars. Grill for 20 minutes and then turn. (They'll brown more evenly but will also have less of a tendency to stick.) Continue to cook until the wings are nicely browned and the meat is no longer pink at the bone, about 20 minutes more.
6. Remove the wings from the grill and pile them on a platter. Serve with the Cajun rémoulade, lemon wedges, and pickled okra (if using).

Pulled Pork Loaded Nachos

Servings: 4
Cooking Time: 10 Minutes

Ingredients:

- 2 cups leftover smoked pulled pork
- 1 small sweet onion, diced
- 1 medium tomato, diced
- 1 jalapeño pepper, seeded and diced
- 1 garlic clove, minced
- 1 teaspoon salt
- 1 teaspoon freshly ground black pepper
- 1 bag tortilla chips
- 1 cup shredded Cheddar cheese
- ½ cup The Ultimate BBQ Sauce, divided
- ½ cup shredded jalapeño Monterey Jack cheese
- Juice of ½ lime
- 1 avocado, halved, pitted, and sliced
- 2 tablespoons sour cream
- 1 tablespoon chopped fresh cilantro

Directions:

1. Supply your smoker with wood pellets and follow the start-up procedure. Preheat, with the lid closed, to 375°F.
2. Heat the pulled pork in the microwave.
3. In a medium bowl, combine the onion, tomato, jalapeño, garlic, salt, and pepper, and set aside.
4. Arrange half of the tortilla chips in a large cast iron skillet. Spread half of the warmed pork on top and cover with the Cheddar cheese. Top with half of the onion-jalapeño mixture, then drizzle with ¼ cup of barbecue sauce.
5. Layer on the remaining tortilla chips, then the remaining pork and the Monterey Jack cheese. Top with the remaining onion-jalapeño mixture and drizzle with the remaining ¼ cup of barbecue sauce.
6. Place the skillet on the grill, close the lid, and smoke for about 10 minutes, or until the cheese is melted and bubbly. (Watch to make sure your chips don't burn!)
7. Squeeze the lime juice over the nachos, top with the avocado slices and sour cream, and garnish with the cilantro before serving hot.

Citrus-infused Marinated Olives

Servings: 6

Cooking Time: 30 Minutes

Ingredients:

- 1½ cups mixed brined olives, with pits
- ½ cup extra virgin olive oil
- 1 tbsp freshly squeezed lemon juice
- 1 garlic clove, peeled and thinly sliced
- 1 tsp smoked Spanish paprika
- 2 sprigs of fresh rosemary
- 2 sprigs of fresh thyme
- 2 bay leaves, fresh or dried
- 1 small dried red chili pepper, deseeded and flesh crumbled, or ¼ tsp crushed red pepper flakes
- 3 strips of orange zest
- 3 strips of lemon zest

Directions:

1. Supply your smoker with wood pellets and follow the start-up procedure. Preheat the grill, with the lid closed, to 180° F.

2. Drain the olives, reserving 1 tablespoon of brine. Spread the olives in a single layer in an aluminum foil roasting pan. Place the pan on the grate and cook the olives for 30 minutes, stirring the olives or shaking the pan once or twice.

3. In a small saucepan on the stovetop over low heat, warm the olive oil. Whisk in the lemon juice and the reserved 1 tablespoon of brine. Stir in the garlic and paprika. Add the rosemary, thyme, bay leaves, chili pepper, and orange and lemon zests. Warm over low heat for 10 minutes. Remove the saucepan from the heat.

4. Transfer the olives and olive oil mixture to a pint jar. Tuck the aromatics around the sides of the jar. Let cool and then cover and refrigerate for up to 5 days. Let the olives come to room temperature before serving.

Chorizo Queso Fundido

Servings: 4-6

Cooking Time: 20 Minutes

Ingredients:

- 1 poblano chile
- 1 cup chopped queso quesadilla or queso Oaxaca
- 1 cup shredded Monterey Jack cheese
- ¼ cup milk
- 1 tablespoon all-purpose flour
- 2 (4-ounce) links Mexican chorizo sausage, casings removed
- ⅓ cup beer
- 1 tablespoon unsalted butter
- 1 small red onion, chopped
- ½ cup whole kernel corn

- 2 serrano chiles or jalapeño peppers, stemmed, seeded, and coarsely chopped
- 1 tablespoon minced garlic
- 1 tablespoon freshly squeezed lime juice
- 1 teaspoon ground cumin
- 1 teaspoon salt
- 1 teaspoon freshly ground black pepper
- 1 tablespoon chopped fresh cilantro
- 1 tablespoon chopped scallions
- Tortilla chips, for serving

Directions:

1. Supply your smoker with wood pellets and follow the start-up procedure. Preheat, with the lid closed, to 350°F.

2. On the smoker or over medium-high heat on the stove top, place the poblano directly on the grate (or burner) to char for 1 to 2 minutes, turning as needed. Remove from heat and place in a closed-up lunch-size paper bag for 2 minutes to sweat and further loosen the skin.

3. Remove the skin and coarsely chop the poblano, removing the seeds; set aside.

4. In a bowl, combine the queso quesadilla, Monterey Jack, milk, and flour; set aside.

5. On the stove top, in a cast iron skillet over medium heat, cook and crumble the chorizo for about 2 minutes.

6. Transfer the cooked chorizo to a small, grill-safe pan and place over indirect heat on the smoker.

7. Place the cast iron skillet on the preheated grill grate. Pour in the beer and simmer for a few minutes, loosening and stirring in any remaining sausage bits from the pan.

8. Add the butter to the pan, then add the cheese mixture a little at a time, stirring constantly.

9. When the cheese is smooth, stir in the onion, corn, serrano chiles, garlic, lime juice, cuvmin, salt, and pepper. Stir in the reserved chopped charred poblano.

10. Close the lid and smoke for 15 to 20 minutes to infuse the queso with smoke flavor and further cook the vegetables.

11. When the cheese is bubbly, top with the chorizo mixture and garnish with the cilantro and scallions.

12. Serve the chorizo queso fundido hot with tortilla chips.

Grilled Guacamole

Servings: 6

Cooking Time: 30 Minutes

Ingredients:

- 3 large avocados, halved and pitted
- 1 lime, halved
- ½ jalapeño, deseeded and deveined
- ½ small white or red onion, peeled
- 2 garlic cloves, peeled and skewered on a toothpick

- 1 tsp coarse salt, plus more
- 1½ tbsp reduced-fat mayo
- 2 tbsp chopped fresh cilantro
- 2 tbsp crumbled queso fresco (optional)
- tortilla chips

Directions:

1. Supply your smoker with wood pellets and follow the start-up procedure. Preheat the grill, with the lid closed, to 225° F.

2. Place the avocados, lime, jalapeño, and onion cut sides down on the grate. Use the toothpicks to balance the garlic cloves between the bars. Smoke for 30 minutes. (You want the vegetables to retain most of their rawness.)

3. Transfer everything to a cutting board. Remove the garlic cloves from the toothpick and roughly chop. Sprinkle with the salt and continue to mince the garlic until it begins to form a paste. Scrape the garlic and salt into a large bowl.

4. Scoop the avocado flesh from the peels into the bowl. Squeeze the juice of ½ lime over the avocado. Mash the avocados but leave them somewhat chunky. Finely dice the jalapeño. Dice 2 tablespoons of onion. (Reserve the remaining onion for another use.) Add the jalapeño, onion, mayo, and cilantro to the bowl. Stir gently to combine. Taste for seasoning, adding more salt, lime juice, and jalapeño as desired.

5. Transfer the guacamole to a serving bowl. Top with the queso fresco (if using). Serve with tortilla chips.

Pigs In A Blanket

Servings: 4-6
Cooking Time: 15 Minutes

Ingredients:

- 2 Tablespoon Poppy Seeds
- 1 Tablespoon Dried Minced Onion
- 2 Teaspoon garlic, minced
- 2 Tablespoon Sesame Seeds
- 1 Teaspoon salt
- 8 Ounce Original Crescent Dough
- 1/4 Cup Dijon mustard
- 1 Large egg, beaten

Directions:

1. When ready to cook, start your smoker at 350 degrees F, and preheat with lid closed, 10 to 15 minutes.

2. Mix together poppy seeds, dried minced onion, dried minced garlic, salt and sesame seeds. Set aside.

3. Cut each triangle of crescent roll dough into thirds lengthwise, making 3 small strips from each roll.

4. Brush the dough strips lightly with Dijon mustard. Put the mini hot dogs on 1 end of the dough and roll up.

5. Arrange them, seam side down, on a greased baking pan. Brush with egg wash and sprinkle with seasoning mixture.

6. Bake in smoker until golden brown, about 12 to 15 minutes.

7. Serve with mustard or dipping sauce of your choice. Enjoy!

Simple Cream Cheese Sausage Balls

Servings: 5
Cooking Time: 30 Minutes

Ingredients:

- 1 pound ground hot sausage, uncooked
- 8 ounces cream cheese, softened
- 1 package mini filo dough shells

Directions:

1. Supply your smoker with wood pellets and follow the start-up procedure. Preheat, with the lid closed, to 350°F.

2. In a large bowl, using your hands, thoroughly mix together the sausage and cream cheese until well blended.

3. Place the filo dough shells on a rimmed perforated pizza pan or into a mini muffin tin.

4. Roll the sausage and cheese mixture into 1-inch balls and place into the filo shells.

5. Place the pizza pan or mini muffin tin on the grill, close the lid, and smoke the sausage balls for 30 minutes, or until cooked through and the sausage is no longer pink.

6. Plate and serve warm.

Deviled Eggs With Smoked Paprika

Servings: 6
Cooking Time: 30 Minutes

Ingredients:

- 6 large eggs
- 3 tbsp reduced-fat mayo, plus more
- 1 tsp Dijon or yellow mustard
- ½ tsp Spanish smoked paprika or regular paprika, plus more
- dash of hot sauce
- coarse salt
- freshly ground black pepper
- for garnishing
- small sprigs of fresh parsley, dill, tarragon, or cilantro
- chopped chives
- minced scallions
- Mustard Caviar
- sliced green or black olives
- celery leaves
- sliced radishes
- diced bell peppers
- sliced cherry tomatoes
- fresh or pickled jalapeños
- sliced or diced pickles
- slivers of sun-dried tomatoes

- bacon crumbles
- smoked salmon
- Hawaiian black salt
- Caviar

Directions:

1.   Supply your smoker with wood pellets and follow the start-up procedure. Preheat the grill, with the lid closed, to 180° F.

2.   On the stovetop over medium-high heat, bring a saucepan of water to a boil. (Make sure there's enough water in the saucepan to cover the eggs by 1 inch [5cm].) Use a slotted spoon to gently lower the eggs into the water. Lower the heat to maintain a simmer. Set a timer for 13 minutes.

3.   Prepare an ice bath by combining ice and cold water in a large bowl. Carefully transfer the eggs to the ice bath when the timer goes off.

4.   When the eggs are cool enough to handle, gently tap them all over to crack the shell. Carefully peel the eggs. Rinse under cold running water to remove any clinging bits of shell, but don't dry the eggs. (A damp surface will help the smoke adhere to the egg whites.)

5.   Place the eggs on the grate and smoke until the eggs take on a light brown patina from the smoke, about 25 minutes. Transfer the eggs to a cutting board, handling them as little as possible.

6.   Slice each egg in half lengthwise with a sharp knife. Wipe any yolk off the blade before slicing the next egg. Gently remove the yolks and place them in a food processor. Pulse to break up the yolks. Add the mayo, mustard, paprika, and hot sauce. Season with salt and pepper to taste. Pulse until the filling is smooth. Add additional mayo 1 teaspoon at a time if the mixture is a little dry. (It shouldn't be too loose either.)

7.   Spoon the filling into each egg half or pipe it in using a small resealable plastic bag. You can also use a pastry bag fitted with a fluted tip.

8.   Place the eggs on a platter and lightly dust with paprika. Accompany with one or more of the suggested garnishes.

Smoked Cashews

Servings: 6
Cooking Time: 60 Minutes

Ingredients:

- 1 pound roasted, salted cashews

Directions:

1.   Supply your smoker with wood pellets and follow the start-up procedure. Preheat the grill, with the lid closed, to 120°F.

2.   Pour the cashews onto a rimmed baking sheet and smoke for 1 hour, stirring once about halfway through the smoking time.

3.   Remove the cashews from the grill, let cool, and store in an airtight container for as long as you can resist.

Pig Pops (sweet-hot Bacon On A Stick)

Servings: 24
Cooking Time: 30 Minutes

Ingredients:

- Nonstick cooking spray, oil, or butter, for greasing
- 2 pounds thick-cut bacon (24 slices)
- 24 metal skewers
- 1 cup packed light brown sugar
- 2 to 3 teaspoons cayenne pepper
- ½ cup maple syrup, divided

Directions:

1.   Supply your smoker with wood pellets and follow the start-up procedure. Preheat, with the lid closed, to 350°F.

2.   Coat a disposable aluminum foil baking sheet with cooking spray, oil, or butter.

3.   Thread each bacon slice onto a metal skewer and place on the prepared baking sheet.

4.   In a medium bowl, stir together the brown sugar and cayenne.

5.   Baste the top sides of the bacon with ¼ cup of maple syrup.

6.   Sprinkle half of the brown sugar mixture over the bacon.

7.   Place the baking sheet on the grill, close the lid, and smoke for 15 to 30 minutes.

8.   Using tongs, flip the bacon skewers. Baste with the remaining ¼ cup of maple syrup and top with the remaining brown sugar mixture.

9.   Continue smoking with the lid closed for 10 to 15 minutes, or until crispy. You can eyeball the bacon and smoke to your desired doneness, but the actual ideal internal temperature for bacon is 155°F

10. Using tongs, carefully remove the bacon skewers from the grill. Let cool completely before handling.

Chuckwagon Beef Jerky

Servings: 6
Cooking Time: 300 Minutes

Ingredients:

- 2½lb (1.2kg) boneless top or bottom round steak, sirloin tip, flank steak, or venison
- 1 cup sugar-free dark-colored soda
- 1 cup cold brewed coffee
- ½ cup light soy sauce
- ¼ cup Worcestershire sauce
- 2 tbsp whiskey (optional)
- 2 tsp chili powder
- 1½ tsp garlic salt
- 1 tsp onion powder
- 1 tsp pink curing salt

Directions:

1. Slice the meat into ¼-inch-thick (.5cm) strips, trimming off any visible fat or gristle. (Slice against the grain for more tender jerky and with the grain for chewier jerky.) Place the meat in a large resealable plastic bag.

2. In a small bowl, whisk together the soda, coffee, soy sauce, Worcestershire sauce, whiskey (if using), chili powder, garlic salt, onion powder, and curing salt (if using). Whisk until the salt dissolves. Pour the mixture over the meat and reseal the bag. Refrigerate for 24 to 48 hours, turning the bag several times to redistribute the brine.

3. Supply your smoker with wood pellets and follow the start-up procedure. Preheat the grill, with the lid closed, to 150° F.

4. Drain the meat and discard the brine. Place the strips of meat in a single layer on paper towels and blot any excess moisture.

5. Place the meat in a single layer on the grate and smoke for 4 to 5 hours, turning once or twice. (If you're aware of hot spots on your grate, rotate the strips so they smoke evenly.) To test for doneness, bend one or two pieces in the middle. They should be dry but still somewhat pliant. Or simply eat a piece to see if it's done to your liking.

6. For the best texture, when you remove the meat from the grill, place the still-warm jerky in a resealable plastic bag and let rest for 30 minutes. (You might see condensation form on the inside of the bag, but the moisture will be reabsorbed by the meat.) Or let the meat cool completely and then store in a resealable plastic bag or covered container. The jerky will last a few days at room temperature but will last longer (up to 2 weeks) if refrigerated.

Smoked Cheese

Servings: 4
Cooking Time: 150 Minutes

Ingredients:
- 1 (2-pound) block medium Cheddar cheese, or your favorite cheese, quartered lengthwise

Directions:
1. Supply your smoker with wood pellets and follow the start-up procedure. Preheat the grill, with the lid closed, to 90°F.

2. Place the cheese directly on the grill grate and smoke for 2 hours, 30 minutes, checking frequently to be sure it's not melting. If the cheese begins to melt, try flipping it. If that doesn't help, remove it from the grill and refrigerate for about 1 hour and then return it to the cold smoker.

3. Remove the cheese, place it in a zip-top bag, and refrigerate overnight.

4. Slice the cheese and serve with crackers, or grate it and use for making a smoked mac and cheese.

Roasted Red Pepper Dip

Servings: 8
Cooking Time: 45 Minutes

Ingredients:
- 4 red bell peppers, halved, destemmed, and deseeded
- 1 cup English walnuts, divided
- 1 small white onion, peeled and coarsely chopped
- 2 garlic cloves, peeled and smashed with a chef's knife
- ¼ cup extra virgin olive oil, plus more
- 1 tbsp balsamic vinegar or balsamic glaze
- 1 tsp honey (eliminate if using balsamic glaze)
- 1 tsp coarse salt, plus more
- 1 tsp ground cumin
- 1 tsp smoked paprika
- ½ to 1 tsp Aleppo red pepper flakes, plus more
- ¼ cup fresh white breadcrumbs (optional)
- distilled water (optional)
- assorted crudités or wedges of pita bread

Directions:
1. Supply your smoker with wood pellets and follow the start-up procedure. Preheat the grill, with the lid closed, to 400° F.

2. Place the peppers skin side down on the grate and grill until the skins blister and the flesh softens, about 30 minutes. Transfer the peppers to a bowl and cover with plastic wrap. Let cool to room temperature. Remove the skins with a paring knife or your fingers. Coarsely chop or tear the peppers.

3. Place ¾ cup of walnuts in an aluminum foil roasting pan. Place the pan on the grate and toast for 10 to 15 minutes, stirring twice. Remove the pan from the grill and let the walnuts cool.

4. Place the peppers, onion, garlic, and walnuts in a food processor fitted with the chopping blade. Pulse several times. Add the olive oil, balsamic vinegar, honey, salt, cumin, paprika, and red pepper flakes. Process until the mixture is fairly smooth. Taste for seasoning, adding more salt or red pepper flakes (if desired). (If the mixture is too loose, add breadcrumbs until the texture is to your liking. If it's too thick, add olive oil or water 1 tablespoon at a time.)

5. Transfer the dip to a serving bowl. Use the back of a spoon to make a shallow depression in the center. Top with the remaining ¼ cup of walnuts and drizzle olive oil in the depression. Serve with crudités or pita bread.

Delicious Deviled Crab Appetizer

Servings: 30
Cooking Time: 10 Minutes

Ingredients:

- Nonstick cooking spray, oil, or butter, for greasing
- 1 cup panko breadcrumbs, divided
- 1 cup canned corn, drained
- ½ cup chopped scallions, divided
- ½ red bell pepper, finely chopped
- 16 ounces jumbo lump crabmeat
- ¾ cup mayonnaise, divided
- 1 egg, beaten
- 1 teaspoon salt
- 1 teaspoon freshly ground black pepper
- 2 teaspoons cayenne pepper, divided
- Juice of 1 lemon

Directions:

1. Supply your smoker with wood pellets and follow the start-up procedure. Preheat, with the lid closed, to 425°F.
2. Spray three 12-cup mini muffin pans with cooking spray and divide ½ cup of the panko between 30 of the muffin cups, pressing into the bottoms and up the sides. (Work in batches, if necessary, depending on the number of pans you have.)
3. In a medium bowl, combine the corn, ¼ cup of scallions, the bell pepper, crabmeat, half of the mayonnaise, the egg, salt, pepper, and 1 teaspoon of cayenne pepper.
4. Gently fold in the remaining ½ cup of breadcrumbs and divide the mixture between the prepared mini muffin cups.
5. Place the pans on the grill grate, close the lid, and smoke for 10 minutes, or until golden brown.
6. In a small bowl, combine the lemon juice and the remaining mayonnaise, scallions, and cayenne pepper to make a sauce.
7. Brush the tops of the mini crab cakes with the sauce and serve hot.

Smoked Turkey Sandwich

Servings: 1
Cooking Time: 15 Minutes

Ingredients:

- 2 slices sourdough bread
- 2 tablespoons butter, at room temperature
- 2 (1-ounce) slices Swiss cheese
- 4 ounces leftover Smoked Turkey
- 1 teaspoon garlic salt

Directions:

1. Supply your smoker with wood pellets and follow the start-up procedure. Preheat the grill, with the lid closed, to 375°F.
2. Coat one side of each bread slice with 1 tablespoon of butter and sprinkle the buttered sides with garlic salt.
3. Place 1 slice of cheese on each unbuttered side of the bread, and then put the turkey on the cheese.
4. Close the sandwich, buttered sides out, and place it directly on the grill grate. Cook for 5 minutes. Flip the sandwich and cook for 5 minutes more. Remove the sandwich from the grill, cut it in half, and serve.

Sriracha & Maple Cashews

Servings: 10
Cooking Time: 60 Minutes

Ingredients:

- 2 tbsp unsalted butter
- 3 tbsp pure maple syrup
- 1 tbsp sriracha
- 1 tsp coarse salt (use only if nuts are unsalted)
- 2½ cups unsalted cashews

Directions:

1. Supply your smoker with wood pellets and follow the start-up procedure. Preheat the grill, with the lid closed, to 250° F.
2. In a small saucepan on the stovetop over low heat, melt the butter. Add the maple syrup, sriracha, and salt (if using). Stir until combined. Add the nuts and stir gently to coat thoroughly.
3. Spread the nuts in a single layer in an aluminum foil roasting pan coated with cooking spray. Place the pan on the grate and smoke the nuts until they're lightly toasted, about 1 hour, stirring once or twice.
4. Remove the pan from the grill and let the nuts cool for 15 minutes. They'll be sticky at first but will crisp up. Break them up with your fingers and store at room temperature in an airtight container, such as a lidded glass jar.

Jalapeño Poppers With Chipotle Sour Cream

Servings: 8
Cooking Time: 45 Minutes

Ingredients:

- 3 strips of thin-sliced bacon
- 12 large jalapeños, red, green, or a mix
- 8oz (225g) light cream cheese, at room temperature
- 1 cup shredded pepper Jack, Monterey Jack, or Cheddar cheese
- 1 tsp chili powder
- ½ tsp garlic salt
- smoked paprika
- for the sour cream
- 1¼ cups light sour cream

- juice of ½ lime
- ½ to 1 canned chipotle peppers in adobo sauce, finely minced, plus 1 tsp of sauce, plus more
- 1 tbsp minced fresh cilantro leaves
- ½ tsp coarse salt, plus more

Directions:

1. Supply your smoker with wood pellets and follow the start-up procedure. Preheat the grill, with the lid closed, to 375° F.

2. Line a rimmed sheet pan with aluminum foil and place a wire rack on top. Place the bacon in a single layer on the wire rack. Place the pan on the grate and grill until the bacon is crisp and golden brown, about 20 minutes. Transfer the bacon to paper towels to cool and then crumble. Set aside.

3. In a small bowl, make the chipotle sour cream by whisking together the ingredients. Add more salt, chipotle peppers, or adobe sauce to taste. Cover and refrigerate.

4. Slice the jalapeños lengthwise through their stems. Scrape out the veins and seeds with the edge of a small metal spoon.

5. In a small bowl, beat together the cream cheese, shredded cheese, chili powder, and garlic salt. Stir in the crumbled bacon. Mound the cream cheese mixture in the jalapeño halves. Line another rimmed sheet pan with aluminum foil and place a wire rack on top. Place the jalapeños filled side up in a single layer on the wire rack.

6. Place the sheet pan on the grate and roast the jalapeños until the filling has melted and the peppers have softened, about 20 to 25 minutes. (They should no longer look bright in color.) Remove the pan from the grill and let the peppers rest for 5 minutes.

7. Transfer the poppers to a platter and lightly dust with paprika. Serve with the chipotle sour cream.

Cold-smoked Cheese

Servings: 6
Cooking Time: 180 Minutes

Ingredients:
- 2lb (1kg) well-chilled hard or semi-hard cheese, such as:

- Edam
- Gouda
- Cheddar
- Monterey Jack
- pepper Jack
- goat cheese
- fresh mozzarella
- Muenster
- aged Parmigiano-Reggiano
- Gruyère
- blue cheese

Directions:

1. Unwrap the cheese and remove any protective wax or coating. Cut into 4-ounce (110g) portions to increase the surface area.

2. If possible, move your smoker to a shady area. Place 1 resealable plastic bag filled with ice on top of the drip pan. This is especially important on a warm day because you want to keep the interior temperature of the grill between 70 and 90°F (21 and 32°C) or below.

3. Place a grill mat on one side of the grate. Place the cheese on the mat and allow space between each piece.

4. Fill your smoking tube or pellet maze (see Cast Iron Skillets and Grill Pans) with pellets or sawdust and light according to the manufacturer's instructions. Place the smoking tube on the grate near—but not on—the grill mat. When the tube is smoking consistently, close the grill lid.

5. Smoke the cheese for 1 to 3 hours, replacing the pellets or sawdust and ice if necessary. Monitor the temperature and make sure the cheese isn't beginning to melt. Carefully lift the mat with the cheese to a rimmed baking sheet and let the cheese cool completely before handling.

6. Package the smoked cheese in cheese storage paper or bags or vacuum-seal the cheese, labeling each. (While you can wrap the cheese tightly in plastic wrap, the cheese will spoil faster.) Let the cheese rest for at least 2 to 3 days before eating. It will be even better after 2 weeks.

COCKTAILS RECIPES

Smoked Berry Cocktail

Servings: 2

Cooking Time: 15 Minutes

Ingredients:

- 1/2 Cup strawberries, stemmed
- 1/2 Cup blackberries
- 1/2 Cup blueberries
- 8 Ounce bourbon or iced tea
- 2 Ounce lime juice
- 3 Ounce simple syrup
- soda water
- fresh mint, for garnish

Directions:

1. Supply your smoker with wood pellets and follow the start-up procedure. Preheat the grill, with the lid closed, to 180° F.
2. Wash berries well, spread them on a clean cookie sheet and place on the grill. Smoke berries for 15 minutes. Grill: 180 °F
3. Remove berries from grill and transfer to a blender. Puree berries until smooth then pass through a fine mesh strainer to remove seeds.
4. To create a layered cocktail, pour 2 ounces of berry puree in the bottom of a glass. Next, pour 2 ounces of bourbon or iced tea over the back of a spoon into the glass, then 1/2 ounce lime juice and 1/2 ounce simple syrup, top with soda water and ice. Finish with mint or extra berries for garnish.
5. Repeat the same process for 3 more servings. Enjoy!

Smoking Gun Cocktail

Servings: 2

Cooking Time: 45 Minutes

Ingredients:

- 2 Jar vermouth soaked cocktail onions
- 3 Ounce vodka
- 1 Ounce dry vermouth

Directions:

1. Supply your smoker with wood pellets and follow the start-up procedure. Preheat the grill, with the lid closed, to 180° F.
2. To make the smoked onion vermouth: Pour jar of vermouth soaked cocktail onions onto a shallow sheet pan. Smoke for 45 minutes. Remove from grill and set aside to chill. Grill: 180 °F
3. To make the cocktail: Add vodka, 1 teaspoon liquid from the smoked onions and dry vermouth to a mixing glass. Shake and strain into a chilled martini glass.
4. Garnish with smoked cocktail onions on a skewer. Enjoy!

Traeger Smoked Daiquiri

Servings: 2

Cooking Time: 25 Minutes

Ingredients:

- 2 limes, sliced
- 2 Tablespoon granulated sugar
- 3 Ounce Rum
- 1 Ounce Smoked Simple Syrup
- 1 1/2 Ounce lime juice

Directions:

1. Supply your smoker with wood pellets and follow the start-up procedure. Preheat the grill, with the lid closed, to 350° F.
2. Toss the lime slices with granulated sugar and place directly on the grill grate. Cook 20-25 minutes or until grill marks form. Remove from grill and cool. Grill: 350 °F
3. In a mixing glass add rum, Traeger Simple Syrup, and fresh lime juice. Add ice to the mixing glass and shake. Strain contents into a chilled glass.
4. Garnish with a grilled lime wheel. Enjoy!

In Traeger Fashion Cocktail

Servings: 2

Cooking Time: 20 Minutes

Ingredients:

- 2 Whole orange peel
- 2 Whole lemon peel
- 3 Ounce bourbon
- 1 Ounce Smoked Simple Syrup
- 6 Dash Bitters Lab Charred Cedar & Currant Bitters

Directions:

1. Supply your smoker with wood pellets and follow the start-up procedure. Preheat the grill, with the lid closed, to 350° F.
2. Place the lemon and orange peel directly on the grill grate and cook 20 to 25 minutes or until lightly browned. Grill: 350 °F
3. Add bourbon, Traeger Smoked Simple Syrup and bitters to a mixing glass and stir over ice. Stir until glass is chilled and contents are well diluted.
4. Strain into a new glass over fresh ice and garnish with grilled lemon and orange peel. Enjoy!

Smoked Apple Cider

Servings: 2

Cooking Time: 30 Minutes

Ingredients:

- 32 Ounce apple cider
- 2 cinnamon sticks
- 4 whole cloves
- 3 star anise
- 2 Pieces orange peel
- 2 Pieces lemon peel

Directions:

1. Supply your smoker with wood pellets and follow the start-up procedure. Preheat the grill, with the lid closed, to 225° F.

2. Combine the cider, cinnamon stick, star anise, clove, lemon and orange peel in a shallow baking dish.

3. Place directly on the grill grate and smoke for 30 minutes. Remove from grill, strain and transfer to four mugs. Grill: 225 °F

4. Finish with a slice of apple and a cinnamon stick to serve. Enjoy!

Grilled Blood Orange Mimosa

Servings: 4

Cooking Time: 15 Minutes

Ingredients:

- 3 blood orange, halved
- 2 Tablespoon granulated sugar
- 1 Bottle sparkling wine
- thyme sprigs, for garnish

Directions:

1. Supply your smoker with wood pellets and follow the start-up procedure. Preheat the grill, with the lid closed, to 375° F.

2. When the grill is hot, dip the cut side of the orange halves in sugar and place cut side down directly on the grill grate. Grill: 375 °F

3. Grill the oranges for 10-15 minutes or until grill marks develop. Grill: 375 °F

4. Remove from the grill and let cool at room temperature.

5. When cool enough to handle, juice the oranges and strain through a fine strainer removing any pulp.

6. Pour 5 oz of sparkling wine into each glass and top with 1 oz blood orange juice.

7. Garnish with a sprig of thyme. Enjoy!

Sunset Margarita

Servings: 2

Cooking Time: 55 Minutes

Ingredients:

- 4 oranges
- 2 Cup plus 1 teaspoon agave
- 1/2 Cup water
- 1 Ounce burnt orange agave
- 3 Ounce reposado tequila
- 1 1/2 Ounce fresh squeezed lime juice
- Jacobsen Salt Co. Cherrywood Smoked Salt

Directions:

1. Supply your smoker with wood pellets and follow the start-up procedure. Preheat the grill, with the lid closed, to 350° F.

2. For the Burnt Orange Agave Syrup: Cut one orange in half and brush cut side with agave. Place cut side down directly on the grill grate and grill for 15 minutes or until grill marks develop. Grill: 350 °F

3. While the orange halves are grilling, slice the other orange and brush both sides of the slices with agave. Place slices directly on the grill grate next to the halves and cook for 15 minutes or until grill marks develop. Grill: 350 °F

4. Remove orange halves from grill grate and let cool. After they have cooled, juice halves and strain. Set aside.

5. Combine 1/4 cup water and agave in a shallow dish and mix well. Remove orange slices from the grill and place in the agave mixture, reserving a few for garnish.

6. Reduce the grill temperature to 180 degrees F and place the shallow dish with agave and oranges directly on the grill grate. Smoke for 40 minutes. Remove from heat and strain. Set aside. Grill: 180 °F

7. To Mix Drink: Rim glass with Jacobsen Smoked Salt. Combine tequila, fresh lime juice, grilled orange juice and burnt orange agave syrup in a glass. Add ice and shake well.

8. Strain into a rimmed glass over clean ice. Garnish with a grilled orange slice. Enjoy!

Ryes And Shine Cocktail

Servings: 2

Cooking Time: 30 Minutes

Ingredients:

- 2 lemon, cut into wheels for garnish
- 6 Tablespoon granulated sugar
- 2 Ounce rye
- 1 Ounce bourbon
- 3 Ounce lemon juice
- 1 Ounce Smoked Simple Syrup
- 6 Dash Fernet-Branca

Directions:

1. Supply your smoker with wood pellets and follow the start-up procedure. Preheat the grill, with the lid closed, to 325° F.

2. Toss lemon wheels with granulated sugar to coat on both sides. Place wheels directly on the grill grate and cook for 15 minutes on each side or until grill marks form. Grill: 325 ˚F

3. Add rye, bourbon, lemon juice, Traeger Smoked Simple Syrup and Fernet-Branca to a shaker and shake until slightly diluted (about 10 to 15 seconds).

4. Pour into a fresh glass, serve neat and garnish with a grilled lemon wheel. Enjoy!

Grilled Peach Sour Cocktail

Servings: 2
Cooking Time: 15 Minutes

Ingredients:
- 2 peach, sliced
- 2 Tablespoon sugar
- 1 1/2 Ounce Smoked Simple Syrup
- 4 Ounce bourbon
- 6 Dash Bitters Lab Apricot Vanilla Bitters
- 2 Sprig fresh thyme, for garnish

Directions:
1. Supply your smoker with wood pellets and follow the start-up procedure. Preheat the grill, with the lid closed, to 325° F.

2. Toss peach slices with granulated sugar and place directly on grill grate. Cook for 20 minutes or until grill marks form. Remove from grill and let cool. Grill: 325 ˚F

3. Place peaches and Traeger Smoked Simple Syrup into tin and muddle. Peaches should form about an ounce of juice during the muddling. Once completed, add remaining ingredients and shake.

4. Pour contents into glass over fresh ice and garnish with fresh thyme. Enjoy!

Zombie Cocktail Recipe

Servings: 2
Cooking Time: 45 Minutes

Ingredients:
- fresh squeezed orange juice
- pineapple juice
- 2 Ounce light rum
- 2 Ounce dark rum
- 2 Ounce lime juice
- 1 Ounce Smoked Simple Syrup
- 6 Ounce smoked orange and pineapple juice
- 2 grilled orange peel, for garnish
- 2 grilled pineapple chunks, for garnish

Directions:
1. Supply your smoker with wood pellets and follow the start-up procedure. Preheat the grill, with the lid closed, to 180° F.

2. Smoked Orange and Pineapple Juice: Pour equal parts fresh squeezed orange juice and pineapple juice into a shallow sheet pan and smoke for 45 minutes. Remove and let cool. Measure out 3 ounces of juice and reserve any remaining juice in the refrigerator for future use. Grill: 180 ˚F

3. Add dark and light rums, 3 ounces smoked orange and pineapple juice, lime juice and Traeger Smoked Simple Syrup to a mixing glass.

4. Add ice, shake and strain over clean ice into a Tiki glass.

5. Garnish with a grilled orange peel and grilled pineapple. Enjoy!

Smoked Hot Buttered Rum

Servings: 4
Cooking Time: 30 Minutes

Ingredients:
- 2 Cup water
- 1/4 Cup brown sugar
- 1/2 Stick butter, melted
- 1 Teaspoon ground cinnamon
- 1/4 Teaspoon ground nutmeg
- ground cloves
- salt
- 6 Ounce Rum

Directions:
1. Supply your smoker with wood pellets and follow the start-up procedure. Preheat the grill, with the lid closed, to 180° F.

2. In a shallow baking dish, combine 2 cups water with all ingredients except for the rum and place directly on the grill grate. Smoke for 30 minutes. Grill: 180 ˚F

3. Remove from the grill and pour into the pitcher of a blender. Process until somewhat frothy.

4. Pour 1.5 ounces of rum each into 4 glasses. Split hot butter mixture evenly between the four glasses.

5. Garnish with a cinnamon stick and freshly grated nutmeg. Enjoy!

Strawberry Mule Cocktail

Servings: 2
Cooking Time: 15 Minutes

Ingredients:
- 8 grilled strawberries, plus more for serving
- 3 Ounce vodka
- 1 Ounce Smoked Simple Syrup
- 1 Ounce lemon juice
- 6 Ounce ginger beer
- fresh mint leaves

Directions:

1. Supply your smoker with wood pellets and follow the start-up procedure. Preheat the grill, with the lid closed, to 400° F.
2. Place strawberries directly on the grill grate and cook 15 minutes or until grill marks appear. Grill: 400 °F
3. For the cocktail: Add vodka, grilled strawberries, Traeger Smoked Simple Syrup and lemon juice to a shaker. Shake vigorously.
4. Double strain into a fresh glass or copper mug with crushed ice.
5. Top with ginger beer and garnish with extra grilled strawberries and fresh mint. Enjoy!

Garden Gimlet Cocktail

Servings: 2
Cooking Time: 45 Minutes

Ingredients:
- 2 Cup honey
- 4 lemons, zested
- 4 Sprig rosemary, plus more for garnish
- 1/2 Cup water
- 4 Slices cucumber
- 1 1/2 Ounce lime juice
- 3 Ounce vodka

Directions:
1. Supply your smoker with wood pellets and follow the start-up procedure. Preheat the grill, with the lid closed, to 180° F.
2. To make smoked lemon and rosemary honey syrup, thin 1 cup honey by adding 1/4 cup water to a shallow pan. Add lemon zest and 2 sprigs rosemary.
3. Place the pan directly on the grill grate and smoke 45 minutes to an hour. Remove from heat, strain and cool. Grill: 180 °F
4. In a cocktail shaker, muddle the cucumbers and 1oz of the smoked lemon and rosemary honey syrup.
5. After muddling, add lime juice, vodka, and ice. Shake and double strain into a coup glass.
6. Garnish with a sprig of rosemary. Enjoy!

Grilled Hawaiian Sour

Servings: 2
Cooking Time: 15 Minutes

Ingredients:
- 2 Whole pineapple, trimmed and sliced
- 1/2 Cup palm sugar
- 3 Ounce bourbon
- 2 Ounce grilled pineapple juice
- 2 Ounce Smoked Simple Syrup
- 10 Ounce lemon juice

- 2 grilled pineapple chunk, for garnish
- 2 pineapple leaf, for garnish

Directions:
1. Supply your smoker with wood pellets and follow the start-up procedure. Preheat the grill, with the lid closed, to 350° F.
2. For the Grilled Pineapple Juice: Dust pineapple slices with palm sugar. Place directly on the grill grate and cook for 8 minutes per side. Grill: 350 °F
3. Remove from grill and let cool. Reserve a few pieces for garnish. Run remaining pineapple pieces through centrifugal juicer to extract juice.
4. To Make the Drink: Add bourbon, grilled pineapple juice, simple syrup and lemon juice to a cocktail strainer with ice. Shake vigorously. Double strain into a chilled coupe glass. Garnish with grilled pineapple chunk and pineapple leaf. Enjoy!

Smoked Pomegranate Lemonade Cocktail

Servings: 2
Cooking Time: 45 Minutes

Ingredients:
- 32 Ounce POM Juice
- 2 Cup pomegranate seeds
- 3 Ounce vodka
- 8 Ounce lemonade
- lemon wheel, for garnish
- fresh mint, for garnish

Directions:
1. Supply your smoker with wood pellets and follow the start-up procedure. Preheat the grill, with the lid closed, to 225° F.
2. For the Smoked Pomegranate Ice Cubes: Pour one small container of POM juice and 1 cup of pomegranate seeds into a shallow sheet pan. Smoke on the Traeger for 45 minutes. Pull off grill and let sit until cooled. Grill: 180 °F
3. Pour smoked POM juice into ice molds of your choice and put into freezer.
4. When ready to serve, place the frozen pomegranate cubes into a mason jar. Pour vodka and lemonade over the ice cubes.
5. Garnish with a lemon wheel and fresh mint. Enjoy!

Smoked Mulled Wine

Servings: 10
Cooking Time: 60 Minutes

Ingredients:
- 2 Bottle red wine
- 1/2 Cup whiskey
- 1/2 Cup white rum

- 1/2 Cup honey
- 1 cinnamon stick
- 2 pods star anise
- 4 whole cloves
- 1 (3 in) orange peel

Directions:

1. Supply your smoker with wood pellets and follow the start-up procedure. Preheat the grill, with the lid closed, to 180° F.
2. In a shallow baking dish, combine wine, whiskey, rum, honey, cinnamon stick, star anise, cloves and orange peel. Stir well until combined.
3. Place the dish directly on the grill grate and smoke for one hour until the mixture is warm. Grill: 180 °F
4. Remove from grill and ladle into mugs leaving the mulling spices behind. Garnish with fresh cinnamon sticks, anise, orange zest or a combination. Enjoy!

Batter Up Cocktail

Servings: 2
Cooking Time: 60 Minutes

Ingredients:

- 2 whole nutmeg
- 4 Ounce Michter's Bourbon
- 3 Teaspoon pumpkin puree
- 1 Ounce Smoked Simple Syrup
- 2 Large egg

Directions:

1. Supply your smoker with wood pellets and follow the start-up procedure. Preheat the grill, with the lid closed, to 180° F.
2. Place whole nutmeg on a sheet tray and place in the grill. Smoke 1 hour. Remove from grill and let cool. Grill: 180 °F
3. Add everything to a shaker and shake without ice. Add ice, then shake and strain into a chilled highball glass.
4. Garnish with grated, smoked nutmeg. Enjoy!

Smoked Ice Mojito Slurpee

Servings: 2
Cooking Time: 30 Minutes

Ingredients:

- water
- 1 Cup white rum
- 1/2 Cup lime juice
- 1/4 Cup Smoked Simple Syrup
- 12 Whole fresh mint leaves
- 4 Sprig mint
- 4 Whole lime wedge, for garnish

Directions:

1. Supply your smoker with wood pellets and follow the start-up procedure. Preheat the grill, with the lid closed, to 180° F.
2. For optimal flavor, use Super Smoke if available. Grill: 180 °F
3. Remove water from grill and pour smoked water into ice cube trays. Place in freezer until frozen.
4. Add rum, lime juice, Traeger Smoked Simple Syrup, mint and smoked ice to a blender.
5. Blend until a slushy consistency and pour into glasses.
6. Garnish with a mint sprig and lime wedge. Enjoy!

Grilled Frozen Strawberry Lemonade

Servings: 4
Cooking Time: 15 Minutes

Ingredients:

- 1 Pound fresh strawberries
- 1/2 Cup turbinado sugar
- 8 lemon, halved
- 1/4 Cup Cointreau
- 1/4 Cup simple syrup
- 2 Cup ice
- 1 Cup Titos Vodka

Directions:

1. Supply your smoker with wood pellets and follow the start-up procedure. Preheat the grill, with the lid closed, to High heat.
2. Dip the lemon halves in turbinado sugar and place directly on the grill grate. Toss the strawberries with remaining sugar and place next to the lemons.
3. Cook until grill marks develop on both, about 15 min for lemons and 10 min for strawberries.
4. Remove from heat and let cool.
5. Juice grilled lemons straining out any seeds or pulp. Pour into a blender pitcher.
6. Remove stems from grilled strawberries and place in blender pitcher with lemon juice. Add simple syrup, vodka, cointreau, and 2 cups of ice.
7. Puree until smooth and transfer to 4-6 glasses. Garnish with grilled strawberries and grilled lemon slices if desired. Enjoy!

Smoked Sangria

Servings: 6
Cooking Time: 45 Minutes

Ingredients:

- 1 (750 ml) medium-bodied red wine
- 1/4 Cup Grand Marnier
- 1/4 Cup Smoked Simple Syrup
- 1 Cup fresh cranberries
- 1 Whole apple, sliced
- 2 Whole limes, sliced

- 4 cinnamon stick
- soda water

Directions:

1. Supply your smoker with wood pellets and follow the start-up procedure. Preheat the grill, with the lid closed, to 180° F.

2. In a shallow dish, combine red wine, Grand Marnier, Traeger Smoked Simple Syrup and cranberries, and place directly on the grill grate.

3. Smoke for 30 to 45 minutes or until the liquid picks up desired amount of smoke. Remove from grill and place in the fridge to cool. Grill: 180 ˚F

4. When the mixture has cooled, place in a large pitcher. Add sliced apples, limes, cinnamon sticks and ice to pitcher.

5. Top with soda water, if desired. Enjoy!

Smoked Pumpkin Spice Latte

Servings: 4

Cooking Time: 45 Minutes

Ingredients:

- 1 Small sugar pumpkin
- olive oil
- 1 Can sweetened condensed milk
- 1 Cup whole milk
- 2 Tablespoon Smoked Simple Syrup
- 1 Teaspoon pumpkin pie spice
- pinch of salt
- cinnamon
- whipped cream
- shaved nutmeg
- 8 Ounce smoked cold brew coffee

Directions:

1. Supply your smoker with wood pellets and follow the start-up procedure. Preheat the grill, with the lid closed, to 325° F.

2. Cut the sugar pumpkin in half, scoop out the seeds and discard. Place the pumpkin halves cut side up on a baking sheet and brush lightly with olive oil.

3. Place the sheet tray directly on the grill grate and cook 45 minutes or until the flesh is tender. Remove from heat and place on the counter to cool. Grill: 325 ˚F

4. When the pumpkin is cool enough to handle, scoop out the flesh and mash until smooth.

5. Place 3 Tbsp of the pumpkin puree in a separate bowl and reserve the remaining for another use.

6. Add the sweetened condensed milk, whole milk, Traeger Smoked Simple Syrup, pumpkin pie seasoning and salt to the pumpkin puree. Whisk to combine.

7. Pour the cold brew over ice, add desired amount of pumpkin spice creamer and top with whipped cream, cinnamon, and shaved nutmeg if desired. Enjoy!

Fig Slider Cocktail

Servings: 2

Cooking Time: 15 Minutes

Ingredients:

- 2 peach, halved
- 4 oranges
- honey
- sugar
- 2 Teaspoon orange fig spread
- 1 Ounce fresh lemon juice
- 4 Ounce bourbon
- 3 Ounce honey glazed grilled orange juice

Directions:

1. Supply your smoker with wood pellets and follow the start-up procedure. Preheat the grill, with the lid closed, to 325° F.

2. Pit the peach and cut in half. Cut one of the oranges in half. Glaze the peach and orange cut sides with honey and set directly on the grill grate until the honey caramelizes and fruit has grill marks. Grill: 325 ˚F

3. Cut the second orange into wheels and coat with granulated sugar on both sides. Place directly on the grill grate and cook 15 minutes each side or until grill marks form. Grill: 325 ˚F

4. In a mixing tin, add grilled peaches, bourbon, orange fig spread, fresh lemon juice and honey glazed orange juice.

5. Shake vigorously to blend the juices and fig spread. Strain over clean ice. Garnish with grilled orange wheel. Enjoy!

Bacon Old-fashioned Cocktail

Servings: 2

Cooking Time: 20 Minutes

Ingredients:

- 16 Slices bacon
- 1/2 Cup warm water (110˚F to 115˚F)
- 1500 mL bourbon
- 1/2 Fluid Ounce maple syrup
- 4 Dash Angostura bitters
- 2 fresh orange peel

Directions:

1. Smoke bacon prior to making Old Fashioned using this recipe for Applewood Smoked Bacon.

2. To Make Bacon: Supply your smoker with wood pellets and follow the start-up procedure. Preheat the grill, with the lid closed, to 325° F.

3. Place bacon in a single layer on a cooling rack that fits inside a baking sheet pan. Cook in Traeger for 15-20 minutes or until bacon is browned and crispy. Reserve bacon for later. Let the fat cool slightly; you'll use the fat to infuse the bourbon. Grill: 325 ˚F

4. Combine 1/4 cup of warm (not hot) liquid bacon fat with the entire contents of a 750ml bottle of bourbon in a glass or heavy plastic container.

5. Use a fork to stir well. Let it sit on the counter for a few hours, stirring every so often.

6. After about four hours, put bourbon fat mixture into the freezer. After about an hour, the fat will congeal and you can simply scoop it out with a spoon. You can fine-strain the mixture through a sieve to remove all fat if desired.

7. Combine ingredients with ice and stir until cold. Strain over fresh ice in an Old Fashioned glass and garnish with reserved bacon and orange peel. Enjoy!

Smoked Salted Caramel White Russian

Servings: 4
Cooking Time: 20 Minutes

Ingredients:

*   16 Ounce half-and-half
*   salted caramel sauce
*   6 Ounce vodka
*   6 Ounce Kahlúa

Directions:

1. Supply your smoker with wood pellets and follow the start-up procedure. Preheat the grill, with the lid closed, to 180° F.

2. Pour the half-and-half in a shallow baking dish and place directly on the grill grate. In another shallow baking dish, pour 2 to 3 cups of water and place on the grill next to the half-and-half.

3. Smoke both the half-and-half and water for 20 minutes. Remove from the grill and let cool. Grill: 180 °F

4. Place the half-and-half in the fridge until ready to use. Pour the smoked water into ice cube trays and transfer to the freezer until completely frozen.

5. Separate the smoked ice cubes into four glasses. Drizzle the salted caramel sauce around the inside of the glass.

6. Pour 1-1/2 ounce vodka and 1-1/2 ounce Kahlúa into each of the glasses and top with the smoked half-and-half. Enjoy!

Smoky Scotch & Ginger Cocktail

Servings: 2
Cooking Time: 60 Minutes

Ingredients:

*   1 Ounce ginger syrup
*   1/2 Ounce brandied cherry juice
*   1/2 Ounce agave nectar
*   4 Ounce scotch
*   1 1/2 Ounce lemon juice
*   2 Slices grilled lemon, for garnish
*   2 cherry, for garnish

Directions:

1. Supply your smoker with wood pellets and follow the start-up procedure. Preheat the grill, with the lid closed, to 180° F.

2. For the smoked ginger cherry syrup: Place ginger syrup, cherry juice and agave nectar in a shallow dish and place the dish directly on the grill grate.

3. Smoke for 60 minutes, or until the mixture has picked up the smoke flavor. Remove from grill and allow to cool for 30 minutes. Grill: 180 °F

4. Place smoked ginger cherry syrup, scotch and lemon juice into a shaker tin and shake with ice. Strain into a glass over fresh ice and garnish with a grilled lemon wheel and cherry. Enjoy!

A Smoking Classic Cocktail

Servings: 2
Cooking Time: 60 Minutes

Ingredients:

*   2 Bottle Angostura orange bitters
*   10 sugar cubes
*   8 Ounce Champagne
*   lemon twist

Directions:

1. Supply your smoker with wood pellets and follow the start-up procedure. Preheat the grill, with the lid closed, to 180° F.

2. For the Smoked Orange Bitters: In a small skillet, combine 1 bottle of Angostura orange bitters with a splash of water and 4 sugar cubes.

3. Place skillet on the grill grate and smoke for 60 minutes. Cool the smoked bitters and put back into the bottle. Grill: 180 °F

4. Add a sugar cube to each Champagne flute and soak the sugar cubes with the smoked bitters.

5. Add champagne and a lemon twist in a flute glass. Enjoy!

Cran-apple Tequila Punch With Smoked Oranges

Servings: 2
Cooking Time: 15 Minutes

Ingredients:

*   6 Cup apple juice, chilled
*   6 Cup light cranberry cocktail
*   1 Cup cranberries, fresh or thawed
*   3 Large oranges, halved
*   1 Cup sugar, for rimming glasses
*   2 Tablespoon lemon juice
*   2 Cup reposado tequila
*   1 Cup orange-flavored liqueur, such as Grand Marnier or Cointreau
*   2 Bottle sparkling wine (such as prosecco) or sparkling water

Directions:

1. Combine 1 cup each of the apple and cranberry juices, then pour into ice cube trays. If the cube molds are big enough, place a few cranberries into each cube. Freeze for 6 hours to overnight.

2. Supply your smoker with wood pellets and follow the start-up procedure. Preheat the grill, with the lid closed, to 180° F.

3. Place the orange halves cut-side down on the grill and smoke for 15 minutes. Remove from the grill and juice oranges. Reserve smoked orange juice. Grill: 180 °F

4. When ready to serve, place the sugar on a flat plate. Pour the lemon juice into a bowl that will fit the rim of each glass.

5. Carefully dip the rim of each glass in the lemon juice, then dip in the sugar to create a 1/8" sugar rim. Turn the glass right-side up and allow to dry for a few minutes before using.

6. Just before serving, mix the remaining apple juice, cranberry cocktail and smoked orange juice with the tequila, orange liqueur, and sparkling wine in a large bowl or pitcher. Taste, adding more of any ingredient to meet your preference.

7. When ready to serve, place a few ice cubes in each glass, then pour a cup of the punch over the top. Alternatively, place all of the ice cubes in the punch bowl and allow guests to help themselves. Enjoy!

Smoked Cold Brew Coffee

Servings: 8
Cooking Time: 120 Minutes

Ingredients:

- 12 Ounce coarse ground coffee
- heavy cream or milk
- sugar

Directions:

1. Place half the coffee grounds in a plastic container and slowly pour 3-1/2 cups water over the top of the grounds. Add remaining grounds and pour another 3-1/2 cups water over the top in a circular motion.

2. Press the grounds down into the water using the back of a spoon. Cover and transfer to the refrigerator and let sit for 18 to 24 hours.

3. Remove from refrigerator and strain into a clean container through a fine mesh strainer or double layer of cheese cloth.

4. Supply your smoker with wood pellets and follow the start-up procedure. Preheat the grill, with the lid closed, to 180° F.

5. Pour cold brew into a shallow baking dish and place directly on the grill grate. Smoke for 1 to 2 hours depending on desired level of smoke. Grill: 180 °F

6. Remove from grill and place over an ice bath to cool. Drink as is over ice, with cream or sugar or use in your favorite coffee recipes. Enjoy!

Smoked Hibiscus Sparkler

Servings: 4
Cooking Time: 30 Minutes

Ingredients:

- 1/2 Cup sugar
- 2 Tablespoon dried hibiscus flowers
- 1 Bottle sparkling wine
- crystallized ginger, for garnish

Directions:

1. Supply your smoker with wood pellets and follow the start-up procedure. Preheat the grill, with the lid closed, to 180° F.

2. Place water in a shallow baking dish and place directly on the grill grate. Smoke the water for 30 minutes or until desired smoke flavor is achieved. Grill: 180 °F

3. Pour water into a small saucepan and add sugar and hibiscus flowers. Bring to a simmer over medium heat and cook until sugar is dissolved.

4. Strain out the hibiscus flowers and transfer your simple syrup to a small container and refrigerate until chilled.

5. Pour 1/2 ounce smoked hibiscus simple syrup in the bottom of a champagne glass and top with sparkling wine.

6. Drop in a few pieces of crystallized ginger to garnish. Enjoy!

Smoked Jacobsen Salt Margarita

Servings: 2
Cooking Time: 1 Day

Ingredients:

- kosher sea salt
- 3 Cup Jacobsen Co. Honey
- 6 Ounce tequila
- 4 Ounce fresh squeezed lime juice
- 1/2 Cup Jacobsen Salt Co. Cherrywood Smoked Salt or smoked kosher salt
- 2 Ounce simple syrup
- 2 Teaspoon orange liqueur

Directions:

1. If making your own smoked salt, take kosher sea salt (however much you want to smoke) and spread it out on a tray.

2. Supply your smoker with wood pellets and follow the start-up procedure. Preheat the grill, with the lid closed, to 165° F.

3. Place tray of salt directly on the grill grate and smoke for about 24 hours, stirring the salt every 8 hours. Once it has smoked for 24 hours, take off grill and use in all your favorite dishes. Note: If you want to skip the long smoke session, use Jacobsen Salt Co. Cherrywood Smoked Salt. Grill: 165 °F

4. Simple Syrup: Put the honey and 1 cup water in a small saucepan. Cook over low heat, stirring, for about 20 min.

5. Fill a cocktail shaker with ice. Add tequila, lime juice, simple syrup and orange liqueur. Cover and shake until mixed and chilled, about 30 seconds.

6. Place smoked salt on a plate. Press the rim of a chilled rocks glass into the salt to rim the edge. Strain margarita into the glass. Enjoy!

Smoked Barnburner Cocktail

Servings: 2
Cooking Time: 45 Minutes

Ingredients:
- 16 Ounce fresh raspberries
- 1/2 Cup Smoked Simple Syrup
- 1 1/2 Ounce smoked raspberry syrup
- 3 Ounce reposado tequila
- 1 Ounce lime juice
- 1 Ounce lemon juice
- 2 grilled lime wheel, for garnish

Directions:
1. Supply your smoker with wood pellets and follow the start-up procedure. Preheat the grill, with the lid closed, to 180° F.

2. For Smoked Raspberry Syrup: Place fresh raspberries on a grill mat and smoke for 30 minutes. After the raspberries have been smoked, reserve a few for garnish and place the remainder into a shallow sheet pan with Traeger Smoked Simple Syrup. Grill: 180 °F

3. Place sheet pan on the grill grate and smoke for 45 minutes. Remove from grill and let cool. Strain through a fine mesh sieve discarding solids. Transfer the syrup to the refrigerator until ready to use. Makes about 1/2 cup of smoked raspberry syrup. Grill: 180 °F

4. For cocktail: Add 3/4 ounce smoked raspberry syrup, tequila, lime juice and lemon juice with ice into a mixing glass. Shake and pour over clean ice. Garnish with smoked raspberries and a grilled lime wheel. Enjoy!

Smoked Pineapple Hotel Nacional Cocktail

Servings: 2
Cooking Time: 20 Minutes

Ingredients:
- 2 pineapple
- 1/2 Cup water
- 1/2 Cup sugar
- 3 Fluid Ounce white rum
- 1 1/2 Fluid Ounce lime juice
- 1 1/2 Fluid Ounce Pineapple Syrup
- 1 Fluid Ounce apricot brandy

- 2 Dash Angostura bitters

Directions:
1. For the Syrup: Supply your smoker with wood pellets and follow the start-up procedure. Preheat the grill, with the lid closed, to 180° F.

2. Trim both ends of the pineapple, discard the ends. Cut the pineapple into slices about 3/4" thick. Don't worry about the skin, it doesn't hurt to leave it on. Place the pineapple slices on the grill and smoke for about 15 minutes on each sideTrim both ends of the pineapple and discard the ends. Cut the pineapple into slices about 3/4 inch thick. Don't worry about the skin, it doesn't hurt to leave it on. Place the pineapple slices on the grill and smoke for about 15 minutes per side. Grill: 180 °F

3. While the pineapple is smoking, combine 1/4 cup water and sugar in a saucepan over low heat, stirring constantly, until sugar is dissolved. Pour syrup into a large bowl and set aside.

4. When the pineapple is done cooking, cut each slice into eight or so wedges and add the wedges to the bowl with the simple syrup, tossing to coat and cover.

5. Leave the mixture to macerate for at least 4 hours (or up to 24) in the refrigerator, stirring from time to time.

6. Strain the syrup into a clean bowl through a fine-mesh strainer and press on the pineapple with a ladle to extract as much liquid as possible. You can bottle and refrigerate the syrup for up to 4 days.

7. To make the cocktail: Combine the rum, lime juice, pineapple syrup, apricot brandy, and bitters in a cocktail shaker or mixing glass. Fill with ice cubes and shake until cold.

8. Strain into a chilled cocktail glass. Garnish with a lime wheel and serve. Enjoy!

Dublin Delight Cocktail

Servings: 2
Cooking Time: 20 Minutes

Ingredients:
- 2 orange, sliced
- 3 Fluid Ounce Teeling Whiskey
- 1 1/2 Fluid Ounce Smoked Simple Syrup
- 6 Dash aromatic bitters
- 6 Fluid Ounce Guinness beer
- 2 Amarena cherry, for garnish

Directions:
1. Supply your smoker with wood pellets and follow the start-up procedure. Preheat the grill, with the lid closed, to 450° F.

2. Place orange slices directly on the grill grate and cook 20 to 25 minutes. Remove from grill and let cool. Grill: 450 °F

3. In a mixing glass, add whiskey, Traeger Smoked Simple Syrup and bitters. Add ice and shake. Pour over a beer glass filled with ice and top off with cold Guinness.

4. Garnish with a grilled orange slice and Amarena cherry. Enjoy!

Grilled Peach Mint Julep

Servings: 2

Cooking Time: 45 Minutes

Ingredients:

- 2 Whole peach
- 4 Ounce whiskey
- 2 Cup sugar
- 4 Tablespoon pink peppercorns
- 20 Whole fresh mint leaves, plus more for garnish
- 2 lime wedge, for garnish
- 4 Ounce bourbon

Directions:

1. For the Grilled Whiskey Peaches: cut peach into slices, then soak peach slices in whiskey in the refrigerator for 4 to 6 hours.
2. For the Pink Peppercorn Simple Syrup: In a shallow pan, combine sugar, 1 cup water and pink peppercorns.
3. Supply your smoker with wood pellets and follow the start-up procedure. Preheat the grill, with the lid closed, to 180° F.
4. Cook syrup down on the grill for 30 minutes, or until desired smoke flavor has been reached. Remove from the grill. Grill: 180 °F
5. Increase Traeger temperature to 350°F and preheat. Place the whiskey peach slices directly on the grill grate and cook 10 to 12 minutes or until peaches soften and get grill marks. Grill: 350 °F
6. To make the Julep: Muddle 1/2 ounce Pink Peppercorn Simple Syrup with 10 fresh mint leaves and 4 slices of grilled whiskey peaches.
7. Add crushed ice over the rim of the glass. Pour bourbon over the crushed ice and stir. Garnish with 1 large sprig of mint and fresh lime. Enjoy!

Smoked Irish Coffee

Servings: 2

Cooking Time: 15 Minutes

Ingredients:

- 10 Ounce hot coffee
- 1/2 Cup heavy cream
- 1 Tablespoon sugar
- 2 Ounce Irish whiskey
- freshly grated nutmeg, for garnish (optional)

Directions:

1. Supply your smoker with wood pellets and follow the start-up procedure. Preheat the grill, with the lid closed, to 180° F.
2. Place the coffee and cream in separate shallow baking dishes and place both directly on the grill grate. Smoke for 10 to 15 minutes until the liquids pick up a slight smoke flavor. Grill: 180 °F

3. Remove from the grill and cool the cream. When the cream is cool, add sugar and whip in a stand mixer or by hand to soft peaks.
4. Pour the hot coffee into two mugs then add 2 ounces of whiskey to each.
5. Top with smoked whipped cream and finish with freshly grated nutmeg, if desired. Enjoy!

Smoked Texas Ranch Water

Servings: 4

Cooking Time: 60 Minutes

Ingredients:

- 3 Whole limes
- 1 Tablespoon Blackened Saskatchewan Rub
- 12 Ounce blanco tequila
- 24 Ounce Topo Chico or other sparkling mineral water
- 8 Slices jalapeño, optional

Directions:

1. Supply your smoker with wood pellets and follow the start-up procedure. Preheat the grill, with the lid closed, to 225° F.
2. Cut two of the limes in half and sprinkle with Traeger Blackened Saskatchewan Rub. Place the four lime halves on the edge of the grill grate and smoke for 1 hour. Remove from grill and set aside to cool. Grill: 225 °F
3. Pour some of the rub onto a small plate. Cut the third lime into 1/4 wedges and use the lime to rub the rim of 4 cocktail glasses, turn the glasses upside down, and into the rub to salt the rim.
4. Place several ice cubes into your rimmed glasses and pour 3 ounces tequila, 6 ounces Topo Chico, squeeze the juice of one smoked lime (discard after squeezing), and add one fresh lime wedge to each. If using the jalapeño, add one or two slices to each glass (muddle if desired).
5. Stir to combine and enjoy!

Traeger Old Fashioned

Servings: 2

Cooking Time: 60 Minutes

Ingredients:

- 2 orange
- 2 Cup cherries
- 3 Ounce bourbon
- 1 Ounce Smoked Simple Syrup
- 8 Dash Bitters Lab Apricot Vanilla Bitters

Directions:

1. Supply your smoker with wood pellets and follow the start-up procedure. Preheat the grill, with the lid closed, to 180° F.
2. While Traeger preheats, slice whole orange into wheels.

3. Place cherries on a small sheet pan and place in the Traeger. Place orange slices directly on the grill grate.

4. Smoke cherries for 1 hour and oranges for 25 minutes, depending on taste, before removing from the grill. Let oranges and cherries cool. Grill: 180 ˚F

5. Pour bourbon into glass, followed by Traeger Smoked Simple Syrup and bitters. Add ice and stir for 45 seconds or until drink is well-diluted.

6. Strain contents into new glass over fresh ice. Skewer orange wheel and add cherry for garnish. Enjoy!

Traeger Boulevardier Cocktail

Servings: 2
Cooking Time: 60 Minutes

Ingredients:

- 4 oranges
- 1/2 Cup honey
- 1500 mL rye whiskey
- 1 1/2 Ounce Campari
- 1 1/2 Ounce sweet vermouth
- 2 Tablespoon granulated sugar
- 3 Ounce grilled orange infused rye

Directions:

1. Supply your smoker with wood pellets and follow the start-up procedure. Preheat the grill, with the lid closed, to 350° F.

2. Slice 2 oranges in half and coat cut side with honey. Peel remaining orange and place peels on the grill. Cook 20 to 25 minutes. Grill: 350 ˚F

3. Remove from grill and let cool. Place orange halves cut side down directly on the grill grate and cook 20 to 30 minutes or until dark grill marks appear. Remove orange halves and allow to cool. Grill: 350 ˚F

4. Place orange halves into a bottle of rye whiskey and let steep for 10 to 12 hours. The longer they steep, the sweeter and more pronounced the orange flavor will be.

5. Add all ingredients into a mixing glass and stir until diluted. Strain into a fresh coupe glass and serve neat.

6. Garnish with grilled orange peel. Enjoy!

Grilled Rabbit Tail Cocktail

Servings: 2
Cooking Time: 25 Minutes

Ingredients:

- 1 1/2 Ounce lemon juice
- 4 Ounce Apple Brandy
- 1 Ounce orange juice
- 1 Ounce Smoked Simple Syrup

Directions:

1. Supply your smoker with wood pellets and follow the start-up procedure. Preheat the grill, with the lid closed, to 350° F.

2. Place lemon halves directly on the grill grate and cook for 20-25 minutes or until grill marks appear. Remove from grill and let cool. Once cool enough to handle, juice the lemons then chill and reserve the juice. Grill: 350 ˚F

3. Using the proportions listed above and considering the size and consumption rate of your tailgate crew or party, mix all the above ingredients in a large thermos and top with a bit of ice.

4. Using 6-8 oz glasses or cups, guests can serve themselves from the thermos and garnish each drink with a grilled apple slice. Enjoy!

Traeger Paloma Cocktail

Servings: 2
Cooking Time: 25 Minutes

Ingredients:

- 4 grapefruit, halved
- Smoked Simple Syrup
- 10 Stick cinnamon
- 3 Ounce reposado tequila
- 1 Ounce lime juice
- 1 Ounce Smoked Simple Syrup
- grilled lime, for garnish
- cinnamon stick, for garnish

Directions:

1. Supply your smoker with wood pellets and follow the start-up procedure. Preheat the grill, with the lid closed, to 350° F.

2. Grilled Grapefruit Juice: Cut 2 grapefruits in half. Place a cinnamon stick in each grapefruit half and glaze with Traeger Smoked Simple Syrup. Place on grill grate and cook for 20 minutes or until edges start to burn and it acquires grill marks. Remove from heat and let cool. Grill: 350 ˚F

3. After grapefruits have cooled, squeeze and strain juice. It should yield 10 to 12 ounces of juice.

4. In a mixing glass, add tequila, lime juice, Traeger Smoked Simple Syrup and 2 ounces of the grilled grapefruit juice.

5. Add ice and shake. Strain over ice in an old fashioned glass.

6. Add a grilled lime slice and cinnamon stick to garnish. Enjoy!

Smoked Grape Lime Rickey

Servings: 4
Cooking Time: 45 Minutes

Ingredients:

- 1/2 Pound red grapes
- 1/2 Cup plus 1 tablespoon sugar
- 1/2 Cup water
- 1 limes, sliced

- 2 limes, halved
- 1 Tablespoon sugar
- 1 L lemon lime soda

Directions:

1. Supply your smoker with wood pellets and follow the start-up procedure. Preheat the grill, with the lid closed, to 180° F.
2. Rinse grapes well and place in a shallow baking dish. Combine 1/2 cup sugar and water and stir until sugar dissolves. Pour over grapes.
3. Place the baking dish directly on the grill grate and smoke for 30 to 40 minutes until grapes are tender. Grill: 180 ˚F
4. Remove from the grill and pour entire contents of the baking dish in a blender. Puree on high until smooth then pass the mixture through a fine mesh strainer.
5. Increase Traeger temperature to 350˚F . Grill: 350 ˚F
6. Toss the lime slices and lime halves with 1 tablespoon sugar and place directly on the grill grate. Cook for 15 to 20 minutes or until grill marks develop. Remove from grill and set slices aside. When cool enough to handle, juice grilled lime halves. Grill: 350 ˚F
7. To build the drink, fill a pint glass with ice. Pour in 1-1/2 ounce grilled lime juice, 1-1/2 ounce smoked grape syrup and top off with soda. Garnish with grilled lime slice. Enjoy!

Honey Glazed Grapefruit Shandy Cocktail

Servings: 2

Cooking Time: 20 Minutes

Ingredients:

- 4 grapefruits
- 4 Tablespoon honey
- granulated sugar
- 2 Ounce bourbon
- 1 Ounce Smoked Simple Syrup
- 4 Ounce honey glazed grilled grapefruit, juiced
- 2 Bottle Ballast Point Grapefruit Sculpin

Directions:

1. Supply your smoker with wood pellets and follow the start-up procedure. Preheat the grill, with the lid closed, to 375° F.
2. For the honey glazed grapefruit: Slice one grapefruit in half and coat with 2 tablespoons honey.
3. Take the other grapefruit and slice into wheels. Toss the wheels in granulated sugar until well coated.
4. Place the grapefruit halves and wheels directly on the grill grate, cut side down, and cook for 20 to 30 minutes. Remove from grill and set the wheels aside. Grill: 375 ˚F
5. Squeeze the grapefruit halves into a measuring cup. It should yield about 2 oz juice.

6. Pour the grapefruit juice into a shaker and add bourbon and Traeger Smoked Simple Syrup then top with ice. Shake for 10-15 seconds.
7. Strain into glass, add ice and fill with beer. Garnish with the grilled grapefruit wheel. Enjoy!

Smoked Plum And Thyme Fizz Cocktail

Servings: 2

Cooking Time: 60 Minutes

Ingredients:

- 6 fresh plums
- 4 Fluid Ounce vodka
- 1 1/2 Fluid Ounce fresh lemon juice
- 2 Ounce smoked plum and thyme simple syrup
- 4 Fluid Ounce club soda
- 2 Slices smoked plum, for garnish
- 2 Sprig fresh thyme, for garnish
- 8 Sprig thyme
- 2 Cup Smoked Simple Syrup

Directions:

1. Supply your smoker with wood pellets and follow the start-up procedure. Preheat the grill, with the lid closed, to 180° F.
2. Cut plums in half and remove the pit. Place the plum halves directly on the grill grate and smoke for 25 minutes. Grill: 180 ˚F
3. For the Plum and Thyme Simple Syrup: After 25 minutes, remove plums from the grill and cut into quarters. Add plums and thyme sprigs to 1 cup of Traeger Smoked Simple Syrup. Smoke the mixture for 45 minutes. Remove from grill, strain and let cool. Grill: 180 ˚F
4. Add vodka, fresh lemon juice and smoked plum and thyme simple syrup to a mixing glass.
5. Add ice and shake. Strain over clean ice, top off with club soda and garnish with a piece of thyme and slice of smoked plum. Enjoy!

Grilled Peach Smash Cocktail

Servings: 2

Cooking Time: 10 Minutes

Ingredients:

- 2 peach, sliced and grilled
- 10 fresh mint leaves
- 1 1/2 Ounce Smoked Simple Syrup
- 4 Ounce bourbon
- 2 mint sprig, for garnish

Directions:

1. Supply your smoker with wood pellets and follow the start-up procedure. Preheat the grill, with the lid closed, to 375° F.

2. Cut the peach into 6 slices and brush with Traeger Smoked Simple Syrup. Place directly on the grill grate and cook 10 to 12 minutes or until peaches soften and get grill marks. Grill: 375 °F

3. In a mixing glass, add 3 slices of grilled peaches, 5 mint leaves and Traeger Smoked Simple Syrup.

4. Muddle ingredients to release oils of the mint and juices from the grilled peaches. Add bourbon and crushed ice.

5. Shake and pour into a stemless wine glass. Top off with more crushed ice. Garnish with a grilled peach and mint sprig. Enjoy!

Smoked Eggnog

Servings: 4
Cooking Time: 60 Minutes

Ingredients:
- 2 Cup whole milk
- 1 Cup heavy cream
- 4 egg yolk
- Cup sugar
- 3 Ounce bourbon
- 1 Teaspoon vanilla extract
- 1 Teaspoon nutmeg
- 4 egg white
- whipped cream

Directions:
1. Plan ahead, this recipe requires chill time.

2. Supply your smoker with wood pellets and follow the start-up procedure. Preheat the grill, with the lid closed, to 180° F.

3. Pour the milk and the cream into a baking pan and smoke on the Traeger for 60 minutes. Grill: 180 °F

4. Meanwhile, in the bowl of a stand mixer, beat the egg yolks until they lighten in color. Gradually add 1/3 cup sugar and continue to beat until sugar completely dissolves.

5. After the milk and cream have smoked, add them along with the bourbon, vanilla and nutmeg into the egg mixture and stir to combine.

6. Place the egg whites in the bowl of a stand mixer and beat to soft peaks. When you lift the beaters the whites will make a peak that slightly curls down.

7. With the mixer still running, gradually add 1 tablespoon of sugar and beat until stiff peaks form.

8. Gently fold the egg whites into the cream mixture and then whisk to thoroughly combine.

9. Chill eggnog for a couple hours to let the flavors meld. Garnish with a dash of nutmeg and whipped cream on top. Enjoy!

Traeger Gin & Tonic

Servings: 2
Cooking Time: 45 Minutes

Ingredients:
- 1/2 Cup berries
- 2 orange, sliced
- 4 Tablespoon granulated sugar
- 3 Ounce gin
- 1 Cup tonic water
- 2 Sprig fresh mint, for garnish

Directions:
1. Supply your smoker with wood pellets and follow the start-up procedure. Preheat the grill, with the lid closed, to 180° F.

2. For the Smoked Berries: Spread mixed fresh berries on a sheet pan and place directly on the grill grate. Smoke for 30 minutes then remove from grill. Grill: 180 °F

3. For the Orange Slices: Increase the grill temperature to 450°F and preheat, lid closed for 15 minutes. Grill: 450 °F

4. Toss the orange slices with granulated sugar and place directly on grill grate. Cook for about 5 minutes, turning once or until the slices have developed grill marks. Grill: 450 °F

5. Pour gin into a glass, add ice and berries, then top with tonic water. Garnish with a fresh mint sprig and grilled orange wheel. Enjoy!

Smoke And Bubz Cocktail

Servings: 2
Cooking Time: 45 Minutes

Ingredients:
- 16 Ounce POM Juice
- 2 Cup pomegranate seeds
- 6 Ounce sparkling white wine
- 2 lemon twist, for garnish
- 2 Teaspoon pomegranate seeds

Directions:
1. Supply your smoker with wood pellets and follow the start-up procedure. Preheat the grill, with the lid closed, to 180° F.

2. For the Smoked Pomegranate Juice: Pour POM juice and a cup of pomegranate seeds into a shallow sheet pan. Smoke on the Traeger for 45 minutes. Pull off grill, strain, discard seeds and let sit until chilled. Grill: 180 °F

3. Add 1-1/2 ounces of the smoked pomegranate juice to the bottom of a champagne flute.

4. Add sparkling white wine, a few fresh pomegranate seeds and a lemon twist to garnish. Enjoy!

Smoked Raspberry Bubbler Cocktail

Servings: 2
Cooking Time: 45 Minutes

Ingredients:
- 2 Cup fresh raspberries

- Smoked Simple Syrup
- 8 Ounce sparkling wine

Directions:

1. Supply your smoker with wood pellets and follow the start-up procedure. Preheat the grill, with the lid closed, to 180° F.

2. Smoked Raspberry Syrup: Place 1 cup fresh raspberries on a grill mat and smoke for 30 minutes. Grill: 180 °F

3. After the raspberries have been smoked, set a few aside for garnish. Place the remainder into a shallow sheet pan with Traeger Smoked Simple Syrup. Place back on the grill grate and let smoke for 45 minutes. Remove from heat and allow to cool. Strain and refrigerate until ready to use. Grill: 180 °F

4. Place 1 ounce of the smoked raspberry syrup in the bottom of a champagne flute and top off with sparkling white wine or champagne.

5. Garnish with smoked raspberries. Enjoy!

Smoky Mountain Bramble Cocktail

Servings: 2
Cooking Time: 15 Minutes

Ingredients:

- 16 Ounce blackberries
- 2 Cup sugar
- 10 smoked blackberries
- 3 Ounce vodka
- 1 1/2 Ounce Alpine Distilling Preserve Liqueur
- 1 1/2 Ounce lemon juice
- 1 Ounce smoked blackberry syrup

Directions:

1. Supply your smoker with wood pellets and follow the start-up procedure. Preheat the grill, with the lid closed, to 180° F.

2. To make Smoked Blackberry Simple Syrup: Place blackberries on a grill mat and smoke for 15 to 20 minutes. Grill: 180 °F

3. Combine 1 cup water and sugar in a small sauce pan and warm over medium heat until sugar dissolves. Remove from heat and place 2/3 of blackberries in the simple syrup and macerate.

4. Strain through a fine mesh strainer and store for up to 14 days.

5. To make the cocktail: Muddle 4 to 5 smoked blackberries in a cocktail shaker. Add vodka, Preserve Liqueur, lemon and smoked blackberry syrup. Add ice and shake vigorously. Double strain into an old fashioned glass.

6. Garnish with a smoked blackberry and lemon twist. Enjoy!

PORK RECIPES

First-timer's Pulled Pork

Servings: 8
Cooking Time: 540 Minutes

Ingredients:

- 1 bone-in pork shoulder, about 5 to 7lb (2.3 to 3.2kg)
- coarse salt
- freshly ground black pepper
- 1½ cups low-carb beer or sugar-free dark-colored soda
- for the sauce
- 1½ cups apple cider vinegar
- ½ cup distilled water
- 2 tbsp ketchup
- 1½ tbsp granulated brown sugar or low-carb substitute
- 1 tsp coarse salt, plus more
- 1 tsp freshly ground black pepper
- ½ to 1 tsp crushed red pepper flakes

Directions:

1. Supply your smoker with wood pellets and follow the start-up procedure. Preheat the grill, with the lid closed, to 250° F.

2. In a medium saucepan on the stovetop over medium-high, make the vinegar sauce by bringing the ingredients to a boil. Whisk to dissolve the sugar and salt. Let the sauce cool to room temperature and then transfer to a jar with a tight-fitting lid. Set aside.

3. Season the pork shoulder on all sides with salt and pepper. Place the pork on the grate and smoke until the bone releases easily from the meat and the internal temperature reaches 200°F (93°C), about 7 to 9 hours. Wrap the pork tightly in a large piece of heavy-duty aluminum foil and let rest in an insulated cooler for up to 1 hour.

4. Carefully remove the pork from the foil and reserve the juices. Wear heatproof gloves to pull the pork into chunks. Discard the bone and any large lumps of fat. Pull the meat into shreds and transfer to a clean aluminum foil roasting pan. Moisten with some of the reserved juices. Taste, adding more salt and pepper. Serve with the vinegar sauce.

Roasted Bacon Weave Holiday Ham

Servings: 6
Cooking Time: 180 Minutes

Ingredients:

- 1 1/2 Pound Bacon, sliced
- 1 Large Ham, Bone-In
- whole cloves
- 1 1/2 Cup pineapple juice

- 2 Cup ginger beer
- 1/4 Cup brown sugar
- 2 Tablespoon mustard

Directions:

1. Create a bacon weave on parchment paper.

2. Put the ham in a disposable roasting pan. Gently transfer the bacon weave to the top of the ham and stud the bacon with the cloves (if desired).

3. Pour 1 cup of pineapple juice and 1 cup of ginger beer/ale into the bottom of the roasting pan.

4. Supply your smoker with wood pellets and follow the start-up procedure. Preheat the grill, with the lid closed, to 300° F.

5. Cover the roasting pan with foil and put on the Traeger. Cook the ham until it reaches 145°F (somewhere between 2 to 3 hours). Grill: 300 °F Probe: 145 °F

6. Meanwhile mix together the glaze. Combine the remaining 1/2 cup of pineapple juice, 1 cup ginger beer/ale, brown sugar and mustard in a saucepan on the stovetop. Cook until it thickens slightly, then brush on the ham.

7. Put the uncovered ham back on Traeger and cook until the temperature reaches 160°F. Grill: 300 °F Probe: 160 °F

8. Let the ham rest 5 minutes before slicing and serving. Reserve the juices to pour over the ham. Enjoy!

Bbq 3-2-1 St. Louis Ribs

Servings: 6
Cooking Time: 360 Minutes

Ingredients:

- 2 Rack St. Louis-style ribs
- Pork & Poultry Rub
- 1/2 Cup brown sugar, divided
- 1/3 Cup honey, divided
- 1 Cup BBQ Sauce
- BBQ Sauce

Directions:

1. If your butcher has not done so already, remove the thin silverskin membrane from the bone-side of the ribs by working the tip of a butter knife underneath the membrane over a middle bone. Use paper towels to get a firm grip, then tear the membrane off.

2. Season both sides of the ribs generously with Traeger Pork & Poultry Rub.

3. Supply your smoker with wood pellets and follow the start-up procedure. Preheat the grill, with the lid closed, to 180° F.

4. Smoke the ribs, meat-side up for 3 hours. Transfer the ribs to a rimmed baking sheet and increase the grill temperature to 225°F. Preheat the grill with the lid closed. Grill: 225 °F

5. Tear off four long sheets of heavy-duty aluminum foil. Top with a rack of ribs. Sprinkle half the brown sugar on the rack then top with half the honey. Tightly wrap the ribs with the foil to create a leak-proof pouch. Repeat with remaining rack of ribs. Grill: 225 ˚F

6. Return the foiled ribs to the grill, meat side down and cook for an additional two hours. Grill: 225 ˚F

7. Carefully remove the foil from the ribs – watch out for hot steam – and brush the ribs on both sides with your favorite Traeger BBQ sauce. Discard the foil. Arrange the ribs directly on the grill grate, bone side down and continue to grill until the sauce tightens, about 30 minutes to 60 minutes more. Let the ribs rest for a few minutes before serving. Enjoy! Grill: 225 ˚F

Apple & Bourbon Glazed Ham

Servings: 6
Cooking Time: 60 Minutes

Ingredients:

- 1 Large ham
- 1 Cup apple jelly
- 2 Tablespoon Dijon mustard
- 2 Tablespoon bourbon
- 2 Teaspoon fresh lemon juice
- 1/2 Teaspoon ground cloves
- 2 Cup apple juice or cider

Directions:

1. Supply your smoker with wood pellets and follow the start-up procedure. Preheat the grill, with the lid closed, to 325° F.

2. When the grill is hot, place ham directly on the grill grate. Cook for 30 minutes. Grill: 325 ˚F

3. Meanwhile, in a small saucepan over medium-low heat, melt the apple jelly. Whisk in the apple juice, mustard, bourbon, lemon juice and ground cloves, then remove from the heat and set aside.

4. After 30 minutes, glaze ham with the apple bourbon mixture. Continue cooking for another 30 minutes or until a thermometer that is inserted into the thickest part of the meat reaches an internal temperature of 135˚F. Grill: 325 ˚F Probe: 135 ˚F

5. Remove ham from grill and allow to rest for 20 minutes before serving. Warm remaining sauce and serve with ham if desired. Enjoy!

Championship Ribs With Kansas City Style

Servings: 4
Cooking Time: 210 Minutes

Ingredients:

- Apple Juice
- 2 Racks Baby Back Rib

- 2 Cups Brown Sugar
- 24 Oz Dijon Mustard
- 4 Tbsp Sweet Rib Rub
- Spray Bottle

Directions:

1. Pour Dijon Mustard into a mixing bowl. Mix in brown sugar until mustard taste diminishes and a sweet taste takes over.

2. Generally, you will use a half bag of brown sugar for 2 bottles and the whole bag for 4 bottles. The key is for the tangy mustard taste to turn sweet.

3. When this mix is brushed on the ribs the mix of pork flavor and this glaze will produce a sweet and sassy result. The easiest way to mix is with an electric mixer but a whisk will do nicely. This will become very thick and sticky.

4. Supply your smoker with wood pellets and follow the start-up procedure. Preheat the grill, with the lid open, to 275° F.

5. Place ribs, back side down, on the cooking grid. Note: If you are doing multiple slabs, I suggest you use a rib rack. Most Rib Racks will hold 6 slabs. This will allow ribs to cook evenly. The rib rack allows for more slabs since ribs will sit in rack on their edge. Try to put meatier side up.

6. Spray ribs thoroughly with apple juice every 30-40 minutes. Apple Juice not only helps to keep meat moist and juicy while cooking, the acidity also helps to break down the muscles, thus tenderizing as well. I have had people tell me they prefer Pineapple juice or a mixture of apple and pineapple. Personally, I can't tell the difference, but you can experiment for yourself if you want to. The result will be same.

7. Note: How to tell when ribs are done? It is hard to measure temp of a rib with a meat thermometer due to the meat between the bones being so tight. You can get a false reading if the thermometer is touching a bone. Take your tongs and pick up slab in the middle. If the rib folds over and is limp and the meat just begins to pull away from the bone, they are done.

8. Remove ribs from grill and place in a pan (long enough for ribs to fit)

9. Glaze both sides of ribs with a light coat of the sassy glaze. This is a flavor enhancer, not a cover up. Just a light coat is plenty. If you really like the glaze there will generally always be some left over, and you can add to your desire while on the plate.

10. Wrap ribs in foil and let stand for 15 minutes

11. Serve (you can serve in slab form and let each guest cut his own or I like to cut ribs and serve as single bones.

12. Enjoy!

Sweet And Spicy Pork Roast

Servings: 2
Cooking Time: 60 Minutes

Ingredients:

- 2 Pound Pork, Loins
- 2/3 habanero peppers, seeded
- 2/3 Can coconut milk
- 1/3 Teaspoon Chinese five-spice powder
- 2/3 Tablespoon paprika
- 2/3 Teaspoon curry powder
- 2/3 Tablespoon lime juice
- 2/3 Tablespoon garlic, minced
- 2/3 Teaspoon freshly grated ginger

Directions:

1. Mix all ingredients, except pork, in a bowl. Rub the mixture onto your pork and let it sit overnight.
2. Supply your smoker with wood pellets and follow the start-up procedure. Preheat the grill, with the lid closed, to 300° F.
3. Place pork on hot grill. Cook for 1 to 1-1/2 hours, or until it reaches an internal temperature of 145-150°F for medium-rare to medium. Enjoy! Grill: 300 °F Probe: 150 °F

Pulled Pork Shoulder And Chicken

Servings: 6 - 8
Cooking Time: 300 Minutes

Ingredients:

- 1/3 Cup Apple Cider Vinegar
- 4 Cups Chicken Broth
- 1/3 Cup Ketchup
- 2 Tbsp Pulled Pork Seasoning
- 4 Lbs. Pork Shoulder, Bone In

Directions:

1. Supply your smoker with wood pellets and follow the start-up procedure. Preheat the grill, with the lid open, to 350° F. In a bowl, combine the chicken broth, ketchup, apple cider vinegar, and 1 tablespoon of Pulled Pork Seasoning. Whisk well to combine and set aside.
2. Generously season the pork shoulder with the remaining 3 tablespoons of Pulled Pork Seasoning on all sides of the pork shoulder, then place on the grill and sear on all sides until golden brown, about 10 minutes.
3. Remove the pork shoulder from the grill and place in the disposable aluminum pan. Pour the chicken broth mixture over the pork shoulder. It should come about 1/3 to ½ way up the side of the pork shoulder. Cover the top of the pan tightly with aluminum foil.

4. Reduce the temperature of your grill to 250°F. Place the foil pan on the grill and grill for four to five hours, or until the pork is tender and falling off the bone.
5. Remove the pork from the grill and allow to cool slightly. Drain the liquid from the pan, reserving about a cup, then shred the pork and cover with the reserved liquid. Serve and enjoy!

Smoked Blt Sandwich

Servings: 4
Cooking Time: 20 Minutes

Ingredients:

- 2 Pound thick-cut bacon
- 1/2 Cup mayonnaise
- 8 Slices Texas toast
- 2 Head butter lettuce
- 3 heirloom tomato, sliced

Directions:

1. Supply your smoker with wood pellets and follow the start-up procedure. Preheat the grill, with the lid closed, to 350° F.
2. When the grill is hot, place the bacon slices directly on the grill grate and cook for 15-20 minutes or until crispy. Grill: 350 °F
3. To build the sandwich, smear mayo on two pieces of toast. Layer lettuce leaves, tomatoes, bacon and top with the other piece of toast. Enjoy!

Bbq Pulled Coleslaw Pork Sandwiches

Servings: 12
Cooking Time: 480 Minutes

Ingredients:

- 1 Bottle Bbq Sauce
- Coleslaw, Prepared
- 12 Kaiser Rolls
- 8-10Lbs Pork Butt Roast, Bone-In
- 5 Oz Sugar
- 1 Cup Yellow Mustard

Directions:

1. Supply your smoker with wood pellets and follow the start-up procedure. Preheat the grill, with the lid open, to 225° F. While your grill is heating, remove the pork roast from its packaging and place on a cookie sheet. Rub the pork roast down with yellow mustard.
2. Mix BBQ sauce and sugar in a bowl. Rub the roast down with entire mixture, allowing time for the rub to melt into the meat.
3. Place the roast in the smoker and cook for 6 hours.
4. After 6 hours, remove the roast and double wrap in tin foil. Turn the grill up to 250°F and cook the roast for another 2 hours or until the roast is probe tender (around an internal temperature

of 204°F). Let the pork butt rest in the foil for up to an hour before pulling.

5.   Cut each Kaiser roll in half, mix pulled pork with some more barbecue sauce and pile on each half of roll. Top with coleslaw and green onions. Don't mix all the pulled pork with barbecue sauce so that you can use the extra pulled pork for different recipes. Serve hot and enjoy!

Bbq Pulled Pork Hash

Servings: 4
Cooking Time: 30 Minutes

Ingredients:
- 1/2 Cup carrots, peeled and cut into 1 inch pieces
- 1/2 Cup beets
- 1/2 Cup small new potatoes
- 1/2 Cup asparagus
- 1 Tablespoon olive oil
- leftover pulled pork
- 3 egg

Directions:
1.   Supply your smoker with wood pellets and follow the start-up procedure. Preheat the grill, with the lid closed, to 375° F.
2.   Chop all vegetables into even pieces, about 1/2 inch cubes. Pre heat a cast iron pan over Medium-High heat.
3.   Add a Tablespoon of olive oil then the carrots, new potatoes, and beets. Season with salt and pepper to taste and sauté stirring every few minutes until vegetables are cooked through (about 8 to 10 minutes).
4.   Add the asparagus and cook an additional 2 minutes. Add a layer of pulled pork over vegetables. Crack 3 eggs over that being careful not to break the yokes.
5.   Place into preheated Traeger and cook for about 10 minutes or until eggs are just set. Remove from grill and serve immediately with your favorite hot sauce. Enjoy! Grill: 375 °F

Cuban Onion Pork Sandwich

Servings: 4
Cooking Time: 270 Minutes

Ingredients:
- 1 Tbsp Butter
- 3 Cups Chicken Stock
- 4 Ciabatta Bread Or Torta Rolls, Halved
- 1/4 Cup Dijon Mustard
- 4 Dill Pickle, Slice
- 1 Lb Ham Or Prosciutto
- 1/4 Cup Mayonnaise
- Pulled Pork Rub
- 3 1/2 Lbs Pork Shoulder

- 8 Oz Swiss Cheese, Sliced
- 1 Tbsp Vegetable Oil
- 1 White Onion, Sliced

Directions:
1.   Supply your smoker with wood pellets and follow the start-up procedure. Preheat the grill, with the lid open, to 250° F. If using a gas or charcoal grill, set it up for low, indirect heat.
2.   Generously season pork shoulder with Pulled Pork Rub, then transfer to the grill grate. Smoke for 1 hour, then flip pork and smoke for an additional hour.
3.   Place onion and chicken stock in a deep cast iron skillet, or metal grill pan. Transfer the pork to the skillet, then cover with a shallow cast iron skillet, or aluminum foil. Braise for 2 hours, then increase grill temperature to 300° F, and braise for 1 more hour.
4.   Remove the cover then pull pork with tongs while still on the grill. The stock will have reduced, so be sure and toss the pork in the reduced, seasoned stock and onions. Remove from the grill and set aside.
5.   Preheat the griddle to medium-low flame. If using a different grill, preheat a clean cast iron skillet on medium low heat.
6.   Heat butter and oil on the griddle, then toast rolls, pressing down by hand or with a metal spatula. Combine mustard and mayonnaise, then spread onto both sides of rolls. Set aside.
7.   Divide pork into 4 portions, and place on the griddle, along with the sliced ham. Cook for 2 to 3 minutes, rotating ham and pork. Layer pork, ham, cheese, and pickles. Cover for 1 minute to allow cheese to melt. Return rolls to the griddle, cut each portion of filling in half, then stack 2 per prepared rolls. Press each sandwich down with the bottom of a metal spatula. Carefully flip, and press down again.
8.   Remove sandwiches from the griddle and serve warm.

Spiced Pulled Pork Shoulder

Servings: 16
Cooking Time: 600 Minutes

Ingredients:
- 5-8 lb Bone-in Pork Shoulder
- Maple Chili Rub
- Maple Sugar
- Kosher Salt
- Fresh Ground Black Pepper
- Roasted Garlic Powder
- Onion Powder
- Cumin
- Chipotle Powder
- Chili Powder
- Cinnamon Powder

Directions:

1. Supply your smoker with wood pellets and follow the start-up procedure. Preheat the grill, with the lid closed, to 225° F. Using apple pellets for this dish will impart a slightly sweeter smoke that goes great with the rub.
2. In a bowl combine rub ingredients.
3. Trim excess fat from pork shoulder, score fat with a sharp knife (only slice about 1/8" into pork), then cover with rub. Reserve some rub to be sprinkled on the meat after it has been shredded.
4. Place the pork onto the smoker.
5. Continue to smoke pork until internal temperature reaches 203 °F, about 10 hours. You can wrap pork in butcher paper once it reaches 160 °F if you want to speed up cooking time (your final bark won't be as good though).
6. Once Pork reaches 203 °F, remove from smoker then wrap tightly in aluminum foil. Place wrapped Pork into a cooler for 1 hour.
7. After 1 hour remove pork from the foil, pull out the bones, using 2 forks shred the pork to your desired consistency.
8. Sprinkle left over rub onto the pork and toss to coat.
9. Enjoy!

Grilled Raspberry Chipotle Pork Ribs

Servings: 4
Cooking Time: 180 Minutes

Ingredients:
- Baby Back Rib
- Original Bbq Sauce
- Raspberry Chipotle Spice Rub

Directions:
1. Begin by gently rinsing off your ribs in cool water. Pat dry and remove the flavor blocker (thin membrane on the underside of the ribs) to allow the seasoning to permeate right into the meat.
2. Generously season your ribs with Raspberry Chipotle seasoning and place in the refrigerator for an hour for flavor to set in.
3. Supply your smoker with wood pellets and follow the start-up procedure. Preheat the grill, with the lid open, to 250° F. Place your seasoned rack of ribs on the grill and let cook for 2 hours. Next, lather on a thick coating of Original BBQ Sauce, turn up the grill to 300°F and let your ribs roast for another hour. Remove, cut and serve for a meal that will surely make its way into the weekly rotation.

Baby Back Ribs With Mustard Slather

Servings: 4
Cooking Time: 120 Minutes

Ingredients:

- 2 racks of baby back ribs, each about 2lb (1kg)
- all-purpose barbecue rub
- low-carb barbecue sauce (optional)
- for the mustard
- ½ cup yellow or brown mustard
- 2 tbsp dill pickle juice or apple cider vinegar

Directions:
1. Supply your smoker with wood pellets and follow the start-up procedure. Preheat the grill, with the lid closed, to 325° F.
2. Remove the thick membrane on the bone side of the ribs. Don't remove the thin membrane on top of the bones because it holds them together. Trim off any odd bits of meat or excess fat. Place the ribs on a rimmed sheet pan.
3. In a small bowl, make the mustard slather by combining the mustard and pickle juice. Brush the ribs on both sides with the mixture and then season with the barbecue rub.
4. Place the ribs on the grate and smoke until the ribs are tender, about 1½ to 2 hours. (A toothpick inserted between bones should go in with little resistance. The meat will also have pulled back from the bone about ½ inch [1.25cm].) Brush the ribs with barbecue sauce (if using) during the last 10 minutes of smoking. Place the ribs meat side down on the grate for 5 minutes. Turn and grill for 5 minutes more. This sets the sauce.
5. Transfer the ribs to a cutting board. Use a sharp knife to cut the slabs in half or into individual ribs. Serve immediately with more barbecue sauce.

Delicious Smoked Bone-in Pork Chops

Servings: 4
Cooking Time: 90 Minutes

Ingredients:
- 1/2 Cup Apple Cider Vinegar
- 4 Pork Butt Roast, Bone-In
- 2 Tbsp Salt
- 1 Tbsp Sugar
- 4 Tablespoons Tennessee Apple Butter Seasoning
- 1/4 Cup Vinegar, Red Wine
- 1/4 Cup Water

Directions:
1. Supply your smoker with wood pellets and follow the start-up procedure. Preheat the grill, with the lid closed, to 250° F.
2. In a large mixing bowl, combine the sugar, red wine vinegar, salt, 2 tablespoons of Tennessee Apple Butter and water to create a brine for the pork chops. Whisk the brine well until the sugar, salt and Tennessee Apple Butter have dissolved.
3. Generously rub the pork chops on all sides with olive oil and season on all sides with the Tennessee Apple Butter. Make sure the meat is coated on all sides.

4. Place the pork chops in the smoker, insert a temperature probe into the thickest part of one of the pork chops, and smoke until the internal temperature reaches 145°F, or about 1 hour 30 minutes. The pork chops should have developed a good color and be juicy, but no longer be pink in the center.

5. Remove the pork chops from the smoker and allow them to rest for 5-10 minutes under tented aluminum foil, then slice along the grain and serve.

Hawaiian Pineapple Pork Butt

Servings: 8 - 10
Cooking Time: 720 Minutes

Ingredients:
- 6 - 8 Pineapple Rings
- 2 Cups Pineapple, Juice
- 1 8-10Lb Pork Butt Roast, Bone-In
- ¼ Cup Sweet Heat Rub

Directions:
1. Supply your smoker with wood pellets and follow the start-up procedure. Preheat the grill, with the lid open, to 225° F. If not using a pellet smoker, set up the smoker for indirect smoking.
2. Remove the pork butt from its packaging and drain any excess liquid from the pork butt. Pat the pork butt dry with paper towels and discard the paper towels.
3. Generously season the pork butt with the Sweet Heat seasoning, making sure that the roast is coated on all sides.
4. Place the pineapple rings evenly over the pork shoulder, fat side up, and pin with toothpicks. Place the pork butt into the 9x13 pan and pour the pineapple juice over the top.
5. Set the pan into the smoker. Make sure that the pork butt is placed as close to the center of the rack as possible for even cooking.
6. Place a temperature probe into the thickest part of the pork butt, and smoke the pork until it reaches an internal temperature of 201°F. The pork should be deeply browned and smell very porky.
7. Once the pork butt reaches its internal temperature, remove the pork butt from the grill and wrap it tightly in foil. Allow the roast to rest for at least 1 hour before shredding.
8. After the roast has rested for an hour, shred the pork with your meat claws, discarding any large chunks of fat. Serve immediately.

Bacon Stuffed Smoked Pork Loin

Servings: 4-6
Cooking Time: 60 Minutes

Ingredients:
- 3 Pound Pork Loin, Butterflied

- As Needed Pork Rub
- 1/4 Cup Walnuts, Chopped
- 1/3 Cup Craisins
- 1 Tablespoon Oregano, fresh
- 1 Tablespoon fresh thyme
- 6 Pieces Asparagus, fresh
- 6 Slices Bacon, sliced
- 1/3 Cup Parmesan cheese, grated
- As Needed Bacon Grease

Directions:
1. Lay down 2 large pieces of butcher's twine on your work surface. Place butterflied pork loin perpendicular to twine.
2. Season the inside of the pork loin with the pork rub.
3. On one end of the loin, layer in a line all of the ingredients, beginning with the chopped walnuts, craisins, oregano, thyme, and asparagus.
4. Add bacon and top with the parmesan cheese.
5. Starting at the end with all of the fillings, carefully roll up the pork loin and secure on both ends with butcher's twine.
6. Roll the pork loin in the reserved bacon grease and season the outside with more Pork Rub.
7. When ready to cook, set temperature to 180°F and preheat, lid closed for 15 minutes. Place stuffed pork loin directly on the grill grate and smoke for 1 hour.
8. Remove the pork loin; increase the temperature to 350°F and allow to preheat.
9. Place the loin back on the smoker and grill for approximately 30 to 45 minutes or until the temperature reads 135°F on an instant-read thermometer.
10. Move the pork loin to a plate and tent it with aluminum foil. Let it rest for 15 minutes before slicing and serving. Enjoy!

Smoked Rendezvous Ribs

Servings: 4
Cooking Time: 120 Minutes

Ingredients:
- 1/2 Cup apple cider vinegar
- 1/2 Cup water
- 1/2 Cup BBQ Sauce
- 2 Tablespoon Pork & Poultry Rub
- 3 Rack baby back pork ribs, membrane removed
- 1 As Needed Pork & Poultry Rub

Directions:
1. In a mixing bowl, combine vinegar, water, barbecue sauce, and Traeger Pork and Poultry rub. Set the sauce and a barbecue mop or basting brush grill-side.
2. Supply your smoker with wood pellets and follow the start-up procedure. Preheat the grill, with the lid closed, to 325° F.
3. Arrange the ribs on the grill grate, meat-side up.

4. Grill for 30 minutes, then start mopping. Mop every 15 minutes. After 2 hours, check the ribs for doneness. Grill: 325 °F

5. Insert a toothpick between the bones in the center of a rack. If there is little or no resistance, the ribs are done (or close to it). If the ribs are not to your liking, continue to grill them in 30-minute increments, mopping every 15 minutes. Grill: 325 °F

6. When the ribs are done, transfer them to a cutting board and give them a final dose of the mop sauce. Sprinkle lightly with Traeger Pork and Poultry Rub.

7. Let the ribs rest for a few minutes before cutting into half slabs or individual ribs. Enjoy!

Grilled Bbq Pork Chops

Servings: 6
Cooking Time: 12 Minutes

Ingredients:
- 6 Thick-Cut Pork Chops
- Generous amounts BBQ rub

Directions:
1. Supply your smoker with wood pellets and follow the start-up procedure. Preheat the grill, with the lid closed, to 450° F. Place seasoned pork chops on grill. Cook 6 minutes per side, or until internal temps reach 145 °F.

2. Remove from heat and let sit for 5-10 minutes before serving.

Buffalo Pork Tenderloin

Servings: 4
Cooking Time: 20 Minutes

Ingredients:
- 2 Pork Tenderloins (about 12 to 15 oz. each)
- 6 Tablespoon butter, melted
- 6 Tablespoon Louisiana-style hot sauce
- Cajun Shake

Directions:
1. Trim any silverskin from the tenderloins with a sharp knife.

2. Combine the melted butter and the hot sauce and roll the tenderloins in the mixture.

3. Supply your smoker with wood pellets and follow the start-up procedure. Preheat the grill, with the lid closed, to 400° F.

4. Arrange the tenderloins on the grill grate and grill for 6 to 8 minutes per side, rolling with tongs, or until the internal temperature is 145F when read on an instant-read meat thermometer. (The pork will still be slightly pink in the center. If you prefer your pork well-done, cook it to 160F.) Grill: 400 °F Probe: 150 °F

5. Transfer the tenderloins to a cutting board. Let rest for several minutes before carving on a diagonal into 1/2-inch slices. Enjoy!

Beer Braised Pork Belly And Beef

Servings: 4
Cooking Time: 90 Minutes

Ingredients:
- 1, Dark Beer, Any Brand
- 3 Cups Broth, Beef
- 1 Tablespoon Chinese Cooking Wine (Such As Shaoxing) Or Dry Sherry Wine
- 1 Teaspoon Chinese Five Spice Powder
- 2, Smashed Garlic, Cloves
- 1 Inch Knob Ginger, Peeled And Thinly Sliced
- 1 Onion, Sliced
- 2 Pounds Pork Belly, Cut Into 1 Inch Chunks
- 2 Tablespoons Rice Wine Vinegar
- 2 Tablespoons, Dark Soy Sauce, Low Sodium
- 3 Tablespoons Sugar

Directions:
1. Place a heavy dutch oven on a stovetop over medium high heat. Add the pork belly and brown on all sides, about 5 minutes. Once the pork belly has browned, add in the onion, ginger, and garlic, and stir well.

2. Pour the beer, beef broth, soy sauce, dark soy sauce, sugar, Chinese cooking wine, rice wine vinegar, and Chinese five spice powder into the pan. Place a lid on the pan and bring it to a boil. Once it boils, remove it from the heat.

3. Supply your smoker with wood pellets and follow the start-up procedure. Preheat the grill, with the lid open, to 325° F. Place the pan of pork belly on the grill and braise for 1 ½ hours, or until the pork belly is falling apart tender and glazed.

4. Remove the pork belly from the grill and serve immediately.

Simple Smoked Baby Backs

Servings: 4-8
Cooking Time: 360 Minutes

Ingredients:
- 2 (2- or 3-pound) racks baby back ribs
- 2 tablespoons yellow mustard
- 1 batch Pork Rub

Directions:
1. Supply your smoker with wood pellets and follow the start-up procedure. Preheat the grill, with the lid closed, to 225°F.

2. Remove the membrane from the backside of the ribs. This can be done by cutting just through the membrane in an X pattern and working a paper towel between the membrane and the ribs to pull it off.

3. Coat the ribs on both sides with mustard and season them with the rub. Using your hands, work the rub into the meat.

4. Place the ribs directly on the grill grate and smoke until their internal temperature reaches between 190°F and 200°F.

5. Remove the racks from the grill and cut into individual ribs. Serve immediately.

Bourbon Chile Glazed Ham

Servings: 8 – 10
Cooking Time: 90 Minutes

Ingredients:

- ¼ Cup Apple Cider Vinegar
- 2 Cups Bourbon
- 1 Cup Brown Sugar
- 2 Canned Chipotle Chiles In Adobo Sauce
- 2 Cups Chicken Stock
- 2 Dried Ancho Chiles
- 1 Dried Arbol Chile
- 2 Dried Guajillo Chiles
- 2 Tbsp Extra Virgin Olive Oil
- 4 Fresh Garlic, Roughly Chopped
- 4 Cloves Roasted Garlic
- Salt
- 2 Shallots, Roughly Chopped
- 1 Spiral Cut Ham

Directions:

1. Supply your smoker with wood pellets and follow the start-up procedure. Preheat the grill, with the lid open, to 450° F.
2. In a large, heavy-bottomed skillet, heat the oil over medium-high heat. Add the shallots and cook for 5 minutes, or until softened.
3. Add the roasted and fresh garlic and cook, stirring occasionally, for 3 to 4 minutes, until the garlic is browned.
4. Remove the skillet from the heat and add the bourbon.
5. Return the skillet to medium-high heat, add the vinegar, and cook until the liquid is reduced by one third, about 10 minutes.
6. Add the ancho, guajillo, árbol, and chipotle chiles and the brown sugar, then add the chicken stock and continue to cook until the mixture reduces by two thirds, about 15 minutes.
7. Strain the reduction through a fine-mesh strainer into a bowl, then pour it into a small saucepan.
8. Return to the heat over medium and reduce until the glaze coats the back off a spoon. Taste and add salt if needed.

Rub-injected Pork Shoulder

Servings: 8-12
Cooking Time: 1200 Minutes

Ingredients:

- 1 (6- to 8-pound) bone-in pork shoulder
- 2 cups Tea Injectable made with Pork Rub
- 2 tablespoons yellow mustard
- 1 batch Pork Rub

Directions:

1. Supply your smoker with wood pellets and follow the start-up procedure. Preheat the grill, with the lid closed, to 225°F.
2. Inject the pork shoulder throughout with the tea injectable.
3. Coat the pork shoulder all over with mustard and season it with the rub. Using your hands, work the rub into the meat.
4. Place the shoulder directly on the grill grate and smoke until its internal temperature reaches 160°F and a dark bark has formed on the exterior.
5. Pull the shoulder from the grill and wrap it completely in aluminum foil or butcher paper.
6. Increase the grill's temperature to 350°F.
7. Return the pork shoulder to the grill and cook until its internal temperature reaches 195°F.
8. Pull the shoulder from the grill and place it in a cooler. Cover the cooler and let the pork rest for 1 or 2 hours.
9. Remove the pork shoulder from the cooler and unwrap it. Remove the shoulder bone and pull the pork apart using just your fingers. Serve immediately.

3-2-1 Spare Ribs

Servings: 4
Cooking Time: 180 Minutes

Ingredients:

- 2 racks of St. Louis–cut pork spare ribs, each about 3lb (1.4kg)
- all-purpose barbecue rub
- 3 tbsp unsalted butter, cut into cubes
- 1 cup apple juice or apple cider
- low-carb barbecue sauce

Directions:

1. Supply your smoker with wood pellets and follow the start-up procedure. Preheat the grill, with the lid closed, to 225° F.
2. Place the ribs on a rimmed sheet pan and dust with the rub. Place the ribs bone side down on the grate and smoke for 3 hours.
3. Tear off 2 large sheets of heavy-duty aluminum foil. Place one rack of ribs bone side down on the foil and top with half the butter cubes. Place the second rack of ribs bone side down on the butter cubes and top with the remaining butter cubes.
4. Bring up all 4 sides of the foil and pour in the apple juice. Crimp the edges of the foil so the ribs are tightly enclosed. Place the foil package on the grate and smoke for 2 hours more.
5. Transfer the ribs to a workspace and carefully open the foil package. (Be careful of escaping steam.) Discard the foil and any accumulated juices. Brush the ribs on both sides with barbecue sauce. Place the ribs on the grate and smoke for 1 hour more to set the sauce and firm up the bark.
6. Transfer the ribs to a cutting board. Use a sharp knife to cut the slabs in half or into individual ribs. Serve immediately.

Grilled Pork Loin

Servings: 4
Cooking Time: 30 Minutes

Ingredients:

- 2 Tablespoons Balsamic Vinegar
- 2 Cups Fresh Washed And Dried Blackberries
- ¼ Cup Seedless Blackberry Preserve
- ½ Teaspoon Dijon Mustard
- Pinch Of Kosher Salt
- 1 Tablespoon Olive Oil
- 1 Pound Silver Skin And Extra Fat Removed Pork Loin
- 2 Tablespoons Sweet Rib Rub
- 1 Tablespoon Worcestershire Sauce

Directions:

1. Place your pork loin on a flat work surface. Trim the pork loin if necessary. Rub the tenderloin all over with olive oil until it is fully coated. Once the pork loin is completely coated, generously season all over with Sweet Rib Rub until every part of the pork loin is coated. Allow the pork tenderloin to rest at room temperature for 30 minutes.

2. While the pork loin rests, make the blackberry sauce. In a small bowl, place a metal strainer on top combine the fresh blackberries, seedless blackberry preserves, balsamic vinegar, Worcestershire sauce, Dijon mustard, and Sweet Rib Rub. Mix well and set aside.

3. Supply your smoker with wood pellets and follow the start-up procedure. Preheat the grill, with the lid open, to 350° F. If you're using a gas or charcoal grill, set it up for medium heat. Insert a temperature probe into the thickest part of the pork loin and smoke at 225°F for 4-5 hours, flipping once, until the pork loin is golden brown and charred in some spots, and reaches an internal temperature of 145°-165°F. Remove the pork loin from the grill and allow it to rest for 5 minutes.

4. Slice the pork loin thinly and serve with the blackberry sauce.

Pork & Pepperoni Burgers

Servings: 4
Cooking Time: 60 Minutes

Ingredients:

- 1lb (450g) bulk pork sausage, preferably Italian
- 1lb (450g) ground pork, well chilled
- 8 slices of bacon, preferably thick-cut
- 8oz (225g) grated mozzarella cheese, plus more
- 1 tsp Italian seasoning
- ½ cup pizza sauce
- 1½oz (40g) pepperoni, roughly chopped

Directions:

1. Wet your hands with cold water. In a large bowl, combine the sausage and ground pork until well mixed. Line a rimmed sheet pan with aluminum foil. Divide the meat into 4 equal-sized balls and place on the sheet pan. Spray the lower third of a soda can (including the bottom) with cooking spray. Firmly press the can into one of the meatballs to create a meat bowl with uniform sides. Gently twist or rock the can to remove. Use your hands to repair any cracks in the bowl.

2. Wrap 2 slices of bacon around the circumference of the bowl and secure with toothpicks. Repeat with the remaining meatballs, respraying the can with cooking spray as necessary. Chill for 1 hour.

3. Supply your smoker with wood pellets and follow the start-up procedure. Preheat the grill, with the lid closed, to 300° F.

4. Place the patties cup side up on the grate and grill for 30 minutes. Use paper towels to blot any grease that pools at the bottom of the cups.

5. Sprinkle 2 tablespoons of cheese into each cup. Top each patty with equal amounts of Italian seasoning, pizza sauce, and pepperoni. Generously sprinkle more cheese over the top. Continue to grill until the bacon crisps, the cheese melts, and the internal temperature reaches 160°F (71°C), about 20 to 30 minutes more.

6. Remove the burgers from the grill and rest for 3 minutes. Remove the toothpicks and serve immediately.

Bbq Baby Back Ribs With Bacon Pineapple Glaze By Scott Thomas

Servings: 4
Cooking Time: 180 Minutes

Ingredients:

- 2 Rack baby back ribs
- 1 As Needed salt and pepper
- 1 As Needed Your Favorite Spicy Rub
- 6 Slices bacon
- 6 Fluid Ounce pineapple juice
- 1 Teaspoon garlic, minced
- 2 Tablespoon honey

Directions:

1. Remove the membrane from the bone side of the ribs and apply the salt, pepper and rub to that side. Flip the ribs over and season the meat side.

2. Supply your smoker with wood pellets and follow the start-up procedure. Preheat the grill, with the lid closed, to 350° F.

3. While the grill heats up, cook the bacon in a frying pan. As the bacon is cooking, pour the pineapple juice, garlic and honey into an oven safe pot.

4. Remove the bacon from the grease and let the pan and bacon fat cool down. After the pan has cooled for a while, pour the bacon grease in with the pineapple juice, garlic and honey and stir to combine.

5. Place the ribs and the pot on the grill and close the lid. After an hour, the slurry will have reduced down a bit and can be applied to the ribs. Slather the ribs with the reduction every 15 minutes. When the bones peek out about a quarter to a third of an inch, the ribs are done which is about 2 hours and 15 minutes. Grill: 350 ˚F

6. For fall off the bone ribs, go another 30-45 minutes, continuing to glaze every 15 minutes. Grill: 350 ˚F

7. The sweet and savory of the reduction will temper the heat of the spicy rub forming an outstanding and complex blend of flavors. Enjoy!

Bacon-draped Injected Pork Loin Roast

Servings: 4
Cooking Time: 180 Minutes

Ingredients:

- 1 Cup apple juice
- 1/4 Cup water
- 1 Teaspoon salt
- 1 Teaspoon Worcestershire sauce
- 3 Pound (3 lb) center-cut pork loin
- Sweet Rub
- 10 Slices bacon

Directions:

1. In a small bowl combine apple juice, water, salt, and Worcestershire; stir to dissolve the salt crystals. Plunge the injector into the sauce and retract the needle to draw up the liquid. Liberally inject the meat.

2. Plunge the injector into the sauce and retract the needle to draw up the liquid. Liberally inject the meat.

3. Season the meat all over with the Traeger Sweet Rub.

4. Supply your smoker with wood pellets and follow the start-up procedure. Preheat the grill, with the lid closed, to 225˚ F.

5. Drape the loin with the bacon slices. Put the roast directly on the grill grate and smoke for 3 to 4 hours, or until the internal temperature of the meat is at least 145 degrees F on an instant-read thermometer. Grill: 225 ˚F Probe: 145 ˚F

6. Transfer the pork to a cutting board and let rest for 10 minutes before carving and serving. Enjoy!

Cheese Potato Stuffed Pork Chops

Servings: 4
Cooking Time: 45 Minutes

Ingredients:

- 4 Bone-In Pork Chops
- 1 Package Frozen Shredded Hash Browns, Thawed
- 1 Tbsp Parsley, Minced Fresh
- Pulled Pork Seasoning
- 1 Cup Shredded Cheddar Cheese
- ¼ Cup Sour Cream
- White Onion, Diced

Directions:

1. Place the pork chops on a flat work surface. Using a sharp knife, cut a pocket into the side of each pork chop, being careful not to cut all the way through the sides of the chop. Season the pork chops generously on both sides with Pulled Pork Seasoning.

2. In a large mixing bowl, mix together the hash browns, shredded cheddar, sour cream, diced onion, parsley, and 1 tablespoon of Pulled Pork seasoning. Stuff each pork chop with about ¼ cup of the potato filling. Use a toothpick to securely close the chop if needed.

3. Supply your smoker with wood pellets and follow the start-up procedure. Preheat the grill, with the lid open, to 350˚ F. If you're using a gas or charcoal grill, set it up for medium heat. Insert a temperature probe into the thickest part of one of the chops and place the meat on the grill. Grill the chops on one side for 10-15 minutes, then flip and grill for another 10-15, or until the internal temperature of the chops reach 145˚F.

4. Remove the chops from the grill, take the toothpicks out of the meat, and serve immediately.

Baked Pig Candy

Servings: 4
Cooking Time: 60 Minutes

Ingredients:

- 1 Pound thin sliced bacon
- 1/2 Cup maple syrup or corn syrup
- 2 Cup light brown sugar, packed
- 3 Tablespoon chipotle chile powder

Directions:

1. Supply your smoker with wood pellets and follow the start-up procedure. Preheat the grill, with the lid closed, to 250˚ F.

2. Place the bacon slices in a single layer on a large disposable, perforated aluminum pan. Brush each bacon slice with maple syrup. Sprinkle generously with brown sugar, then chipotle powder.

3. Place the pan on the grill and cook until the bacon has absorbed the brown sugar and is crispy, about 1 hour. Remove the bacon from the pan and place in a single layer on a wire rack set over a rimmed baking sheet. Grill: 250 ˚F

4. Set aside at room temperature until the surface of the bacon is dry. Refrigerate in an airtight container with parchment paper between the layers and use within 1 week. Enjoy!

Smoked Bacon Roses

Servings: 2

Cooking Time: 60 Minutes

Ingredients:

- 1 Pack Bacon, Thick Cut
- 1 Dozen Roses, Fake

Directions:

1. Supply your smoker with wood pellets and follow the start-up procedure. Preheat the grill, with the lid open, to 225° F.
2. Roll each piece of bacon tightly, starting on the thicker side of the strip. Take a toothpick and skewer the middle of the bottom of the bacon roll to keep the bacon from unraveling. With a second toothpick, skewer the bacon roll so that the two toothpicks form an "X" at the bottom of the roll of bacon. Do this to every piece of bacon.
3. Place the bacon rolls directly on the grates of your preheated Grill and smoke for an hour, checking on them every 20 minutes.
4. While the bacon is smoking, rip the petals of the fake roses off of the steams.
5. Once the bacon is fully cooked, remove the toothpicks and pierce the bacon in the head of the steam (where the fake flowers once were). If the bacon isn't staying, you can break a toothpick in half and stick it in the tip of the steam, press firmly and try piercing the bacon again.
6. Place in a nice vase with some babies breath and gift to your Valentine.

3-2-1 Bbq Baby Back Ribs

Servings: 6

Cooking Time: 360 Minutes

Ingredients:

- 2 Rack baby back pork ribs
- 1/3 Cup yellow mustard
- 1/2 Cup apple juice, divided
- 1 Tablespoon Worcestershire sauce
- Pork & Poultry Rub
- 1/2 Cup dark brown sugar
- 1/3 Cup honey, warmed
- 1 Cup 'Que BBQ Sauce

Directions:

1. If your butcher has not already done so, remove the thin silverskin membrane from the bone-side of the ribs by working the tip of a butter knife or a screwdriver underneath the membrane over a middle bone. Use paper towels to get a firm grip, then tear the membrane off.
2. In a small bowl, combine the mustard, 1/4 cup of apple juice (reserve the rest) and the Worcestershire sauce. Spread the mixture thinly on both sides of the ribs and season with Traeger Pork & Poultry Rub.
3. Supply your smoker with wood pellets and follow the start-up procedure. Preheat the grill, with the lid closed, to 180° F. Smoke the ribs, meat-side up for 3 hours.
4. After the ribs have smoked for 3 hours, transfer them to a rimmed baking sheet and increase the grill temperature to 225°F.
5. Tear off four long sheets of heavy-duty aluminum foil. Top with a rack of ribs and pull up the sides to keep the liquid enclosed. Sprinkle half the brown sugar on the rack, then top with half the honey and half the remaining apple juice. Use a bit more apple juice if you want more tender ribs. Lay another piece of foil on top and tightly crimp the edges so there is no leakage. Repeat with the remaining rack of ribs.
6. Return the foiled ribs to the grill and cook for an additional 2 hours.
7. Carefully remove the foil from the ribs and brush the ribs on both sides with Traeger 'Que Sauce. Discard the foil. Arrange the ribs directly on the grill grate and continue to grill until the sauce tightens, 30 to 60 minutes more.
8. Let the ribs rest for a few minutes before serving. Enjoy!

Beer Pork Belly Chili Con Carne

Servings: 4

Cooking Time: 120 Minutes

Ingredients:

- Avocado, Diced
- 2 Bay Leaves
- 1 Lbs Beef Stew Meat
- 12 Oz Beef Stock
- 12 Oz Beer, Bottle
- 15 Oz Black Beans, Rinsed And Drained
- 3 Tbsp Chili Powder
- Cilantro, Chopped
- 1 Tsp Coriander, Ground
- 2 Tsp Cumin, Ground
- 1 Tbsp Flour
- 4 Garlic Cloves, Minced
- 2 Tsp Mexican Oregano, Dried
- 2 Tbsp Olive Oil
- 2 Oz Pancetta, Diced
- Pork Belly, Cut Into 1 Inch Chunks
- 2 Red Onion, Chopped
- Rice, Cooked
- To Taste, Salt & Pepper
- Scallion, Sliced Thin
- 1/4 Cup Tomato Purée

Directions:

1. Supply your smoker with wood pellets and follow the start-up procedure. Preheat the grill, with the lid open, to 425° F. If using a gas or charcoal grill, set it up for medium-high heat. Place Dutch oven on grill and allow to preheat.
2. Heat the olive oil in the Dutch oven, then sauté the pancetta until crisp. Add the onions and sauté for 3 minutes, then add the garlic and sauté 1 minute, until fragrant. Remove mixture with a slotted spoon and set aside.
3. Add the pork belly and beef to the pot to brown, then add the chili powder, cumin, oregano, and coriander. Add the flour and cook for 2 minutes, stirring constantly.
4. Add the beer, beef stock, and tomato purée. Stir well, then return the pancetta mixture to the pot. Add the black beans and bay leaves, then season with salt and pepper.
5. Bring chili to a simmer, then reduce temperature to 325°F and simmer, uncovered, for 2 hours, stirring occasionally, until meat is tender, and sauce has thickened.
6. Remove the chili from the grill, then serve warm with cooked rice, avocado, fresh cilantro, and scallions.

Bbq Pork Belly Burnt Ends

Servings: 8
Cooking Time: 240 Minutes

Ingredients:
- 1 (5-7 lb) skinless pork belly, cut into 1 inch cubes
- Meat Church Honey Hog, Honey Hog Hot or The Gospel Rub
- 1 Cup apple juice, for spritzing
- 1 1/2 Cup Apricot BBQ Sauce
- 1/2 Cup clover honey

Directions:
1. Supply your smoker with wood pellets and follow the start-up procedure. Preheat the grill, with the lid closed, to 275° F.
2. Thoroughly coat all sides of the pork belly cubes with your choice of Meat Church Honey Hog, Honey Hog Hot or The Gospel Rub. I prefer a spicier rub because I finish these with a sweet sauce.
3. Allow the rub to adhere on all sides for at least 15 minutes. Place the pork belly in the Traeger fat-side down. I prefer to do this on a wire rack.
4. Cook the pork belly for 3 hours, spritzing with apple juice every 45 minutes or whenever it starts to look dry. Grill: 275 °F
5. Pull the belly when the meat reaches an internal temperature of 190°F to 195°F. Some people pull the belly a lot earlier, but I want it really tender. Grill: 275 °F Probe: 190 °F
6. Place the cubes in the half-size aluminum pan. Season and toss the cubes with more Meat Church rub.

7. Cover the cubes with Traeger Apricot BBQ Sauce. Drizzle clover honey across the top. Finally, toss the cubes thoroughly to ensure they are completely covered.
8. Return the pan (uncovered) to the Traeger and cook for another hour or until all liquid has reduced and caramelized. Grill: 275 °F
9. Allow them to cool for 15 minutes before serving. Enjoy!

Beer-braised Cabbage With Bacon

Servings: 4
Cooking Time: 30 Minutes

Ingredients:
- 1/4 Pound Bacon, bulk unsliced
- 1 Cup yellow onion, diced
- 1 Cup Apple, diced small
- 2 Pound Cabbage, green, sliced
- salt
- ground black pepper
- 12 Ounce Beer, light

Directions:
1. Supply your smoker with wood pellets and follow the start-up procedure. Preheat the grill, with the lid closed, to 325° F.
2. On a stovetop, heat a large heavy pot or Dutch oven over medium heat. Add the bacon and cook until crisp (about 5 mins). Transfer to a plate lined with paper towels.
3. Return the pot to medium heat. Add the onion and cook for 5 minutes, or until golden brown. Add the apple, stir, then add the cabbage. Sprinkle generously with salt and a touch of black pepper and stir for 3 minutes.
4. Pour in the beer and bring to a boil over medium-high heat. Cover and move the pot immediately into the Traeger.
5. Cook at 325 degrees F (160 C) for 10 minutes. Remove lid and cook for an additional 10-15 more minutes, or until cabbage is tender and most of the liquid has evaporated. Grill: 325 °F
6. Add the reserved bacon and stir into the cabbage. Enjoy!

Lip-smackin' Pork Loin

Servings: 8
Cooking Time: 180 Minutes

Ingredients:
- ¼ cup finely ground coffee
- ¼ cup paprika
- ¼ cup garlic powder
- 2 tablespoons chili powder
- 1 tablespoon packed light brown sugar
- 1 tablespoon ground allspice
- 1 tablespoon ground coriander
- 1 tablespoon freshly ground black pepper

- 2 teaspoons ground mustard
- 1½ teaspoons celery seeds
- 1 (1½- to 2-pound) pork loin roast

Directions:

1. Supply your smoker with wood pellets and follow the start-up procedure. Preheat, with the lid closed, to 250°F.

2. In a small bowl, combine the ground coffee, paprika, garlic powder, chili powder, brown sugar, allspice, coriander, pepper, mustard, and celery seeds to create a rub, and generously apply it to the pork loin roast.

3. Place the pork loin on the grill, fat-side up, close the lid, and roast for 3 hours, or until a meat thermometer inserted in the thickest part of the meat reads 160°F.

4. Let the pork rest for 5 minutes before slicing and serving.

Turkey Stuffing Bacon Balls

Servings: 8
Cooking Time: 25 Minutes

Ingredients:

- 1 Can Cranberry Sauce, Whole Berry (16oz) Can
- 1 jalapeño, diced
- 3 Cup Your Favorite Stuffing, Prepared According to the Package Directions, or Homemade
- 1 Cup Shredded Cooked Turkey
- 6 Slices bacon

Directions:

1. In a small saucepan, combine cranberry sauce and jalapenos. Bring to a boil over medium high heat then reduce the heat to a simmer. Cook for 4-5 minutes then remove from the heat and allow to cool.

2. Supply your smoker with wood pellets and follow the start-up procedure. Preheat the grill, with the lid closed, to 375° F.

3. Start by filling the palm of your hand with approximately 1/4 cup of the stuffing. Use your thumb to create an indentation. Fill the indentation with a heaping tablespoon of the shredded turkey and then close the stuffing all around to form into a ball.

4. Wrap the ball of stuffing with a half a piece of bacon and hold in place with a toothpick, if necessary. Repeat until all of the bombs are made.

5. When ready to cook, place the stuffing balls directly on the grill grate and cook for 25-30 minutes, turning once. The bacon should be crisp. Grill: 375 °F

6. Serve with cranberry jalapeno jelly. Enjoy!

Apple Cider Maple Glazed Ham

Servings: 10 - 14
Cooking Time: 190 Minutes

Ingredients:

- 1 1/2 Cups Apple Cider
- 3 Tbsp Apple Cider Vinegar
- 1/2 Cup Packed Light Brown Sugar
- 2 Tbsp Unsalted Butter
- ¼ Tsp Chili Powder
- 2 Tsp Cornstarch
- 3 Tbsp Dijon Mustard
- ½ Tsp Ground Cinnamon
- ¼ Tsp Ground Cloves
- Large Cast Iron Skillet
- 1/2 Cup Pure Maple Syrup
- 2 Tsp Tennessee Apple Butter Rub
- 1 Spiral-Sliced Ham, Bone-In
- ¼ Tsp Thyme, Dried
- 3 Tbsp Yellow Mustard

Directions:

1. Remove ham from refrigerator and let rest at room temperature for 2-3 hours.

2. Supply your smoker with wood pellets and follow the start-up procedure. Preheat the grill, with the lid open, to 300° F. If using a gas or charcoal grill, set heat to medium-high heat.

3. Create a bed of foil in the bottom of a large cast iron pan, making sure to have enough to seal entire ham. Set ham inside foil and add one cup of water to the bottom of pan. Pour some glaze (about ⅓ of mixture) over ham, making sure to coat in between slices. Wrap ham tightly in foil and grill for 2 hours.

4. Remove ham from grill and increase temperature to 400° F. Carefully unfold foil to expose ham and pour an additional ⅓ of glaze over ham. Leave ham exposed and grill for 30 minutes or until edges are golden brown and caramelized.

5. Remove ham from grill and carefully remove foil from underneath ham, so that ham is directly sitting on cast iron. Return to grill, brush with more glaze, and grill another 15 minutes. Remove ham from grill, let rest for 15 minutes, then carve and serve with remaining glaze.

Bacon Grilled Cheese Sandwich

Servings: 4
Cooking Time: 10 Minutes

Ingredients:

- mayonnaise
- 8 Slices Texas toast
- 16 Slices cheddar cheese
- 1 Pound applewood smoked bacon slices, cooked
- butter, softened

Directions:

1. Supply your smoker with wood pellets and follow the start-up procedure. Preheat the grill, with the lid closed, to 350° F.

2. Spread a little bit of mayonnaise on each piece of bread.

3. Place 1 piece of cheddar cheese on bread slice then top with a couple slices of bacon. Add another slice of cheese then top with the other piece of bread. Spread softened butter on the exterior of the top piece of bread.

4. When the grill is hot, place the grilled cheese directly on a cleaned, oiled grill grate buttered side down. Spread softened butter on the exterior of the top slice. Grill: 350 °F

5. Cook the grilled cheese on the first side for 5 to 7 minutes until grill marks develop and the cheese has begun to melt. Flip the sandwich and repeat on the other side. Grill: 350 °F

6. Remove from the grill when the cheese is melted and the exterior is lightly toasted. Enjoy!

Smoked Chili Con Queso By Doug Scheiding

Servings: 8
Cooking Time: 45 Minutes

Ingredients:
- 1 Pound hot pork sausage
- 1 (2 lb) block Velveeta cheese
- 1 Pound smoked Gouda cheese
- 1 (10 oz) can RO*TEL Original Diced Tomatoes and Green Chilies
- 1 (10 oz) can RO*TEL Fire Roasted Diced Tomatoes and Green Chilies
- 1 (10 oz) can cream of mushroom soup
- 4 Tablespoon Coffee Rub
- 1/2 Cup chopped cilantro

Directions:
1. Heat a medium cast iron skillet over medium heat and fully cook pork sausage, breaking into small chunks as you go. Remove the sausage and drain and discard the fat.

2. Supply your smoker with wood pellets and follow the start-up procedure. Preheat the grill, with the lid closed, to 350° F.

3. Use a 4 to 5 quart cast iron Dutch oven or other oven safe dish. Divide the block of Velveeta into 5 to 6 large pieces and cut the smoked Gouda into small 1 inch cubes. Add the canned ingredients including the liquid. Add the sausage and Traeger Coffee Rub last. Grill: 350 °F

4. Smoke the queso for 45 minutes on the Traeger, stirring 3 to 4 times. Grill: 350 °F

5. Add most of the cilantro the last 5 minutes of smoking. Sprinkle remaining cilantro on the top before serving. Enjoy!

Leftover Pulled Pork With Eggs

Servings: 4
Cooking Time: 20 Minutes

Ingredients:

- 1 Teaspoon Coarse Black Pepper
- 4 Eggs
- 1 Green Bell Pepper, Diced
- 1 Teaspoon Kosher Salt
- 3 Tablespoons Olive Oil
- 1 Small Onion, Diced
- 1 Tablespoon Hickory Bacon Seasoning
- 2 Cups Of Leftover Pulled Pork
- 1 Red Bell Peppers, Diced
- 1 ½ Pounds Red Potatoes, Diced

Directions:
1. Supply your smoker with wood pellets and follow the start-up procedure. Preheat the grill, with the lid open, to 350° F.

2. In a large bowl, toss the potatoes with 2 tablespoons of olive oil and Hickory Bacon seasoning. You want to get the potatoes coated well and evenly with the oil and seasoning.

3. Add the potatoes to the skillet and cook on the grill for 12-15 minutes or until they're cooked all the way through and browned. Remove from the pan and set aside.

4. Add 1 more tablespoon of olive to the pan and cook the peppers and onion for 2-3 minutes or until soft. Remove from the pan and set aside.

5. Add the pork to the pan and cook until warmed through. Because the pork is already cooked this should only be 1-2 minutes so the meat stays moist.

6. Add the potatoes, peppers and onions back to the pan, then give everything in the skillet a quick mix, so the hash is evenly blended.

7. Crack the 4 eggs on top of the hash. Try to space them evenly around. Sprinkle the teaspoons of salt and pepper on top of the eggs, then place the lid on top of the pan and allow the eggs to cook for 5-6 minutes, or until the whites are firm and the yolks are still runny.

8. Remove from the grill and serve immediately.

Mini Sausage Rolls

Servings: 4
Cooking Time: 25 Minutes

Ingredients:
- 3/4 Cup dry mustard
- 3/4 Cup distilled white vinegar
- 1/2 Cup honey
- 4 egg yolk, beaten
- 2 Pound Sausage, Uncooked
- ground sage
- 1 Small onion, diced small
- 17 1/2 Ounce frozen puff pastry

Directions:

1. Make the mustard: Combine the mustard and vinegar in a small mixing bowl. Cover with plastic wrap and let sit overnight at room temperature to develop the flavors. Transfer the mustard mixture to a small heavy saucepan and add the honey and egg yolks. Cook over low heat, whisking constantly, until thickened, about 7 minutes. Cool, then refrigerate until serving time.

2. In a medium mixing bowl, thoroughly combine the sausage and onion. On a lightly floured work surface, roll each sheet of thawed puff pastry - there are two to a package - into an 11 by 10-1/2 inch rectangle.

3. Using a pizza cutter or knife, cut each rectangle widthwise into three strips, each 3-1/2 inches wide. Wet your hands and mold some of the sausage into a tube-like shape. Lay it down the center of one of the puff pastry strips.

4. Wrap the pastry around the sausage and seal the seams with a bit of beaten egg. Repeat with the remaining sausage and puff pastry. Put all the rolls seam side down on your work surface and brush the tops lightly with the egg.

5. Cut the rolls into pieces about 1-1/2 inches long and transfer to a rimmed baking sheet lined with parchment paper. Leave about an inch between each roll. Supply your smoker with wood pellets and follow the start-up procedure. Preheat the grill, with the lid closed, to 350° F.

6. Bake the sausage rolls for about 25 minutes, or until the sausage is cooked through and the pastry is golden brown. Serve hot with the honey mustard. Grill: 350 °F

Cajun Double-smoked Ham

Servings: 12-15
Cooking Time: 300 Minutes

Ingredients:
- 1 (5- or 6-pound) bone-in smoked ham
- 1 batch Cajun Rub
- 3 tablespoons honey

Directions:
1. Supply your smoker with wood pellets and follow the start-up procedure. Preheat the grill, with the lid closed, to 225°F.
2. Generously season the ham with the rub and place it either in a pan or directly on the grill grate. Smoke it for 1 hour.
3. Drizzle the honey over the ham and continue to smoke it until the ham's internal temperature reaches 145°F.
4. Remove the ham from the grill and let it rest for 5 to 10 minutes, before thinly slicing and serving.

Pickled-pepper Pork Chops

Servings: 4
Cooking Time: 50 Minutes

Ingredients:

- 4 (1-inch-thick) pork chops
- ½ cup pickled jalapeño juice or pickle juice
- ¼ cup chopped pickled (jarred) jalapeño pepper slices
- ¼ cup chopped roasted red peppers
- ¼ cup canned diced tomatoes, well-drained
- ¼ cup chopped scallions
- 2 teaspoons poultry seasoning
- 2 teaspoons salt
- 2 teaspoons freshly ground black pepper

Directions:
1. Pour the jalapeño juice into a large container with a lid. Add the pork chops, cover, and marinate in the refrigerator for at least 4 hours or overnight, supplementing with or substituting pickle juice as desired.
2. In a small bowl, combine the chopped pickled jalapeños, roasted red peppers, tomatoes, scallions, and poultry seasoning to make a relish. Set aside.
3. Remove the pork chops from the marinade and shake off any excess. Discard the marinade. Season both sides of the chops with the salt and pepper.
4. Supply your smoker with wood pellets and follow the start-up procedure. Preheat, with the lid closed, to 325°F.
5. To serve, divide the chops among plates and top with the pickled pepper relish.

Jamaican Jerk Pork Chops

Servings: 4
Cooking Time: 720 Minutes

Ingredients:
- 4 thick pork rib or loin chops, each about 12oz (340g) and 1 inch (2.5cm) thick
- for the marinade
- ½ to 1 Scotch bonnet or habanero pepper, destemmed, deseeded, and coarsely chopped, plus more
- 2 scallions, trimmed, white and green parts coarsely chopped
- 1 garlic clove, peeled and coarsely chopped
- juice of 1 lime
- 2 tbsp vegetable oil
- 2 tbsp distilled water
- 1 tbsp light soy sauce
- 2 tsp coarsely chopped fresh thyme leaves
- 2 tsp peeled and minced fresh ginger
- 2 tsp dark brown sugar or low-carb substitute, plus more
- 1 tsp coarse salt, plus more
- ½ tsp freshly ground black pepper
- ½ tsp ground allspice
- ½ tsp ground nutmeg
- ½ tsp ground cinnamon

Directions:

1. In a blender, make the jerk marinade by combining the ingredients. Blend until fairly smooth. Taste for seasoning, adding more Scotch bonnet, brown sugar, or salt. Place the pork chops in a resealable plastic bag and pour the marinade over them, turning and massaging the bag to thoroughly coat the meat. Refrigerate for 2 to 4 hours.

2. Supply your smoker with wood pellets and follow the start-up procedure. Preheat the grill, with the lid closed, to 425° F.

3. Remove the pork from the marinade and scrape off the excess. (Discard the marinade.) Grill the chops until the internal temperature reaches 145°F (63°C), about 6 to 8 minutes per side.

4. Transfer the chops to a platter. Let rest for 2 minutes before serving.

Brats In Beer

Servings: 4
Cooking Time: 60 Minutes

Ingredients:
- 4 Can (12 oz) cans beer
- 2 Large onions, peeled and sliced into rings
- 2 Tablespoon butter
- 10 uncooked bratwurst
- 10 hot dog buns
- mustard, for serving

Directions:
1. Pour beer into a large saucepan. Add onions and butter. Bring to a simmer on the stovetop.

2. Supply your smoker with wood pellets and follow the start-up procedure. Preheat the grill, with the lid closed, to 350° F.

3. Put a deep disposable aluminum foil pan on one side of the Traeger. Carefully pour the beer and onions from the saucepan into the pan on the grill.

4. Arrange the brats on the other side of the grill grate. Grill the brats until cooked through, turning frequently with tongs, about 20 to 25 minutes. Grill: 350 °F

5. Transfer the brats to the beer mixture and cover the pan tightly with aluminum foil.

6. Let the brats simmer until the onions are tender, 45 minutes to an hour. Grill: 350 °F

7. Butter the cut sides of the buns and toast on the grill.

8. To serve, lift a brat out of the mixture and put it on a bun. Top it with onions and mustard. Enjoy!

Orange & Maple Baked Ham

Servings: 2
Cooking Time: 120 Minutes

Ingredients:
- 2/3 Cup orange juice

- 1/3 Cup maple syrup
- 1/3 Cup Marmalade, Orange
- 1/8 Cup Dijon mustard
- 1 1/3 Tablespoon apple cider vinegar
- 1/2 Teaspoon ground cinnamon
- 1/8 Teaspoon ground cloves
- 2/3 ham

Directions:
1. Supply your smoker with wood pellets and follow the start-up procedure. Preheat the grill, with the lid closed, to 325° F.

2. Meanwhile, make the glaze: In a small saucepan, combine the orange juice, the maple syrup, marmalade, mustard, vinegar, cinnamon, and cloves.

3. Warm over low heat, whisking to combine the ingredients. Remove from the heat and reserve.

4. Place ham in large roasting pan lined with aluminum foil. Place pan on grill and cook for 1.5 hours. Grill: 325 °F

5. Open grill and glaze ham with reserved mixture. Continue cooking for another 30 minutes or until a thermometer is inserted into the thickest part of the meat and reaches an internal temperatures of 135 degrees F. Grill: 325 °F Probe: 135 °F

6. Remove ham from grill and allow to rest for 20 minutes before serving.

7. Warm remaining sauce and serve with ham if desired. Enjoy!

St. Louis Bbq Ribs

Servings: 4
Cooking Time: 240 Minutes

Ingredients:
- 2 Rack St. Louis-style ribs
- 1/4 Cup Pork & Poultry Rub
- 1 Cup apple juice
- 1 Bottle Sweet & Heat BBQ Sauce

Directions:
1. Trim ribs and peel off membrane from the back of ribs. Apply an even coat of rub to the front and back of ribs. Let sit for 20 minutes and up to 4 hours if refrigerated.

2. Supply your smoker with wood pellets and follow the start-up procedure. Preheat the grill, with the lid closed, to 225° F.

3. Place ribs bone side down on grill grate. Put apple juice in a spray bottle and evenly spray ribs. Grill: 225 °F

4. After 3 hours, remove ribs from grill and wrap them in aluminum foil. Leave an opening at one end, pour in remainder of apple juice (about 6 oz) into the foil and wrap tightly.

5. Place ribs back on grill, meat side down and smoke for an additional 3 hours. Grill: 225 °F Probe: 203 °F

6. After 1 hour, start checking the internal temperature of ribs. Ribs are done when the internal temperature reaches 203°F. Grill: 225 °F

7. When ribs are done, remove from the foil and brush a light layer of sauce on the front and back on the ribs.

8. Return to the grill and cook an additional 10 minutes to set the sauce. Grill: 225 °F

9. After sauce has set, take ribs off the grill and let rest for 10 minutes. To serve, slice ribs in between the bones. Enjoy!

Baked Beans

Servings: 12
Cooking Time: 180 Minutes

Ingredients:
- 1 Pack Bacon
- 1/2 Cup Brown Sugar
- 1 Coca Cola, Can
- 2 Cans Mixed Beans
- 1/3 Cup Molasses
- 4 Cans Pork And Beans
- 1 Red Onion, Chopped
- 1/3 Cup Yellow Mustard

Directions:
1. Supply your smoker with wood pellets and follow the start-up procedure. Preheat the grill, with the lid closed, to 275° F.
2. Combine all the ingredients and stir until combined.
3. Smoked for 2.5 hours covered. For the last 30 minutes, smoke uncovered.
4. Serve hot. Enjoy!

Spiced Pork Belly

Servings: 4
Cooking Time: 130 Minutes

Ingredients:
- 2lb (1kg) skinless pork belly
- for the rub
- 2 tbsp fine kosher salt
- 2 tbsp granulated white or light brown sugar or low-carb substitute
- 2 tsp freshly ground black pepper
- 2 tsp ground mustard
- 2 tsp Chinese five-spice powder

Directions:
1. In a small bowl, make the rub by combining the ingredients. Mix well. Lightly season the pork belly on all sides with the rub. Cover and refrigerate overnight.
2. Supply your smoker with wood pellets and follow the start-up procedure. Preheat the grill, with the lid closed, to 450° F.
3. Place the pork belly on the grate and roast for 30 minutes, turning once. Lower the temperature to 275°F (135°C). Roast the pork until tender and the internal temperature reaches 185°F (85°C), about 1 to 1½ hours more.

4. Remove the pork belly from the grill and let cool completely. Wrap tightly in plastic wrap and refrigerate until firm and well chilled.

5. Preheat the grill to 450°F (232°C).

6. Cut the pork belly into slices, slabs, or cubes. Place the pork on the grate and grill until the edges crisp, about 8 to 10 minutes, turning as needed.

7. Remove the pork from the grill and serve immediately.

Cider Glazed Baked Holiday Ham

Servings: 6
Cooking Time: 120 Minutes

Ingredients:
- 3 apples, cored and cut into thick slices
- 1 Large ham
- 4 Cup apple cider, divided
- 1/4 Cup bourbon
- 1/4 Cup Dijon mustard
- 1/4 Cup honey or maple syrup
- 1/2 Teaspoon ground cinnamon
- 1/4 Teaspoon ground cloves
- 1 Pinch ground nutmeg or allspice

Directions:
1. Supply your smoker with wood pellets and follow the start-up procedure. Preheat the grill, with the lid closed, to 325° F.
2. Line a roasting pan with heavy-duty foil for easier clean-up.
3. Arrange the apple slices in the bottom of the roasting pan for a natural roasting rack. Place ham on top of the apple slices and pour remaining 1 cup of apple cider around the ham.
4. Place roasting pan directly on grill grate and bake for 1-1/2 hours. Grill: 325 °F
5. For the glaze, combine remaining 3 cups of apple cider and bourbon in a small saucepan and bring to a boil over medium-high heat. Simmer until reduced by one-third. Whisk in the mustard, honey, cinnamon, cloves and nutmeg.
6. Glaze ham with apple cider mixture as needed (use any left over for serving) and continue cooking for another 30 minutes or until a thermometer inserted into the thickest part of the meat reaches an internal temperatures of 140°F. Grill: 325 °F Probe: 140 °F
7. Remove ham from grill and allow to rest for 20 minutes before serving.
8. Warm remaining sauce and serve with ham if desired. Enjoy!

Baked Sage & Sausage Stuffing

Servings: 4
Cooking Time: 45 Minutes

Ingredients:

- 1 Pound Sage-Flavored Sausage, Such as Bob Evans Or Jimmy Dean
- 1/2 Cup onion, diced
- 1/2 Cup celery, diced
- 14 Ounce (14 oz) package herb seasoned stuffing
- 1/2 Cup dried sweetened cranberries
- 2 Cup low sodium chicken broth
- 6 Tablespoon butter
- butter

Directions:

1. Brown the sausage in a large frying pan, breaking up the sausage with a wooden spoon.
2. Add the onion and celery and cook until softened. Drain any excess fat. Transfer to a large mixing bowl. Add the stuffing mix and cranberries, if using.
3. Warm the chicken broth over medium-low heat; add butter and cook until melted. Toss with the bread/sausage mixture and mix lightly.
4. Butter a 3-qt casserole or baking dish. Do not compress the mixture or it will be dense.
5. Supply your smoker with wood pellets and follow the start-up procedure. Preheat the grill, with the lid closed, to 350° F.
6. Bake the stuffing, covered, for 35 to 45 minutes; uncover during the last 20 minutes of cooking if you prefer a crunchier texture. Grill: 350 °F
7. Remove from grill and serve. Enjoy!

Grilled Dr. Pepper Ribs

Servings: 4
Cooking Time: 300 Minutes

Ingredients:

- Aluminum Foil
- 2 Racks Baby Back Ribs
- 1 Cup Bbq Sauce
- 1 Stick Butter, Melted
- 1/2 Cup Dark Brown Sugar
- 12 Oz Dr. Pepper Soda
- 1/4 Cup Sweet Rib Rub
- 1/4 Cup Yellow Mustard

Directions:

1. Supply your smoker with wood pellets and follow the start-up procedure. Preheat the grill, with the lid open, to 225° F. If using a gas or charcoal grill, set it up for low, indirect heat.

2. After the grill comes to temp, place the ribs directly on the grill grates, close the lid, and smoke for 2 hours.
3. In a glass measuring cup, whisk together butter, brown sugar, and 8 ounces of Dr. Pepper.
4. Pour half of the mixture on a foil-lined sheet tray.
5. Place ribs, meat-side down, on top of the mixture, then pour remaining mixture on the bone-side. Tent the sheet tray with foil, then return to the grill for another 2 hours.
6. Remove ribs from liquid and set meat-side up directly on the grill grate.
7. Whisk together BBQ sauce and 4 ounces of Dr. Pepper, then brush half of the sauce all over the ribs.
8. Increase temperature to 275°F and cook an additional 30 to 60 minutes until ribs are tender, and meat pulls away from the bones.
9. Place ribs on a sheet tray, allow to rest for 10 minutes, then slice and serve with remaining BBQ sauce.

Pineapple-pepper Pork Kebabs

Servings: 12-15
Cooking Time: 240 Minutes

Ingredients:

- 1 (20-ounce) bottle hoisin sauce
- ½ cup Sriracha
- ¼ cup honey
- ¼ cup apple cider vinegar
- 2 tablespoons canola oil
- 2 teaspoons minced garlic
- 2 teaspoons onion powder
- 1 teaspoon ground ginger
- 1 teaspoon salt
- 1 teaspoon freshly ground black pepper
- 2 pounds thick-cut pork chops or pork loin, cut into 2-inch cubes
- 10 ounces fresh pineapple, cut into chunks
- 1 red onion, cut into wedges
- 1 bag mini sweet peppers, tops removed and seeded
- 12 metal or wooden skewers (soaked in water for 30 minutes if wooden)

Directions:

1. In a small bowl, stir together the hoisin, Sriracha, honey, vinegar, oil, minced garlic, onion powder, ginger, salt, and black pepper to create the marinade. Reserve ¼ cup for basting.
2. Toss the pork cubes, pineapple chunks, onion wedges, and mini peppers in the remaining marinade. Cover and refrigerate for at least 1 hour or up to 4 hours.
3. Supply your smoker with wood pellets and follow the start-up procedure. Preheat, with the lid closed, to 450°F.

4. Remove the pork, pineapple, and veggies from the marinade; do not rinse. Discard the marinade.

5. Use the double-skewer technique to assemble the kebabs (see Tip below). Thread each of 6 skewers with a piece of pork, a piece of pineapple, a piece of onion, and a sweet mini pepper, making sure that the skewer goes through the left side of the ingredients. Repeat the threading on each skewer two more times. Double-skewer the kebabs by sticking another 6 skewers through the right side of the ingredients.

6. Place the kebabs directly on the grill, close the lid, and smoke for 10 to 12 minutes, turning once. They are done when a meat thermometer inserted in the pork reads 160°F.

Grilled German Sausage With A Smoky Traeger Twist

Servings: 8
Cooking Time: 120 Minutes

Ingredients:
- 2 Tablespoon Jacobsen Salt Co. Pure Kosher Sea Salt
- 1 Teaspoon The Sausage Maker Instacure #1
- 1 Tablespoon ground nutmeg
- 2 Teaspoon ground mace
- 1 Teaspoon ground ginger
- 4 Pound ground pork, 80% lean
- 1 Pound ground veal or ground beef
- 2 Large eggs
- 1 Cup nonfat dry milk powder

Directions:
1. Combine salt, Instacure #1, nutmeg, mace and ginger in a large pitcher or small bowl. Add the milk and eggs. Beat until well combined. Pour the egg mixture over the ground meat and mix gently. Using your hands, mix in the milk powder until evenly distributed.

2. Form the meat into sausage links, roughly 4 to 6 inches in length.

3. Supply your smoker with wood pellets and follow the start-up procedure. Preheat the grill, with the lid closed, to 225° F.

4. Smoke for approximately 2 hours, or until the internal temperature reaches 175°F. Serve immediately or refrigerate until ready to serve. Enjoy! Grill: 225 °F Probe: 175 °F

Honey Glazed Pork Chops

Servings: 6
Cooking Time: 16 Minutes

Ingredients:
- 4-6 Pork Chop
- 1/2 Cup of Honey
- 4 Tablespoons Soy Sauce
- 2 Tablespoons Olive Oil
- 2 Garlic Cloves, pressed
- Salt & Pepper

Directions:
1. Supply your smoker with wood pellets and follow the start-up procedure. Preheat the grill, with the lid closed, to 350° F.

2. Mix together the honey, soy sauce, and garlic in a small dish.

3. Brush the olive oil over the pork chops and sprinkle with salt and pepper.

4. Place the pork chops on the grill and brush the honey mixture over the top side.

5. When you flip the pork chops over, brush the second side with the honey mixture.

6. Grill for about 8 minutes on each side or until a thermometer inserted reads 170 degrees. Brush a final layer of the honey glaze over the pork chops before serving. Enjoy!

Maple Syrup Bacon Wrapped Tenderloin

Servings: 5
Cooking Time: 30 Minutes

Ingredients:
- 1 Package Bacon, Thick Cut
- 1/4 Cup Maple Syrup
- 2 Tbsp Olive Oil
- 3 Tbsp Competition Smoked Rub
- 1 Trimmed With Silver Skin Removed Pork, Tenderloin

Directions:
1. Lay the strips of bacon out flat, with each strip slightly overlapping the other.

2. Sprinkle the pork tenderloin with 1 tablespoon of the Competition Smoked Rub and lay in the center.

3. Wrap with bacon over the tenderloin and tuck in the ends.

4. In a small bowl, mix the olive oil, maple syrup and remaining seasoning together and brush onto the wrapped tenderloin.

5. Supply your smoker with wood pellets and follow the start-up procedure. Preheat the grill, with the lid open, to 350° F.

6. When the grill is ready, place your tenderloin on the grill and cook, turning, for 15 minutes.

7. Increase the grill temperature to 400°F and grill for another 15 minutes or until the internal temperature is 145°F. Serve and enjoy!

St Louis Style Bbq Ribs With Texas Spicy Bbq Sauce

Servings: 8
Cooking Time: 300 Minutes

Ingredients:
- 3 Rack St. Louis-style ribs, membrane removed
- 4 Tablespoon Rub
- 6 Tablespoon butter
- 1 1/2 Cup brown sugar
- 1 1/2 Cup agave
- 1 1/2 Cup Texas Spicy BBQ Sauce

Directions:
1. Supply your smoker with wood pellets and follow the start-up procedure. Preheat the grill, with the lid closed, to 250° F.
2. Season ribs with Traeger rub and place directly on grill grate rib side down or in a Traeger rib rack with the bone resting on the rack. Cook for 3 hours. Grill: 250 °F
3. Stack 2 pieces of tin foil on the table large enough to cover one rack of ribs. In the center of the foil place 3 tablespoons butter, 1/2 cup brown sugar, and 1/2 cup agave. Place the rib rack meat side down on top of the brown sugar mixture and wrap tightly. Repeat with remaining 2 racks.
4. Place all ribs directly on the grill grate meat side down and cook an additional 1-1/2 to 2 hours or until internal temperature reaches 203°F. Grill: 250 °F Probe: 203 °F
5. Remove ribs from the grill and cover each rack with 1/2 cup Texas Spicy BBQ sauce.
6. Rewrap and return to grill an additional 10 minutes allowing sauce to thicken. Grill: 250 °F
7. Remove ribs from the grill, slice and enjoy!

Pulled Pork Taquitos With Sour Cream

Servings: 4
Cooking Time: 300 Minutes

Ingredients:
- ⅓ Cup Apple Cider Vinegar
- ½ Cup, Plus Extra For Dipping Bbq Sauce
- 4 Cups Chicken Broth
- 1 Teaspoon Chili Powder
- ⅓ Cup Mustard
- 2 Tbsp Olive Oil
- 6 Tbsp Pulled Pork Rub
- 4 Lb. Pork Shoulder, Bone In
- 1 ½ Cup Sharp Cheddar Cheese, Shredded
- ¼ Cup Sour Cream
- 10 Flour Tortillas

Directions:

1. Supply your smoker with wood pellets and follow the start-up procedure. Preheat the grill, with the lid open, to 400° F. If using a gas or charcoal grill, set the temp to medium heat. In a bowl, combine the chicken broth, mustard, apple cider vinegar, and 1 tablespoon of Pulled Pork Seasoning. Whisk well to combine and set aside.
2. Generously season the pork shoulder with the remaining 3 tablespoons of Pulled Pork Seasoning on all sides of the pork shoulder, then place on the grill and sear on all sides until golden brown, about 10 minutes.
3. Remove the pork shoulder from the grill and place in the disposable aluminum pan. Pour the chicken broth mixture over the pork shoulder. It should come about 1/3 to ½ way up the side of the pork shoulder. Cover the top of the pan tightly with aluminum foil.
4. Reduce the temperature of your grill to 250°F. Place the foil pan on the grill and grill for four to five hours, or until the pork is tender and falling off the bone.
5. Remove the pork from the grill and allow to cool slightly. Place on a cutting board and shred with meat claws, reserving about 2.5 cups. Fire up grill to 425°F.
6. In a mixing bowl, combine sour cream, BBQ sauce, and chili powder. Stir in cheddar cheese and pork until well combined.
7. Lay each tortilla flat on your work surface and scoop about ¼ cup of pork mixture in the center, lengthwise. Roll up tightly and place seam side down on baking sheet. Repeat with all tortillas, then brush tops lightly with olive oil.
8. Transfer baking sheet to grill and cook for 15-20 minutes at 400°F, or until cheese has melted and tortilla edges have turned a golden brown. Serve with extra BBQ sauce for dipping and enjoy!

Bacon Onion Ring

Servings: 6
Cooking Time: 60 Minutes

Ingredients:
- 16 Slices bacon
- 2 Whole Vidalia onion, sliced
- 1 Tablespoon Chili Garlic Sauce
- 1 Tablespoon yellow mustard
- 1 Teaspoon honey

Directions:
1. Wrap a piece of bacon around an individual onion ring; continue until bacon is gone. Some onion slices may be larger and require 2 pieces of bacon to complete a ring.
2. Place a skewer through the bacon-wrapped onion slice, to keep bacon from unraveling while cooking.
3. Supply your smoker with wood pellets and follow the start-up procedure. Preheat the grill, with the lid closed, to 400° F.

4. Meanwhile, mix chili garlic sauce and yellow mustard in a small bowl until incorporated; add honey.

5. Place skewers on the grill grate and cook for approximately 90 minutes, flipping after 45 minutes. Enjoy! Grill: 400 °F

Grilled St. Louis Style Ribs With Tequila Bbq

Servings: 8
Cooking Time: 240 Minutes

Ingredients:

- 1/2 Cup Brown Sugar
- 2 Garlic, Cloves
- 3 Tbsp Honey
- 1 Cup Ketchup
- 1/2 Squeezed Lime
- 3 Tbsp Molasses
- 1 Jar Mustard
- 2 Slabs Slabs St. Louis-Style Rib Racks
- 1 Bottle Sweet Heat Rub
- 1/4 Cup Tequila Blanco

Directions:

1. First, make the barbecue sauce. In a mixing bowl, add the ketchup, brown sugar, garlic cloves, molasses, honey, tequila, lime, and 1 tbsp Sweet Heat Rub. Mix together well until glaze is blended together. Set aside.

2. Prepare the ribs. Pat the ribs dry with paper towels, then pull the thin membrane off the back of the ribs and discard. Using a basting brush, coat the meat on both sides with a thin layer of mustard and season heavily with Sweet Heat Rub until the ribs are completely coated. Repeat with the second rack of ribs. Place the ribs on a baking sheet and refrigerate overnight, or for 12 hours if you choose to.

3. Once the ribs have finished marinating, remove them from the refrigerator and set out two sheets of large, heavy duty aluminum foil. Place one rack of ribs on each sheet of foil, meat-side down, and fold the edges over to form a sealed pouch.

4. Supply your smoker with wood pellets and follow the start-up procedure. Preheat the grill, with the lid open, to 225° F. If you're using a gas or charcoal grill, set it up for low, indirect heat. Place the rib packets on the grill, meat-side up, and smoke for 2-3 hours, or until the ribs are nearly tender.

5. Remove the ribs from the grill and take the aluminum foil off the ribs and place them back onto the grill for another hour. Brush generously with the tequila barbecue sauce on both sides, then grill for 5 minutes, meat- side up. Baste the ribs one more time with the barbecue sauce, then flip them meat-side down and grill for a final 5 minutes. The ribs should be sticky and caramelized.

Remove the ribs from the grill and serve immediately with the remaining barbecue sauce.

Grilled Bacon Dog

Servings: 4
Cooking Time: 25 Minutes

Ingredients:

- 16 hot dogs
- 16 Slices Bacon, sliced
- 2 Vidalia onion, sliced
- 16 hot dog buns
- 'Que BBQ Sauce
- Velveeta cheese

Directions:

1. Supply your smoker with wood pellets and follow the start-up procedure. Preheat the grill, with the lid closed, to 375° F.

2. Wrap bacon strips around the hot dogs, and grill directly on the grill grate for 10 minutes each side. Grill onions at the same time as the hot dogs, and cook for 10 -15 minutes.

3. Open hot dog buns and spread Traeger 'Que sauce, the grilled hot dogs, cheese sauce and grilled onions. Top with vegetables. Serve, enjoy!

Grilled Lasagna With Cold-smoked Mozzarella

Servings: 8-12
Cooking Time: 70 Minutes

Ingredients:

- 15 Oz. Ricotta Cheese
- 3 Cups Cold-Smoked Mozzarella, Grated Divided
- 2 Eggs
- 6 Garlic Cloves, Chopped
- 1 Tsp Garlic Powder
- 1 Cup Grated Parmesan Cheese, Divided
- 1 Lb. Italian Sausage
- 1 Tbsp Italian Seasoning
- 1 Pkg."No-Bake" Lasagna Noodles
- 48 Oz. Marinara Sauce
- 1 Lb. Mozzarella Block
- 1 Tbsp Olive Oil
- 1 Tbsp Chopped Oregano
- ¼ Cup Italian Parsley, Chopped
- 1 Yellow Onion, Chopped

Directions:

1. In a glass bowl, mix together the eggs, Italian seasoning, garlic powder, ricotta cheese, ½ cup parmesan cheese, and 1 cup of

smoked mozzarella, and 2 tablespoons of parsley. Cover and refrigerate for 1 hour.

2.   Supply your smoker with wood pellets and follow the start-up procedure. Preheat the grill, with the lid open, to 400° F. If using a gas or charcoal grill, set it up for medium-high heat. Place a cast iron skillet on the grill grates and allow to preheat.

3.   Heat olive oil in skillet, then add Italian sausage and cook for 5 minutes, then add in onion and garlic, and cook an additional 3 minutes. Remove from heat and stir in 1 tablespoon of parsley and dried oregano. Set aside and reduce grill temperature to 350° F.

4.   To assemble, begin by covering the bottom of a 9x13 pan with 1 cup of sauce. For the first layer, place a single layer of uncooked noodles over the sauce, followed by ⅓ of the ricotta cheese mixture, half of the Italian sausage, 1 cup of mozzarella cheese, and 1 cup of sauce. Repeat for layer two with a single layer of uncooked lasagna noodles, ⅓ of the ricotta cheese mixture, and 1 ½ cups of sauce. Repeat for layer three with a layer of uncooked lasagna noodles, remaining ricotta mixture, remaining Italian sausage, 1 cup of sauce. For the final layer, add a layer of uncooked lasagna noodles, remaining sauce, and remaining 1 cup mozzarella plus ½ cup parmesan.

5.   Transfer lasagna to grill and cook, covered with foil, for 35 minutes. Remove foil and continue cooking for 10 minutes, sprinkle with additional parmesan and parsley, if desired. Remove from grill and let stand 15 minutes before serving.

Crown Roast Of Pork

Servings: 4
Cooking Time: 60 Minutes

Ingredients:
- 1 Whole Crown Roast of Pork, 12-14 ribs
- 1/4 Cup Pork & Poultry Rub
- 1 Cup apple juice
- 1 Cup Apricot BBQ Sauce

Directions:
1.   Supply your smoker with wood pellets and follow the start-up procedure. Preheat the grill, with the lid closed, to 375° F.

2.   Season the pork roast liberally with Traeger Pork and Poultry Rub. Let sit at room temperature for 30 minutes. Wrap each tip of the crown roast in a small piece of aluminum foil. This will protect the bones during the cook and prevent them from turning black.

3.   Place the roast directly on the grill grate and cook for about 90 minutes spraying with apple juice every 30 minutes or so.

4.   When the roast reaches an internal temperature of 125 degrees F, remove the aluminum foil from the bones and return to the grill.

5.   Spray again with apple juice and continue to cook until the internal temperature reaches 135 degrees F in the thickest part of the roast. In the last ten minutes, baste the roast with the Apricot BBQ Sauce to let the glaze set.

6.   Remove from the grill, tent with foil, and let it rest 15-20 minutes before slicing. Enjoy!

Spiced Coffee-rubbed Ribs

Servings: 6 - 8
Cooking Time: 360 Minutes

Ingredients:
- 1 Tbsp Ancho Chili Powder
- Ground Black Pepper
- ½ Tsp Cocoa Powder
- 2 Tbsp Coffee
- ½ Tsp Coriander, Ground
- 1 Tbsp Dark Brown Sugar
- 1 Tsp Garlic Powder
- 2 Tbsp Kosher Salt
- 1 Tsp Onion Powder
- 1 Tsp Oregano
- 2 Tbsp Paprika
- 8 Lbs. Pork Spareribs

Directions:
1.   Begin by preparing the dry rub. In a mixing bowl, whisk together the coffee, salt, paprika, brown sugar, oregano, garlic powder, onion powder, black pepper, cocoa powder and coriander. Set aside.

2.   Remove the membrane from the back of your ribs: Take a butter knife and wedge it just underneath the membrane to loosen it. Using your hands or a paper towel to grip, pull the membrane up and off the bone. Place the ribs on a sheet tray, then rub each rack generously with dry rub. Wrap ribs in foil, then refrigerate overnight.

3.   When ready to cook, remove ribs from the refrigerator and let come to room temp. Supply your smoker with wood pellets and follow the start-up procedure. Preheat the grill, with the lid open, to 225° F. If using a gas or charcoal grill, set it up for low indirect heat.

4.   Place foil-wrapped ribs on the grill and close lid. Cook for 4 hours then remove foil from ribs and pour accumulated juices into a glass measuring cup. Pour the sauce over the ribs, then continue to cook for an additional 1 ½ - 2 hours or until tender. Remove from grill, slice and serve.

Spiced Pulled Pork Nachos

Servings: 4 - 6
Cooking Time: 270 Minutes

Ingredients:
- ½ Cup Apple Cider
- ½ Avocado, Diced
- 2 Tbsp Cilantro, Chopped
- ¼ Cup Crema
- 2 Tbsp Jalapeno, Chopped
- 1 Cup Marble Jack, Grated
- 2 Tbsp Sweet Heat Rub
- 2 Lbs Pork Shoulder
- 1 Cup Queso Fresco, Crumbled
- ¼ Cup Red Bell Pepper, Chopped
- 1 Tsp Red Chili Flakes
- 2 Tbsp Red Onion, Chopped
- 2 Tbsp Scallions, Chopped
- 10 Oz. Tortilla Chips
- 1 Cup Water

Directions:
1. Supply your smoker with wood pellets and follow the start-up procedure. Preheat the grill, with the lid closed, to 225° F. If using a gas or charcoal grill, set it up for low, indirect heat.
2. Combine Sweet Heat and chili flakes, then sprinkle over pork shoulder, rubbing to coat all sides.
3. Place seasoned pork shoulder directly on the grill grate, fat side up, then close the lid and smoke the pork until it reaches an internal temperature of 175° F, about 2 ½ hours.
4. Transfer pork to a disposable aluminum pan, with cider and water. Cover with aluminum foil and cook another 2 hours, or until the pork reaches an internal temperature of 202° F.
5. Remove the pork shoulder from the grill and allow it to rest for 30 minutes before shredding with meat claws.
6. In a cast-iron skillet, build 2 layers of toppings beginning with chips, followed by cheese, red onion, scallions, bell pepper, jalapeno, and cilantro. Transfer to grill for 10 minutes, until cheese is melted.
7. Top nachos with avocado and crema. Serve hot.

Triple Threat Pork Fattywith Stuffed Jalapeños

Servings: 10
Cooking Time: 150 Minutes

Ingredients:
- 16 strips of bacon, about 1¼lb (565g) total, not thick cut
- 1½ tsp Tajin seasoning, plus more
- 8oz (225g) light cream cheese, at room temperature
- 3 large jalapeños, decored, destemmed, and deseeded
- 1lb (450g) seasoned breakfast sausage
- 1lb (450g) ground pork
- 6 to 8oz (170 to 225g) thinly sliced pepper Jack cheese

Directions:
1. Supply your smoker with wood pellets and follow the start-up procedure. Preheat the grill, with the lid closed, to 275° F.
2. Moisten a workspace with a damp towel. Place a 15-inch (38cm) rectangle of plastic wrap on the workspace. Place 8 strips of bacon, sides touching, parallel to the edge of the plastic. Fold back the even-numbered strips at the halfway point and place a 9th snugly against the folds (perpendicular to the first 8). Unfold.
3. Fold back the odd-numbered strips and place a 10th snugly against the folds. Unfold. Repeat until the weave is complete. Place another sheet of plastic over the weave. Use a rolling pin to thin and tighten the weave.
4. In a small bowl, combine the Tajin and cream cheese. Tightly stuff each jalapeño with the mixture. Reserve any extra filling.
5. Place the sausage and pork in a large bowl. Wet your hands with cold water and knead the meats to combine. Transfer to a resealable plastic bag. Use a rolling pin to create a rectangle that's smaller than the dimensions of your bacon weave. (For reference, place the weave alongside the bag.) Slit the sides of the bag to release the meat and then position the bag over the weave and remove the remaining plastic.
6. Cover the meat with the pepper Jack, leaving 1 inch (2.5cm) around the edges. Pipe the reserved cream cheese mixture randomly over the surface. Position the stuffed jalapeños end to end on the long side of the meat. Use the plastic under the weave to tightly roll up the fatty from the side with the jalapeños. Use bamboo skewers to secure the weave. Lightly season the outside with more Tajin seasoning.
7. Place the fatty seam side down on the grate and smoke until the internal temperature reaches 160°F (71°C), about 2 to 2½ hours.
8. Transfer the fatty to a cutting board and let rest for 10 minutes. Use an electric knife to slice the fatty into 1-inch (2.5cm) rounds before serving.

Pork Tenderloin

Servings: 2
Cooking Time: 15 Minutes

Ingredients:
- 1 Pound pork tenderloin
- 1/3 Cup Kentucky bourbon or apple juice
- 1/4 Cup low sodium soy sauce
- 1/4 Cup brown sugar, packed
- 2 Tablespoon Dijon mustard
- 2 Teaspoon Worcestershire sauce
- 1 Teaspoon ground black pepper

- 1 Medium onion, chopped
- 2 Clove garlic, minced

Directions:

1. Trim any silverskin from the tenderloins with a sharp knife. Place meat in a large resealable plastic bag.

2. For the marinade: In a small mixing bowl or resealable bag, combine the bourbon, soy sauce, brown sugar, mustard, Worcestershire sauce and pepper, whisk to mix. Stir in the onion and garlic. Pour over the tenderloins and refrigerate for 8 hours or overnight.

3. Supply your smoker with wood pellets and follow the start-up procedure. Preheat the grill, with the lid closed, to 400° F.

4. Remove the pork from the marinade and scrape off any solid ingredients (onion or bits of garlic). Discard the marinade.

5. Arrange the tenderloins on the grill grate and grill for 6 to 8 minutes per side or until the internal temperature is 145℉. The pork will still be slightly pink in the center. If you prefer your pork well-done, cook it to 160℉. Grill: 400 ℉ Probe: 145 ℉

6. Transfer the tenderloins to a cutting board. Let rest for several minutes before carving on a diagonal into 1/2 inch slices. Enjoy!

Honey Pork Belly Burnt Ends

Servings: 4
Cooking Time: 270 Minutes

Ingredients:

- 2/3 Cup Bbq Sauce
- 2 Tbsp Butter, Melted
- 2 Tbsp Honey
- 2 Tbsp Olive Oil
- Blackened Sriracha Rub
- 3 Lbs Pork Belly, Skin Removed

Directions:

1. Supply your smoker with wood pellets and follow the start-up procedure. Preheat the grill, with the lid open, to 225° F. If using a gas or charcoal grill, set it up for low, indirect heat.

2. Cut pork belly into 2-inch cubes and place into a large mixing bowl.

3. Drizzle olive oil over pork belly, then generously season with Blackened Sriracha.

4. Transfer seasoned pork belly to a wire rack and place on the grill grate. Cook for 3 hours.

5. Remove the pork belly from the wire rack and transfer into a foil-lined aluminum pan or disposable foil pan.

6. Whisk together BBQ sauce, melted butter, and honey, then pour mixture over pork.

7. Toss to coat, then cover the pan with aluminum foil and return to the grill rack.

8. Cook for another 1 to 1 ½ hours, until the internal temperature reaches 200° F.

9. Remove the foil, transfer pork belly to a cast iron skillet and place in the center of the grill.

10. Open the sear slide and continue cooking for another 5 to 7 minutes, turning halfway, to crisp up the pork.

11. Remove pork belly from the grill, and serve warm.

Smoked Ribs

Servings: 4
Cooking Time: 315 Minutes

Ingredients:

- 2 Racks Baby Back Rib
- Sweet Rib Rub

Directions:

1. Supply your smoker with wood pellets and follow the start-up procedure. Preheat the grill, with the lid open, to 225° F.

2. Remove the membrane on the reverse side of the ribs by sliding a butter knife under the membrane and breaking it. With a piece of paper towel, grab the broken membrane and peel back until the entire membrane is removed.

3. Season both sides of the ribs with Sweet Rib Rub.

4. Place the ribs, meat side up, on the grates of the grill and close the lid. Smoke for about 4 1/2 hours.

5. Wrap in foil and return to the grill at 350℉ for another 45 minutes.

6. Pull your ribs off the grill and rest for 10 minutes.

7. Slice and serve hot. Enjoy!

Onion Pork Shoulder

Servings: 8 - 10
Cooking Time: 240 Minutes

Ingredients:

- Aluminum Foil
- 1 Diced Apple
- 1 Cup Broth, Chicken
- 2 Tbsp Butter, Salted
- 1 Diced Onion
- 1 Pork Shoulder Or Pork Butt Roast
- 1 Box Or Bag Of Stovetop Stuffing Mix
- Champion Chicken Seasoning

Directions:

1. Prepare the pork shoulder. Place the pork shoulder on the cutting board, and with a sharp knife, trim any very fatty sections of the pork shoulder and remove. Then, butterfly the shoulder. Beginning on one side, carefully cut a slit horizontally into one side of the pork shoulder and carefully continue to slice almost all

the way to the right side, rolling the shoulder as you cut, unfolding the meat like a book, until the pork shoulder is one long strip.

2.   Began to make the stuffing by using a medium sized pan and adding 2 tbsp of salted butter to the pan. Add in the onion and apple and let cook for about 5 minutes making sure to stir in between. Add 2 tbsp of Champion Chicken Seasoning. Add the 1 cup of chicken broth followed by a bag of stuffing mix. Let reduce and mix together very well and remove from heat. Transfer to a bowl and set aside.

3.   Once the pork shoulder is butterflied, place some stuff on the roast making sure to leave enough space to roll and tie the roast as well.

4.   Starting on one end of the pork shoulder, roll the pork shoulder up into a tight spiral, and set onto the cutting board, seam side down. Cut four even lengths of butcher's twine, and wiggle under the pork shoulder, two inches apart from each other. Tie tightly to hold the roast together and place on a sheet pan.

5.   Supply your smoker with wood pellets and follow the start-up procedure. Preheat the grill, with the lid open, to 250° F. If you're using a gas or charcoal grill, set it up for medium low heat. Place the aluminum pan in the center of the grill and cook for 3-4 hours, or until the temperature of the pork shoulder reaches an internal temperature of 180°F and is very tender.

6.   Remove the pork shoulder from the grill and allow to rest for 15 minutes, then slice and serve.

Smoky Pork Tenderloin

Servings: 4
Cooking Time: 20 Minutes

Ingredients:
- 2 Pork Tenderloins (3-5 Pounds Total), Trimmed of Excess Fat or Silver Skin
- 1 Tablespoon Olive Oil
- 1-2 Tablespoons Fresh Lime Juice
- 1/4 Cup Light Brown Sugar
- 2 Teaspoons Smoked Paprika
- 1 Teaspoon Onion Powder
- 1 Teaspoon Garlic Powder
- 1 Teaspoon Coarse, Kosher Salt
- Pinch of Coarsely Ground Black Pepper

Directions:
1.   Stir together the olive oil, lime juice, brown sugar, paprika, onion powder, garlic powder, salt, and pepper in a small bowl.
2.   Rub the mixture over the pork and place the meat in a shallow dish. You can grill right away, but for more flavor, cover the dish and refrigerate up to 24 hours.
3.   Supply your smoker with wood pellets and follow the start-up procedure. Preheat the grill, with the lid closed, to 375° F.

4.   Grill the pork tenderloin for 10 minutes, flip and continue to cook until internal temperature at the thickest part of the meat registers 145 degrees F on an instant-read thermometer, about 8-10 minutes.

5.   Remove the pork from the grill and cover with aluminum foil for 10-15 minutes before slicing and serving.

Traeger Roasted Easter Ham

Servings: 8
Cooking Time: 60 Minutes

Ingredients:
- 1 (6-7 lb) bone-in ham
- 1 Cup Sweet & Heat BBQ Sauce
- 2 Cup brown sugar
- 1/2 Cup pineapple juice

Directions:
1.   Supply your smoker with wood pellets and follow the start-up procedure. Preheat the grill, with the lid closed, to 225° F.
2.   Place ham in grill and cook for 60 minutes. Grill: 225 °F
3.   While the ham is cooking, mix together the Traeger Sweet & Heat BBQ Sauce, brown sugar and pineapple juice.
4.   Glaze ham with the sauce every 10 minutes during the last 30 minutes. Remove ham from grill and serve. Enjoy!

Unique Carolina Mustard Ribs

Servings: 4
Cooking Time: 300 Minutes

Ingredients:
- 1 Rack St. Louis Style Ribs
- 2 Cups Apple Juice
- 1/4 Cup Cider Vinegar
- 1/4 Cup Dark Brown Sugar
- 1/4 Cup Honey
- 1 Tablespoon Hot Sauce
- 2 Tablespoons Ketchup
- 7 Tablespoon Sweet Rib Rub
- 1 Tablespoon Worcestershire Sauce
- 2 Cups, Prepared Yellow Mustard

Directions:
1.   Make the sauce for the ribs. In a large mixing bowl, combine 1 cup of the yellow mustard, cider vinegar, dark brown sugar, honey, ketchup, Worcestershire sauce, hot sauce, and 1 tablespoon of the Sweet Rib Rub. Mix well to combine and set in the refrigerator until ready to use.
2.   Make the ribs. Using a paper towel, peel the membrane off of the backs of the rib racks and discard. Generously coat the ribs in a thin coat of mustard, and sprinkle all over with Sweet Rib Rub.

3. Supply your smoker with wood pellets and follow the start-up procedure. Preheat the grill, with the lid closed, to 275° F. If you're using a gas or charcoal grill set it up for low, indirect heat. Place the ribs meaty-side up and grill for 2-3 hours. Once the ribs have grilled for 2-3 hours, fill a spray bottle with 2 cups of apple juice and spray the ribs to keep them moist. Continue to grill the ribs, spraying every 45 minutes, until the meat bends slightly at the ends when lifted and is a deep mahogany color, about another 2-3 hours.

4. Remove the ribs from the grill and brush with mustard sauce, then slice and serve immediately.

Teriyaki Pork Tenderloin

Servings: 12-15
Cooking Time: 120 Minutes

Ingredients:
- 2 (1-pound) pork tenderloins
- 1 batch Quick and Easy Teriyaki Marinade
- Smoked salt

Directions:
1. In a large zip-top bag, combine the tenderloins and marinade. Seal the bag, turn to coat, and refrigerate the pork for at least 30 minutes—I recommend up to overnight.
2. Supply your smoker with wood pellets and follow the start-up procedure. Preheat the grill, with the lid closed, to 180°F.
3. Remove the tenderloins from the marinade and season them with smoked salt.
4. Place the tenderloins directly on the grill grate and smoke for 1 hour.
5. Increase the grill's temperature to 300°F and continue to cook until the pork's internal temperature reaches 145°F.
6. Remove the tenderloins from the grill and let them rest for 5 to 10 minutes, before thinly slicing and serving.

Spiced Orange Ribs

Servings: 4
Cooking Time: 180 Minutes

Ingredients:
- 1 Tablespoon Adobo Sauce
- 2 (2 1/2-Pound) Racks Baby Back Rib
- 1/3 Cup Firmly Packed Light Brown Sugar
- 1 Tablespoon Chili Powder
- 5 In Adobo Sauce Chipotle Peppers
- 1/3 Cup Leaves Cilantro, Fresh
- 1 Teaspoon Ground Cumin
- 1/4 Cup Honey
- 1/4 Cup Ketchup
- 2 Tablespoons Lime Juice

- 1 Cup Orange Juice, Fresh
- 5 Tablespoons Sweet Heat Rub

Directions:
1. First, make the barbecue sauce. Into the bowl of a blender, add ¾ cup of orange juice, cilantro, honey, ketchup, lime juice, 2 chipotles in adobo, adobo sauce, and 1 tablespoon of the Sweet Heat Rub. Place the lid on the blender and blend until completely smooth. Pour into a bowl, reserve ½ cup and set aside.
2. Prepare the ribs. Using the paper towels, pull the membrane off of the back of the ribs and discard. In the bowl of a blender, add the orange juice, brown sugar, chipotle peppers, chili powder, ground cumin, and Sweet Heat. Place the lid on the blender and blend until smooth. Pour this mixture over the ribs and massage into the meat. Place the ribs in the refrigerator and marinade for 8 hours.
3. Supply your smoker with wood pellets and follow the start-up procedure. Preheat the grill, with the lid open, to 275° F. Place the ribs, meat side up, and grill for 1 ½ hours. Baste the ribs with the reserved barbecue sauce, then BBQ for another 1 ½ hours, or until the ribs are extremely tender. Remove the ribs from the grill and serve with barbecue sauce.

Bacon Weave Smoked Country Sausage

Servings: 4
Cooking Time: 120 Minutes

Ingredients:
- Pound Sausage, Uncooked
- Pork & Poultry Rub
- 8 Slices bacon

Directions:
1. Using your hands, form sausage into a loaf-shape. Season lightly with Traeger Pork and Poultry Shake.
2. Supply your smoker with wood pellets and follow the start-up procedure. Preheat the grill, with the lid closed, to 180° F.
3. Put the sausage loaf directly on the grill grate and smoke for 1-1/2 hours.
4. While sausage is smoking, assemble the bacon weave on a piece of wax paper. First, lay out 4 pieces of bacon so they are touching each other on the wax paper. Next, lay the 5th piece of bacon so it crosses the others. Tuck every other slice under the 5th piece of bacon. Find the two pieces of bacon that were under the 5th piece of bacon and fold them back on top of themselves.
5. Lay down the 6th piece of bacon and unfold the two that were laid back. Continue folding the bacon back that was most recently under the last piece of bacon, two pieces at a time, laying the next piece of bacon on top until your weave is complete. Set aside. After your sausage has smoked for 1-1/2 hours, take it off the grill and increase the heat of your Traeger, lid closed to 350°F and preheat. Grill: 350 °F

6. While the grill is heating, wrap your sausage loaf in the bacon weave. Lay the middle of the weave directly on top of the sausage loaf and press the bacon all around the sausage.

7. Flip the sausage and bacon over to finish the weave on the bottom of the sausage. Alternate the bacon ends across the bottom and tuck the ends around each other.

8. Put your sausage back on the grill and cook for 25-30 minutes until the internal temperature of the sausage reaches 160℉. Enjoy! Probe: 160 ℉

Barbecued Tenderloin

Servings: 4-6
Cooking Time: 30 Minutes

Ingredients:
- 2 (1-pound) pork tenderloins
- 1 batch Sweet and Spicy Cinnamon Rub

Directions:
1. Supply your smoker with wood pellets and follow the start-up procedure. Preheat the grill, with the lid closed, to 350℉.
2. Generously season the tenderloins with the rub. Using your hands, work the rub into the meat.
3. Place the tenderloins directly on the grill grate and smoke until their internal temperature reaches 145℉.
4. Remove the tenderloins from the grill and let them rest for 5 to 10 minutes, before thinly slicing and serving.

Holiday Smoked Cheese Log

Servings: 8
Cooking Time: 60 Minutes

Ingredients:
- 16 Ounce cream cheese
- 3 Cup shredded cheddar cheese
- 1 Tablespoon Worcestershire sauce
- 1 Teaspoon hot sauce
- 8 Slices bacon
- 2 green onion
- 1 Cup coarsely chopped pecans

Directions:
1. In a mixing bowl, using an electric mixer or large spoon, combine the cream cheese (room temperature) and the cheddar cheese.
2. Add in the Worcestershire sauce and hot sauce. Mix again.
3. Add in the cooked and crumbled bacon and chopped green onions. Mix until combined.
4. Cover the bowl with plastic wrap and refrigerate for 4 hours or until the cheese mixture is firm enough to mold. Shape it into a log and layer the outside with the toasted pecans.

5. Cover with plastic wrap. Freeze the cheese log overnight to make sure it doesn't get too soft while it's smoking.
6. The next day supply your smoker with wood pellets and follow the start-up procedure. Preheat the grill, with the lid closed, to 180° F.
7. Take the cheese log out of the freezer and unwrap. Place on a cooking sheet and smoke for 1 hour. Keep an eye on it to make sure it doesn't get too soft. Grill: 180 ℉
8. Move the cheese log to a serving tray and serve with your favorite crackers. (If the cheese is too soft, throw it in the fridge for an hour or two.)

Bbq Brown Sugar Bacon Bites

Servings: 2
Cooking Time: 25 Minutes

Ingredients:
- 1/2 Cup brown sugar
- 1 Tablespoon Fennel, ground
- 2 Teaspoon kosher salt
- 1 Teaspoon ground black pepper
- 1 Pound Pork Belly, diced

Directions:
1. Fold a 12" x 36" piece of aluminum foil in half and crimp the edges so there is a rim. Using a fork, poke holes in the bottom of the foil. This way some of the bacon fat will be rendered out and the bacon bites will crisp.
2. Supply your smoker with wood pellets and follow the start-up procedure. Preheat the grill, with the lid closed, to 350° F.
3. In a large bowl, combine the brown sugar, ground fennel, salt, and black pepper. Stir to combine.
4. Place the diced pork belly into the mixture and toss until well-coated. Transfer the pork pieces to the foil.
5. Place on the grill and bake until the pieces are crispy, glazed, and bubbly, about 20-30 minutes. Enjoy!

Stuffed Pork Crown Roast

Servings: 2-4
Cooking Time: 180 Minutes

Ingredients:
- 10 Pound Crown Roast of Pork, 12-14 ribs
- 1 Cup apple juice or cider
- 2 Tablespoon apple cider vinegar
- 2 Tablespoon Dijon mustard
- 1 Tablespoon brown sugar
- 2 Clove garlic, minced
- 2 Tablespoon Thyme or Rosemary, fresh
- 1 Teaspoon salt
- 1 Teaspoon coarse ground black pepper, divided

- 1/2 Cup olive oil
- 8 Cup Your Favorite Stuffing, Prepared According to the Package Directions, or Homemade

Directions:

1. Set the pork on a flat rack in a shallow roasting pan. Cover the end of each bone with a small piece of foil.
2. Make the marinade: Bring the apple cider to a boil over high heat and reduce by half. Remove from the heat, and whisk in the vinegar, mustard, brown sugar, garlic, thyme, and salt and pepper. Slowly whisk in the oil.
3. Using a pastry brush, apply the marinade to the roast, coating all surfaces. Cover it with plastic wrap and allow it to sit until the meat comes to room temperature, about 1 hour.
4. When ready to cook, set grill temperature to High and preheat, lid closed for 15 minutes.
5. Arrange the roasting pan with the pork on the grill grate. Roast for 30 minutes.
6. Reduce the heat to 325°F. Loosely fill the crown with the stuffing, mounding it at the top. Cover the stuffing with foil. (Alternatively, you can bake the stuffing in a separate pan alongside the roast.)
7. Roast the pork for another 1-1/2 hours. Remove the foil from the stuffing and continue to roast until the internal temperature of the meat is 150°F, about 30 minutes to an hour. Make sure the temperature probe doesn't touch bone or you will get a false reading.
8. Remove roast from grill and allow to rest for 15 minutes. Remove the foil covering the bones, but leave the butcher's string on the roast until ready to carve. Transfer to a warm platter.
9. To serve, carve between the bones. Enjoy!

Chinese Alcoholic Bbq Pork Tenderloin

Servings: 4
Cooking Time: 30 Minutes

Ingredients:

- 14 Cup Bbq Sauce
- 2 Garlic Cloves, Minced
- 14 Cup Hoisin Sauce
- 2 Lbs Pork Tenderloin, Trimmed With Silver Skins Removed
- 1 Tbsp Sugar, Granulated
- 1 Tsp Sweet Rib Rub Seasoning
- 14 Cup Tamari
- 14 Cup White Wine

Directions:

1. In a glass measuring cup, whisk together the hoisin sauce, tamari, wine, garlic, sugar, and Sweet Rib Rub.

2. Place pork tenderloin in a resealable bag, then pour the marinade over the pork and allow to marinate in the refrigerator for 4 to 6 hours.
3. Supply your smoker with wood pellets and follow the start-up procedure. Preheat the grill, with the lid open, to 400° F. If using a gas or charcoal grill, preheat to medium-high heat.
4. Remove the pork from the marinade, then pour the marinade into a grill-safe pan.
5. Place the marinade on the grill and bring to a boil for 3 minutes. Add the BBQ sauce and simmer for 2 minutes. Remove from the grill, and set aside.
6. Place the pork on the grill and cook for 18 to 20 minutes, until an internal temperature of 145° F. Flip and baste the pork with the sauce every 3 to 5 minutes.
7. Remove the pork from the grill and allow it to rest on a cutting board for 10 minutes, prior to serving warm with additional sauce.

Bbq Pork Shoulder Roast With Sugar Lips Glaze

Servings: 8
Cooking Time: 540 Minutes

Ingredients:

- 1 (8-10 lb) bone-in pork butt
- 1/4 Cup Pork & Poultry Rub, divided
- 1 1/2 Cup apple juice, divided
- 4 Tablespoon brown sugar
- 1 Tablespoon salt
- 1/2 Cup apple juice
- Sugar Lips Glaze

Directions:

1. Trim pork butt of all excess fat leaving 1/4 inch of the fat cap attached.
2. Combine 2 tablespoons Traeger Pork & Poultry Rub, 1 cup apple juice, brown sugar and salt in a small bowl stirring until most of the sugar and salt are dissolved. Inject the pork butt every square inch or so with the apple juice mixture.
3. Season the exterior of the pork butt with remaining Traeger Pork & Poultry Rub.
4. Supply your smoker with wood pellets and follow the start-up procedure. Preheat the grill, with the lid closed, to 250° F.
5. Place pork butt directly on the grill grate and cook for about 6 hours or until the internal temperature reaches 160°F. Grill: 250 °F Probe: 160 °F
6. Wrap the pork butt in two layers of foil and pour in 1/2 cup of apple juice. Secure tin foil tightly to contain the apple juice.
7. Increase Traeger temperature to 275°F and return wrapped pork butt to grill in a pan large enough to hold the pork butt in

case it leaks. Cook an additional 3 hours or until internal temperature reaches 195°F. Grill: 275 °F Probe: 195 °F

8. Remove from the grill and allow to rest 10 to 15 minutes. Slice the pork butt around the bone and top with Traeger Sugar Lips BBQ Sauce. Serve with your favorite sides. Enjoy!

Home-cured Picnic Ham With Mustard Caviar

Servings: 8
Cooking Time: 420 Minutes

Ingredients:
- 1 pork shoulder roast, about 5lb (2.3kg) total
- 1 cup distilled water, apple cider, or apple juice, plus more
- Mustard Caviar
- for the brine
- 1 cup kosher salt
- 5 tsp pink curing salt #1
- 1 cup light brown sugar or turbinado sugar or low-carb substitute
- ¼ cup molasses or honey
- 1 gallon (3.8 liters) distilled water, divided, plus more

Directions:
1. Trim any excess fat from the pork shoulder, leaving at least ¼ inch. Use a sharp knife to score the skin of the ham in the classic diamond pattern, making the cuts about 1 inch (2.5cm) apart, but don't penetrate the meat. (If you purchased a shoulder without skin, skip this step.)
2. In a stockpot on the stovetop over medium-high heat, make the brine by combining the salts, brown sugar, molasses, and water. Bring the mixture to a boil. Whisk to dissolve the salts and sugar. Remove the stockpot from the stovetop and let the brine cool to room temperature.
3. Submerge the pork shoulder in the brine. If it floats, place a resealable bag of ice on top. Refrigerate for 3 days.
4. Place the ham in a clean container and cover with cold water. Let the ham soak for 30 minutes. Drain and pat dry with paper towels.
5. Supply your smoker with wood pellets and follow the start-up procedure. Preheat the grill, with the lid closed, to 225° F.
6. Place the ham on the grate and grill until the internal temperature in the thickest part of the meat reaches 160°F (71°C), about 4 to 5 hours. Remove the ham from the grill. Let the ham come to room temperature. Cover and refrigerate for up to 3 days. This helps establish the ham's smokiness.
7. Preheat the grill to 325°F (163°C).
8. Transfer the ham to an aluminum foil roasting pan and add the water to the bottom of the pan. Place the pan on the grate and

roast the ham until the skin is nicely browned and the internal temperature reaches 145°F (63°C), about 1½ to 2 hours.

9. Remove the ham from the grill and let rest for 10 minutes. Carve the ham and serve with the mustard caviar.

Smoked Pork Tomato Tamales

Servings: 6-8
Cooking Time: 60 Minutes

Ingredients:
- 1 Boneless, Netted Pork Roast
- 1 Cup, Fresh Cilantro, Chopped
- 3 Cloves Garlic, Peeled
- 20 Dried Cornhusks
- 1 Tbsp Lime Juice
- ¼ Cup Olive Oil
- 1 Onion, Quartered
- 4 - 6 Cups Prepared Masa Harina Tamale Dough
- 3 – 4 Serrano Peppers, Deseeded
- 1 Tbsp Sweet Heat Rub
- 1 Lb. Tomatillos, Husked And Washed

Directions:
1. Began by soaking the corn husks in a pan filled with water. Soak for 2 – 4 hours, or if needed, overnight.
2. Unwrap the tomatillos from their shell and place all of them into a grill basket followed by a few Serranos, deseeded, garlic cloves and 1 onion cut into quarters.
3. Supply your smoker with wood pellets and follow the start-up procedure. Preheat the grill, with the lid open, to 400° F. If you're using a gas or charcoal grill, set it up for medium low heat, and use smoke chips to fill your grill with smoke for 15 minutes. Place the grill basket filled with your vegetables and roast them over an open flame on your smoker until vegetables have become charred.
4. Place tomatillos, peppers, garlic and onions in a bowl, cover with plastic wrap, and let stand until cool enough to handle, 10 to 15 minutes.
5. Season the pork roast generously with Sweet Heat Rub and grill at 350°F for 1 hour until the roast has a nice crust on the outside.
6. While the pork roast is cooking, add a handful of cilantro, charred vegetables, 1 tbsp of Sweet Heat Rub, 1 tbsp lime juice, and ¼ cup of olive oil to a food processor. Pulse in food processor until mixture is consistent. Set aside
7. After the pork roast has been grilled for an hour, turn heat down to 275°F. Put roast in pan with about a cup of water, cover with aluminum foil and cook for another 4 hours or until the roast can be shredded. Pour chile verde sauce over shredded pork and toss to combine.
8. To being assembling tamales, place a corn husk on a work surface. Place 2-3 tablespoons of tamale dough on larger end of

husk and spread into a rectangle, about ¼" thick, leaving a small border along the edge. Place large tablespoon of chili and pork filling on top of dough. Fold over sides of husk so dough surrounds filling, then fold bottom of husk up and secure closed by tying a thin strip of husk around tamale.

9.   To cook tamales, place them in a large metal colander over a large stockpot filled with water. Cover and let steam for 1 hour. After the tamales have been steamed, take them off and grill them at 350°F for about 10-20 minutes until corn husks have charred marks.

Baked Maple And Brown Sugar Bacon

Servings: 4
Cooking Time: 60 Minutes

Ingredients:
- 1 Pound cold bacon
- 1/2 Cup pure maple syrup, warmed
- 1/2 Cup brown sugar, plus more as needed

Directions:
1.   Supply your smoker with wood pellets and follow the start-up procedure. Preheat the grill, with the lid closed, to 300° F.
2.   Line a rimmed baking sheet with foil and place a wire rack on top. Lay bacon strips in a single layer on the wire rack.
3.   Using a pastry brush, brush each strip of bacon on both sides with the warmed maple syrup, then sprinkle brown sugar evenly on both sides.
4.   Put the baking sheet in the grill and cook bacon for 60-75 minutes, or until bacon browns and appears to be crisping. Grill: 300 °F
5.   Allow the bacon to cool slightly before eating. Enjoy!

Roasted Pork With Balsamic Strawberry Sauce

Servings: 2
Cooking Time: 35 Minutes

Ingredients:
- 2 Pound pork tenderloin
- salt and pepper
- 2 Tablespoon dried rosemary
- 2 Tablespoon extra-virgin olive oil
- 12 Large fresh strawberries
- 1 Cup balsamic vinegar
- 4 Tablespoon sugar

Directions:
1.   Supply your smoker with wood pellets and follow the start-up procedure. Preheat the grill, with the lid closed, to 350° F.

2.   Rinse pork and pat dry. Sprinkle both sides with salt, pepper, and rosemary.
3.   In a large Dutch oven skillet, heat oil on High until almost smoking. Add the tenderloin and sear on each side until the skin is golden brown, about 2 minutes per side.
4.   Set the skillet in the Traeger and cook until pork is no longer pink and internal temperature reaches 150°F, about 20 minutes. Grill: 350 °F Probe: 150 °F
5.   Remove from grill and let the pork rest for 5-10 minutes.
6.   Add strawberries to the skillet over the stove on medium heat and quickly sear on both sides for less than a minute. Remove berries from the pan.
7.   Add balsamic vinegar to the same pan and scrape the browned bits from the bottom.
8.   Bring to a boil and then reduce heat to medium low. Add the sugar, stirring frequently. Sauce is ready when it has reduced by half and texture is thick.
9.   Slice the pork and place the seared strawberries on top. Serve with a drizzle of the balsamic vinegar sauce. Enjoy!

Baked Eggs In Bacon Nest

Servings: 4
Cooking Time: 30 Minutes

Ingredients:
- 6 Strips bacon
- 6 Whole eggs
- 1/4 Teaspoon salt
- 1/4 Teaspoon pepper

Directions:
1.   Supply your smoker with wood pellets and follow the start-up procedure. Preheat the grill, with the lid closed, to 375° F.
2.   Place bacon strips directly on the grill grate and cook about 15 minutes. Transfer to a paper towel and pat dry.
3.   Spray a muffin tin liberally with cooking spray. Line each muffin cup with one slice of bacon then crack one egg into each cup. Season each cup with salt and pepper.
4.   Transfer muffin tin to the grill and cook for 15-20 minutes until the bacon is crisp, whites are just set, and yolk is still runny. Enjoy!

Bbq Pork Short Ribs

Servings: 4

Cooking Time: 360 Minutes

Ingredients:

- 2 Pork Short Rib Racks With At Least 1 1/2-2" of Meat On Bone
- Pork & Poultry Rub

Directions:

1. Clean and trim short ribs. Season generously on all sides with Traeger Pork and Poultry rub.
2. Supply your smoker with wood pellets and follow the start-up procedure. Preheat the grill, with the lid closed, to 250° F.
3. Place ribs directly on the grill grate and cook for 4-6 hours or until the internal temperature reaches 202-204°F when an instant read thermometer is inserted in the thickest part of meat. Spritz with apple juice every hour if desired. Grill: 250 °F Probe: 202 °F
4. Remove from grill and allow to rest 10 minutes before slicing. Cut into individual ribs and serve with your favorite sides. Enjoy!

POULTRY RECIPES

Buffalo Wings

Servings: 2-3
Cooking Time: 35 Minutes

Ingredients:
- 1 pound chicken wings
- 1 batch Chicken Rub
- 1 cup Frank's Red-Hot Sauce, Buffalo wing sauce, or similar

Directions:
1. Supply your smoker with wood pellets and follow the start-up procedure. Preheat the grill, with the lid closed, to 300°F.
2. Season the chicken wings with the rub. Using your hands, work the rub into the meat.
3. Place the wings directly on the grill grate and smoke until their internal temperature reaches 160°F.
4. Baste the wings with the sauce and continue to smoke until the wings' internal temperature reaches 170°F.

Smoked Honey Chicken Drumsticks

Servings: 4
Cooking Time: 30 Minutes

Ingredients:
- 1/2 Cup Apple Cider Vinegar
- 12 Chicken Drumsticks
- 2 Tablespoons Dijon Mustard
- 1/4 Cup Honey
- 1/4 Cup Ketchup
- 1 Tablespoon Sweet Heat Rub
- 1/2 Cup Soy Sauce

Directions:
1. Supply your smoker with wood pellets and follow the start-up procedure. Preheat the grill, with the lid open, to 225° F. Remove the wings from the marinade and place the drumsticks into the Buffalo Wing Rack.
2. Smoke for 60 minutes, or until a thermometer inserted into the thickest part of the drumstick registers at 170°F.
3. Turn the heat up to 350°F and cook for 5 to 10 minutes to make the skin crisp.
4. Remove from the smoker, serve immediately and enjoy!

Wild West Wings

Servings: 4
Cooking Time: 60 Minutes

Ingredients:
- 2 pounds chicken wings

- 2 tablespoons extra-virgin olive oil
- 2 packages ranch dressing mix (such as Hidden Valley brand)
- ¼ cup prepared ranch dressing (optional)

Directions:
1. Supply your smoker with wood pellets and follow the start-up procedure. Preheat, with the lid closed, to 350°F.
2. Place the chicken wings in a large bowl and toss with the olive oil and ranch dressing mix.
3. Arrange the wings directly on the grill, or line the grill with aluminum foil for easy cleanup, close the lid, and smoke for 25 minutes.
4. Flip and smoke for 20 to 35 minutes more, or until a meat thermometer inserted in the thickest part of the wings reads 165°F and the wings are crispy. (Note: The wings will likely be done after 45 minutes, but an extra 10 to 15 minutes makes them crispy without drying the meat.)
5. Serve warm with ranch dressing (if using).

Roasted Tin Foil Dinners

Servings: 4
Cooking Time: 25 Minutes

Ingredients:
- 4 boneless, skinless chicken breast
- Chicken Rub
- 1/2 Pound new potatoes, quartered
- 8 Ounce cremini mushrooms, cleaned and quartered
- salt and pepper
- 1/2 Pound green beans, ends trimmed
- 1 Medium lemon, cut into 3/4 inch slices

Directions:
1. Supply your smoker with wood pellets and follow the start-up procedure. Preheat the grill, with the lid closed, to 400° F.
2. Season chicken breast with salt, pepper and Traeger Chicken Rub. Place the potatoes, mushrooms and chicken in the middle of a large sheet of foil, season with more salt and pepper as needed, and wrap up tightly.
3. Place foil pack directly on the grill grate and cook for 15 minutes. Grill: 400 °F
4. Open up the foil pack and add green beans, lemon and additional salt and pepper, if needed. Wrap back up and return to the Traeger for an additional 10 minutes. Grill: 400 °F
5. Remove from the Traeger, open packet and enjoy!

Savory Smoked Chicken Breasts

Servings: 2
Cooking Time: 30 Minutes

Ingredients:
- 1 lb Boneless Skinless Chicken Breasts
- 2-3 Tbsp BBQ Chicken Rub

Directions:
1. Supply your smoker with wood pellets and follow the start-up procedure. Preheat the grill, with the lid closed, to 250° F.
2. Pound chicken breasts flat, about 1/2" thick. Rub the dry rub all over chicken breasts.
3. Place chicken breasts on the grill grate. Close pellet grill lid and cook at 250 °F for about 30 minutes or until the chicken reaches an internal temperature of 165 °F.
4. Remove from pellet grill and let rest 5-10 minutes.

Bbq Turkey Breast With Meat Church Holy Cow

Servings: 8
Cooking Time: 180 Minutes

Ingredients:
- 1 Large boneless, skinless turkey breast
- 1/4 Cup Duke's Mayonnaise
- Meat Church Holy Cow BBQ Rub
- 1/2 Cup honey
- 1/4 Cup Dijon mustard
- 2 Tablespoon Meat Church Holy Cow BBQ Rub

Directions:
1. Rinse off the breast and pat dry. Slather it liberally in mayonnaise, this will act as a binder for the seasoning. Apply Meat Church Holy Cow BBQ Rub generously to all sides.
2. Supply your smoker with wood pellets and follow the start-up procedure. Preheat the grill, with the lid closed, to 275° F.
3. Place the breast directly on the grill grate and cook for 2 to 3 hours, or until the internal temperature reaches 160°F in the thickest part. (The breast will continue to cook another 5° or so after it is removed from the grill.) Grill: 275 °F Probe: 160 °F
4. While the turkey is cooking you can go ahead and prepare your glaze (if using). Mix all glaze ingredients in a small saucepan and bring to a simmer. Reduce by 1/3. Remove from the heat and set aside.
5. Drizzle the glaze on the turkey during the last 15 minutes of the cook. I recommend doing this around 158 - 160°F, internal temperature. (This turkey is also delicious as-is, without the optional glaze.)
6. Remove from the grill and let the turkey breast rest 5 to 10 minutes before slicing. Enjoy!

Grilled Parmesan Chicken Wings

Servings: 4
Cooking Time: 25 Minutes

Ingredients:
- 4 Tbsp Butter
- 4 Lbs Chicken Wings, Trimmed And Patted Dry
- 4 Garlic Cloves, Chopped
- 2 Tbsp Olive Oil
- 1/2 Cup Parmesan Cheese, Grated
- 2 Tbsp Parsley, Chopped
- Champion Chicken Seasoning

Directions:
1. Lay chicken wings out on a sheet tray, blot with paper towel, then season with Champion Chicken.
2. Supply your smoker with wood pellets and follow the start-up procedure. Preheat the grill, with the lid open, to 400° F. If using a gas or charcoal grill, set it up for medium-high heat.
3. Transfer wings to grill and cook for 20 to 25 minutes, turning every 5 minutes, until lightly browned. Remove wings from the grill and set on a sheet tray. Place in the smoking cabinet to keep warm while preparing the garlic butter.
4. Melt butter and olive oil in a cast iron skillet, then add garlic and simmer until fragrant. Remove from the grill.
5. Transfer chicken wings to a large bowl and pour garlic butter over the wings. Add cheese and parsley, then toss well to coat. Serve warm with additional sprinkling of parmesan cheese.

Garlic Sriracha Buffalo Chicken Wings

Servings: 6-8
Cooking Time: 160 Minutes

Ingredients:
- 1 Cup Buffalo Sauce
- 6 Lbs Chicken Wings
- 2 Tbsp Garlic Powder
- 1 Tsp Pepper
- Divided By 2 Tbsp And ½ Tbsp Sweet Heat Rub
- 1 Tsp Salt
- ⅓ Cup, Divided Sriracha Sauce

Directions:
1. In a non-stick sauce pot, add the remaining Sriracha and buffalo sauce. Stir to combine and set aside.
2. Supply your smoker with wood pellets and follow the start-up procedure. Preheat the grill, with the lid open, to 250° F. If using a gas or charcoal grill, set it to low heat with indirect heat. Place marinated wings directly on grill grate and cook (covered) for 1 hour 15 minutes.

3. Flip wings and baste each piece with Sriracha sauce. Season with additional Sweet Heat Rub, cover, and continue to grill for an additional 1 hour 15 minutes.

4. Remove wings from grill and place on sheet tray. Baste with additional sauce, then open Sear Slide and return wings to the grill. Grill for 3-5 minutes, rotating often, until wings begin to char lightly.

5. Transfer wings to a serving tray, baste with remaining sauce and serve!

Bbq Chicken Tostada

Servings: 4
Cooking Time: 50 Minutes

Ingredients:
- 4 Whole boneless, skinless chicken thighs
- salt and pepper
- 8 Whole Corn Tostada
- Refried Beans
- lettuce
- green onion, coarsely chopped
- cilantro, chopped
- guacamole

Directions:
1. Supply your smoker with wood pellets and follow the start-up procedure. Preheat the grill, with the lid closed, to 350° F.
2. While grill heats, trim excess fat and skin from chicken thighs.
3. Season with a light layer of salt and pepper.
4. Place chicken thighs on the grill grate and cook for 35 minutes.
5. Check internal temperature; chicken is done when a thermometer inserted reads 175 degrees F. Remove from the grill and let rest for 10 minutes before shredding.
6. Place tostadas on grill while chicken is resting for 5 minutes.
7. Build tostadas starting with refried beans, sliced lettuce, shredded chicken, tomatoes, green onions, cilantro, guacamole. Enjoy!

Crispy Spiced Chicken Wings

Servings: 10
Cooking Time: 75 Minutes

Ingredients:
- 5 pounds of chicken wings (flats and drumettes)
- 2 1/2 Tablespoons baking powder
- 1 teaspoon salt

Directions:
1. Dry your chicken wings thoroughly on all sides with a paper towel. Place them in a zip-top bag.

2. Add the baking powder and salt to the wings, close the bag, and toss to coat evenly.

3. Supply your smoker with wood pellets and follow the start-up procedure. Preheat the grill, with the lid closed, to 250° F, using your favorite wood. Place the wings directly on the grill grates, close the lid, and smoke for 30 minutes.

4. Increase the heat in your smoker to 425 degrees F and continue cooking for 45 more minutes, or until the internal temperature of the wing reads 175 degrees F. You can rotate or flip the wings as needed to maintain even cooking and avoid any hot spots on the grill.

5. Remove the wing from the grill and serve. You can serve plain, toss in your favorite BBQ seasoning, or hot sauce.

Big Game Roast Chicken

Servings: 4
Cooking Time: 60 Minutes

Ingredients:
- 1 whole chicken
- Big Game Rub

Directions:
1. Supply your smoker with wood pellets and follow the start-up procedure. Preheat the grill, with the lid closed, to 375° F.
2. Remove the neck and gizzards from the cavity of the bird. Rinse and wipe the outside and inside of the chicken with a paper towel. Tie chicken legs together with butcher twine and tuck wings.
3. Apply an even coat of the Traeger Big Game Rub to the inside and outside of the chicken.
4. Place chicken on the grill grate and cook for 60 minutes. After an hour, check the temperature of the bird in the thickest part of the leg. The temperature needs to be between 165 and 180°F. Check every 15 minutes if not up to temperature. When the leg reaches desired internal temperature, check the temperature of the breast. The breast needs to reach an internal temperature of 165°F before it is done. Grill: 375 °F Probe: 165 °F
5. Let bird rest for 15 to 20 minutes for slicing. Enjoy!

Flavoured Hibachi Chicken

Servings: 4
Cooking Time: 10 Minutes

Ingredients:
- To Taste, Blackened Sriracha Rub Seasoning
- To Taste, Blackened Sriracha Rub Seasoning (For Vegetables)
- 2 Cups Broccoli Florets, Blanched
- 1 Tbsp Brown Sugar
- 1 Tbsp Butter, Unsalted
- 1 1/2 Lbs Chicken Breast, Boneless, Skinless, Sliced Thin

- 1 Tbsp Cilantro, Chopped
- 3 Garlic Cloves, Minced
- 2 Garlic Cloves, Minced (For Vegetables)
- 1 Tsp Ginger, Grated
- 1 Tsp Ginger, Grated (For Vegetables
- 1/2 Lime, Juiced
- 1/2 Red Bell Pepper, Sliced Thin
- For Serving, Rice Noodles, Cooked
- 2 Scallions, Chopped
- 1 Tbsp Sesame Oil
- 2 Tbsp Sesame Oil, Divided
- 1 Cup Snap Peas, Blanched
- 1/4 Cup Tamari
- For Serving, Toasted Sesame Seeds
- 1 Tbsp Vegetable Oil
- 1 Tbsp Vegetable Oil (For Vegetables)
- For Serving, Yum-Yum Sauce

Directions:

1. Supply your smoker with wood pellets and follow the start-up procedure. Preheat the grill, with the lid open, to medium-high heat. When hot, add 1 tablespoon of sesame oil and vegetable oil. Immediately add the chicken and season with Blackened Sriracha. When the chicken starts to brown, flip it over to brown the other side.

2. Add the garlic, ginger, soy sauce, brown sugar, butter, and the remaining tablespoon of sesame oil and stir. Turn the heat down to medium-low and let the mixture simmer for 3 minutes, until it thickens and adheres to the chicken. Add lime juice, cilantro, and scallions, then remove the mixture from the griddle.

3. After starting the sauce for the chicken, sauté the vegetables: Add sesame oil and vegetable oil to the other side of the griddle. Quickly sauté broccoli, snap peas, and red bell pepper with garlic and ginger. Season with Blackened Sriracha. Remove from the griddle after 2 minutes.

4. Serve hibachi chicken warm with sautéed vegetables, toasted sesame seeds, rice noodles, and Yum-Yum sauce if desired.

Green Chile Chicken Enchiladas

Servings: 6
Cooking Time: 45 Minutes

Ingredients:

- 2 Cups Chicken, Shredded
- 1 (12 Oz) Package Colby Jack Cheese, Shredded
- 1 Enchilada Sauce, Can
- 1 Can Green Chile, Drained
- 1 Onion, Diced
- 1 Tablespoon Sweet Rib Rub
- 1 Cup Sour Cream
- 1 Package Flour Tortilla

Directions:

1. Supply your smoker with wood pellets and follow the start-up procedure. Preheat the grill, with the lid open, to 300° F.

2. In a bowl, mix - the chicken, green chiles, Sweet Heat seasoning, sour cream, diced onion, and half the bag of shredded cheese.

3. Place a large spoonful of the chicken mixture in the center of a tortilla and roll it up. Repeat with the remaining tortillas, then place in the baking pan, and pour the enchilada sauce over the tortilla pans. Top with the remainder of the shredded cheese.

4. Wrap the top of the pan tightly in aluminum foil and grill for 45 minutes or until the enchilada sauce is bubbly. Remove from the grill and serve.

Kansas City Hot Fried Chicken

Servings: 4
Cooking Time: 25 Minutes

Ingredients:

- 1 Whole Chicken, cut into pieces
- 1 1/2 Cup buttermilk
- 2 Tablespoon hot sauce
- 4 Cup all-purpose flour
- 1 Teaspoon salt
- 1/2 Teaspoon black pepper
- 1/2 Tablespoon red pepper flakes
- 12 Ounce Bacon, Uncooked, Chopped
- vegetable oil

Directions:

1. Supply your smoker with wood pellets and follow the start-up procedure. Preheat the grill, with the lid closed, to 180° F.

2. Smoke the 4 pieces of chicken for about 10 min. Grill: 180 °F

3. Mix buttermilk and hot sauce together in a large bowl, keep mixture ultra chilled.

4. In a separate bowl, mix the dry ingredients and bacon together, set aside.

5. Remove chicken and place in ice-cold buttermilk mixture for about an hour in the refrigerator.

6. Heat Vegetable Oil in a frying pan to 370°F (195 C).

7. Remove chicken from the liquid and batter it in dry ingredient mixture, drop into frying oil for about 10-15 minutes.

8. Serve with pickled hot peppers. Enjoy!

Roasted Whole Chicken

Servings: 6-8
Cooking Time: 120 Minutes

Ingredients:
- 1 whole chicken
- 2 tablespoons olive oil
- 1 batch Chicken Rub

Directions:
1. Supply your smoker with wood pellets and follow the start-up procedure. Preheat the grill, with the lid closed, to 375°F.
2. Coat the chicken all over with olive oil and season it with the rub. Using your hands, work the rub into the meat.
3. Place the chicken directly on the grill grate and smoke until its internal temperature reaches 170°F.
4. Remove the chicken from the grill and let it rest for 10 minutes, before carving and serving.

Savory Smoked Turkey Legs

Servings: 4
Cooking Time: 150 Minutes

Ingredients:
- 1 Cup Chicken Stock
- 2 Tbsp Blackened Sriracha Rub
- 4 Turkey Legs (Drumsticks)

Directions:
1. Fire up your pellet grill on SMOKE mode. With the lid open, let it run for 10 minutes.
2. Supply your smoker with wood pellets and follow the start-up procedure. Preheat the grill, with the lid closed, to 225° F. If using a gas or charcoal grill, set it up for low, indirect heat.
3. Combine turkey stock with 2 teaspoons of Blackened Sriracha Rub.
4. Place turkey legs on a sheet tray, then inject each with seasoned stock. Season the outside of the legs with remaining Blackened Sriracha.
5. Place turkey legs directly on the grate of the smoking cabinet, and cook for 1 ½ hours.
6. Increase temperature to 325°F, then transfer turkey legs to the bottom grill and cook for another 45 to 60 minutes, until the internal temperature reaches 170°F.
7. Remove turkey from the grill, allow to rest for 10 minutes, then serve warm.

Mandarin Chicken Breast

Servings: 4
Cooking Time: 25 Minutes

Ingredients:

- 1/2 Cup kosher salt
- 1/4 Cup brown sugar
- 1/2 Cup soy sauce
- 8 (6 oz) boneless, skinless chicken breasts
- sweet chili sauce
- steamed rice, for serving
- thinly sliced scallions, for garnish

Directions:
1. Pour 2 quarts water into a large mixing bowl, then add salt, brown sugar, and soy sauce. Stir until sugar and salt dissolve. Grill: 350 °F Probe: 170 °F
2. Submerge chicken breasts in the brine, cover and refrigerate for 2 hours.
3. Drain the chicken, rinse and pat dry with paper towels. Discard the brine.
4. Supply your smoker with wood pellets and follow the start-up procedure. Preheat the grill, with the lid closed, to 350° F.
5. Arrange the chicken breasts on the grill grate and cook for 25 to 30 minutes or until the internal temperature on an instant-read thermometer is 170°F. Turn chicken breasts once halfway through the cooking time. Grill: 350 °F Probe: 170 °F
6. Brush chicken breasts with the sweet chili sauce during the last few minutes of cooking.
7. Remove to a platter or plates and serve with steamed rice. Sprinkle the chicken breasts with thinly sliced scallions for garnish. Enjoy!

Cider-brined Turkey

Servings: 8
Cooking Time: 180 Minutes

Ingredients:
- 1 whole turkey, about 12 to 14lb (4.5 to 5.4kg), thawed if frozen
- 1 white onion, peeled and sliced into quarters
- 1 apple, cut into wedges
- 2 celery stalks, sliced into 2-inch (5cm) pieces
- sprigs of fresh sage, rosemary, parsley, or thyme
- 8 tbsp unsalted butter, at room temperature
- coarse salt
- freshly ground black pepper
- for the brine
- 1 quart (1 liter) apple cider or apple juice
- 3 quarts (3 liters) cold distilled water
- ¾ cup coarse salt
- ½ cup light brown sugar or low-carb substitute
- 3 garlic cloves, peeled and smashed with a chef's knife
- 3 bay leaves

Directions:

1. In a large food-safe bucket, make the brine by combining the apple cider, water, salt, and brown sugar. Stir until the salt and sugar dissolve. Add the garlic and bay leaves. Submerge the turkey in the brine. If it floats, place a resealable bag of ice on top. Refrigerate for at least 8 hours and up to 16 hours.

2. Supply your smoker with wood pellets and follow the start-up procedure. Preheat the grill, with the lid closed, to 350° F.

3. Remove the turkey from the brine and pat dry with paper towels. Discard the brine. Place the onion, apple, celery, and herbs in the main cavity. Tie the legs together with butcher's twine. Fold the wings behind the back. Rub the outside with butter. Lightly season with salt and pepper.

4. Place the turkey breast side up on a wire rack in a shallow roasting pan. Place the pan on the grate and roast the turkey until the internal temperature in the thickest part of a thigh reaches 165°F (74°C), about 2½ to 3 hours.

5. Transfer the turkey to a cutting board and let rest for 20 minutes. (Save the drippings to make from-scratch turkey gravy.) Carve the turkey and arrange the meat on a large platter before serving.

Chicken Parmesan Sliders With Pesto Mayonnaise

Servings: 4
Cooking Time: 30 Minutes

Ingredients:
- 2 Pound Chicken, ground
- 1 Cup Parmesan cheese
- 1 Tablespoon Worcestershire sauce
- black pepper
- 1 Cup mayonnaise
- 2 Tablespoon Pesto Sauce
- 3 Roma tomatoes
- 1 red onion, sliced
- Baby Spinach

Directions:
1. Line a baking sheet with plastic wrap. In a large mixing bowl, combine the ground chicken, the Parmesan, the Worcestershire, and a few grinds of black pepper. Wet your hands with cold water, and use them to mix the ingredients.

2. Divide the meat mixture in half, then form six 2-inch patties out of each half. Place the patties on the baking sheet, cover with another sheet of plastic wrap, and refrigerate for at least 1 hour.

3. Combine the mayonnaise and pesto in a small bowl and whisk together. Cover and refrigerate until serving time.

4. Supply your smoker with wood pellets and follow the start-up procedure. Preheat the grill, with the lid closed, to 300° F.

5. Arrange the chicken patties on the grill grate and grill, turning once, until the patties are cooked through (165F), about 30 minutes. Grill: 300 °F Probe: 165 °F

6. To serve, put a chicken patty on the bottom of a slider bun and top with a dollop of the pesto mayonnaise. Add tomato, onion, and spinach as desired. Replace the top of the bun and skewer with a frilled toothpick, if desired.

Asian Chicken Sliders

Servings: 4
Cooking Time: 10 Minutes

Ingredients:
- 1½lb (680g) ground chicken, preferably a mix of breast and thigh meat
- 1 large egg, beaten
- ½ cup panko breadcrumbs or crushed chicharróns
- 2 scallions, trimmed, white and green parts finely minced
- 2 garlic cloves, peeled and finely minced
- ¼ cup loosely packed minced cilantro leaves
- 2 tbsp sambal oelek
- 1 tbsp light soy sauce
- 2 tsp peeled and minced fresh ginger
- 1 tsp coarse salt
- 1 tsp freshly ground black pepper
- vegetable oil
- for serving
- 8 slider buns
- reduced-fat mayo
- fresh baby arugula or spinach leaves
- pickled onions (optional)

Directions:
1. Supply your smoker with wood pellets and follow the start-up procedure. Preheat the grill, with the lid closed, to 450° F.

2. In a large bowl, combine all the ingredients except the vegetable oil. Wet your hands with cold water. Knead the mixture until it's somewhat sticky and the ingredients are incorporated. Form the mixture into 8 equal-sized patties. Lightly oil the patties on both sides with the oil.

3. Place the patties on the grate and grill until the internal temperature reaches 165°F (74°C), about 4 to 5 minutes per side.

4. Transfer each patty to the bottom half of each bun. Top with a dollop of mayo, a few arugula or spinach leaves, and drained pickled onions (if using). Top each slider with the top half of the bun. Run a knotted bamboo skewer through the top of each slider before serving.

Bbq Chicken Legs

Servings: 6
Cooking Time: 60 Minutes

Ingredients:

- 8 chicken drumsticks
- 2 Tablespoon Chicken Rub
- 1 Cup Apricot BBQ Sauce
- 1 Cup 'Que BBQ Sauce
- 1 Cup apple jelly, melted

Directions:

1. Pat drumsticks dry with a paper towel and season generously Traeger Chicken Rub.
2. Supply your smoker with wood pellets and follow the start-up procedure. Preheat the grill, with the lid closed, to 180° F.
3. Arrange the chicken legs on the grill grate and smoke for 30 minutes. Grill: 180 °F
4. Increase the grill temperature to 350 degrees F and cook for an additional 30 minutes. Grill: 350 °F
5. While the drumsticks are cooking, combine the two BBQ sauces and the jelly in a small sauce pan. Bring to a simmer over medium heat then set aside until ready to use.
6. Brush the BBQ sauce on the chicken legs. Cook for an additional 10 minutes, or until an instant-read meat thermometer inserted into the thickest part of the leg (but not touching the bone) reaches 165 degrees F. Enjoy! Grill: 350 °F Probe: 165 °F

Fried Chicken Sliders

Servings: 8
Cooking Time: 30 Minutes

Ingredients:

- 8 Slider Buns
- ½ Cup Buttermilk
- 4 Horizontally Cut Chicken Breasts
- 2 Cups Flour, All-Purpose
- 1 Tablespoon Hot Sauce
- ¼ Cup Mayonnaise
- 2 Quarts Cooking Canola Or Soybean Oil
- ½ Cup Spicy Bread And Butter Pickle Slices
- ½ Tablespoon Champion Chicken Seasoning

Directions:

1. Supply your smoker with wood pellets and follow the start-up procedure. Preheat the grill, with the lid open, to 350° F. If you're using a gas or charcoal grill, set it up for medium heat.
2. Place a deep cast iron pan on the grill and fill it with about 3 inches of cooking oil. Place a temperature probe into the oil.
3. While the oil heats, combine the buttermilk, hot sauce and Champion Chicken seasoning in a resealable plastic bag. Seal and shake to mix, then place the chicken in the bag and turn to coat.

4. Place the flour on a plate and dip the chicken in the flour to coat. Place the chicken on a wire rack set on a baking sheet and allow the coated chicken to set for 10 minutes, then dip again in the flour.
5. Once the oil in the cast iron pan reaches 350°F, place a temperature probe in a piece of chicken and fry the chicken, 2-3 pieces at a time. The oil temperature in the pan will drop by 25-30 degrees, so make sure not to put more than 3 pieces of chicken in the pan or your chicken will be greasy.
6. Fry the chicken until golden brown, crispy, and the internal temperature of the chicken is 170°F. Remove the chicken and place on a plate lined with paper towels. Allow the chicken to drain and rest for 5 minutes. Fry the remaining chicken pieces, reinserting the temperature probe.
7. Once the chicken is all fried, place the chicken on the slider buns, top with spicy bread and butter pickles, and a swoop of mayo, serve immediately.

Cheese Chicken Cordon Bleu

Servings: 8
Cooking Time: 75 Minutes

Ingredients:

- 8 Chicken, Boneless/Skinless
- 1 Cup Mozzarella Cheese, Shredded
- Lemon Pepper Garlic Seasoning
- 8 Prosciutto, Sliced

Directions:

1. Supply your smoker with wood pellets and follow the start-up procedure. Preheat the grill, with the lid closed, to 250° F.
2. Pound each chicken breast with a mallet or cast iron pan so that it's about ½ inch thick.
3. On a piece of prosciutto, sprinkle mozzarella cheese and roll up. Place in the middle of a chicken breast and wrap the chicken around the prosciutto roll. Sprinkle with Lemon Pepper seasoning.
4. Smoke for an hour to 75 minutes, or until internal temperature reaches 165 degrees F.

Bacon Weaved Stuffed Turkey Breast

Servings: 8
Cooking Time: 60 Minutes

Ingredients:

- 1/2 Cup celery, diced
- 14 Ounce Stuffing Mix
- 2 Tablespoon chopped sage
- 4 Tablespoon Chicken Rub
- 1/2 Cup dried sweetened cranberries
- 2 Cup apple cider
- 20 Strips thick-cut bacon

Directions:

1. Prepare the stuffing: Add all stuffing ingredients into a large bowl and toss to mix together.

2. Create a bacon weave and lay it out in a 5x5 pattern on cutting board.

3. Using a long, thin knife, butterfly each of the turkey breasts. Stuff each breast with a generous amount of stuffing and close.

4. Place turkey breast on prepared bacon weave, carefully wrap turkey, and secure with tooth picks. Repeat for the second breast.

5. Supply your smoker with wood pellets and follow the start-up procedure. Preheat the grill, with the lid closed, to 375° F.

6. Place the breasts seam side down on a rimmed baking sheet. Transfer directly to grill.

7. Place the bacon wrapped turkey breasts directly to the Traeger and cook for approximately 45 mins to 1 hour or until an instant read thermometer inserted into the center of the stuffing reaches 165 degrees F. Grill: 375 °F Probe: 165 °F

8. If the bacon gets too dark, cover with foil. Slice and enjoy!

Cheesy Buffalo Chicken Pinwheels

Servings: 8
Cooking Time: 10 Minutes

Ingredients:

- 2 T Bleu Cheese, Crumbled
- ½ Cup Buffalo Wing Sauce, Divided
- 1-2, Boneless And Skinless Chicken Breast
- ½ Cup Colby Cheese, Shredded
- 4 Oz. Cream Cheese
- 4, 10" Diameter Flour Tortillas
- 2 Scallions, Thinly Sliced [Reserve 1 Tsp Of Green For Garnish]

Directions:

1. Supply your smoker with wood pellets and follow the start-up procedure. Preheat the grill, with the lid closed, to 375° F. If you're using a gas or charcoal grill, set it up for medium heat. Remove chicken from refrigerator place on grill. Grill chicken for 10 min, turning once. Allow to rest 10 minutes, then shred.

2. In a food processor, add remaining buffalo wing sauce, cream cheese, Colby cheese, bleu cheese, and scallions. Process on low for 20 seconds. Add shredded chicken breast to mixture and pulse about 8 times, or until mixture is fully combined.

3. Place tortillas on a flat work surface and divide filling into quarters. Spread mixture evenly over each tortilla with a rubber spatula.

4. Roll up tortillas and place seam side down on cutting board. Refrigerate for 10 minutes, then slice into ½ inch pieces. Transfer to serving platter and garnish with remaining scallions. Serve with extra buffalo sauce or ranch dressing.

Savory Jerk Chicken Wings

Servings: 4
Cooking Time: 20 Minutes

Ingredients:

- 1 Tsp Allspice, Ground
- 3 Lbs Chicken Wings, Split
- 1/2 Tsp Cinnamon, Ground
- 4 Garlic Cloves, Smashed
- 2 Tsp Ginger, Grated
- 1 Habanero Pepper, Chopped
- 2 Tbsp Honey
- 2 Tbsp Lemon Juice
- 1/3 Cup Lime Juice
- 1/2 Tsp Nutmeg, Ground
- 1/2 Cup Olive Oil
- 1/4 Cup Poblano Pepper, Chopped
- 1 Tbsp Tamari
- 2 Tsp Thyme, Dried
- 1/2 Cup Yellow Onion, Chopped

Directions:

1. Add chicken to a large resealable plastic bag.

2. In the bowl of a food processor, add the garlic, onion, ginger, peppers, tamari, honey, lime juice, lemon juice, thyme, allspice, cinnamon, nutmeg, and oil. Process on low for 1 minute, then transfer marinade to the bag. Seal the bag and place in the refrigerator for at least 2 hours, up to overnight.

3. Supply your smoker with wood pellets and follow the start-up procedure. Preheat the grill, with the lid open, to 425° F. If using a gas or charcoal grill, set it up for medium-high heat.

4. Remove wings from the marinade, and discard remaining marinade. Place wings on the grill and cook for 15 to 20 minutes, flipping every 5 minutes, until an internal temperature of 165 F is reached.

5. Remove wings from the grill and serve warm.

Smoked Turkey Jerky

Servings: 6
Cooking Time: 240 Minutes

Ingredients:

- 1/2 Cup soy sauce
- 1/4 Cup water
- 2 Tablespoon honey
- 2 Tablespoon Asian chili garlic sauce
- 2 Tablespoon lime juice
- 1 Tablespoon Morton Tender Quick Home Meat Cure
- 2 Pound (4-5 lb) boneless turkey breast

Directions:

1. In a mixing bowl, combine the soy sauce, water, honey, chili-garlic paste, lime juice, and curing salt, if using. With a sharp knife, slice the turkey into 1/4" thick slices with the grain, which helps it hold together better as it dries. (This is easier if the meat is partially frozen.) Trim any fat, membrane, or connective tissue.

2. Put the turkey slices in a large resealable plastic bag. Pour the marinade mixture over the turkey, and massage the bag so that all the slices get coated with the marinade. Seal the bag and refrigerate for several hours, or overnight.

3. Supply your smoker with wood pellets and follow the start-up procedure. Preheat the grill, with the lid closed, to 180° F.

4. Remove the turkey from the marinade and discard the marinade. Dry the turkey slices between paper towels. Arrange in a single layer directly on the grill grate.

5. Smoke for 2 to 4 hours, or until the jerky is dry but still chewy and somewhat pliant when you bend a piece. Grill: 180 °F

6. Transfer to a resealable plastic bag while the jerky's still warm. Let the jerky rest for an hour at room temperature. Squeeze any air from the bag, and refrigerate the jerky. It will keep for several weeks. Enjoy!

Green Goddess Chicken Legs

Servings: 4
Cooking Time: 40 Minutes

Ingredients:
- 2 Pound chicken legs
- 2 Cup Prepared "Green Goddess" Dressing
- 1/4 Cup parsley, chopped
- 1 Tablespoon paprika

Directions:
1. Place the chicken legs in a large resealable plastic bag. Combine the Green Goddess dressing as well as the parsley and paprika. Pour over the chicken legs. Refrigerate for 2 to 8 hours.

2. Supply your smoker with wood pellets and follow the start-up procedure. Preheat the grill, with the lid closed, to 350° F. Drain the chicken legs. Arrange the legs directly on the grill grate and grill, turning once, for 40 to 50 minutes, or until the legs are golden brown and cooked through. Serve at once. Grill: 350 °F

Bbq Turkey Drumsticks

Servings: 6
Cooking Time: 120 Minutes

Ingredients:
- 1/2 Tbsp Black Pepper
- 1 Tbsp Brown Sugar
- 1/2 Tsp Cayenne Pepper
- 1/2 Tbsp Coriander, Ground
- 1/2 Tbsp Granulated Garlic

- 1 Package, Approx 4 Lbs Honeysuckle White® Turkey Drumsticks
- 1 Tbsp Kosher Salt
- 2 Tbsp Olive Oil

Directions:
1. Supply your smoker with wood pellets and follow the start-up procedure. Preheat the grill, with the lid open, to 225° F. If using a gas or charcoal grill, set it up for low, indirect heat.

2. Place Honeysuckle White® Turkey Legs on a sheet tray, coat with olive oil, then season with a blend of salt pepper, cayenne, brown sugar, granulated garlic, and ground coriander.

3. Place turkey legs in the smoking cabinet and smoke for 1 ½ hours, checking the internal temperature after 1 hour.

4. Increase the temperature to 325°F, transfer the turkey legs to the bottom grill grate and cook for another 25 to 30 minutes, until the internal temperature reaches 170°F.

5. Remove turkey drumsticks from the grill, allow to rest for 10 minutes, then serve warm.

Bbq Game Day Chicken Wings And Thighs

Servings: 6
Cooking Time: 50 Minutes

Ingredients:
- 10 chicken thighs
- 30 chicken wings
- 1/2 Cup olive oil
- 1/2 Cup Chicken Rub

Directions:
1. Place thighs and wings in a large bowl. Add the olive oil and Traeger Chicken Rub and mix well. Cover bowl and refrigerate for 3 to 8 hours.

2. Supply your smoker with wood pellets and follow the start-up procedure. Preheat the grill, with the lid closed, to 375° F.

3. Place chicken directly on the grill grate and cook for 45 minutes. Check the internal temperature of the chicken, it is considered done at 165°F, however, a finished temperature of 175 to 180°F results in a better texture in dark meat. Grill: 375 °F Probe: 165 °F

4. Once the finished temperature is reached, remove chicken from the grill and let rest for 5 to 10 minutes before serving. Enjoy!

Wood-fired Chicken Breasts

Servings: 2-4

Cooking Time: 45 Minutes

Ingredients:

- 2 (1-pound) bone-in, skin-on chicken breasts
- 1 batch Chicken Rub

Directions:

1. Supply your smoker with wood pellets and follow the start-up procedure. Preheat the grill, with the lid closed, to 350°F.
2. Season the chicken breasts all over with the rub. Using your hands, work the rub into the meat.
3. Place the breasts directly on the grill grate and smoke until their internal temperature reaches 170°F. Remove the breasts from the grill and serve immediately.

Savory-sweet Turkey Legs

Servings: 4

Cooking Time: 300 Minutes

Ingredients:

- 1 gallon hot water
- 1 cup curing salt (such as Morton Tender Quick)
- ¼ cup packed light brown sugar
- 1 teaspoon freshly ground black pepper
- 1 teaspoon ground cloves
- 1 bay leaf
- 2 teaspoons liquid smoke
- 4 turkey legs
- Mandarin Glaze, for serving

Directions:

1. In a large container with a lid, stir together the water, curing salt, brown sugar, pepper, cloves, bay leaf, and liquid smoke until the salt and sugar are dissolved; let come to room temperature.
2. Submerge the turkey legs in the seasoned brine, cover, and refrigerate overnight.
3. When ready to smoke, remove the turkey legs from the brine and rinse them; discard the brine.
4. Supply your smoker with wood pellets and follow the start-up procedure. Preheat, with the lid closed, to 225°F.
5. Arrange the turkey legs on the grill, close the lid, and smoke for 4 to 5 hours, or until dark brown and a meat thermometer inserted in the thickest part of the meat reads 165°F.
6. Serve with Mandarin Glaze on the side or drizzled over the turkey legs.

Yucatán-spiced Chicken Thighs

Servings: 4

Cooking Time: 40 Minutes

Ingredients:

- 8 skin-on, bone-in chicken thighs, about 2½lb (1.2kg) total
- for the marinade
- 2oz (55g) achiote paste
- ¼ cup hot distilled water
- ¼ cup freshly squeezed orange juice
- 2 tbsp freshly squeezed lime juice
- 2 tbsp apple cider vinegar or distilled white vinegar
- 2 tbsp vegetable oil or extra virgin olive oil
- 2 garlic cloves, peeled and minced
- 1 tsp kosher salt, plus more
- 1 tsp dried Mexican oregano
- ½ tsp ground cumin
- ¼ tsp ground cinnamon

Directions:

1. In a small bowl, make the marinade by using a fork to crumble the achiote paste. Add the hot water and mash the paste with the fork until blended. Whisk in the orange juice, lime juice, vinegar, oil, garlic, salt, oregano, cumin, and cinnamon.
2. Place the chicken thighs in a resealable plastic bag. Pour the marinade over the chicken, turning and massaging the bag to thoroughly coat the chicken. Refrigerate for 2 hours.
3. Supply your smoker with wood pellets and follow the start-up procedure. Preheat the grill, with the lid closed, to 400° F.
4. Remove the chicken thighs from the marinade and let any excess drip off. (Discard the marinade.) Place the chicken thighs skin side down on the grate at an angle to the bars. Grill for 20 minutes and then turn. Continue to grill until the internal temperature in the thighs reaches 165°F (74°C), about 20 minutes more.
5. Transfer the thighs to a platter and serve immediately.

Turkey & Bacon Kebabs With Ranch-style Dressing

Servings: 8

Cooking Time: 25 Minutes

Ingredients:

- 1½lb (680g) skinless turkey tenders or boneless, skinless turkey breasts, cut into 1-inch (2.5cm) chunks
- 8 strips of thick-cut bacon
- 12 fresh bay leaves (optional)
- for the dressing
- 1 cup reduced-fat mayo
- 1 cup light sour cream
- ½ cup buttermilk or whole milk, plus more
- 2 tbsp minced fresh parsley
- 2 tbsp minced fresh chives
- 1 tbsp minced fresh dill

- 2 tsp freshly squeezed lemon juice
- 1 tsp Worcestershire sauce
- 1 tsp garlic salt
- 1 tsp onion powder
- ½ tsp coarse salt, plus more
- ½ tsp freshly ground black pepper, plus more

Directions:

1. In a large bowl, make the dressing by whisking together the mayo, sour cream, and buttermilk until smooth. Whisk in the remaining ingredients. Pour half the mixture into a small bowl. Cover and refrigerate.

2. Add the turkey to the mixture remaining in the bowl and toss to coat thoroughly. If the dressing seems too thick (dip-like), add more buttermilk 1 tablespoon at a time. Cover and refrigerate for 2 to 4 hours.

3. Supply your smoker with wood pellets and follow the start-up procedure. Preheat the grill, with the lid closed, to 375° F.

4. Place the bacon on the grate and cook until some of the fat has rendered and the bacon begins to brown, about 15 minutes. Remove the bacon from the grill to cool. Cut the bacon into 1-inch (2.5cm) squares. Set aside.

5. Drain the tenders and discard any excess dressing. Alternate threading the turkey, bacon pieces, and 3 bay leaves on a bamboo skewer. Repeat the threading with 3 more skewers.

6. Place the kebabs on the grate and grill until the turkey is cooked through, about 4 to 5 minutes per side, turning as needed.

7. Transfer the skewers to a platter. Serve with the reserved dressing.

Roasted Beer Can Chicken

Servings: 4
Cooking Time: 60 Minutes

Ingredients:

- 1 Whole (3-5 lb) chicken
- Chicken Rub
- 1 Can beer

Directions:

1. Season chicken generously with Traeger Chicken Rub, including inside the cavity.

2. Tuck the wing tips back.

3. Supply your smoker with wood pellets and follow the start-up procedure. Preheat the grill, with the lid closed, to 350° F.

4. Open the can of beer and set the chicken on top of the beer. Make sure all but the bottom 1-1/2 inch of the beer can is in the cavity of the chicken. Tip: you can also place the beer can directly on the grill grates, then place the chicken on top.

5. Place the entire chicken and beer can directly on the grill grate. Cook for 60 to 75 minutes, or until the internal temperature

registers 165°F in the thickest part of the breast. Grill: 350 °F Probe: 165 °F

6. Remove from the grill and onto a sheet tray and let rest 5 to 10 minutes. Before carving, lay the bird on its back and remove the beer can. Carve and enjoy!

Smoked Ditch Chicken

Servings: 2
Cooking Time: 60 Minutes

Ingredients:

- 3 pheasant breasts or quarters
- Blackened Saskatchewan Rub
- 3 Tablespoon Smoky Okie's Rooster Booster Poultry Seasoning
- 1 white onion
- 1 red bell pepper
- 4 Tablespoon olive oil
- salt and pepper
- 1 Box Uncle Ben's Ready Rice Pilaf

Directions:

1. Supply your smoker with wood pellets and follow the start-up procedure. Preheat the grill, with the lid closed, to 275° F.

2. Clean and rinse pheasant breasts and thighs; place in a large resealable bag.

3. Add a liberal amount of Traeger Blackened Saskatchewan Rub and Rooster Booster. Shake vigorously and set aside.

4. Slice the onions into thin sections. Quarter the peppers, removing the core.

5. Brush onions and peppers lightly with olive oil and lightly apply salt and pepper.

6. Place the vegetables on tin foil on one side of the grill. Give the vegetables an ample head start on the pheasant (at least an hour), as pheasant is lean and will cook quickly.

7. After allowing the vegetables to smoke for at least an hour, place the pheasant on the grill, keeping the grill at 275°F. Cook for 30 to 45 minutes. Remove the pheasant and vegetables from the grill and serve over a bed of rice pilaf. Enjoy! Grill: 275 °F

Bbq Smoked Turkey Jerky

Servings: 4 - 6
Cooking Time: 120 Minutes

Ingredients:

- 2 Tablespoons Apple Cider Vinegar
- 2 Tablespoons (Any Kind) Barbecue Sauce
- 1 Tablespoon Quick Curing Salt
- ½ Cup Soy Sauce
- 4 Tablespoons Sweet Sweet Rib Rub
- 2 Pounds Boneless Skinless Turkey Breast

- ¼ Cup Water

Directions:

1. In a large bowl, combine the soy sauce, water, barbecue sauce, apple cider vinegar, quick curing salt, and 2 tablespoons of the Sweet Rib Rub. Whisk together until well combined and pour into a large, resealable plastic bag.

2. Using a sharp knife, slice the turkey into ¼ inch slices with the grain (this is easier if the meat is partially frozen). Trim off any fat, skin or connective tissue and discard.

3. Place the turkey slices into the plastic bag, seal, and massage the marinade into the turkey. Refrigerate for 24 hours.

4. Once the jerky is ready to go, remove the turkey from the refrigerator, drain the marinade and discard. Pat the turkey dry with paper towels and sprinkle all sides generously with the remaining Sweet Rib Rub.

5. Supply your smoker with wood pellets and follow the start-up procedure. Preheat the grill, with the lid closed, to 180° F. If you're using a sawdust or charcoal smoker, set it up for medium low heat.

6. Place the turkey slices directly onto the smoker grates and smoke for 2-4 hours, or until the jerky is chewy but still bends slightly.

7. Transfer the jerky to a resealable plastic bag while the jerky is still warm and allow it to sit at room temperature for 1 hour. Squeeze any air from the bag and place in the refrigerator. It will keep for several weeks.

Bbq Chicken Thighs

Servings: 4
Cooking Time: 35 Minutes

Ingredients:

- 6 bone-in, skin-on chicken thighs
- salt and ground black pepper
- Big Game Rub

Directions:

1. Supply your smoker with wood pellets and follow the start-up procedure. Preheat the grill, with the lid closed, to 350° F.

2. While grill is heating, trim excess fat and skin from chicken thighs. Season with a light layer of salt and pepper then a layer of Traeger Big Game Rub.

3. Place chicken thighs on the grill grate and cook for 35 minutes. Check internal temperature, chicken is done at 165°F, but there is enough fat that they will stay moist at an internal temperature of 180°F and the texture is better. Grill: 350 °F Probe: 165 °F

4. Remove from the grill and let rest for 5 minutes before serving. Enjoy!

Lollipop Drumsticks

Servings: 4-6
Cooking Time: 75 Minutes

Ingredients:

- 1 Cup Barbecue Sauce
- 10 Tablespoons Butter, Salted
- 12 Chicken Drumsticks
- 1 Cup Hot Sauce
- Champion Chicken Seasoning
- Blue Cheese Or Ranch Dressing

Directions:

1. Supply your smoker with wood pellets and follow the start-up procedure. Preheat the grill, with the lid open, to 300° F.

2. Rinse chicken and pat dry with a paper towel.

3. Chop the very top of the drumstick on the larger, meaty side so the lollipops sit flatly. On the small end of the drumstick, about an inch above the knuckle, use a sharp knife or kitchen shears to cut the skin and tendons all the way down to the bone and pull the skin and cartilage off the knuckle.

4. Remove the tiny, sharp bone that sits right against the exposed chicken leg. Then, push all the meat and skin down to form the lollipop ball. Use your knife or shears to remove any excess tendons.

5. Season each lollipop generously with Champion Chicken seasoning and place in the aluminum pan with the flat side done and bones standing straight up. Then, cut 10 tablespoons of butter into cubes of 1 tablespoon each and place evenly throughout the rows of lollipops.

6. Cook lollipop drumsticks on your   at 300°F for 1 hour; checking back every 20 minutes to baste the meat with the melted butter on the bottom of the pan.

7. For the Sauce: add your favorite bbq sauce into one aluminum loaf pan. Then, add 1 cup of hot sauce and 10 tablespoons of butter into the other aluminum loaf pan. Place them on the grill 5 minutes before your chicken is done. Stir well once it's warm and the butter has melted.

8. After 1 hour, use a thermometer to check the internal temperature of the lollipops. They will be ready to glaze when the temperature reaches 165°F.

9. Once ready, dip 6 lollipops in the bbq sauce and 6 in the buffalo sauce making sure to hold the leg and cover the meat entirely. Then, place the lollipops on the wing rack and put back on the grill for 15 more minutes or until the sauce is set.

Smoked Deviled Eggs

Servings: 4
Cooking Time: 30 Minutes

Ingredients:

- 7 hard boiled eggs, cooked and peeled
- 3 Tablespoon mayonnaise
- 3 Teaspoon diced chives
- 1 Teaspoon brown mustard
- 1 Teaspoon apple cider vinegar
- hot sauce
- salt and pepper
- 2 Tablespoon cooked bacon, crumbled
- paprika

Directions:

1. Supply your smoker with wood pellets and follow the start-up procedure. Preheat the grill, with the lid closed, to 180° F.
2. Place cooked and peeled eggs directly on the grill grate and smoke eggs for 30 minutes. Grill: 180 °F
3. Remove from grill and allow eggs to cool. Slice the eggs lengthwise and scoop the egg yolks into a gallon zip top bag.
4. Add mayonnaise, chives, mustard, vinegar, hot sauce, salt, and pepper to the bag. Zip the bag closed and, using your hands, knead all of the ingredients together until completely smooth.
5. Squeeze the yolk mixture into one corner of the bag and cut a small part of the corner off. Pipe the yolk mixture into the hard boiled egg whites. Top the deviled eggs with crumbled bacon and paprika. Chill until ready to serve. Enjoy!

Smoked Chicken Leg & Thigh Quarters

Servings: 6
Cooking Time: 120 Minutes

Ingredients:

- 8 chicken legs (thigh and drumstick)
- 3 Tablespoon olive oil
- Pork & Poultry Rub

Directions:

1. Place the chicken pieces in a large mixing bowl. Pour oil over the chicken to coat each piece, then season to taste with the Traeger Pork & Poultry Rub. Massage the chicken pieces to encourage the oil and seasonings get under the skin. Cover and refrigerate for at least 1 to 2 hours.
2. Supply your smoker with wood pellets and follow the start-up procedure. Preheat the grill, with the lid closed, to 180° F.
3. Remove the chicken from the refrigerator, letting any excess oil drip back into the bowl. Grill: 180 °F
4. Arrange the chicken on the grill grate and smoke for 1 hour. Increase Traeger temperature to 350°F and continue to roast the chicken until the internal temperature in the thickest part of a thigh is 165°F or the chicken is golden brown and the juices run clear, about 50 to 60 minutes. Grill: 350 °F Probe: 165 °F
5. Remove from the grill and allow the chicken to rest for 8 to 10 minutes and serve. Enjoy!

Smoked Drumsticks

Servings: 2-4
Cooking Time: 25 Minutes

Ingredients:

- 1 pound chicken drumsticks
- 2 tablespoons olive oil
- 1 batch Sweet and Spicy Cinnamon Rub

Directions:

1. Supply your smoker with wood pellets and follow the start-up procedure. Preheat the grill, with the lid closed, to 350°F.
2. Coat the drumsticks all over with olive oil and season with the rub. Using your hands, work the rub into the meat.
3. Place the drumsticks directly on the grill grate and smoke until their internal temperature reaches 170°F. Remove the drumsticks from the grill and serve immediately.

County Fair Turkey Legs

Servings: 4
Cooking Time: 90 Minutes

Ingredients:

- 4 turkey legs, each about 1lb (450g)
- for the brine
- ½ gallon (1.9 liters) distilled water
- ½ cup kosher salt
- ¼ cup light brown sugar or low-carb substitute
- 2½ tsp pink curing salt #1
- 1 tsp liquid smoke (optional)

Directions:

1. In a stockpot on the stovetop over medium-high heat, make the brine by combining the ingredients. Bring the mixture to a boil. Stir until the salts and sugar dissolve. Remove the pot from the stovetop and let the brine cool to room temperature. Cover and refrigerate until cool.
2. Submerge the turkey legs in the brine. If they float, place a resealable bag of ice on top. Refrigerate for 24 hours, turning from time to time so the legs cure evenly.
3. Supply your smoker with wood pellets and follow the start-up procedure. Preheat the grill, with the lid closed, to 325° F.
4. Remove the turkey legs from the brine and discard the liquid. Rinse the legs under cold running water and pat dry with paper towels.
5. Place the turkey legs on the grate and grill for 45 minutes. Turn and continue to cook until the turkey skin is nicely browned

and the internal temperature in a leg reaches 170 to 175°F (77 to 79°C), about 45 minutes. (Turkey legs have a lot of connective tissue and they seem to turn out better when cooked to a slightly higher temperature.)

6. Remove the legs from the grill and serve warm or cold.

Smoked Chicken Fajita Quesadillas

Servings: 4
Cooking Time: 45 Minutes

Ingredients:

- 2 Chicken, Boneless/Skinless
- 1 Tsp Chilli, Powder
- 1 Tsp Garlic Powder
- 1/2 Green Bell Pepper, Sliced
- 1 Cup Mexican Cheese, Shredded
- 1/2 Onion, Sliced
- 1/2 Tsp Oregano
- 1 Tsp Paprika, Powder
- 1/4 Tsp Pepper
- 1/2 Red Bell Peppers
- Salsa
- Sour Cream
- 4 Tortilla
- 1/2 Yellow Bell Pepper, Sliced

Directions:

1. Supply your smoker with wood pellets and follow the start-up procedure. Preheat the grill, with the lid open, to 350° F.
2. Combine spices in a bowl and season chicken breasts. Leave a little bit of seasoning for the vegetables.
3. Place chicken on the grates and cook for 30 minutes, flipped halfway through.
4. In a Vegetable Basket, combine all vegetables and season with the remaining spice mixture.
5. Open up the flame broiler and saute over the open flame for about 15 minutes, or until the vegetables are cooked to your liking.
6. On a tortilla, layer cheese, vegetables, sliced chicken and more cheese. Fold the tortilla and place over the open flame on your Grill. Sear until the tortilla is nicely toasted and the cheese is melted. Cut and serve with salsa and sour cream.

Sweet Cajun Wings

Servings: 4
Cooking Time: 30 Minutes

Ingredients:

- 2 Pound chicken wings
- Pork & Poultry Rub
- Cajun Shake

Directions:

1. Coat wings in Traeger Sweet rub and Traeger Cajun shake.
2. Supply your smoker with wood pellets and follow the start-up procedure. Preheat the grill, with the lid closed, to 350° F.
3. Cook for 30 minutes or until skin is brown and center is juicy and an instant-read thermometer reads at least 165°F. Serve, enjoy! Grill: 350 °F Probe: 165 °F

Grilled Greek Chicken With Garlic & Lemon

Servings: 4
Cooking Time: 60 Minutes

Ingredients:

- 2 Whole Roasting Chicken, 3.5-4lbs, each cut into 8 pieces
- 2 Whole lemons, quartered
- Cup extra-virgin olive oil
- 4 Clove garlic, minced
- 1 1/2 Tablespoon Oregano, fresh
- 1 As Needed Chicken Rub
- 1 Cup Broth, chicken

Directions:

1. Arrange the chicken pieces in a single layer in a large roasting pan. Squeeze the juice from each piece of lemon over the chicken, catching any seeds in your fingers. Tuck the lemon rinds in with the chicken. Drizzle the olive oil over all.
2. Sprinkle the garlic over the chicken. Dust the chicken with the fresh oregano, and season it generously with the Traeger Chicken rub, or salt and black pepper. Pour the chicken broth into the pan.
3. Supply your smoker with wood pellets and follow the start-up procedure. Preheat the grill, with the lid closed, to 350° F.
4. Roast the chicken for an hour, or until the juices run clear or the internal temperature reaches 165°F on an instant-read meat thermometer. Grill: 350 °F Probe: 165 °F
5. Transfer to a platter or plates and spoon some of the juices on top. Let rest 3 minutes before serving. Enjoy!

Dry Brine Traeger Turkey

Servings: 6
Cooking Time: 360 Minutes

Ingredients:

- 1 farm fresh turkey, any size
- 1 Teaspoon kosher salt per pound of turkey
- fresh thyme
- fresh rosemary
- fresh sage
- fresh parsley

Directions:

1. Make sure to plan ahead, this recipe requires multiple days of brine time.

2. Combine desired amounts of thyme, rosemary, sage and/or parsley with kosher salt. Rub kosher salt and spice mixture over entire surface of the turkey, including the cavity.

3. Place turkey in a bag or plastic wrap and seal tight. Place turkey in the fridge for 2 days. On day 3, take the turkey out of the bag or unwrap plastic wrap. Place the turkey back in the fridge, uncovered for 24 hours.

4. Supply your smoker with wood pellets and follow the start-up procedure. Preheat the grill, with the lid closed, to 180° F.

5. Place the turkey on grill, breast up. Smoke the turkey for 3 to 4 hours. Grill: 180 °F

6. After 3 to 4 hours, increase the grill temperature to 325°F and continue to cook turkey until it reaches an internal temperature of 165°F. Enjoy!

Roasted Stuffed Turkey Breast

Servings: 6
Cooking Time: 40 Minutes

Ingredients:
- 1 (4-5 lb) boneless turkey breast
- 5 Slices thick-cut bacon, chopped
- 3/4 Cup assorted mushrooms
- 1 Bunch scallions, chopped
- 1/8 Cup white wine
- 3 Tablespoon panko breadcrumbs
- salt
- black pepper

Directions:
1. Supply your smoker with wood pellets and follow the start-up procedure. Preheat the grill, with the lid closed, to 375° F.

2. Slice the turkey breast horizontally, making sure not to slice all the way through. Lay breast open flat.

3. Cook bacon in a skillet over medium heat until crispy. Remove bacon and set aside. Sauté mushrooms in the bacon grease until browned. Add scallions and cook for an additional two minutes. Add white wine and cook down until no wine remains. Stir in breadcrumbs and bacon, adding salt and pepper to taste.

4. Transfer filling to fridge to cool for 15 to 20 minutes. Once chilled, spread the filling onto the turkey breast, pressing lightly to make sure it adheres. Roll the turkey breast tightly and tie with butcher's twine at about 1 inch intervals. Tuck the ends of the turkey breast under and tie with twine lengthwise.

5. Season the outside of the turkey breast with salt and pepper. Place in grill for 40 minutes. Check the internal temperature, desired temperature is 165°F. Once the finished temperature is reached, remove turkey from the grill and let rest for 10 minutes. Slice and serve. Enjoy! Grill: 375 °F Probe: 165 °F

Peanut Butter Chicken Wings

Servings: 4
Cooking Time: 35 Minutes

Ingredients:
- 1 Tsp Black Peppercorns, Ground
- 2 Tbsp Brown Sugar
- 4 Lbs Chicken Wings, Trimmed And Patted Dry
- 2 Tbsp Honey
- 1/4 Cup Peanut Butter
- 10 Oz Peanuts, Whole
- 2 Tsp Sweet Rib Rub
- 1/2 Red Onion, Minced
- 1/2 Cup Strawberry Preserves
- 1 Tbsp Thai Chili Sauce
- 1/4 Cup Worcestershire Sauce

Directions:
1. Place chicken wings in a 9 x13 glass baking dish. Pour mixture over chicken, cover with plastic wrap, and refrigerate for 2 hours.

2. Supply your smoker with wood pellets and follow the start-up procedure. Preheat the grill, with the lid open, to 400° F. Preheat griddle to medium-low flame. If using a gas or charcoal grill, set it to medium-high heat.

3. Place wings directly on grill grate, over indirect heat, and cook for 20 to 25 minutes, rotating wings every 5 minutes.

4. Meanwhile, place shelled peanuts on the griddle, turning occasionally with a metal spatula for 5 to 7 minutes, to lightly roast. Remove from the griddle and set aside to cool.

5. Remove wings from grill and allow to rest for 5 minutes. While wings are resting, shell the peanuts, and transfer to a resealable plastic bag. Use a rolling pin to crush the peanuts, then scatter peanuts on top of the chicken wings. Serve warm.

Baked Prosciutto-wrapped Chicken Breast With Spinach And Boursin

Servings: 4
Cooking Time: 60 Minutes

Ingredients:
- 1 Tablespoon olive oil
- 10 Ounce baby spinach leaves, washed and dried
- 2 Whole packs (5.2 oz) Boursin Garlic & Fine Herbs Gournay Cheese
- 2 Pound boneless, skinless chicken breasts
- Pork & Poultry Rub
- 14 Slices prosciutto

Directions:

1. Heat olive oil in a medium sauté pan. Add spinach and sauté until wilted, about 3 to 5 minutes. Transfer to a strainer and squeeze out excess liquid. Place spinach and cheese in a medium bowl. Mix well and set aside.

2. Butterfly each chicken breast and open like a book. Cover with plastic wrap and using a meat mallet, pound out thinly. Season the chicken with Pork & Poultry Rub.

3. Lay a sheet of plastic wrap about 2 feet long down on a flat, clean surface. Lay down slices of prosciutto, slightly overlapping and double-wide. Place the chicken on top of the prosciutto leaving a 1- 1/2 inch border.

4. Spread the spinach mixture on top of the chicken. Roll it up tightly to create a log. Tie off the ends tightly and transfer to the refrigerator. Refrigerate 2 to 3 hours or overnight.

5. Supply your smoker with wood pellets and follow the start-up procedure. Preheat the grill, with the lid closed, to 300° F.

6. Carefully remove the plastic wrap and place directly on the grill grate. Bake for an hour and a half, or until the internal temperature reaches 162°F to 165°F. Remove from Traeger and let rest for 10 minutes before slicing. Enjoy! Grill: 300 °F Probe: 162 °F

Traeger Bbq Half Chickens

Servings: 2

Cooking Time: 60 Minutes

Ingredients:

- 1 (3 to 3-1/2 lb) fresh young chicken
- Leinenkugel's Summer Shandy Rub
- Apricot BBQ Sauce

Directions:

1. Place the chicken breast side down, on a cutting board with the neck pointing away from you. Cut along one side of the backbone, staying as close to the bone as possible, from the neck to the tail. Repeat on the other side of the backbone then remove it.

2. Open the chicken and slice through the white cartilage at the tip of the breastbone to pop it open. Cut down either side of the breast bone then use your fingers to pull it out. Flip the chicken over so it is skin side up and cut down the center splitting the chicken in half. Tuck the wings back on each chicken half.

3. Season on both sides with Traeger Leinenkugel's Summer Shandy Rub.

4. Supply your smoker with wood pellets and follow the start-up procedure. Preheat the grill, with the lid closed, to 375° F.

5. Place chicken directly on the grill grate skin side up and cook until the internal temperature reaches 160°F, about 60-90 minutes. Grill: 375 °F Probe: 160 °F

6. Brush the BBQ sauce all over the chicken skin and cook for an additional 10 minutes. Remove from grill and let rest 5 minutes before serving. Enjoy! Grill: 375 °F

Tandoori Chicken Leg Quarters

Servings: 4

Cooking Time: 40 Minutes

Ingredients:

- 4 skinless chicken leg quarters, about 2½lb (1.2kg) total
- juice of 2 lemons
- ¼ cup cold distilled water
- 1½ tsp coarse salt
- ½ tsp ground turmeric
- 3 tbsp vegetable oil, plus more
- 3 garlic cloves, peeled and minced
- 1½-inch (3.75cm) piece of fresh ginger, peeled and minced
- 2 tsp sweet paprika
- 1 tsp chili powder, preferably Kashmiri
- 1 tsp ground coriander
- 1 tsp ground cumin
- ½ tsp ground cayenne
- ¼ tsp ground nutmeg
- ½ cup plain Greek yogurt
- 4 tbsp unsalted butter, melted
- for serving
- 1 large red onion, peeled and thinly sliced crosswise
- ½ cup cilantro leaves
- lemon wedges

Directions:

1. Use a sharp, thin-bladed knife to cut several deep slashes in the fleshy side of each leg quarter to increase the surface area exposed to the marinade and to help the chicken cook faster. Place the chicken legs in a resealable plastic bag.

2. In a small bowl, combine the lemon juice, water, salt, and turmeric. Stir until the salt dissolves. Pour the mixture over the chicken legs and massage the bag to thoroughly coat the chicken, forcing the liquid into the slashes. Refrigerate for 15 minutes.

3. In a medium bowl, combine the vegetable oil, garlic, ginger, paprika, chili powder, coriander, cumin, cayenne, and nutmeg. Whisk in the yogurt. Add this mixture to the plastic bag and again massage the bag to thoroughly coat the chicken legs. Refrigerate for 4 to 8 hours.

4. Supply your smoker with wood pellets and follow the start-up procedure. Preheat the grill, with the lid closed, to 400° F.

5. Remove the chicken from the plastic bag and discard the marinade. Place the leg quarters fleshy side down on the grate and grill until the chicken is nicely browned and the temperature in the thickest part of the thigh reaches 170°F (77°C), about 35 to 40 minutes, turning once or twice.

6. Remove the chicken leg quarters from the grill and let rest for 2 minutes. Brush on both sides with butter. Place the legs on a platter. Scatter the red onion, cilantro leaves, and lemon wedges on the platter. Serve immediately.

Smoked Whole Chicken

Servings: 6-8
Cooking Time: 240 Minutes

Ingredients:
- 1 whole chicken
- 2 cups Tea Injectable (using Not-Just-for-Pork Rub)
- 2 tablespoons olive oil
- 1 batch Chicken Rub
- 2 tablespoons butter, melted

Directions:
1. Supply your smoker with wood pellets and follow the start-up procedure. Preheat the grill, with the lid closed, to 180°F.
2. Inject the chicken throughout with the tea injectable.
3. Coat the chicken all over with olive oil and season it with the rub. Using your hands, work the rub into the meat.
4. Place the chicken directly on the grill grate and smoke for 3 hours.
5. Baste the chicken with the butter and increase the grill's temperature to 375°F. Continue to cook the chicken until its internal temperature reaches 170°F.
6. Remove the chicken from the grill and let it rest for 10 minutes, before carving and serving.

Onion Turkey Burger Sliders

Servings: 5
Cooking Time: 30 Minutes

Ingredients:
- 1 Sweet Onion, Chopped
- 1 Pepper, Anaheim
- Bacon Cheddar Burger Seasoning
- Spinach
- 16 Oz Turkey, Ground

Directions:
1. Supply your smoker with wood pellets and follow the start-up procedure. Preheat the grill, with the lid closed, to 400° F.
2. Put the ground turkey into a bowl and generously add the Bacon Cheddar Burger seasoning to the mixture.
3. Dice the Anaheim pepper and add it to the bowl as well.
4. Dice about 1/3 of the sweet onion and add it to the bowl.
5. Mix with your hands until the meat looks evenly coated in seasoning and the veggies are evenly mixed.
6. Separate the meat out into 3oz balls, disperse or toss the remnants.

7. Use the 3-in-1 Burger press to create the perfect patty! Place the patties on the grill and cook for 15-20 minutes depending on their thickness. Flip every 5ish minutes.
8. Add the buns to the grill if you'd like them toasted!
9. Remove the turkey sliders (and the buns) from the grill, add spinach, and whatever you think will taste good!

Crispy Chicken Quarters

Servings: 4
Cooking Time: 55 Minutes

Ingredients:
- 2 Cups Alabama White Sauce
- 1 Tbsp Champion Chicken
- 4 Chicken Leg Quarters
- 1 Tbsp Olive Oil

Directions:
1. Place chicken leg quarters on a sheet tray lined with aluminum foil. Gently pull away the skin from the chicken leg quarters, then drizzle inside and out with olive oil. Season the chicken leg quarters all over and under the skin with Champion Chicken. Let chicken sit out at room temperature for 1 hour.
2. Supply your smoker with wood pellets and follow the start-up procedure. Preheat the grill, with the lid open, to 450° F. If using a gas or charcoal grill, set it up for medium-high heat and direct heat.
3. Sear the leg quarters on all sides over direct flame until crispy and golden brown. Transfer to indirect heat and close the sear slide. Reduce temperature to 350° F and grill the chicken for 45 minutes, turning occasionally, until chicken registers an internal temperature of 165° F.
4. Remove chicken from grill and allow to rest for 10 minutes. Serve chicken hot with a generous drizzling of Alabama white sauce*.

Fig Glazed Chicken Stuffed Cornbread

Servings: 10
Cooking Time: 120 Minutes

Ingredients:
- Black Pepper
- 6 Tablespoons (For The Chicken) Butter, Unsalted
- 3 Chicken, Whole
- 2 1/5 Cups (Replace With Craisins For A Different Flavor) Dried Figs, Chopped
- 1 Egg
- 2 Tablespoon Extra-Virgin Olive Oil
- 1/2 Cup Heavy Cream
- 1/2 Cup Honey
- Kosher Salt

- 4 Tablespoon Lemon, Juice
- 1/2 Onion, Chopped
- Champion Chicken Seasoning
- 1 1/2 Teaspoon Finely Chopped Rosemary, Fresh
- 1 Pound Sweet Italian Sausage
- 3 Cups Water, Warm

Directions:

1. Mix figs, honey, lemon juice, and warm water. Cover with plastic wrap and let figs soften for 30 minutes. Strain the figs and reserve the liquid for glaze.

2. Heat olive oil over medium heat and sauté the onions with rosemary. Add the sausage. Cook until browned. Place into a large bowl, add the cornbread and figs. Season with Champion Chicken Seasoning. Stir. In a separate bowl, Stir together egg, heavy whipping cream, and chicken stock. Pour over the cornbread/fig mix and stir together. Set aside.

3. Rinse chickens and pat dry. Season liberally with Champion Chicken Seasoning, kosher salt and black pepper. Don't forget the cavity! Stuff cavities with Stuffing. Top each Chicken with 2 tablespoons butter.

4. Supply your smoker with wood pellets and follow the start-up procedure. Preheat the grill, with the lid closed, to 300° F. Place in a roasting tray and cook until internal temp reads 165°F.

5. While chickens cook, place the fig liquid, balsamic vinegar and butter over. Reduce to thicken and baste chickens with about 160°F or 10 minutes before finished. Rest for 10 minutes. Carve and serve!

Grilled Chicken Wings

Servings: 6
Cooking Time: 50 Minutes

Ingredients:

- 4 Lbs Chicken Wings, Whole
- 1 Cup Cornmeal
- 2 Eggs
- 1 Cup Flour
- 2 Tbsp Champion Chicken Rub
- 1 Cup Milk

Directions:

1. Supply your smoker with wood pellets and follow the start-up procedure. Preheat the grill, with the lid open, to 300° F. If using a gas or charcoal grill, set it up for medium-low heat.

2. Place chicken wings on a sheet tray, then cut off the tip of each wing with a knife, or scissors. Pat dry with a paper towel.

3. In a mixing bowl, whisk together flour, cornmeal, and Champion Chicken. Set aside.

4. In another mixing bowl, whisk together milk and eggs. Set aside.

5. Form "breading" station: wings, egg wash, seasoned flour, sheet tray. Dunk each wing in egg wash, then coat in seasoned flour. Set aside on a sheet tray, while coating the remaining wings.

6. Place wings directly on the grill rack. Flip/rotate wings every 10 minutes for 45-55 minutes, until golden and "fried crisp."

7. Remove from the grill, rest for 10 minutes, then serve warm.

Hot Turkey Sandwich With Gravy

Servings: 4
Cooking Time: 10 Minutes

Ingredients:

- 8 Slices Bread, Sliced
- 1 Cup Gravy, Prepared
- 2 Cups Leftover Turkey, Shredded

Directions:

1. Supply your smoker with wood pellets and follow the start-up procedure. Preheat the grill, with the lid closed, to 400° F.

2. Place the BBQ Grill Mat on the grates of your preheated grill and lay the shredded turkey evenly across the mat to reheat for about 10 minutes.

3. Prepare or reheat the gravy. You"ll want to have the gravy warmed and ready as soon as the turkey is reheated and the bread is toasted.

4. Hold each slice of bread over the flame broiler to toast to your liking.

5. When all of your ingredients are hot, scoop 1/2 cup of the shredded turkey onto a piece of bread, generously cover with gravy and top with another piece of toasted bread. Serve immediately.

Grilled Honey Chicken Wings

Servings: 4 - 8
Cooking Time: 30 Minutes

Ingredients:

- 2 Chipotles Chopped In Adobo
- 1 Apple Cider Vinegar
- 2 Tablespoons Balsamic Vinegar
- ¼ Cup Brown Sugar
- 2 ½ Lbs Chicken Wings, Trimmed And Patted Dry
- ¼ Cup Honey
- ½ Cup Ketchup
- ¼ Cup Adobo Sauce
- 2 Tablespoons Sweet Rib Rub
- 2 Teaspoons Worcestershire Sauce

Directions:

1. Supply your smoker with wood pellets and follow the start-up procedure. Preheat the grill, with the lid open, to 350° F. If you're using a charcoal or gas grill, set up the grill for medium high heat.

144

2. In a large bowl, whisk together the apple cider vinegar, ketchup, brown sugar, honey, chopped chipotle peppers with adobo sauce, balsamic vinegar, Worcestershire sauce, and Sweet Rib Rub. Whisk the glaze until it's well combined.

3. Add the wings to the glaze and place the bowl in the refrigerator. Marinade the chicken wings for up to 12 hours. Once the wings have finished marinating, remove the chicken wings from the marinade and place the chicken wings onto the wing rack.

4. Once all the wings have been placed on the wing rack, place the wing rack on the grill. Insert a temperature probe into the thickest part into one of the wings and grill the wings for 5 minutes, and then rotate the rack 180° and grill for another 5 minutes. Remove the wings once they have an internal temperature of 165°F and the juice from the chicken runs clear.

5. Remove the wings from the grill and serve immediately.

Smoked Wings

Servings: 6
Cooking Time: 50 Minutes

Ingredients:
- 24 chicken wings, flats and drumettes separated
- 12 Ounce Italian dressing
- 3 Ounce Chicken Rub
- 5 Ounce 'Que BBQ Sauce
- 3 Ounce chili sauce

Directions:
1. Wash all wings and place into resealable bag. Add Italian dressing to the resealable bag containing the wings. Place in refrigerator and allow to marinate for 6 to 12 hours.

2. Supply your smoker with wood pellets and follow the start-up procedure. Preheat the grill, with the lid closed, to 225° F.

3. Remove wings from marinade and shake off excess marinade. Season all sides of the wings with Traeger Chicken Rub and let sit for 15 minutes before putting wings on the Traeger.

4. In a small bowl, combine the BBQ and chili sauces. Set aside.

5. Cook wings to an internal temperature of 160°F. Remove the wings and toss in chili barbecue sauce. Grill: 225 °F Probe: 160 °F

6. Increase the grill temperature to 375°F and preheat. Once at temperature, place the wings on the Traeger and sear both sides until the internal temperature reaches 165°F. Grill: 375 °F Probe: 165 °F

7. Remove the wings from grill and let rest for 5 minutes. Serve with your favorite side wing dressing or sauce. Enjoy!

Skinny Smoked Chicken Breasts

Servings: 4-6
Cooking Time: 85 Minutes

Ingredients:

- 2½ pounds boneless, skinless chicken breasts
- Salt
- Freshly ground black pepper

Directions:
1. Supply your smoker with wood pellets and follow the start-up procedure. Preheat the grill, with the lid closed, to 180°F.

2. Season the chicken breasts all over with salt and pepper.

3. Place the breasts directly on the grill grate and smoke for 1 hour.

4. Increase the grill's temperature to 325°F and continue to cook until the chicken's internal temperature reaches 170°F. Remove the breasts from the grill and serve immediately.

Spatchcocked Chicken With Toasted Fennel & Garlic

Servings: 6
Cooking Time: 45 Minutes

Ingredients:
- 6 Pound whole chicken
- 1 Tablespoon toasted fennel seed
- 2 Clove garlic, minced
- 1 Tablespoon salt
- 1/2 Tablespoon pepper

Directions:
1. To Spatchcock the chicken, remove the backbone by cutting down both sides of the backbone.

2. Next turn the bird over and make a cut down the keel bone, which is right in the center. This will allow the chicken to lay flat.

3. Supply your smoker with wood pellets and follow the start-up procedure. Preheat the grill, with the lid closed, to 450° F.

4. While the grill is preheating, rub the chicken with the fennel, garlic, salt, and pepper, and let it come almost to room temperature (this will help it cook faster).

5. Place the chicken, skin-side down on the grill. Cook 8 to 10 minutes, or until there are good grill marks. Grill: 450 °F

6. Turn the chicken over and cook until the meat reaches an internal temperature of 160 degrees. Enjoy! Grill: 450 °F Probe: 160 °F

Roasted Prosciutto Stuffed Chicken

Servings: 2
Cooking Time: 35 Minutes

Ingredients:
- 2 Whole boneless, skinless chicken breast
- salt and pepper
- 2 Tablespoon Dijon mustard
- 2 Slices Prosciutto Ham

- 4 Pieces mozzarella cheese
- 1 Large Tomatoes, sliced
- 4 Large basil leaves
- 2 Tablespoon olive oil
- Toothpicks

Directions:

1. Supply your smoker with wood pellets and follow the start-up procedure. Preheat the grill, with the lid closed, to 225° F.

2. While grill heats up, use a sharp knife to fillet each chicken breast in two. Open up each half, by pounding with a meat tenderizer.

3. Season each breast half with salt and pepper to taste. Rub mustard on both sides. Place a slice of proscuitto on the inside of the breast followed by a slice of mozzarella, a slice of tomato and a basil leaf. Drizzle olive oil on top.

4. Fold chicken breast back in half and secure with toothpicks. Brush outside of stuffed breast with olive oil.

5. Place directly on the grill grate. Cook for 6 to 7 minutes per side, or until chicken reaches an internal temperature of 160 degrees F.

Bbq Pulled Turkey Sandwiches

Servings: 6
Cooking Time: 120 Minutes

Ingredients:

- 6 Whole Turkey Thighs
- Pork & Poultry Rub
- 1 1/2 Cup chicken broth
- 1 Cup 'Que BBQ Sauce
- 6 Whole Kaiser Buns, Split

Directions:

1. Season turkey thighs on both sides with the Traeger Pork & Poultry rub.

2. Supply your smoker with wood pellets and follow the start-up procedure. Preheat the grill, with the lid closed, to 180° F.

3. Arrange the turkey thighs directly on the grill grate and smoke for 30 minutes.

4. Transfer the thighs to a sturdy disposable aluminum foil or roasting pan. Pour the broth around the thighs. Cover the pan with foil or a lid.

5. Increase temperature to 325°F and preheat, lid closed. Roast the thighs until they reach an internal temperature of 180°F. Grill: 325 °F Probe: 180 °F

6. Remove pan from the grill, but leave grill on. Let the turkey thighs cool slightly until they can be comfortably handled.

7. Pour off the drippings and reserve. Remove the skin and discard.

8. Pull the turkey meat into shreds with your fingers and return the meat to the roasting pan.

9. Add 1 cup or more of your favorite Traeger BBQ Sauce along with some of the drippings.

10. Recover the pan with foil and reheat the BBQ turkey on the Traeger for 20 to 30 minutes.

11. Serve with toasted buns if desired. Enjoy!

Chicken Nachos

Servings: 6-8
Cooking Time: 10 Minutes

Ingredients:

- 1 Can Black Beans, Rinsed And Drained
- 1 Cup Cheddar Cheese, Shredded
- 2 Cups Chicken, Diced
- (If Desired) Cilantro
- 1 Can Corn Kernels, Drained
- (If Desired) Pickled Jalapeno Peppers
- 1/2 Tablespoon Champion Chicken Seasoning
- 1/2 Red Onion, Diced
- 1/2 Cup Salsa
- 1/4 Cup Sour Cream

Directions:

1. On a large sheet pan, spread out half the tortilla chips, then cover with half the shredded cheese and one cup of chicken. Sprinkle with half of Champion Chicken seasoning. Top with the rest of the tortilla chips, cheese, chicken and remaining seasoning.

2. Supply your smoker with wood pellets and follow the start-up procedure. Preheat the grill, with the lid closed, to 350° F. Grill for 5-7 minutes, or until the cheese is melted and bubbly and everything is warmed all the way through. Remove the pan from the grill.

3. Top the nachos with the black beans, corn, diced red onion, sour cream, cilantro and pickled jalapenos. Serve and enjoy!

Grilled Garlic Chicken Kabobs

Servings: 6
Cooking Time: 15 Minutes

Ingredients:

- 3 (Cut Into 1 Inch Cubes) Chicken Breast, Raw
- 2 Cloves Garlic, Minced
- 2 Tablespoons Honey
- 1 Pound Of Button (Destemmed And Cut In Half) Mushroom
- 1/2 Cup Olive Oil
- 1 Red (Cut Into Quarters And Seperated) Onion
- 1 Green (Cut Into Large Chunks) Bell Pepper
- 2 Tablespoons Competition Smoked Seasoning
- 2 Tablespoons Soy Sauce

Directions:

1. To make the marinade: In a large bowl, combine the olive oil, soy sauce, honey, garlic and Competition Smoked. Add the chicken and mix well. When the chicken is covered completely, allow it to marinate for 2-12 hours.
2. In a large, shallow baking dish, soak the kabob skewers for a minimum of 2 hours and up to 12 hours.
3. Once the chicken has finished marinating and the skewers are finished soaking, drain the water from the skewers and remove the chicken from the marinade.
4. Supply your smoker with wood pellets and follow the start-up procedure. Preheat the grill, with the lid closed, to 350° F.
5. Thread a piece of chicken, followed by a piece of pepper, mushroom, and onion. Repeat until the skewers are full.
6. Grill the kabobs for 5 minutes on one side, then flip and grill for 5 more minutes or until the chicken reaches an internal temperature of 180°F. Remove from the grill and serve.

Cornish Game Hen

Servings: 4
Cooking Time: 180 Minutes

Ingredients:
- 4 Cornish game hens
- Extra-virgin olive oil, for rubbing
- 2 teaspoons salt
- 1 teaspoon freshly ground black pepper
- 1 teaspoon celery seeds

Directions:
1. Supply your smoker with wood pellets and follow the start-up procedure. Preheat, with the lid closed, to 275°F.
2. Rub the game hens over and under the skin with olive oil and season all over with the salt, pepper, and celery seeds.
3. Place the birds directly on the grill grate, close the lid, and smoke for 2 to 3 hours, or until a meat thermometer inserted in each bird reads 170°F.
4. Serve the Cornish game hens hot.

Lemon Rosemary Beer Can Chicken

Servings: 4
Cooking Time: 60 Minutes

Ingredients:
- 1 (3 to 3-1/2 lb) whole chicken
- 1 lemon, halved
- 1 Teaspoon kosher salt
- 1 Teaspoon ground black pepper
- 1 Teaspoon fresh finely chopped rosemary
- 1 (12 oz) can beer

Directions:

1. Supply your smoker with wood pellets and follow the start-up procedure. Preheat the grill, with the lid closed, to 400° F.
2. Coat the chicken inside and out with the juice from one lemon. In a small bowl, combine salt, pepper and rosemary, and sprinkle on the inside and outside of chicken.
3. Empty half of the beer from the can and place the can on a solid surface. Place the chicken atop the beer can, tucking the legs in the front.
4. Carefully place the chicken directly on the grill grate using the legs to support if needed. Alternatively, place the chicken atop the beer can on a sheet tray for a more stable surface, then place the sheet tray directly on the grill grate.
5. Cook the chicken until an instant-read thermometer reads 165°F when inserted in the thickest part of the breast, about 60 minutes. Grill: 400 °F Probe: 165 °F
6. Let the chicken rest 10 minutes before carving. Serve with Chardonnay or any of your favorite medium body red or white wines. Enjoy!

Italian Grilled Barbecue Chicken Wings

Servings: 4
Cooking Time: 18 Minutes

Ingredients:
- 1 cup KRAFT Zesty Italian Dressing
- 2 pounds chicken wings/drummettes
- 1/2 cup barbecue sauce

Directions:
1. Pour dressing over chicken in large bowl; toss to coat.
2. Refrigerate at least 30 minutes to marinate.
3. Supply your smoker with wood pellets and follow the start-up procedure. Preheat the grill, with the lid closed, to 400° F. Drain chicken; discard marinade.
4. Grill chicken 8 minutes on each side or until done.
5. Brush with barbecue sauce; grill for another 2 minutes.
6. Remove from grill and serve.

Roasted Duck With Cherry Salsa

Servings: 2-3
Cooking Time: 180 Minutes

Ingredients:
- 1 whole Long Island (Pekin) duck, about 5 to 6lb (2.3 to 2.7kg), thawed if frozen
- coarse salt
- freshly ground black pepper
- 1 white onion, peeled and quartered
- 1 orange, quartered
- 4 garlic cloves, peeled and quartered
- 3 sprigs of fresh thyme or fresh rosemary, plus more

- for the salsa
- 2 cups dark red cherries, washed, destemmed, pitted, and coarsely chopped
- 1 scallion, trimmed, white and green parts sliced crosswise
- 1 jalapeño, destemmed, deseeded, and finely diced
- 1 tbsp granulated sugar, plus more
- 1 tbsp port wine (optional)
- 2 tsp freshly squeezed lime juice
- 2 tsp freshly squeezed orange juice
- 1½ tsp finely chopped orange zest

Directions:

1. Supply your smoker with wood pellets and follow the start-up procedure. Preheat the grill, with the lid closed, to 350° F.
2. In a small bowl, make the salsa by combining the ingredients. Slightly bruise some of the cherries to release their juices. Set aside.
3. Use kitchen shears to cut off the wing tips and trim any excessive neck skin from the duck. Use a sharp knife to score the skin of the breasts in the classic diamond pattern, making the cuts about 1 inch (2.5cm) apart, but don't penetrate the meat. Use a fork with sharp tines to prick the skin on the thighs. Rinse the bird inside and out with cold running water and pat dry with paper towels.
4. Season the duck inside and out with the salt and pepper. Tuck the onion, orange, garlic, and thyme in the cavity. Pull the excess skin over the opening and tie the legs together with butcher's twine.
5. Place a wire rack in a shallow roasting pan and place the duck breast side up on top of the rack. Place the roasting pan on the grate and roast the duck for 1 hour. Use tongs to turn the bird breast side down. Roast for 1 hour more and then turn again, finishing breast side up. Roast until the skin is nicely browned and the internal temperature in the thickest part of a breast reaches 170°F (77°C), about 30 minutes to 1 hour more. (There should also be quite a bit of duck fat in the bottom of the pan. Save in a covered container and refrigerate or freeze for another use.)
6. Remove the pan from the grill and let the duck rest for 15 minutes. Transfer the duck to a cutting board and carve.
7. Place the duck meat on a platter and scatter the fresh thyme over the top. Serve with the cherry salsa.

Roasted Chicken With Wild Rice & Mushrooms

Servings: 2
Cooking Time: 120 Minutes

Ingredients:
- 1 Whole whole chicken
- salt
- pepper

- 2 Tablespoon butter
- 1 Medium onion, chopped
- 4 Strips Bacon, diced
- 1 Cup Rice, wild
- 1 mushrooms, sliced
- salt
- 2 1/4 Cup water
- 2 Tablespoon parsley, chopped

Directions:

1. Supply your smoker with wood pellets and follow the start-up procedure. Preheat the grill, with the lid closed, to 375° F.
2. Season inside and outside of chicken with salt and pepper.
3. In a large saucepan, melt 2 Tbsp butter over medium heat. Add onions and cook until soft, 3-5 minutes. Add bacon to onions and cook, stirring, until bacon and onions are browned. Stir in rice, mushrooms, salt, and pepper.
4. Add 2-1/4 cups of water to mixture and bring to a boil. Reduce heat to low, cover and simmer for 25 minutes, until rice has absorbed liquid. Add fresh parsley and mix.
5. Stuff cavity loosely with rice mixture. Tie chicken legs back with butcher's twine.
6. Place chicken directly on grill grate and roast for 1 hr 15 mins or until an instant-read thermometer inserted into the thickest part of the breast reads 160°F and the thigh 170°F. Grill: 375 °F Probe: 160 °F
7. Remove chicken from grill and allow to rest for 10 minutes.
8. Spoon stuffing out of chicken cavity to a platter and slice chicken. Serve immediately with chicken pieces over rice stuffing. Enjoy!

Spiced Cornish Hens With Cilantro Chutney

Servings: 2
Cooking Time: 60 Minutes

Ingredients:
- 2 Cornish game hens, each about 1 to 1¼lb (450 to 565g), thawed if frozen
- 1 small white onion, peeled and halved
- 4 slices of fresh ginger
- 4 garlic cloves, peeled
- 3 tbsp vegetable oil
- 2 tsp garam masala
- for the brine
- ½ gallon (1.9 liters) distilled water
- ½ cup kosher salt
- for the chutney
- 1 bunch of cilantro, washed and roughly chopped
- 4 scallions, trimmed and roughly chopped

- 2 garlic cloves, peeled and roughly chopped
- 2 small green chili peppers, deseeded and minced
- 1-inch (2.5cm) piece of fresh ginger, peeled and minced
- 1 tbsp dry-roasted peanuts
- 1 tsp coarse salt
- 1 tsp ground cumin
- ½ tsp ground coriander
- 3 tbsp freshly squeezed lemon juice
- ¼ cup extra virgin olive oil

Directions:

1. In a stockpot on the stovetop over medium-high heat, make the brine by bringing the water and salt to a boil. Stir until the salt dissolves. Remove the pot from the stovetop and let the brine cool to room temperature. Cover and refrigerate until cool.

2. Submerge the hens in the brine. If they float, place a resealable bag of ice on top. Cover and refrigerate for 4 hours or as long as 8 hours.

3. Supply your smoker with wood pellets and follow the start-up procedure. Preheat the grill, with the lid closed, to 350° F.

4. In a blender, make the chutney by combining all the ingredients except the olive oil. Blend until the ingredients begin to move, adding 1 tablespoon of water if they need help. When a paste has formed, add the olive oil in a thin stream until the chutney is smooth. If it seems too thick, add a small bit of water. If it's too thin, add a little more oil. Store in a covered container in the refrigerator until ready to use.

5. Remove the hens from the brine. Rinse inside and out under cold running water and pat dry with paper towels. Place half an onion, 2 slices of ginger, and 2 garlic cloves in the cavity of each hen. Tie the legs together with butcher's twine.

6. In a small bowl, combine the vegetable oil and garam masala. Rub the mixture thinly and evenly on the outside of the hens.

7. Place the hens on the grate and roast until they're nicely browned and the internal temperature in the thickest part of a thigh reaches 165°F (74°C), about 1 hour.

8. Transfer the hens to a platter. Serve with the chutney.

Smoked Beer Garlic Chicken

Servings: 4
Cooking Time: 120 Minutes

Ingredients:
- 1 whole chicken
- 2 tbsp olive oil
- 1 tbsp salt
- 2 tsp thyme
- 2 tsp dill
- 2 tsp garlic powder
- 1 can beer

Directions:

1. Spray or rub olive oil on the outside of the chicken. In a bowl, mix all other ingredients together (except beer).

2. Rub this mixture on the outside of your chicken.

3. Fill the chicken stand with beer(takes about 3/4 of your can of beer).

4. Place chicken on top of the chicken stand. Supply your smoker with wood pellets and follow the start-up procedure. Preheat the grill, with the lid closed, to 350° F. place chicken in the center making sure it is flat and won't tip over(you can lean the chicken against the upper rack).

5. Allow the chicken to cook for 2 hours or until the internal temperature of the chicken reaches at least 165 °F.

6. Remove from the grill and the stand and let rest 5-10 minutes before carving. Serve. Enjoy!

Delicious Asian Bbq Wings

Servings: 6
Cooking Time: 60 Minutes

Ingredients:
- 2 Lbs Chicken, Wing
- 1 Tsp Garlic, Minced
- 1 Tsp Ginger, Fresh
- 1 Tsp Chopped Green Onion
- 1/2 Cup Hoisin Sauce
- 1 Tsp Honey
- 2 Tsp Rice Vinegar
- 2 Tsp Sesame Oil
- 1 Tsp Sesame Seeds
- 1 Tsp Soy Sauce
- 1 Cup Water, Boiling

Directions:

1. Add all ingredients except wings and sesame seeds to a mixing bowl and whisk to incorporate. Add wings to a resealable plastic bag and pour marinade over. Allow marinating for at least 2 hours up to overnight. Remove wings from bag, reserving marinade.

2. Supply your smoker with wood pellets and follow the start-up procedure. Preheat the grill, with the lid closed, to 300° F. Place wings in a grilling basket and cook for 1 hour or until they reach an internal temperature of 165°F.

3. While wings are cooking, pour reserved marinade into a small saucepan and add rice wine vinegar. Over high heat, bring to a boil while whisking often, and reduce by 1/3, or about 10 minutes. Set aside.

4. Brush wings with reduced sauce and allow to cook for 5-10 more minutes or until glaze has set. Remove from smoker, sprinkle with sesame seeds, allow to rest for 5 minutes, and serve.

Crust Chicken Pizza

Servings: 4
Cooking Time: 35 Minutes

Ingredients:

- ½ Cup Alfredo Sauce
- 1 Tbsp Butter
- ¾ Lb. Shredded Chicken
- 2 Large Eggs
- 2 + 6 Divided Garlic Clove, Minced
- 1 ½ Cups Heavy Cream
- ¾ Cup Kale
- ¼ Cup Mushroom
- 1 Cup Grated Parmesan Cheese
- Champion Chicken Rub
- 2 Tbsp Red Onion, Diced
- ½ Tsp Salt

Directions:

1. Supply your smoker with wood pellets and follow the start-up procedure. Preheat the grill, with the lid open, to 400° F. If using a gas or charcoal grill, set heat to medium-high heat. Place pizza stone on grill grates and allow to preheat. Line a pizza peel with parchment paper and set aside.
2. In a medium bowl, stir together the shredded chicken, grated Parmesan cheese, minced garlic, and sea salt. Whisk the eggs lightly in a small bowl then add to chicken mixture. Mix until well combined.
3. Spread the chicken crust pizza "dough" onto the parchment paper on the pizza peel, as thinly as possible (about ¼" thick).
4. Using the pizza peel, transfer the parchment to the preheated pizza stone. Grill for 15 to 20 minutes, until firm and golden on the edges. Remove from the grill and let rest for 5-10 minutes.
5. Top pizza crust with alfredo sauce, kale, mushrooms, red onion and additional parmesan cheese. Return to the grill for 10 to 15 minutes, until the cheese is melted. Slice and serve!

Teriyaki Apple Cider Turkey

Servings: 8-10
Cooking Time: 180 Minutes

Ingredients:

- 1/2 Cup Apple Cider
- 1/4 Cup Melted Butter, Unsalted
- 1 Teaspoon Cornstarch
- 2 Finely Chopped Garlic, Cloves
- 1/2 Teaspoon Ginger, Ground
- 2 Tablespoon Honey
- 2 Tablespoon Champion Chicken Seasoning
- 1 Shady Brook Farms® Whole Turkey, Thawed
- 2 Tablespoon Soy Sauce
- 1 Tablespoon Water, Cold

Directions:

1. Supply your smoker with wood pellets and follow the start-up procedure. Preheat the grill, with the lid closed, to 300° F.
2. In a saucepan, whisk together melted butter, garlic, soy sauce, apple cider, ground ginger, and honey. Bring to a boil then reduce to a simmer.
3. Place the turkey in an aluminum roasting pan.
4. With a marinade injector, fill with the mixture and pierce the meat with the needle while pushing on the plunger, injecting the flavor. You want to inject into the thickest part of the breast, thigh, and wings.
5. Next, rub entire turkey with your favorite poultry seasoning or the Champion Chicken seasoning. For added flavor, throw some extra garlic gloves into the cavity and apple cider in the aluminum pan.
6. Place the turkey in the grill and cook until the internal temperature reaches 165-170°F.
7. In a separate bowl, mix cornstarch and cold water together and add to the leftover original mixture to create a glaze. Glaze the turkey with the remaining mixture with approximately 15-20 minutes left. Skin will darken because of the sugar in the glaze.
8. Let the turkey rest 20-25 minutes before carving and enjoy!

Duck Breast With Pomegranate Sauce

Servings: 4
Cooking Time: 13 Minutes

Ingredients:

- 4 duck breasts, each about 6oz (170g), skin on
- for the rub
- 2 tsp coarse salt
- 1 tsp ground cumin
- 1 tsp ground coriander
- 1 tsp freshly ground black pepper
- ½ tsp ground cinnamon
- ½ tsp ground fennel
- for the sauce
- 1 shallot, peeled and minced
- 1 cup pomegranate juice
- 1 tbsp sherry vinegar or balsamic vinegar
- 1 tsp cornstarch
- ¼ cup chicken stock or chicken broth
- 1 tbsp chilled unsalted butter, cut into 4 pieces
- ¼ cup fresh pomegranate seeds (optional)
- 1 tbsp minced fresh chives

Directions:

1. Place a cast iron skillet on the grate. Supply your smoker with wood pellets and follow the start-up procedure. Preheat the grill, with the lid closed, to 400° F.

2. In a small bowl, make the rub by combining the ingredients. Use a sharp knife to diagonally score the skin of each duck breast—but don't nick the flesh. Lightly season the scored side of each breast.

3. Place the duck breasts skin side down in the skillet and sear until the skin is crisp and golden brown, about 8 to 10 minutes. Turn the breasts and cook until the internal temperature in the thickest part of a breast reaches 130°F (54°C), about 2 to 3 minutes more. Transfer the breasts to a plate.

4. In a large saucepan on the stovetop over medium heat, make the sauce by heating 1 tablespoon of duck fat from the skillet. (Reserve the remainder for another use.) Add the shallot and sauté until soft, about 2 to 3 minutes.

5. Add the pomegranate juice and bring the mixture to a boil over medium-high heat. Reduce the sauce by half, about 3 to 5 minutes. Add the vinegar and lower the heat to medium low.

6. Whisk together the cornstarch and chicken stock until smooth. Whisk into the sauce and cook until the sauce thickens, about 1 to 2 minutes. Whisk in the butter and stir in the pomegranate seeds (if using).

7. Place the duck breasts on a warm platter. Drizzle the pomegranate sauce over the top. Scatter the chives around the platter before serving.

Cranberry Turkey Breast

Servings: 6
Cooking Time: 90 Minutes

Ingredients:

- 1 Bay Leaf
- 1/2 Tsp Black Pepper
- 3 Tbsp Butter, Divided
- 1 Celery Rib, Chopped
- To Taste, Cracked Black Pepper
- 4 Oz Cremini Mushrooms
- 1/2 Cup Dried Cranberries
- 2 Garlic Cloves, Minced
- 1 Package, Approx 2Lbs Honeysuckle White Turkey Breast, Boneless
- 1/2 Cup Marsala Wine
- 1 Tbsp Olive Oil
- 1 Rosemary Sprigs
- 1/2 Tsp Rubbed Sage
- 1/2 Tsp Salt
- To Taste, Sea Salt
- 6 Oz Stuffing Mix
- 1 1/4 Cup Turkey Stock, Divided
- 1 Yellow Onion, Chopped

Directions:

1. Supply your smoker with wood pellets and follow the start-up procedure. Preheat the grill, with the lid closed, to 325° F. If using a gas or charcoal grill, set it up for medium-low heat.

2. Melt the butter 1 tablespoon of butter and olive oil in a large skillet over medium heat. Add the onions and celery and cook, stirring frequently, until soft, 3 minutes.

3. Add the garlic and mushrooms and continue to cook for 5 minutes, until the mushrooms are slightly browned.

4. Deglaze with marsala wine, using a wooden spoon to scrape up any browned bits from the bottom of the pan.

5. Add the dried cranberries, black pepper, sage, and salt and simmer for 2 minutes, then remove from the heat.

6. Fold the stuffing into the vegetable mixture, then slowly pour over turkey stock, until stuffing is moistened.

7. Place the Honeysuckle White® Turkey Breast on a large cutting board, skin-side down, then butterfly it. Season with salt and pepper, then spoon over ⅓ of the stuffing, leaving an inch border.

8. Roll the turkey breast, starting at the side with less skin. Use butcher's twine to truss the turkey breast and secure the stuffing. Place in a cast iron skillet, top remaining butter, season with salt and pepper. Place a sprig of rosemary on top, add remaining ¼ cup of stock around the turkey, along with 1 bay leaf. Transfer to the grill.

9. Cook the turkey for 1 to 1 ½ hours, until an internal temperature of 165°F is reached.

10. Remove stuffed turkey breast from the grill, rest for 15 minutes, then slice and serve warm, with remaining stuffing.

Chicken Egg Rolls With Buffalo Sauce

Servings: 4
Cooking Time: 75 Minutes

Ingredients:

- 1/4 Cup Bleu Cheese, Crumbled
- 1/4 Cup Buffalo Sauce
- 1 Lb Chicken Breasts - Boneless, Skinless
- 4 Oz Cream Cheese, Softened
- 8 Egg Roll Wrappers
- 1/2 Jalapeno Pepper, Minced
- Pinch Sweet Heat Rub
- 1/4 Red Bell Pepper, Chopped
- 4 Scallion, Sliced Thin
- 1/4 Cup Sour Cream
- 2 Cups Vegetable Oil

Directions:

1. Supply your smoker with wood pellets and follow the start-up procedure. Preheat the grill, with the lid open, to 200° F. If using a gas or charcoal grill, set it up for low, indirect heat.

2. Season chicken breasts with Sweet Heat Rub, then place on the grill. Smoke for 1 hour, then remove from the grill, cool, shred, and set aside.

3. Prepare the filling: In a mixing bowl, use a hand mixer to blend cream cheese, bleu cheese, Buffalo sauce and sour cream.

4. Fold in scallions, jalapeño, red bell pepper, and shredded chicken.

5. Prepare egg rolls: Lay an egg roll wrapper on a flat surface and add 3 tablespoons of filling to the middle.

6. Fold the bottom of the wrapper over the top of the filling, then fold over each side. Brush the top point of the wrapper with warm water, then roll the wrapper tight. Transfer to a tray while filling the remaining wrappers.

7. Increase the temperature of the grill to 425°F, then set a cast iron Dutch oven on the grill. Add vegetable oil and heat for 5 minutes.

8. Place 3 egg rolls in heated oil and fry until golden, 1 to 2 minutes per side.

9. Transfer to a wire rack to cool, then fry the remaining egg rolls, in batches.

10. Cool egg rolls for 2 minutes, then slice in half and serve warm with celery sticks and extra Buffalo sauce for dipping.

Chicken Lollipops

Servings: 8
Cooking Time: 60 Minutes

Ingredients:

- 18 Pieces chicken drumsticks
- Cajun Shake
- 1 Stick butter
- 'Que BBQ Sauce
- Louisiana Brand Hot Sauce (Optional)

Directions:

1. To turn regular chicken legs into lollipops, you'll need a sharp knife and a pair of kitchen shears. Start by making a cut all of the way around the leg just below the knuckle, cutting through the skins and tendons using either a sharp knife or a pair of kitchen shears. Push the meat down to the large end and pull/cut the remaining skin and cartilage off the knuckle. You might want to also remove the tiny bone right against the leg. Remove this bone with your fingers or the shears, and trim away the tendons sticking out the top.

2. Season the chicken with the Cajun Shake. Wrap the bones of the drumsticks with a small piece of aluminum foil to keep them from turning too black. Let the chicken sit for an hour in the fridge to allow the flavor to permeate.

3. Supply your smoker with wood pellets and follow the start-up procedure. Preheat the grill, with the lid closed, to 180° F.

4. Place the chicken lollipops on the grill grate and let them smoke for 30 minutes.

5. After you remove the chicken, increase the grill temperature to 350°F and let it preheat, lid closed for 15 minutes. Place the stick of butter in a baking pan or aluminum pan and put it on the grill to allow the butter to melt while the grill is coming to temperature. (The butter doesn't need to cover the chicken. It just keeps the drumstick moist and of course, gives it a little added buttery finish.)

6. Arrange the lollipops in the pan with the bones sticking up straight. Let the chicken cook for about 40 minutes or until the internal temperature registers 165F on an instant-read thermometer. Grill: 350 °F Probe: 165 °F

7. Meanwhile, warm up the barbecue sauce in a small saucepan on the stove over low heat. If you want it to have that Louisiana kick, add in a few squirts of the hot sauce, to your taste. Once it starts to thin, turn down the heat to just keep it warm. If the sauce needs to be thinned, pour in a little bit of the butter used in the pan until it reaches a thickness that is thick enough to adhere to the drumsticks but not gluey.

8. Dip the lollipops into the barbecue sauce so that it is completely covered. You can also brush the barbecue sauce on the bones if you want a uniform look and sheen on the lollipops.

9. Increase the temperature to 450F. Place the chicken directly on the grill grate and cook until the internal temperature registers 175F, about 10 more minutes. Keep an eye on the lollipops to make sure that the glaze doesn't burn. You're looking for that perfect caramelization of the barbecue sauce on the outside with a crisp skin to give a little texture. Grill: 450 °F Probe: 175 °F

Smoked Pulled Chicken

Servings: 6
Cooking Time: 65 Minutes

Ingredients:

- To Taste, Ale House Beer Can Chicken Seasoning
- 1 Lb Chicken Breasts, Boneless, Skinless
- 1 Tbsp Cilantro, Chopped
- 1 Tsp Cumin, Ground
- 2 Jalapeños, Chopped
- 2 Tsp Olive Oil
- 1 Bag Tortilla Chips
- 1 Lb White American Cheese, Cubed
- 1 Cup Milk

Directions:

1. Supply your smoker with wood pellets and follow the start-up procedure. Preheat the grill, with the lid open, to 350° F. If using a gas or charcoal grill, preheat to medium heat.

2. Score the chicken, rub with olive oil, then season with Ale House Beer Can Chicken.

3. Transfer the chicken to the grill and cook for 8 to 10 minutes, turning occasionally.

4. Remove chicken from the grill, and reduce the temperature to 225° F. Allow the chicken to rest for 10 minutes, then pull apart with 2 forks. Set aside.

5. While the chicken is resting, heat a cast iron skillet on the grill. Partially open the sear slide, then to the skillet add the cubed cheese, jalapeño, milk, and cumin. Stir occasionally, for 5 minutes, until the cheese melts. Fold in the pulled chicken, then close the lid and allow the dip to smoke for 30 to 45 minutes.

6. Remove from grill and let rest for 5-10 minutes to thicken. Serve warm with fresh cilantro and tortilla chips.

Grilled Honey Garlic Wings

Servings: 4
Cooking Time: 60 Minutes

Ingredients:
- 2 1/2 Pound chicken wings
- Pork & Poultry Rub
- 4 Tablespoon butter
- 3 Clove garlic, minced
- 1/4 Cup honey
- 1/2 Cup hot sauce
- 1 1/2 Cup blue cheese or ranch dressing

Directions:
1. Start by segmenting the wings into three pieces, cutting through the joints. Discard the wing tips or save them to make a stock.

2. Lay out the remaining pieces on a rimmed baking sheet lined with nonstick foil or parchment paper. Season well with Traeger Pork & Poultry Rub.

3. Supply your smoker with wood pellets and follow the start-up procedure. Preheat the grill, with the lid closed, to 350° F.

4. Place the baking sheet with wings directly on the grill grate and cook for 45 to 50 minutes or until they are no longer pink at the bone. Grill: 350 °F

5. To make the sauce: Melt butter in a small saucepan. Add the garlic and sauté for 2 to 3 minutes. Add in the honey and hot sauce and cook for a few minutes until completely combined. Keep sauce warm while the wings are cooking.

6. After 45 minutes, pour the spicy honey-garlic sauce over the wings, turning with tongs to coat.

7. Place wings back on the grill and cook for an additional 10 to 15 minutes to set the sauce. Grill: 350 °F

8. Serve with ranch or blue cheese dressing. Enjoy!

Buffalo Chicken Wings

Servings: 4

Cooking Time: 20 Minutes

Ingredients:
- 1 1/2 Tbsp Apple Cider Vinegar
- 1/2 Cup Butter, Unsalted, Cubed
- 1/4 Tsp Cayenne Pepper
- 3 Lbs Chicken Wings, Split
- 2 Tsp Chives, Minced (Garnish)
- 1/8 Tsp Garlic, Granulated
- 2/3 Cup Hot Pepper Sauce
- 1 Tbsp Ranch Seasoning
- To Taste, Sweet Heat Rub
- 1/2 Tsp Sweet Heat Rub (For Sauce)
- 1/4 Tsp Worcestershire Sauce

Directions:
1. Supply your smoker with wood pellets and follow the start-up procedure. Preheat the grill, with the lid open, to 425° F. If using a gas or charcoal grill, set it up for medium-high heat.

2. Place chicken wings in a large mixing bowl. Season with Sweet Heat.

3. Prepare sauce: Set a small cast iron pan or saucepan on the grill. Add the hot pepper sauce, apple cider vinegar, Worcestershire sauce, Sweet Heat, cayenne, and granulated garlic to the skillet, and whisk to combine. When the sauce begins to bubble, remove the skillet from the grill and whisk in butter. Transfer the sauce to a mason jar.

4. Combine 1 cup of the buffalo sauce with ranch seasoning. Set aside.

5. Place wings on the grill and cook for 20 minutes, flipping and rotating every 3 to 5 minutes.

6. Remove wings from the grill when an internal temperature of 165° F is reached. Transfer to a mixing bowl, then pour sauce over. Toss to evenly coat. Garnish with fresh chives and serve warm.

Bourbon-brined Turkey Thighs

Servings: 4
Cooking Time: 135 Minutes

Ingredients:
- 4 skin-on, bone-in turkey thighs, about 2lb (1kg) total
- 6 tbsp unsalted butter, at room temperature
- 4 large fresh sage leaves
- coarse salt
- freshly ground black pepper
- for the brine
- 1 quart (1 liter) distilled water
- ¼ cup coarse salt, plus more
- ¼ cup light brown sugar or low-carb substitute
- ¼ cup bourbon (optional)

Directions:

1. In a saucepan on the stovetop over medium-high heat, make the brine by combining the water, salt, brown sugar, and bourbon (if using). Bring to a boil. Stir until the salt and sugar dissolve. Remove the saucepan from the stovetop and let the brine cool to room temperature.

2. Place the turkey in a resealable plastic bag and pour the brine over the thighs. Refrigerate for 4 hours.

3. Supply your smoker with wood pellets and follow the start-up procedure. Preheat the grill, with the lid closed, to 250° F.

4. Drain the turkey thighs and discard the brine. Rinse under cold running water and pat dry with paper towels. Gently lift the skin of each thigh and push 2 teaspoons of butter underneath. Top the butter with a sage leaf, smoothing it out so it lays flat under the skin. Rub the outside of the skin with more butter. Lightly season with salt and pepper.

5. Place the turkey thighs on the grate at an angle to the bars. Smoke for 1½ hours. Raise the temperature to 375°F (191°C) and roast until the skin is golden brown and the internal temperature in the thickest part of the meat reaches 170°F (77°C), about 30 to 45 minutes.

6. Transfer the thighs to a platter. Let rest for 3 minutes before serving.

Sweet And Spicy Smoked Wings

Servings: 2-4
Cooking Time: 85 Minutes

Ingredients:
- 1 pound chicken wings
- 1 batch Sweet and Spicy Cinnamon Rub
- 1 cup barbecue sauce

Directions:
1. Supply your smoker with wood pellets and follow the start-up procedure. Preheat the grill, with the lid closed, to 325°F.

2. Season the chicken wings with the rub. Using your hands, work the rub into the meat.

3. Place the wings directly on the grill grate and cook until they reach an internal temperature of 165°F.

4. Transfer the wings into an aluminum pan. Add the barbecue sauce and stir to coat the wings.

5. Reduce the grill's temperature to 250°F and put the pan on the grill. Smoke the wings for 1 hour more, uncovered. Remove the wings from the grill and serve immediately.

Smoked Quarters

Servings: 2-4
Cooking Time: 120 Minutes

Ingredients:
- 4 chicken quarters

- 2 tablespoons olive oil
- 1 batch Chicken Rub
- 2 tablespoons butter

Directions:
1. Supply your smoker with wood pellets and follow the start-up procedure. Preheat the grill, with the lid closed, to 180°F.

2. Coat the chicken quarters all over with olive oil and season them with the rub. Using your hands, work the rub into the meat.

3. Place the quarters directly on the grill grate and smoke for 1½ hours.

4. Baste the quarters with the butter and increase the grill's temperature to 375°F. Continue to cook until the chicken's internal temperature reaches 170°F.

5. Remove the quarters from the grill and let them rest for 10 minutes before serving.

Carrot Celery Chicken Drumsticks

Servings: 4
Cooking Time: 30 Minutes

Ingredients:
- Buffalo Style Dry Rub
- Carrot, Stick
- Celery, Stick
- 12 Chicken, Drumsticks

Directions:
1. Supply your smoker with wood pellets and follow the start-up procedure. Preheat the grill, with the lid closed, to 350° F.

2. Generously sprinkle the Buffalo Wing Rub all over the drumsticks. Hang each drumstick by the bone on the Wing Rack. Place in the for about 30 minutes.

3. Serve hot with celery and carrot sticks. Enjoy!

Jamaican Jerk Chicken Quarters

Servings: 4
Cooking Time: 120 Minutes

Ingredients:
- 4 chicken leg quarters, scored
- ¼ cup canola oil
- ½ cup Jamaican Jerk Paste
- 1 tablespoon whole allspice (pimento) berries

Directions:
1. Supply your smoker with wood pellets and follow the start-up procedure. Preheat, with the lid closed, to 275°F.

2. Brush the chicken with canola oil, then brush 6 tablespoons of the Jerk paste on and under the skin. Reserve the remaining 2 tablespoons of paste for basting.

3. Throw the whole allspice berries in with the wood pellets for added smoke flavor.

4. Arrange the chicken on the grill, close the lid, and smoke for 1 hour to 1 hour 30 minutes, or until a meat thermometer inserted in the thickest part of the thigh reads 165°F.

5. Let the meat rest for 5 minutes and baste with the reserved jerk paste prior to serving.

Grilled Chipotle Chicken Skewers

Servings: 4
Cooking Time: 25 Minutes

Ingredients:
- BBQ Sauce
- 1 cup spicy BBQ sauce
- 3 chipotle peppers
- 1 Tbsp adobo sauce
- Skewers
- Olive oil
- 2 lbs boneless skinless chicken breasts
- 10 thick-cut bacon strips
- 1 large green bell pepper, cut into 3/4 to 1 inch pieces
- 1 medium red onion, peeled and cut into 3/4 to 1 inch pieces
- Bamboo skewers
- Garnish: freshly chopped garnish

Directions:
1. Supply your smoker with wood pellets and follow the start-up procedure. Preheat the grill, with the lid closed.

2. Soak the wooden skewers in water for at least 10 to 15 minutes before skewering to avoid them burning as much.

3. Add all ingredients for the sauce to a blender. Blend until they are combined well.

4. Cut chicken into 3/4-inch bite-sized pieces. Cut bacon into 3/4-inch strips.

5. Thread bacon (folding the bacon in half before skewering), chicken, peppers, and onion onto the skewers, alternating as you go.

6. Arrange the skewers on the grill grate and cook for 10 minutes, turning every few minutes. Baste the skewers with BBQ sauce on all sides. Continue to baste and turn the skewers every minute or so to caramelize.

7. The chicken is cooked through when it reaches an internal temperature of 165 °F. The bacon should be nice and crispy at this point.

8. Remove the skewers from the grill and sprinkle with freshly chopped parsley.

Smoked Texas Spicy Drumsticks

Servings: 6
Cooking Time: 60 Minutes

Ingredients:
- 8 chicken drumsticks
- salt
- pepper
- 1 Cup Texas Spicy BBQ Sauce

Directions:
1. Pat drumsticks dry with a paper towel and season generously with salt and pepper.

2. Supply your smoker with wood pellets and follow the start-up procedure. Preheat the grill, with the lid closed, to 180° F.

3. Arrange the chicken legs on the grill grate and smoke for 30 minutes. Grill: 180 °F

4. Increase grill temperature to 350°F and cook for an additional 30 minutes. Grill: 350 °F

5. Brush the Texas Spicy BBQ Sauce on each of the drumsticks and cook for an additional 15 to 30 minutes, or until an instant-read meat thermometer inserted into the thickest part of the leg (but not touching bone) reaches 165°F. Enjoy! Grill: 350 °F Probe: 165 °F

VEGETABLES RECIPES

Roasted Hasselback Potatoes By Doug Scheiding

Servings: 6
Cooking Time: 120 Minutes

Ingredients:

- 6 Large russet potatoes
- 1 Pound bacon
- 1/2 Cup butter
- salt
- black pepper
- 1 Cup cheddar cheese
- 3 Whole scallions

Directions:

1. To cut potatoes, place two wooden spoons on either side of the potato (this prevents your knife from going all the way through). Slice potato into thin chips leaving about 1/4" attached on the bottom.
2. Freeze bacon slices for about 30 minutes then cut into small pieces about the size of a stamp. Place these in the cracks between every other slice.
3. Place the potato in a large cast iron skillet. Top the potato with slices of hard butter (you can also place thin slivers of cold butter between the potato slices with the bacon if desired). Season with salt and pepper.
4. Supply your smoker with wood pellets and follow the start-up procedure. Preheat the grill, with the lid closed, to 350° F.
5. Place the cast iron directly on the grill grate and cook for two hours. Top potatoes with more butter and baste with melted butter every 30 minutes.
6. In the last 10 minutes of cooking, sprinkle with cheddar and return to grill to melt.
7. To finish, top with chives or scallions. Enjoy!

Roasted Mashed Potatoes

Servings: 8
Cooking Time: 40 Minutes

Ingredients:

- 5 Pound Yukon Gold potatoes
- 1 1/2 Stick butter, softened
- 1 1/2 Cup heavy whipping cream, room temperature
- kosher salt
- white pepper

Directions:

1. Supply your smoker with wood pellets and follow the start-up procedure. Preheat the grill, with the lid closed, to 300° F.
2. Peel and cut potatoes into 1/2 inch cubes. Place the potatoes in a shallow baking dish with 1/2 cup water and cover. Bake until tender, about 40 minutes. Grill: 300 °F
3. In a medium saucepan, combine cream and butter. Cook over medium heat until butter is melted.
4. Remove potatoes from the grill and drain water.
5. Transfer potatoes to a bowl and mash using a potato masher. Gradually add in cream and butter mixture and mix using the masher. Be careful not to overwork or the potatoes will becomes gluey. Season with salt and pepper to taste. Enjoy!

Broccoli-cauliflower Salad

Servings: 4
Cooking Time: 25 Minutes

Ingredients:

- 1½ cups mayonnaise
- ½ cup sour cream
- ¼ cup sugar
- 1 bunch broccoli, cut into small pieces
- 1 head cauliflower, cut into small pieces
- 1 small red onion, chopped
- 6 slices bacon, cooked and crumbled (precooked bacon works well)
- 1 cup shredded Cheddar cheese

Directions:

1. In a small bowl, whisk together the mayonnaise, sour cream, and sugar to make a dressing.
2. In a large bowl, combine the broccoli, cauliflower, onion, bacon, and Cheddar cheese.
3. Pour the dressing over the vegetable mixture and toss well to coat.
4. Serve the salad chilled.

Roasted Potato Poutine

Servings: 6
Cooking Time: 40 Minutes

Ingredients:

- 4 Large russet potatoes
- Tablespoon olive oil or vegetable oil
- Prime Rib Rub
- Cup chicken or beef gravy (homemade or jarred)
- 1 1/2 Cup white or yellow cheddar cheese curds
- freshly ground black pepper
- 2 Tablespoon scallions

Directions:

1. Supply your smoker with wood pellets and follow the start-up procedure. Preheat the grill, with the lid closed, to 500° F.

2. Scrub the potatoes and slice into fries, wedges or preferred shape.

3. Put potatoes into a large mixing bowl and coat with oil. Season generously with Traeger Prime Rib rub.

4. Tip the potatoes onto a rimmed baking sheet and spread in a single layer, cut sides down.

5. Roast for 20 minutes, then using a spatula, turn the potatoes to the other cut side. Continue to roast until the potatoes are tender and golden brown, about 15 to 20 minutes more.

6. While potatoes cook, warm the gravy on the stovetop or in a heat-proof saucepan on your Traeger.

7. To assemble the poutine, arrange the potatoes in a large shallow bowl or on a serving platter. Distribute the cheese curds on top. Pour the hot gravy evenly over the potatoes and cheese curds.

8. Season with black pepper and garnish with thinly sliced scallions. Serve immediately. Enjoy!

Salt Crusted Baked Potatoes

Servings: 4
Cooking Time: 60 Minutes

Ingredients:

- 6 russet potatoes, scrubbed and dried
- 3 Tablespoon canola oil
- 1 Tablespoon kosher salt
- butter
- sour cream
- Chives, fresh
- Bacon Bits
- cheddar cheese

Directions:

1. In a large bowl, coat the potatoes in canola oil and sprinkle heavily with salt.

2. Supply your smoker with wood pellets and follow the start-up procedure. Preheat the grill, with the lid closed, to 450° F.

3. Place the potatoes directly on the grill grate and bake for 30-40 minutes, or until soft in the middle when pricked with a fork. Serve loaded with your favorite toppings. Enjoy! Grill: 450 °F

Grilled Street Corn

Servings: 6
Cooking Time: 10 Minutes

Ingredients:

- 6 ears corn, husked
- 1 As Needed extra-virgin olive oil

- 1/4 Cup mayonnaise
- 1 Tablespoon ancho or guajillo chile powder
- 1/2 Cup chopped cilantro, plus more for serving
- 1 lime, zested and juiced
- salt
- 1/2 Cup Cotija cheese
- 1 As Needed cilantro, finely chopped

Directions:

1. Supply your smoker with wood pellets and follow the start-up procedure. Preheat the grill, with the lid closed, to 450° F.

2. Brush corn with oil and place on grill, turning occasionally.

3. While corn is on the grill, mix mayonnaise with chile powder, cilantro, lime juice and zest in a bowl. Season with salt.

4. After about 10 minutes corn should be cooked through and slightly charred on the outside. Remove from grill.

5. Top corn with chile mayonnaise then sprinkle on the Cotija cheese and chopped cilantro. Enjoy!

Roasted Asparagus

Servings: 4
Cooking Time: 30 Minutes

Ingredients:

- 1 Bunch asparagus
- 2 Tablespoon olive oil, plus more as needed
- Veggie Rub

Directions:

1. Coat asparagus with olive oil and Veggie Rub, stirring to coat all pieces.

2. Supply your smoker with wood pellets and follow the start-up procedure. Preheat the grill, with the lid closed, to 350° F.

3. Place asparagus directly on the grill grate for 15-20 minutes.

4. Remove from grill and enjoy!

Twice-smoked Potatoes

Servings: 16
Cooking Time: 95 Minutes

Ingredients:

- 8 Idaho, Russet, or Yukon Gold potatoes
- 1 (12-ounce) can evaporated milk, heated
- 1 cup (2 sticks) butter, melted
- ½ cup sour cream, at room temperature
- 1 cup grated Parmesan cheese
- ½ pound bacon, cooked and crumbled
- ¼ cup chopped scallions
- Salt
- Freshly ground black pepper
- 1 cup shredded Cheddar cheese

Directions:

1. Supply your smoker with wood pellets and follow the start-up procedure. Preheat, with the lid closed, to 400°F.
2. Poke the potatoes all over with a fork. Arrange them directly on the grill grate, close the lid, and smoke for 1 hour and 15 minutes, or until cooked through and they have some give when pinched.
3. Let the potatoes cool for 10 minutes, then cut in half lengthwise.
4. Into a medium bowl, scoop out the potato flesh, leaving ¼ inch in the shells; place the shells on a baking sheet.
5. Using an electric mixer on medium speed, beat the potatoes, milk, butter, and sour cream until smooth.
6. Stir in the Parmesan cheese, bacon, and scallions, and season with salt and pepper.
7. Generously stuff each shell with the potato mixture and top with Cheddar cheese.
8. Place the baking sheet on the grill grate, close the lid, and smoke for 20 minutes, or until the cheese is melted.

Bacon Wrapped Corn On The Cob

Servings: 4
Cooking Time: 21 Minutes

Ingredients:
- 4 Whole Corn, ears
- 8 Slices bacon
- 1 Teaspoon freshly ground black pepper
- 1 Teaspoon chili powder
- 1 To Taste Parmesan cheese, grated

Directions:
1. Peel back the corn husks, remove silk strings and rinse corn under cold water.
2. Wrap 2 pieces of bacon around each ear of corn, securing with toothpicks.
3. Dust each ear of corn with some chili powder and cracked black pepper.
4. Supply your smoker with wood pellets and follow the start-up procedure. Preheat the grill, with the lid closed, to 375° F.
5. Place the ears of corn directly on the Traeger and grill for approximately 20 minutes or until the bacon is cooked crisp. Grill: 375 °F
6. Take the corn off the Traeger. Carefully remove the toothpicks and season with a little more chili powder and a grating of parmesan cheese, if desired. Serve & enjoy!

Grilled Asparagus And Hollandaise Sauce

Servings: 4
Cooking Time: 10 Minutes

Ingredients:
- 1 Pound asparagus

- 2 Teaspoon red pepper flakes
- 2 Tablespoon olive oil
- salt and pepper
- 4 egg yolk
- 1 Tablespoon lemon juice
- 1/2 Cup butter, melted
- cayenne pepper
- salt

Directions:
1. Supply your smoker with wood pellets and follow the start-up procedure. Preheat the grill, with the lid closed, to 375° F.
2. In a large bowl, mix asparagus with olive oil, red pepper flakes and salt. Arrange asparagus on a cooking sheet and take to the grill. Cook for approximately 10 to 15 minutes. Grill: 375 °F
3. In an aluminum bowl, whisk the egg yolks well. Add the lemon juice and whisk until creamy.
4. Place bowl over a double boiler, over low heat, making sure that it does not touches the water.
5. While whisking, add the melted butter slowly. Whisk until it doubles the volume. Take off the heat, still whisking and add the cayenne pepper and salt.
6. Arrange asparagus over a serving plater. Pour hollandaise sauce over asparagus and serve. Enjoy!

Traeger Smoked Coleslaw

Servings: 8
Cooking Time: 20 Minutes

Ingredients:
- 1 Head purple cabbage, shredded
- 1 Head green cabbage, shredded
- 1 Cup shredded carrots
- 2 scallions, thinly sliced
- 1 1/2 Cup mayonnaise
- 1/8 Cup white wine vinegar
- 1 Teaspoon celery seed
- 1 Teaspoon sugar
- salt and pepper

Directions:
1. Supply your smoker with wood pellets and follow the start-up procedure. Preheat the grill, with the lid closed, to 180° F.
2. Spread cabbage and carrots out on a sheet tray and place directly on the grill grates. Smoke for 20 to 25 minutes or until cabbage picks up desired amount of smoke. Grill: 180 °F
3. Remove from grill and transfer to the refrigerator immediately to cool. While cabbage is cooling, make the dressing.
4. For the dressing, combine all ingredients in a small bowl and mix well.
5. Place smoked cabbage and carrots in a large bowl and pour dressing over them. Stir to coat well.
6. Transfer to a serving dish and sprinkle with scallions. Enjoy!

Grilled Corn On The Cob With Parmesan And Garlic

Servings: 6
Cooking Time: 30 Minutes

Ingredients:

- 4 Tablespoon butter, melted
- 2 Clove garlic, minced
- salt and pepper
- 8 ears fresh corn
- 1/2 Cup shaved Parmesan
- 1 Tablespoon chopped parsley

Directions:

1. Supply your smoker with wood pellets and follow the start-up procedure. Preheat the grill, with the lid closed, to 450° F.
2. Place butter, garlic, salt and pepper in a medium bowl and mix well.
3. Peel back corn husks and remove the silk. Rub corn with half of the garlic butter mixture.
4. Close husks and place directly on the grill grate. Cook for 25 to 30 minutes, turning occasionally until corn is tender. Grill: 450 °F
5. Remove from grill, peel and discard husks. Place corn on serving tray, drizzle with remaining butter and top with Parmesan and parsley.

Smoked Asparagus Soup

Servings: 4
Cooking Time: 40 Minutes

Ingredients:

- Pound Asparagus Spears
- 1 Tablespoon olive oil
- salt and pepper
- 1/2 yellow onion, diced
- 1 Tablespoon butter
- 2 Clove garlic, minced
- 1 1/2 Cup chicken stock
- 1 1/2 Cup cream
- 2 Stalk Raw Asparagus, Shaved

Directions:

1. Supply your smoker with wood pellets and follow the start-up procedure. Preheat the grill, with the lid closed, to 180° F.
2. Drizzle 1 pound of asparagus with olive oil and season with salt and pepper. Place directly on the grill grate and smoke for 20-30 minutes. Taste along the way to assess smoke level pulling earlier if needed. Grill: 180 °F

3. Place 1 Tbsp butter in a saucepan and melt over medium heat. Add onion and garlic and saute for 2-3 minutes or until onion is translucent.
4. Remove asparagus from the grill and cut into 1" pieces. Place asparagus in the pan with the onions and add stock and cream. Bring to a simmer.
5. Remove from heat and puree using a blender or immersion blender until smooth.
6. Season with salt and pepper and serve. Top with fresh shaved asparagus, sprinkle with salt, pepper, and smoked paprika if desired. Enjoy!

Smoked Pico De Gallo

Servings: 4
Cooking Time: 30 Minutes

Ingredients:

- 3 Cup diced Roma tomatoes
- 1 jalapeño, diced
- 1/2 red onion, diced
- 1/2 Bunch cilantro, finely chopped
- 2 lime, juiced
- salt
- olive oil

Directions:

1. Supply your smoker with wood pellets and follow the start-up procedure. Preheat the grill, with the lid closed, to 180° F.
2. Place the diced tomatoes on a small sheet pan spreading them into a thin layer. Place the sheet pan directly on the grill and smoke for 30 minutes. Grill: 180 °F
3. When the tomatoes are finished, toss all ingredients in a medium bowl and finish with lime juice, salt and olive oil to taste. Serve and enjoy!

Traeger Baked Potato Torte

Servings: 6
Cooking Time: 25 Minutes

Ingredients:

- 6 Yukon Gold potatoes, sliced 1/4 inch thick
- 2 Stick butter, melted
- 3 Clove garlic, crushed
- 2 Tablespoon rosemary, chopped
- 1 Cup Parmesan cheese, grated
- salt and pepper

Directions:

1. Supply your smoker with wood pellets and follow the start-up procedure. Preheat the grill, with the lid closed, to 375° F.

2. While the Traeger is heating up, peel and slice the potatoes (make sure to put them in water so they will not oxidize). Melt the butter and combine it with the crushed garlic.

3. Grease a 12" cast iron pan with butter and start to layer the torte. The layers should go as follows, potatoes, butter garlic mixture, rosemary, parmesan, continue layering to the top of the pan, about 4 to 5 layers.

4. Place the pan in the Traeger and bake for 20 to 25 minutes, or until the potatoes are fully cooked. If the top of the torte starts to darken before it is finished cooking, reduce the heat to 325°F. Serve hot and enjoy! Grill: 375 °F

Smoked Macaroni Salad

Servings: 4
Cooking Time: 20 Minutes

Ingredients:

- 1 Pound macaroni, uncooked
- 1/2 Small red onion, diced
- 1 green bell pepper, diced
- 1/2 Cup shredded carrot
- 1 Cup mayonnaise
- 3 Tablespoon white wine vinegar
- 2 Tablespoon sugar
- salt
- black pepper

Directions:

1. Bring a large stock pot of salted water to a boil over medium heat and cook pasta according to package directions. Make sure to cook to al dente, strain, and rinse under cold water.

2. Supply your smoker with wood pellets and follow the start-up procedure. Preheat the grill, with the lid closed, to 225° F.

3. Spread cooked pasta out on a sheet tray and place sheet tray directly on the grill grate. Smoke for 20 minutes, remove from heat, and transfer directly to the refrigerator to cool. Grill: 225 °F

4. While the pasta is cooling mix the dressing. Place all ingredients in a medium bowl and whisk to combine.

5. When pasta is cool combine chopped veggies, smoked pasta and dressing in a large bowl.

6. Cover with plastic wrap and place in the fridge for 20 minutes before serving. Enjoy!

Roasted Pumpkin Seeds

Servings: 8
Cooking Time: 40 Minutes

Ingredients:

- 1 Whole Pumpkin, seeds
- olive oil or vegetable oil
- Jacobsen Salt Co. Pure Kosher Sea Salt

Directions:

1. As soon as possible after removing the seeds from the pumpkin, rinse pumpkin seeds under cold water in a colander and pick out the pulp and strings.

2. Place the pumpkin seeds in a single layer on an oiled baking sheet, stirring to coat. Supply your smoker with wood pellets and follow the start-up procedure. Preheat the grill, with the lid closed, to 180° F.

3. Place the baking sheet with the seeds on the grill grate, close the lid, and smoke for 20 minutes. Grill: 180 °F

4. Sprinkle your seeds with salt and turn the temperature on your grill up to 325°F. Roast the seeds until toasted, about 20 minutes. Check and stir seeds after the first 10 minutes. Grill: 325 °F

5. Seeds will be brown because they were smoked before being roasted. Enjoy!

Stuffed Jalapenos

Servings: 8
Cooking Time: 60 Minutes

Ingredients:

- 40 Whole jalapeño
- 8 Ounce cream cheese, room temperature
- 1 Cup Sharp Cheddar Grated
- 1 1/2 Teaspoon Pork & Poultry Rub
- 2 Tablespoon sour cream
- 1 Whole (14 oz) cocktail sausages
- 20 Whole Slices of Smoked Bacon, Cut in Half

Directions:

1. Wash and dry the peppers. Cut the stem ends off with a paring knife, and using the same knife or a small metal spoon, carefully scrape the seeds and ribs out of each pepper. Set aside.

2. In a small bowl, combine the cream cheese, grated cheese, Traeger Pork and Poultry Rub, and the sour cream.

3. Transfer the mixture to a sturdy resealable plastic bag and trim 1/2-inch off one of the lower corners with a scissors. Squeeze the cream cheese mixture into each pepper, filling each a little over the halfway point.

4. Stuff one sausage into each pepper. Wrap the outside of each with a piece of bacon, securing with 1 or 2 toothpicks.

5. Arrange the peppers on a foil-lined baking sheet. Supply your smoker with wood pellets and follow the start-up procedure. Preheat the grill, with the lid closed, to 180° F, and smoke the peppers for 1 to 1-1/2 hours.

6. Increase the heat to 350 degrees F and continue to cook for 20 to 30 minutes, or until the bacon begins to render its fat and crisp. Enjoy! Grill: 350 °F

Roasted Olives

Servings: 4
Cooking Time: 45 Minutes

Ingredients:
- 2 Cup mixed olives
- 3 Sprig fresh rosemary
- 2 Clove garlic, minced
- 2 Tablespoon orange zest
- 1/3 Cup extra-virgin olive oil
- 2 Tablespoon orange juice
- 1/2 Teaspoon red pepper flakes

Directions:
1. Combine the olives, rosemary, garlic, orange zest, red pepper flakes, olive oil, and orange juice in a glass oven-safe pie plate or baking dish. Cover with foil.
2. Supply your smoker with wood pellets and follow the start-up procedure. Preheat the grill, with the lid closed, to 300° F.
3. Roast the olives for 45 minutes, stirring once or twice. Serve warm in an attractive bowl. Enjoy! Grill: 300 °F

Grilled Asparagus And Spinach Salad

Servings: 8
Cooking Time: 10 Minutes

Ingredients:
- 4 Fluid Ounce apple cider vinegar
- 8 Fluid Ounce Honey Bourbon BBQ Sauce
- 2 Bunch asparagus, ends trimmed
- 3 Fluid Ounce extra-virgin olive oil
- 2 Ounce Beef Rub
- 24 Ounce Spinach, fresh
- 4 Ounce candied pecans
- 4 Ounce feta cheese

Directions:
1. Combine apple cider vinegar and Traeger Apricot BBQ Sauce to create salad dressing.
2. Supply your smoker with wood pellets and follow the start-up procedure. Preheat the grill, with the lid closed, to High heat.
3. Toss the asparagus with Olive Oil and the Beef Shake. Put asparagus in the Traeger Grilling Basket and move the basket to the grill grate.
4. Grill for about 10 minutes. Remove the asparagus once it is cooked. Grill: 350 °F
5. Place the hot asparagus right on top of the bowl of spinach.
6. Add candied pecans, feta cheese & salad dressing then toss and serve. Enjoy!

Red Potato Grilled Lollipops

Servings: 4
Cooking Time: 25 Minutes

Ingredients:
- 8 Large red bliss potatoes, halved
- 2 Clove garlic, minced
- 2 Sprig rosemary, minced
- 2 Tablespoon olive oil
- 1 Teaspoon salt
- 1/2 Teaspoon black pepper
- 5 Wooden Skewers, soaked in water
- 1/4 Cup Parmesan cheese, grated

Directions:
1. Supply your smoker with wood pellets and follow the start-up procedure. Preheat the grill, with the lid closed, to 450° F.
2. Halve potatoes and poke each several times with a fork.
3. Put the potatoes in a large bowl and toss with the minced garlic, rosemary leaves, a few tablespoons of olive oil, kosher salt, and pepper. Microwave the potatoes for 4 minutes. Gently toss potatoes and microwave for another 3 minutes.
4. Skewer potato halves threading about 4 or 5 potato halves on each skewer. Brush potatoes with olive oil.
5. Place the potato skewers on the Traeger, cut side down, and grill until the sides begin to brown (4-7 minutes).
6. Flip and grill skin side down for another 7-10 minutes.
7. They are done when a sharp knife tip easily penetrates the sides. Remove potatoes from grill and top with grated parmesan cheese. Enjoy!

Baked Breakfast Mini Quiches

Servings: 8
Cooking Time: 15 Minutes

Ingredients:
- cooking spray
- 1 Tablespoon extra-virgin olive oil
- 1/2 yellow onion, diced
- 3 Cup Spinach, fresh
- 10 eggs
- 4 Ounce shredded cheddar, mozzarella or Swiss cheese
- 1/4 Cup fresh basil
- 1 Teaspoon kosher salt
- 1/2 Teaspoon black pepper

Directions:
1. Spray a 12-cup muffin tin generously with cooking spray.
2. In a small skillet over medium heat, warm the oil. Add the onion and cook, stirring frequently, until softened, about 7 minutes. Add the spinach and cook until wilted, about 1 minute longer.

3. Transfer to a cutting board to cool, then chop the mixture so the spinach if broken up a little.

4. Supply your smoker with wood pellets and follow the start-up procedure. Preheat the grill, with the lid closed, to 350° F.

5. In a large bowl, whisk the eggs until frothy. Add the cooled onions and spinach, cheese, basil, 1 tsp salt and 1/2 tsp pepper. Stir to combine. Divide egg mixture evenly among the muffin cups.

6. Place tray on the grill and bake until the eggs have puffed up, are set, and are beginning to brown, about 18 to 20 minutes. Grill: 350 ˚F

7. Serve immediately, or allow to cool on a wire rack, then refrigerate in an air tight container for up to 4 days. Enjoy!

Butternut Squash

Servings: 4
Cooking Time: 45 Minutes

Ingredients:

- 1 Whole butternut squash
- Veggie Rub
- Blackened Saskatchewan Rub
- olive oil

Directions:

1. Cut squash in half and lightly coat with mixture of olive oil, Traeger Veggie Shake, and Traeger Blackened Saskatchewan.

2. Wrap in foil with 1/2 cup (120mL) of water.

3. Supply your smoker with wood pellets and follow the start-up procedure. Preheat the grill, with the lid closed, to 450° F.

4. Place squash on grill for 45 minutes. Remove from grill and unwrap. Enjoy!

Steak Fries With Horseradish Creme

Servings: 6
Cooking Time: 25 Minutes

Ingredients:

- 5 Potatoes, Baking
- 2 Tablespoon extra-virgin olive oil
- 1 Teaspoon butter
- 3 Clove garlic, crushed
- 1 Teaspoon onion powder
- 2 Teaspoon Jacobsen Salt Co. Pure Kosher Sea Salt
- 1 Teaspoon black pepper

Directions:

1. Wash the potatoes thoroughly, and cut them in eighths, then toss them in the olive oil, butter, crushed garlic, onion powder, salt, and pepper.

2. Supply your smoker with wood pellets and follow the start-up procedure. Preheat the grill, with the lid closed, to 450° F.

3. In order to get great grill marks, line up the wedges on the front of the grill and the back of the grill, turning to get grill marks on all sides.

4. Once they have been seared, move them to the center of the grill and finish cooking about ten more minutes, serve hot with the horseradish mayo. Enjoy!

Baked Winter Squash Au Gratin

Servings: 8
Cooking Time: 45 Minutes

Ingredients:

- 2 Cup heavy cream
- salt and pepper
- 3 Cup shredded Gruyere cheese
- 4 Clove garlic, diced
- 2 Tablespoon butter
- 3 yellow potatoes, peeled and cubed
- 1 butternut squash seeded, peeled and cubed
- 1 acorn squash seeded, peeled and cubed

Directions:

1. Supply your smoker with wood pellets and follow the start-up procedure. Preheat the grill, with the lid closed, to 375° F.

2. In a medium saucepan, cook the cream, stirring constantly, until it comes to a low boil. Add salt, pepper, garlic and shredded Gruyere cheese. Stir until cheese is melted.

3. Grease a 9x13 inch baking dish with 2 tablespoons of butter. In a large mixing bowl, combine potatoes, butternut and acorn squash. Stir in the cheese sauce. Place mixture in the prepared baking dish and place in grill.

4. Cook for 45 minutes or until potatoes and squash are fork tender. Remove from grill and let cool for 10 minutes before serving. Enjoy! Grill: 375 ˚F

Parmesan Roasted Cauliflower

Servings: 4
Cooking Time: 40 Minutes

Ingredients:

- 1 Head cauliflower, cut into florets
- 1 Medium onion, sliced
- 4 Clove garlic, unpeeled
- 4 Tablespoon olive oil
- salt
- black pepper
- 1 Teaspoon fresh thyme
- 1/2 Cup Parmesan cheese, grated

Directions:

1. Supply your smoker with wood pellets and follow the start-up procedure. Preheat the grill, with the lid closed, to 400° F.

2. On a baking tray, mix together cauliflower, onion, thyme, garlic, olive oil, salt and pepper.
3. Place tray on preheated grill and cook until cauliflower is firm and almost tender (about 25 minutes). Grill: 400 °F
4. Sprinkle cauliflower with Parmesan cheese and continue to cook on the Traeger for another 10 to 15 minutes. Cauliflower should be tender and the Parmesan crisp. Serve immediately, enjoy!

Smoked Parmesan Herb Popcorn

Servings: 2
Cooking Time: 15 Minutes

Ingredients:
- 4 Tablespoon butter
- 2 Teaspoon Italian Seasoning
- 1 Teaspoon garlic powder
- 1 Teaspoon salt
- 1/4 Cup popcorn kernels
- 1/2 Cup Parmesan cheese, grated

Directions:
1. Supply your smoker with wood pellets and follow the start-up procedure. Preheat the grill, with the lid closed, to 250° F.
2. In a small saucepan, melt the butter over medium heat. Add Italian seasoning, garlic powder, and salt and stir to combine. Remove from heat and set aside.
3. Add 1/4 cup of popcorn to a brown paper lunch bag. Fold the top of the bag over twice to close. Place the bag in the microwave and microwave on high for 1 to 2 minutes, or until there are about 5 seconds between pops. Open the bag with care and dump into a large mixing bowl.
4. Pour butter mixture of popcorn in a bowl and toss to combine. Dump popcorn onto a baking sheet and place in grill.
5. Smoke for 10 minutes; remove from grill. Toss with parmesan cheese to serve. Enjoy! Grill: 250 °F

Baked Heirloom Tomato Tart

Servings: 4
Cooking Time: 45 Minutes

Ingredients:
- 1 Whole Puff Pastry Sheet
- 2 Pound heirloom tomatoes, various shapes and sizes
- 1/2 Tablespoon kosher salt
- 1/2 Cup Ricotta Cheese
- 5 Whole eggs
- 1 To Taste salt and pepper
- 1/2 Teaspoon thyme leaves
- 1/2 Teaspoon red pepper flakes
- 4 Sprig thyme

Directions:

1. Supply your smoker with wood pellets and follow the start-up procedure. Preheat the grill, with the lid closed, to 350° F.
2. Place the puff pastry on a parchment lined sheet tray, and make a cut ¾ of the way through the pastry, ½" from the edge.
3. Slice the tomatoes and season with salt. Place on a sheet tray lined with paper towels.
4. In a small bowl combine the ricotta, 4 of the eggs, salt, thyme leaves, red pepper flakes and black pepper. Whisk together until combined. Spread the ricotta mixture over the puff pastry, staying within ½" from the edge.
5. In a small bowl whisk the last egg. Brush the egg wash onto the exposed edges of the pastry.
6. Place the sheet tray directly on the grill grate and bake for 45 minutes, rotating half-way through. Grill: 350 °F
7. When the edges are browned and the moisture from the tomatoes has evaporated, remove from the grill and let cool 5-7 minutes before serving. Enjoy!

Grilled Ratatouille Salad

Servings: 4
Cooking Time: 25 Minutes

Ingredients:
- 1 Whole sweet potatoes
- 1 Whole red onion, diced
- 1 Whole zucchini
- 1 Whole Squash
- 1 Large Tomato, diced
- vegetable oil
- salt and pepper

Directions:
1. Supply your smoker with wood pellets and follow the start-up procedure. Preheat the grill, with the lid closed, to High heat.
2. Slice all vegetables to a ¼ inch thickness.
3. Lightly brush each vegetable with oil and season with Traeger's Veggie Shake or salt and pepper.
4. Place sweet potato, onion, zucchini, and squash on grill grate and grill for 20 minutes or until tender, turn halfway through.
5. Add tomato slices to the grill during the last 5 minutes of cooking time.
6. For presentation, alternate vegetables while layering them vertically. Enjoy!

Roasted Artichokes With Garlic Butter

Servings: 2
Cooking Time: 60 Minutes

Ingredients:
- 2 Large artichokes
- 3 Tablespoon olive oil

- sea salt
- 1 Stick unsalted butter
- 2 Clove garlic, chopped
- 2 Tablespoon chives, parsley, tarragon or cilantro
- 1 lemon

Directions:

1. Supply your smoker with wood pellets and follow the start-up procedure. Preheat the grill, with the lid closed, to 375° F.

2. Meanwhile, break off and discard any small outer leaves on the artichokes. Use a knife to slice off the tops of the artichokes, then using scissors, cut off any thorns on the remaining artichoke leaves. Trim the very bottom of the stem, then peel the tough and fibrous outer layer of the stem. Finally, cut artichokes in half and rinse off.

3. Transfer artichokes to a large mixing bowl, drizzle with olive oil and generously sprinkle with sea salt. Toss to coat the artichokes thoroughly. Grill: 375 °F

4. Add the artichokes to the grill, cut side down, and roast at 375°F until the artichoke bottoms are tender when poked with a fork or knife, about 50 to 60 minutes. Grill: 375 °F

5. When artichokes are almost done, add butter, chopped garlic and a pinch of sea salt to a small sauce pan and melt slowly over medium-low heat. Once the butter melts all the way and starts to bubble slightly, add the herbs.

6. When the artichokes are done, transfer to a butcher paper lined tray with the cut sides up. Drizzle half the garlic butter and squeeze half of the lemon over the artichokes. Add a small sprinkle of sea salt over the artichokes.

7. Serve with a ramekin of the remaining butter for dipping and extra wedges of lemon. Enjoy! Chef Tip: You can also serve with a ramekin of good mayonnaise mixed with a bit of hot sauce.

Chef Curtis' Famous Chimichurri Sauce

Servings: 4
Cooking Time: 5 Minutes

Ingredients:

- 2 Whole lemon, halved
- 2 Medium flat-leaf Italian parsley, washed and chopped with the majority of stems cut off
- 4 Clove garlic, diced
- 1/4 Cup red wine vinegar
- 1/2 Teaspoon black pepper
- 1/4 Cup extra-virgin olive oil
- 1 Teaspoon salt

Directions:

1. Supply your smoker with wood pellets and follow the start-up procedure. Preheat the grill, with the lid closed, to 450° F.

2. Place lemon halves directly on the grill grate and cook for 5 minutes or until grill marks appear. Grill: 450 °F

3. Take lemons off grill and juice. Combine all of the ingredients in a food processor or blender and purée until smooth, or leave slightly chunky for some texture.

4. Add additional olive oil to taste for a milder flavor if preferred. Serve on protein or as a dip. Enjoy!

Roasted Garlic Herb Fries

Servings: 4
Cooking Time: 45 Minutes

Ingredients:

- 4 Whole russet potatoes
- 1 Teaspoon salt
- 2 Tablespoon avocado oil
- 1 Teaspoon fresh chopped rosemary
- 1 Teaspoon fresh chopped thyme
- 2 Clove garlic, minced
- 2 Teaspoon flake salt
- 1 Teaspoon chopped parsley, for garnish

Directions:

1. Supply your smoker with wood pellets and follow the start-up procedure. Preheat the grill, with the lid closed, to 425° F.

2. Chop potatoes into fries, (a mandolin works great for this) and place directly into an ice water bath with 1 teaspoon salt for 15 to 30 minutes.

3. Combine oil, rosemary, thyme and garlic in a big bowl. Remove potatoes from ice water and dry thoroughly with paper towels.

4. Toss potatoes in the oil mixture and place them on 2 to 3 parchment-lined baking sheets in a single layer. Sprinkle the flake salt over the fries.

5. Place baking sheets on the grill and roast for 30 minutes, flip the fries, then cook for an additional 15 minutes until golden and crispy. Dust with parsley. Grill: 425 °F

6. Serve with your favorite dipping sauce, side dish or as a nacho base.

Grilled Zucchini Squash Spears

Servings: 4
Cooking Time: 10 Minutes

Ingredients:

- 4 Medium zucchini
- 2 Tablespoon olive oil
- 1 Tablespoon sherry vinegar
- 2 thyme, leaves pulled
- salt and pepper

Directions:

1. Clean the zucchini and cut the ends off. Cut each in half lengthwise, then each half into thirds.

2. Combine remaining ingredients in a medium Ziplock bag and add the spears. Toss and mix well to coat the zucchini.

3. Supply your smoker with wood pellets and follow the start-up procedure. Preheat the grill, with the lid closed, to 350° F.

4. Remove the spears from the bag and place directly on the grill grate cut side down.

5. Cook for 3-4 minutes per side, until grill marks appear and zucchini is tender. Grill: 350 °F

6. Remove from grill and finish with more thyme leaves if desired. Enjoy!

Potluck Salad With Smoked Cornbread

Servings: 6
Cooking Time: 45 Minutes

Ingredients:

- 1 cup all-purpose flour
- 1 cup yellow cornmeal
- 1 tablespoon sugar
- 2 teaspoons baking powder
- 1 teaspoon salt
- 1 cup milk
- 1 egg, beaten, at room temperature
- 4 tablespoons (½ stick) unsalted butter, melted and cooled
- Nonstick cooking spray or butter, for greasing
- ½ cup milk
- ½ cup sour cream
- 2 tablespoons dry ranch dressing mix
- 1 pound bacon, cooked and crumbled
- 3 tomatoes, chopped
- 1 bell pepper, chopped
- 1 cucumber, seeded and chopped
- 2 stalks celery, chopped (about 1 cup)
- ½ cup chopped scallions

Directions:

1. For the cornbread:

2. In a medium bowl, combine the flour, cornmeal, sugar, baking powder, and salt.

3. In a small bowl, whisk together the milk and egg. Pour in the butter, then slowly fold this mixture into the dry ingredients.

4. Supply your smoker with wood pellets and follow the start-up procedure. Preheat, with the lid closed, to 375°F.

5. Coat a cast iron skillet with cooking spray or butter.

6. Pour the batter into the skillet, place on the grill grate, close the lid, and smoke for 35 to 45 minutes, or until the cornbread is browned and pulls away from the side of the skillet.

7. Remove the cornbread from the grill and let cool, then coarsely crumble.

8. For the salad:

9. In a small bowl, whisk together the milk, sour cream, and ranch dressing mix.

10. In a medium bowl, combine the crumbled bacon, tomatoes, bell pepper, cucumber, celery, and scallions.

11. In a large serving bowl, layer half of the crumbled cornbread, half of the bacon-veggie mixture, and half of the dressing. Toss lightly.

12. Repeat the layering with the remaining cornbread, bacon-veggie mixture, and dressing. Toss again.

13. Refrigerate the salad for at least 1 hour. Serve cold.

Smoked Pickled Green Beans

Servings: 4
Cooking Time: 45 Minutes

Ingredients:

- 1 Pound Green Beans, blanched
- 1/2 Cup salt
- 1/2 Cup sugar
- 1 Tablespoon red pepper flakes
- 2 Cup white wine vinegar
- 2 Cup ice water

Directions:

1. Supply your smoker with wood pellets and follow the start-up procedure. Preheat the grill, with the lid closed, to 180° F.

2. Place the blanched green beans on a mesh grill mat and place mat directly on the grill grate. Smoke the green beans for 30-45 minutes until they've picked up the desired amount of smoke. Remove from grill and set aside until the brine is ready. Grill: 180 °F

3. In a medium sized saucepan, bring all remaining ingredients, except ice water, to a boil over medium high heat on the stove. Simmer for 5-10 minutes then remove from heat and steep 20 minutes more. Pour brine over ice water to cool.

4. Once brine has cooled, pour over the green beans and weigh them down with a few plates to ensure they are completely submerged. Let sit 24 hours before use. Enjoy!

Sweet Potato Marshmallow Casserole

Servings: 6
Cooking Time: 60 Minutes

Ingredients:

- 5 Yams
- 1 1/2 Stick butter
- 1/2 Cup brown sugar
- 1 Teaspoon vanilla
- 1 Teaspoon kosher salt
- 1 Teaspoon cracked black pepper
- 1 Marshmallows, miniature

- 1/4 Unsalted Butter, Softened

Directions:

1. Supply your smoker with wood pellets and follow the start-up procedure. Preheat the grill, with the lid closed, to 375° F.

2. Pierce the skin of the yams with a fork a few times. Place on a baking sheet or foil tin inside the grill and let roast for 50 minutes or until extremely softened. Grill: 375 °F

3. Remove yams from the grill and set aside until cool enough to handle. While the potatoes cool, with a stiff whisk, whip together 1/2 cup softened butter, the brown sugar, vanilla, salt and pepper.

4. Remove and discard skins from sweet potatoes and mash until smooth. Fold in the butter mixture and transfer to a cast iron pan.

5. Place cast iron on the grill and bake for 15-20 minutes. Remove from the grill, top with marshmallows and dot with remaining 1/4 cup butter.

6. Place back in the grill for 15 minutes until warm and the marshmallows are golden. Enjoy! Grill: 375 °F

Roasted Sheet Pan Vegetables

Servings: 4
Cooking Time: 25 Minutes

Ingredients:

- 1 Small head purple cauliflower, stemmed and cut into 2 inch florets
- 1 Small head yellow cauliflower, stemmed and cut into 2 inch florets
- 4 Cup butternut squash
- 2 Cup oyster or shiitake mushrooms, rinsed and sliced
- 3 Tablespoon olive oil
- 2 Teaspoon kosher salt
- freshly ground black pepper
- 1/4 Cup chopped flat-leaf parsley

Directions:

1. Supply your smoker with wood pellets and follow the start-up procedure. Preheat the grill, with the lid closed, to 450° F.

2. In a large mixing bowl, combine all of the vegetables. Drizzle olive oil over the top, along with kosher salt and a generous grinding of black pepper.

3. Using your hands, toss the vegetables until they are evenly coated.

4. Spread out onto 1 or 2 half sheet pans or baking sheets, ensuring there is a little space between the veggies. (If they are too crowded, the vegetables will steam instead of roast and you won't get that crispy texture.)

5. Place the sheet pans on the grill and cook for 15 minutes. Open and stir, then close the lid and continue to cook until the vegetables are brown around the edges, about 5 to 15 minutes longer. Grill: 450 °F

6. Toss with parsley and serve immediately. The vegetables are also delicious at room temperature. Enjoy!

Roasted Sweet Potato Steak Fries

Servings: 4
Cooking Time: 40 Minutes

Ingredients:

- 3 Whole sweet potatoes
- 4 Tablespoon extra-virgin olive oil
- salt and pepper
- 2 Tablespoon fresh chopped rosemary

Directions:

1. Supply your smoker with wood pellets and follow the start-up procedure. Preheat the grill, with the lid closed, to 450° F.

2. Cut sweet potatoes into wedges and toss with olive oil, salt, pepper and rosemary. Spread on a parchment lined baking sheet and put in the grill. Cook for 15 minutes then flip and continue to cook until lightly browned and cooked through, about 40 to 45 minutes total. Grill: 450 °F

3. Serve with your favorite dipping sauce. Enjoy! Grill: 450 °F

Baked Loaded Tater Tots

Servings: 6
Cooking Time: 35 Minutes

Ingredients:

- 2 Pound frozen tater tots
- 1 Can Black Beans
- 1 1/2 Cup leftover chili
- 1 Cup leftover queso
- 1 red onion, finely diced
- 1/2 Cup chopped cilantro
- 1/2 Cup sour cream
- 1 jalapeños, sliced

Directions:

1. Supply your smoker with wood pellets and follow the start-up procedure. Preheat the grill, with the lid closed, to 375° F.

2. Spread frozen tots out on a sheet tray and place directly on the grill grate.

3. Cook for 20 to 25 minutes or until tots are crispy. Grill: 375 °F

4. Top with warmed chili, queso and beans. Place back on the grill for 15 minutes. Grill: 375 °F

5. Remove from grill and top with red onion, cilantro, sour cream and jalapeño. Enjoy!

Smoked Mushrooms

Servings: 4
Cooking Time: 45 Minutes

Ingredients:
- Pound Mushrooms, fresh
- 1/2 Cup apple cider vinegar
- 1/2 Cup soy sauce
- 1 Teaspoon Blackened Saskatchewan Rub

Directions:
1. Clean mushrooms and place in a large Ziploc bag. Add apple cider vinegar, soy sauce and rub.
2. Mix well and allow to marinate in the refrigerator for at least 2 hours.
3. Supply your smoker with wood pellets and follow the start-up procedure. Preheat the grill, with the lid closed, to 350° F.
4. Place cast iron skillet inside grill for 20 minutes to warm up.
5. Add the mushrooms and marinade slowly into the cast iron skillet.
6. Cook uncovered for 15 minutes, then cover the skillet and cook another 30 minutes until mushrooms are tender. Grill: 350 °F
7. Remove skillet from grill and let mushrooms cool down for 5 minutes before serving. Enjoy!

Roasted New Potatoes

Servings: 4
Cooking Time: 25 Minutes

Ingredients:
- 2 Pound small new potatoes
- 3 Tablespoon butter, melted
- 2 Tablespoon olive oil
- 2 Tablespoon whole mustard seeds
- salt and pepper
- 2 Tablespoon freshly minced chives
- 2 Tablespoon freshly minced parsley

Directions:
1. Place potatoes in a colander and rinse with cold water. Dry on paper towels and transfer to a rimmed baking sheet large enough to hold them in a single layer.
2. Drizzle the potatoes with butter and olive oil, then sprinkle them with the mustard seeds. Season with salt and pepper.
3. Supply your smoker with wood pellets and follow the start-up procedure. Preheat the grill, with the lid closed, to 400° F.
4. Place the baking sheet with the potatoes on the grill grate. Roast for about 25 minutes shaking the pan once or twice, until potatoes are tender and the skins are slightly wrinkled. Grill: 400 °F
5. Transfer potatoes to a bowl or platter. Top with fresh chives and parsley. Enjoy!

Grilled Asparagus & Honey-glazed Carrots

Servings: 4
Cooking Time: 35 Minutes

Ingredients:
- 1 Bunch asparagus, woody ends removed
- 1 Pound Carrots, peeled
- 2 Tablespoon olive oil
- sea salt
- 2 Tablespoon honey
- lemon zest

Directions:
1. Rinse all vegetables under cold water. Drizzle asparagus with olive oil and a generous sprinkling of sea salt. Generously drizzle carrots with honey and lightly sprinkle with sea salt.
2. Supply your smoker with wood pellets and follow the start-up procedure. Preheat the grill, with the lid closed, to 350° F.
3. Place carrots on the grill first and cook for 10-15 minutes, then add asparagus and cook both for another 15 to 20 minutes, or until they're done to your liking. Grill: 350 °F
4. Top the asparagus with some fresh lemon zest. Enjoy!

Baked Bacon Green Bean Casserole

Servings: 6
Cooking Time: 50 Minutes

Ingredients:
- 1 1/2 Pound Green Beans, fresh
- 1 Can cream of mushroom soup
- 1/2 Cup milk
- 1/2 Teaspoon Worcestershire sauce
- 1/2 Teaspoon black pepper
- 2/3 Cup French's Original Crispy Fried Onions
- 8 Slices bacon
- 1/4 Cup red bell pepper, diced
- 2/3 French's Original Crispy Fried Onions

Directions:
1. In a mixing bowl, combine beans, soup, milk, Worcestershire sauce, black pepper, 2/3 cup of the onions, 6 of the slices of crumbled bacon, and red bell pepper. Transfer to a 1-1/2 quart casserole dish.
2. Supply your smoker with wood pellets and follow the start-up procedure. Preheat the grill, with the lid closed, to 350° F.
3. Cook casserole until the filling is hot and bubbling, 35 to 40 minutes. Grill: 350 °F
4. Top with remaining onions and the last 2 slices of crumbled bacon and cook for 5 to 10 minutes more, or until the onions are crisp and beginning to brown. Serve, enjoy! Grill: 350 °F

Baked Sweet Potatoes

Servings: 8

Cooking Time: 60 Minutes

Ingredients:

- 1 Cup butter, softened
- 1/4 Cup pure maple syrup
- 1/2 Teaspoon ground cinnamon
- 8 Medium sweet potatoes

Directions:

1. Make the Maple-Cinnamon Butter: In a mixing bowl, combine the butter, maple syrup, and cinnamon and whip with a wooden spoon. (Alternatively, blend the ingredients using a hand-held mixer or a stand mixer.) Transfer to a small bowl, cover, and chill until serving time.

2. Supply your smoker with wood pellets and follow the start-up procedure. Preheat the grill, with the lid closed, to 375° F. Arrange the sweet potatoes on the grill grate and bake until soft, 1 to 1-1/2 hours, depending on the size of the potatoes. Make a slit in the side of each, and squeeze the ends gently to fluff.

3. Serve hot with the Maple-Cinnamon Butter. Enjoy!

Mashed Red Potatoes

Servings: 4

Cooking Time: 40 Minutes

Ingredients:

- 8 Large red potatoes
- salt
- black pepper
- 1/2 Cup heavy cream
- 1/4 Cup butter

Directions:

1. Supply your smoker with wood pellets and follow the start-up procedure. Preheat the grill, with the lid closed, to 180° F.

2. Slice red potatoes in half, lengthwise then cut in half again to make quarters. Season potatoes with salt and pepper.

3. Increase the heat to High and preheat. Once the grill is hot, set potatoes directly on the grill grate. Grill: 450 °F

4. Every 15 minutes flip potatoes to ensure all sides get color. Continue to do this until potatoes are fork tender.

5. When tender, mash potatoes with cream, butter, salt, and pepper to taste. Serve warm, enjoy!

Smoked Jalapeño Poppers

Servings: 4

Cooking Time: 60 Minutes

Ingredients:

- 12 Medium jalapeño

- 6 Slices bacon, cut in half
- 8 Ounce cream cheese
- 2 Tablespoon Pork & Poultry Rub
- 1 Cup grated cheese

Directions:

1. Supply your smoker with wood pellets and follow the start-up procedure. Preheat the grill, with the lid closed, to 180° F. For optimal flavor, use Super Smoke if available.

2. Slice the jalapeños in half lengthwise. Scrape out any seeds and ribs with a small spoon or paring knife. Mix softened cream cheese with Traeger Pork & Poultry rub and grated cheese. Spoon mixture onto each jalapeño half. Wrap with bacon and secure with a toothpick.

3. Place the jalapeños on a rimmed baking sheet. Place on grill and smoke for 30 minutes. Grill: 180 °F

4. Increase the grill temperature to 375°F and cook an additional 30 minutes or until bacon is cooked to desired doneness. Serve warm, enjoy! Grill: 375 °F

Roasted Vegetable Napoleon

Servings: 4

Cooking Time: 30 Minutes

Ingredients:

- 2 Whole sweet potatoes
- 2 Whole zucchini
- 2 Whole Squash
- 1 Whole red onion
- 2 Whole Bell Pepper, Red
- salt and pepper

Directions:

1. Supply your smoker with wood pellets and follow the start-up procedure. Preheat the grill, with the lid closed, to High heat.

2. Salt and pepper all vegetables and grill them on both sides. Begin with the peppers and onions as they will take a little longer to cook. Grill: 450 °F

Portobello Marinated Mushroom

Servings: 2

Cooking Time: 15 Minutes

Ingredients:

- 1 Teaspoon chopped thyme
- 1 Teaspoon rosemary, chopped
- 1 Teaspoon Oregano, chopped
- 3 Tablespoon extra-virgin olive oil
- 1 To Taste Jacobsen Salt Co. Pure Kosher Sea Salt
- 1 To Taste pepper
- 6 Whole Portobello Mushroom
- 2 Whole russet potatoes

Directions:

1. Supply your smoker with wood pellets and follow the start-up procedure. Preheat the grill, with the lid closed, to 450° F.

2. Mix fresh herbs, olive oil, salt, and pepper together in a bowl. Rub over mushrooms. Grill both sides of mushrooms for approximately 2-3 minutes on each side. Grill: 450 ˚F

3. Clean the potatoes and slice into long strips.

4. Heat the oil on the Traeger in a sauce pan; drop the potatoes in the hot oil and fry for 7-8 minutes. Let the potatoes cool slightly on a sheet pan. Enjoy! Grill: 450 ˚F

Roasted Jalapeño Poppers

Servings: 2
Cooking Time: 30 Minutes

Ingredients:

- 8 Slices Bacon, Center Cut
- 2 Cup cream cheese
- 2 Ounce Cheese, sharp cheddar
- 1/2 Cup green onions, minced
- 2 Teaspoon fresh squeezed lime juice
- 4 Tablespoon Seeded Tomato, Chopped
- 4 Tablespoon cilantro, chopped
- 1/2 Teaspoon kosher salt
- 2 Small garlic clove, minced
- 12 Whole Jalapeños

Directions:

1. Supply your smoker with wood pellets and follow the start-up procedure. Preheat the grill, with the lid closed, to 350° F.

2. Place 2 bacon slices directly on the grill grate and cook 10-15 minutes until cooked through and crispy flipping halfway through. Remove from grill, but leave the grill on. When cool enough to handle, coarsely chop the bacon and reserve. Grill: 350 ˚F

3. In the bowl of a stand mixer, combine cream cheese, cheddar cheese, green onions, chopped bacon, lime juice, tomatoes, cilantro, salt and garlic. Mix on medium speed with a paddle until combined. Transfer mixture to a piping bag.

4. Cut the tops off the jalapeños and remove the seeds and ribs with a small paring knife.

5. Pipe the filling into each pepper so that the filling comes up a 1/4" over the top of the pepper. Place the tops back on each pepper.

6. With a rolling pin, flatten out the remaining six slices of bacon until they are 1/8" thick. Cut each slice in half. Wrap 1/2 a bacon slice around each pepper and secure with a toothpick.

7. Place the peppers in the Traeger Jalapeno Popper Tray. Place the tray directly on the grill grate and cook for 30-40 minutes until the peppers are tender, bacon is crispy, and cheese is melted. Enjoy! Grill: 350 ˚F

Roasted Green Beans With Bacon

Servings: 4
Cooking Time: 20 Minutes

Ingredients:

- 1 1/2 Pound green beans, ends trimmed
- 4 Strips bacon, cut into small pieces
- 4 Tablespoon extra-virgin olive oil
- 2 Clove garlic, minced
- 1 Teaspoon kosher salt

Directions:

1. Supply your smoker with wood pellets and follow the start-up procedure. Preheat the grill, with the lid closed, to 350° F.

2. Toss all ingredients together and spread out evenly on a sheet tray.

3. Place the tray directly on the grill grate and roast until the bacon is crispy and beans are lightly browned, about 20 minutes. Enjoy! Grill: 450 ˚F

Double-smoked Cheese Potatoes

Servings: 12
Cooking Time: 35 Minutes

Ingredients:

- 4 large baking potatoes (12 to 14 ounces each—preferably organic)
- 1 1/2 tablespoons bacon fat or butter, melted, or extra virgin olive oil
- Coarse salt (sea or kosher) and freshly ground black pepper
- 4 strips artisanal bacon (like Nueske's), cut crosswise into 1/4-inch slivers
- 6 tablespoons (3/4 stick) cold unsalted butter, thinly sliced
- 2 scallions, trimmed, white and green parts finely chopped (about 4 tablespoons)
- 2 cups coarsely grated smoked or regular white cheddar cheese (about 8 ounces)
- 1/2 cup sour cream
- Spanish smoked paprika (pimentón) or sweet paprika, for sprinkling

Directions:

1. Supply your smoker with wood pellets and follow the start-up procedure. Preheat the grill, with the lid closed, to 400° F.Add enough wood for 1 hour of smoking as specified by the manufacturer.

2. Scrub the potatoes on all sides with a vegetable brush. Rinse well under cold running water and blot dry with paper towels. Prick each potato several times with a fork (this keeps the spud from exploding and facilitates the smoke absorption). Brush or rub the potato on all sides with the bacon fat and season generously with salt and pepper.

3. Place the potatoes on the smoker rack. Smoke until the skins are crisp and the potatoes are tender in the center (they'll be easy to pierce with a slender metal skewer), about 1 hour.

4. Meanwhile, place the bacon in a cold skillet and fry over medium heat until browned and crisp, 3 to 4 minutes. Drain off the bacon fat (save the fat for future potatoes).

5. Transfer the potatoes to a cutting board and let cool slightly. Cut each potato in half lengthwise. Using a spoon, scrape out most of the potato flesh, leaving a 1/4-inch-thick shell. (It's easier to scoop the potatoes when warm.) Cut the potato flesh into 1/2-inch dice and place in a bowl.

6. Add the bacon, 4 tablespoons of the butter, the scallions, and cheese to the potato flesh and gently stir to mix. Stir in the sour cream and salt and pepper to taste; the mixture should be highly seasoned. Stir as little and as gently as possible so as to leave some texture to the potatoes.

7. Spoon the potato mixture back into the potato shells, mounding it in the center. Top each potato half with a thin slice of the remaining butter and sprinkle with paprika. The potatoes can be prepared up to 24 hours ahead to this stage, covered, and refrigerated.

8. Just before serving, preheat your smoker to 400 °F. Add enough wood for 30 minutes of smoking. Place the potatoes in a shallow aluminum foil pan and re-smoke them until browned and bubbling, 15 to 20 minutes.

Whole Roasted Cauliflower With Garlic Parmesan Butter

Servings: 4
Cooking Time: 45 Minutes

Ingredients:
- 1 Whole head cauliflower
- 1/4 Cup olive oil
- salt and pepper
- 1/2 Cup butter, melted
- 1/4 Cup shredded Parmesan cheese
- 2 Clove garlic, minced
- 1/2 Tablespoon chopped parsley

Directions:
1. Supply your smoker with wood pellets and follow the start-up procedure. Preheat the grill, with the lid closed, to 450° F.
2. Brush the cauliflower with olive oil and season liberally with salt and pepper.
3. Put cauliflower in a cast iron skillet, place directly on the grill grate and cook for 45 minutes until golden brown and the center is tender.
4. While the cauliflower is cooking, combine the melted butter, parmesan, garlic and parsley in a small bowl.

5. During the last 20 minutes of cooking, baste the cauliflower with the melted butter mixture.
6. Remove the cauliflower from the grill and top with extra parmesan and parsley if desired. Enjoy!

Roasted Jalapeno Cheddar Deviled Eggs

Servings: 6
Cooking Time: 30 Minutes

Ingredients:
- 7 Eggs, hard boiled
- 3 Tablespoon mayonnaise
- 1 Teaspoon brown mustard
- 1 Teaspoon apple cider vinegar
- 1 Dash hot sauce
- 1 jalapeño pepper, seeded and minced
- salt and pepper
- 1/2 Cup shredded cheddar cheese
- paprika

Directions:
1. Supply your smoker with wood pellets and follow the start-up procedure. Preheat the grill, with the lid closed, to 180° F.
2. Place your eggs directly on the grill grate and smoke for 30 minutes.
3. Remove from the grill and allow the eggs to cool. Smoking the eggs will give them a slightly yellowed color, but an intense smoky flavor. If a classic white egg is your preference, then skip this step.
4. Slice the eggs lengthwise and scoop the egg yolks directly into a gallon zip top bag.
5. Add the mayo, mustard, vinegar, hot sauce, roasted jalapeños and salt and pepper to the bag.
6. Zip the bag closed and, using your hands, knead all of the ingredients together in the bag until completely smooth.
7. Squeeze the yolk mixture into one corner of the bag and then cut the corner off. Pipe the yolk mixture into the whites.
8. Sprinkle with the finely shredded cheddar or paprika and chill until you are ready to serve. Enjoy!

Roasted Beet & Bacon Salad

Servings: 4
Cooking Time: 45 Minutes

Ingredients:
- 2 Medium raw beets, peeled and thinly sliced
- 8 Slices bacon
- 1/4 Cup raw pecans or walnuts
- 2 Medium ripe pears, sliced
- 2 Large avocados, diced

- 1 Head red leaf lettuce or baby spinach, torn into bite-size pieces
- 1/4 Cup champagne vinaigrette

Directions:

1. Supply your smoker with wood pellets and follow the start-up procedure. Preheat the grill, with the lid closed, to 400° F.
2. Place beets on a foil-lined baking sheet and top with bacon. Place baking sheet directly on the grill grate (while preheating) and cook for 25 minutes. Grill: 400 ˚F
3. Toss to coat beets in rendered bacon fat.
4. Spread everything out in a single layer and continue to cook for another 15 minutes, or until beets are tender and bacon is crispy. Grill: 400 ˚F
5. Add pecans or walnuts and roast for 5 more minutes. Spoon out nuts and place on paper towels to drain and cool.
6. Once bacon is cool to the touch, roughly chop into medium pieces.
7. Place bacon, beets, nuts, pears, avocado and lettuce in a large salad bowl. Drizzle with champagne vinaigrette, toss to coat, and serve. Enjoy!

Grilled Fingerling Potato Salad

Servings: 6
Cooking Time: 15 Minutes

Ingredients:

- 10 Whole scallions
- 2/3 Cup extra-virgin olive oil, divided
- 1 1/2 Pound fingerling potatoes, cut in half lengthwise
- pepper
- 2 Teaspoon kosher salt, divided, plus more as needed
- 2 Tablespoon rice vinegar
- 2 Teaspoon lemon juice
- 1 Small jalapeño, sliced

Directions:

1. Supply your smoker with wood pellets and follow the start-up procedure. Preheat the grill, with the lid closed, to 450° F.
2. Brush the scallions with oil and place on the grill.
3. Cook until lightly charred, about 2 to 3 minutes. Remove and let cool. Grill: 450 ˚F
4. Once the scallions have cooled, slice and set aside.
5. Brush the fingerling potatoes with oil (reserving 1/3 cup for later use), then salt and pepper. Place cut-side down on the grill until cooked through, about 4 to 5 minutes. Grill: 450 ˚F
6. In a bowl, whisk the remaining 1/3 cup olive oil, 1 teaspoon salt, rice vinegar and lemon juice. Next mix in the scallions, potatoes and sliced jalapeño.
7. Season with salt and pepper, and serve. Enjoy!

Butter Braised Green Beans

Servings: 6
Cooking Time: 60 Minutes

Ingredients:

- 24 Ounce thin fresh green beans, trimmed or whole frozen green beans, thawed
- 8 Tablespoon butter, melted
- Veggie Rub or coarse salt
- freshly ground black pepper

Directions:

1. Supply your smoker with wood pellets and follow the start-up procedure. Preheat the grill, with the lid closed, to 325° F.
2. Put the green beans in a pile on a rimmed baking sheet and pour the melted butter over them. Using tongs, spread the beans out in the pan and season with Traeger Veggie Rub and black pepper.
3. Roast the beans for about 1 hour, stirring and lifting with tongs every 20 minutes or so. The beans should be very tender, shriveled, and lightly browned in places. Transfer to a serving bowl and serve while hot. Enjoy!

Roasted Pickled Beets

Servings: 8
Cooking Time: 60 Minutes

Ingredients:

- 6 Medium Red Beets, scrubbed and trimmed
- 1 Cup red wine vinegar
- 1/2 Cup sugar
- 10 Whole peppercorns
- 1 Cup water
- 1 1/2 Teaspoon coarse salt
- 8 whole cloves
- 2 Pieces Star Anise, Broken
- 1 cinnamon stick, broken in half

Directions:

1. Make a foil pouch large enough to enclose the beets. Poke a few holes in the top to allow steam to escape.
2. Supply your smoker with wood pellets and follow the start-up procedure. Preheat the grill, with the lid closed, to 350° F.
3. Roast the beets until they are tender, 50 to 60 minutes. Carefully remove the foil and allow the beets to cool until they can be comfortably handled. Grill: 350 ˚F
4. Slip the skins off with your fingers. (You may wish to wear latex gloves to avoid staining your hands.) Cut the beets into quarters or slices. (Candy cane beets are especially pretty when sliced.)
5. In the meantime, make the brine: Bring the vinegar, sugar, salt, and water to a boil in a small saucepan over high heat.

6.   Put the cloves, peppercorns, star anise, and cinnamon in a clean lidded jar, such as a canning jar

7.   Add the beets to the jar. Pour the hot brine over the beets. Put the lid on the jar. Cool the beets to room temperature, then refrigerate for 3 to 5 days before serving. Enjoy!

Traeger Grilled Whole Corn

Servings: 4
Cooking Time: 25 Minutes

Ingredients:

*   3 green onions
*   6 Tablespoon butter, softened
*   1 Teaspoon chile powder
*   1 Teaspoon toasted sesame seeds
*   4 ears corn, in husk

Directions:

1.   Supply your smoker with wood pellets and follow the start-up procedure. Preheat the grill, with the lid closed, to 325° F.
2.   Place green onions directly on the grill grate and cook 15 minutes until lightly charred. Remove from grill and set aside.
3.   Sesame-Chile Butter: Take butter out of fridge and let soften. Chop up charred green onions and add to butter along with chile powder and sesame seeds. Mash all ingredients together.
4.   Grill corn, rotating occasionally, until husks are blackened (some will flake and fall off) and kernels are tender with some browned and charred spots, about 25 to 35 minutes. Grill: 325 °F
5.   Let corn cool slightly, then shuck. Serve with the Sesame-Chile Butter. Enjoy

Baked Sweet Potato Casserole With Marshmallow Fluff

Servings: 6
Cooking Time: 60 Minutes

Ingredients:

*   3 Pound sweet potatoes
*   1/2 Cup milk
*   1 Cup brown sugar
*   3 eggs
*   4 Tablespoon butter
*   1/2 Teaspoon salt
*   3 egg white
*   1 Pinch salt
*   1 Pinch ground cinnamon

Directions:

1.   Supply your smoker with wood pellets and follow the start-up procedure. Preheat the grill, with the lid closed, to 375° F.

2.   Rinse, dry and pierce the sweet potatoes and place in grill whole. Cook for 45 minutes or until fork tender. Remove from grill and peel. Grill: 375 °F
3.   Once peeled, mash the sweet potatoes in a large bowl with the milk, brown sugar, eggs, butter and salt. Place mashed potatoes in a baking dish and cook for 35 minutes. Grill: 375 °F
4.   While the potatoes bake, make the fluff. Make a double boiler by bringing a small pot of water to a simmer, then placing the bowl of your stand mixer or another large stainless steel bowl atop the water.
5.   Add the 3 egg whites, 2/3 cup brown sugar, a pinch of salt and a pinch of cinnamon to the bowl and whisk continuously until the sugar dissolves and the liquid is warm to the touch.
6.   Transfer the bowl from the stovetop to your stand mixer and use the whisk attachment to whip the whites on medium-high speed until it turns glossy with stiff peaks, about 5-8 minutes.
7.   Once the casserole has finished baking, use a rubber spatula to cover the sweet potato mixture with the fluff. Use the back of the spatula to create dramatic peaks.
8.   Return to the grill for 5-7 minutes, or until the fluff starts to turn golden and the peaks are just shy of burnt. Remove from grill and enjoy!

Tater Tot Bake

Servings: 4
Cooking Time: 15 Minutes

Ingredients:

*   1 Whole frozen tater tots
*   salt and pepper
*   1 Cup sour cream
*   1 Cup shredded cheddar cheese, divided
*   1/2 Cup bacon, chopped
*   1/4 Cup green onion, diced

Directions:

1.   Supply your smoker with wood pellets and follow the start-up procedure. Preheat the grill, with the lid closed, to 375° F.
2.   Line a baking sheet with aluminum foil for easy clean up and spread frozen tater tots onto sheet.
3.   Sprinkle with Veggie Shake or salt and pepper to taste.
4.   Place the baking sheet on the preheated grill grate and cook the tater tots for 10 minutes.
5.   Drizzle sour cream over cooked tater tots.
6.   Sprinkle the cheese, bacon bits and green onions on top of the tater tots.
7.   Turn heat up to High heat and cook for 5 more minutes until the cheese melts and serve immediately. Enjoy!

Smoked & Loaded Baked Potato

Servings: 4
Cooking Time: 60 Minutes

Ingredients:

- 6 Yukon Gold or russet potatoes
- 8 Slices bacon
- 1/2 Cup butter, melted
- 1 Cup sour cream
- 1 1/2 Cup shredded cheddar cheese, divided
- salt and pepper
- 1 Bunch green onions, thinly sliced

Directions:

1. Supply your smoker with wood pellets and follow the start-up procedure. Preheat the grill, with the lid closed, to 375° F.
2. Poke potatoes with a fork, then place straight onto the grill. Cook for 1 hour. Grill: 375 °F
3. At the same time, cook bacon on a baking sheet on the grill for about 20 minutes; remove, cool and crumble. Grill: 375 °F
4. Once potatoes are done, remove and allow to cool for 15 minutes.
5. Cut each potato lengthwise, creating long halves. Use a small spoon to scoop out about 70% of the potato to make a boat, keeping a thick layer of potato near skin.
6. Place excess potato in a bowl and reserve. Lightly mash extra potato with a fork; add butter, sour cream, 1/2 cup cheese and season with salt and pepper.
7. Take the potato skins and fill with potato mixture, then sprinkle with extra cheese and bacon.
8. Place back on grill for about 10 minutes or until warm and cheese has melted. Garnish with green onions and extra sour cream. Enjoy! Grill: 375 °F

Roasted Tomatoes

Servings: 2
Cooking Time: 180 Minutes

Ingredients:

- 3 Large ripe tomatoes
- 1/2 Tablespoon kosher salt
- 1 Teaspoon coarse ground black pepper
- 1/4 Teaspoon sugar
- 1/4 Teaspoon thyme or basil
- olive oil

Directions:

1. Line a rimmed baking sheet with parchment paper.
2. Supply your smoker with wood pellets and follow the start-up procedure. Preheat the grill, with the lid closed, to 225° F.
3. Remove the stem end from each tomato and cut the tomatoes into 1/2 inch thick slices.

4. Combine the salt, pepper, sugar and thyme or basil in a small bowl and mix.
5. Pour olive oil into the well of a dinner plate.
6. Dip one side of each tomato slice in the olive oil and arrange on the baking sheet. Dust the tomato slices with the seasoning mixture.
7. Arrange the pan directly on the grill grate and roast the tomatoes until the juices stop running and the edges have contracted, about 3 hours. Remove from grill and enjoy!

Braised Creamed Green Beans

Servings: 4
Cooking Time: 25 Minutes

Ingredients:

- 6 Tablespoon butter
- 2 Clove garlic, pressed or minced
- 1 shallot, thinly sliced
- 1 Cup heavy cream
- 1 Pinch ground nutmeg
- salt
- 3 Pound mixed greens such as kale, chard or collards; washed, stems removed and torn into bite sized pieces

Directions:

1. Supply your smoker with wood pellets and follow the start-up procedure. Preheat the grill, with the lid closed, to 325° F.
2. In a saucepan, heat 2 tablespoons of the butter over high heat until it foams. Add the garlic and shallot and cook over medium-low heat, stirring, until softened and golden, about 5 minutes.
3. Add the cream, bring to a simmer and cook until slightly thickened, about 10 minutes.
4. Add the nutmeg and salt to taste. Using a hand blender, purée until smooth.
5. In a cast iron pan, heat the remaining 4 tablespoons butter over high heat until it foams.
6. Add the greens and cook until tender but still bright green, about 5 minutes.
7. Sprinkle with salt and add the cream mixture. Cover and transfer to the grill.
8. Braise greens for 15-20 minutes until the cream is bubbling and greens are tender. Grill: 325 °F
9. Season to taste with nutmeg and salt. Serve hot. Enjoy!

Blt Pasta Salad

Servings: 6
Cooking Time: 45 Minutes

Ingredients:

- 1 pound thick-cut bacon
- 16 ounces bowtie pasta, cooked according to package directions and drained
- 2 tomatoes, chopped
- ½ cup chopped scallions
- ½ cup Italian dressing
- ½ cup ranch dressing
- 1 tablespoon chopped fresh basil
- 1 teaspoon salt
- 1 teaspoon freshly ground black pepper
- 1 teaspoon garlic powder
- 1 head lettuce, cored and torn

Directions:

1. Supply your smoker with wood pellets and follow the start-up procedure. Preheat, with the lid closed, to 225°F.
2. Arrange the bacon slices on the grill grate, close the lid, and cook for 30 to 45 minutes, flipping after 20 minutes, until crisp.
3. Remove the bacon from the grill and chop.
4. In a large bowl, combine the chopped bacon with the cooked pasta, tomatoes, scallions, Italian dressing, ranch dressing, basil, salt, pepper, and garlic powder. Refrigerate until ready to serve.
5. Toss in the lettuce just before serving to keep it from wilting.

Grilled Chili-lime Corn

Servings: 8
Cooking Time: 45 Minutes

Ingredients:

- 12 Corn, ears
- 1 Teaspoon chili powder
- 1/2 Teaspoon onion powder
- 1 Teaspoon Leinenkugel's Summer Shandy Rub
- 2 lime, juiced
- 1 Tablespoon lime zest

Directions:

1. Soak the ears of corn, still in their husk, in water for 4 to 8 hours.
2. Supply your smoker with wood pellets and follow the start-up procedure. Preheat the grill, with the lid closed, to 350° F.
3. Place corn directly on grill grates. Turn corn every 15 minutes for 45 minutes total cooking time. Grill: 350 °F
4. Combine chili powder, onion powder, Summer Shandy rub, lime juice, lime zest and butter in an oven safe dish and place in grill for 10 minutes. Remove corn and butter from the grill.

5. Pull corn husk back, but not off and remove corn silk. Using the corn husk as a handle, brush the corn with the melted chili-lime butter. Enjoy!

Smoked Beet-pickled Eggs

Servings: 4
Cooking Time: 30 Minutes

Ingredients:

- 6 Eggs, hard boiled
- 1 Red Beets, scrubbed and trimmed
- 1 Cup apple cider vinegar
- 1 Cup Beet, juice
- 1/4 Onion, Sliced
- 1/3 Cup granulated sugar
- 3 Cardamom
- 1 star anise

Directions:

1. Supply your smoker with wood pellets and follow the start-up procedure. Preheat the grill, with the lid closed, to 275° F.
2. Place the peeled hard boiled eggs directly on the grill and smoke for 30 minutes. Grill: 275 °F
3. Put the smoked eggs in a quart size glass jar with the cooked/chopped beets in the bottom.
4. In a medium sauce pan, add the vinegar, beet juice, onion, sugar, cardamom and anise.
5. Bring to a boil and cook, uncovered, until sugar has dissolved and the onions are translucent (about 5 minutes).
6. Remove from the heat and let cool for a few minutes.
7. Pour the vinegar and onions mixture over the eggs and beets in the jar, covering the eggs completely.
8. Securely close with the jar lid. Refrigerate up to a month. Enjoy!

Smoked Mashed Potatoes

Servings: 6
Cooking Time: 45 Minutes

Ingredients:

- 2 Pound red bliss potatoes, washed and diced medium
- chicken stock or water
- 1/2 Stick salted butter
- 1 Cup whole milk
- 1/2 Cup sour cream
- 1/2 Cup shredded or grated Parmesan cheese
- kosher salt
- freshly ground black pepper
- 1/2 Cup fresh sliced green onions

Directions:

1. Place the diced red potatoes into a small saucepan or stockpot and cover with chicken stock or water.

2. Bring to a boil and cook on a simmer until fork tender, then cook 4 to 5 minutes past that until soft.

3. Supply your smoker with wood pellets and follow the start-up procedure. Preheat the grill, with the lid closed, to 400° F.

4. In a separate ovenproof pan, such as a cast iron skillet, add butter and milk and place in the Traeger during start up, until melted (approximately 7 to 10 minutes). Grill: 400 °F

5. Carefully remove the butter/milk mixture from the Traeger using heatproof gloves.

6. Drain the potatoes and place into a large bowl. Add the melted butter/milk mixture and slowly mash.

7. Add sour cream, cheese and green onions, then season to taste with salt and pepper.

8. Place into the cast iron skillet, then place the skillet back into the Traeger and cook until the potatoes have a slight crust and are bubbling, about 15 minutes. Grill: 400 °F

9. Carefully remove the mashed potatoes from the Traeger using heatproof gloves. Allow to cool for 5 minutes. Scoop and enjoy!

Carolina Baked Beans

Servings: 12-15
Cooking Time: 180 Minutes

Ingredients:
- 3 (28-ounce) cans baked beans (I like Bush's brand)
- 1 large onion, finely chopped
- 1 cup The Ultimate BBQ Sauce
- ½ cup light brown sugar
- ¼ cup Worcestershire sauce
- 3 tablespoons yellow mustard
- Nonstick cooking spray or butter, for greasing
- 1 large bell pepper, cut into thin rings
- ½ pound thick-cut bacon, partially cooked and cut into quarters

Directions:
1. Supply your smoker with wood pellets and follow the start-up procedure. Preheat, with the lid closed, to 300°F.

2. In a large mixing bowl, stir together the beans, onion, barbecue sauce, brown sugar, Worcestershire sauce, and mustard until well combined

3. Coat a 9-by-13-inch aluminum pan with cooking spray or butter.

4. Pour the beans into the pan and top with the bell pepper rings and bacon pieces, pressing them down slightly into the sauce.

5. Place a layer of heavy-duty foil on the grill grate to catch drips, and place the pan on top of the foil. Close the lid and cook

for 2 hours 30 minutes to 3 hours, or until the beans are hot, thick, and bubbly.

6. Let the beans rest for 5 minutes before serving.

Baked Garlic Duchess Potatoes

Servings: 8
Cooking Time: 60 Minutes

Ingredients:
- 12 Medium Potatoes, Yukon gold
- salt
- 5 Large Egg Yolk
- 2 Clove garlic, minced
- 1.24 Cup heavy cream
- 3/4 Cup sour cream
- 10 Tablespoon butter, melted
- black pepper

Directions:
1. Place potatoes in a large pot and fill with water. Season with salt. Bring to a boil over medium-high heat.

2. Reduce heat and simmer until a paring knife easily slides through potatoes, about 25 to 35 minutes. Drain and let cool slightly.

3. Supply your smoker with wood pellets and follow the start-up procedure. Preheat the grill, with the lid closed, to 450° F.

4. Whisk together egg yolks, garlic, cream, sour cream, butter, and pepper in a large bowl. Season with salt.

5. Peel potatoes and push flesh through a ricer or a food mill directly into bowl with egg mixture. Fold in the egg mixture being careful not to overmix.

6. Transfer to a 3-quart baking dish and bake until golden brown and slightly puffed, about 30–40 minutes. Enjoy! Grill: 450 °F

Roasted Fall Vegetables

Servings: 6
Cooking Time: 30 Minutes

Ingredients:
- 1/2 Pound Potatoes, new
- 2 Tablespoon olive oil
- salt and pepper
- 1/2 Pound Butternut Squash, diced
- 1/2 Pound fresh Brussels sprouts
- 1 Pint mushrooms, sliced

Directions:
1. Supply your smoker with wood pellets and follow the start-up procedure. Preheat the grill, with the lid closed, to 200° F.

2. Toss potatoes and squash with olive oil, salt and pepper and spread out on a sheet tray.

3. Place directly on the grill grate and cook for 15 minutes. Add brussels sprouts and mushrooms and toss to coat.
4. Cook another 15-20 minutes until veggies are lightly browned and cooked through.
5. Adjust seasoning as needed. Enjoy!

Skillet Potato Cake

Servings: 4
Cooking Time: 40 Minutes

Ingredients:
- 8 Tablespoon butter, melted
- 2 Pound russet potatoes, peeled and thinly sliced
- 3 Tablespoon kosher salt
- 2 Tablespoon freshly ground black pepper
- thyme

Directions:
1. Supply your smoker with wood pellets and follow the start-up procedure. Preheat the grill, with the lid closed, to 375° F.
2. Brush the bottom of a cast iron skillet with part of the melted butter. Place potato slices vertically around the outer edges then fill in the middle in the same fashion.
3. Pour additional melted butter over the top of the layers and sprinkle with salt and pepper.
4. Place skillet in grill and cook for 35 to 40 minutes or until potatoes are fork tender and golden brown.
5. Garnish with a sprinkle of fresh thyme over the top of the potatoes. Enjoy!

Baked Artichoke Parmesan Mushrooms

Servings: 8
Cooking Time: 30 Minutes

Ingredients:
- 8 Cremini Mushroom Caps
- 6 1/2 Ounce artichoke hearts
- 1/3 Cup Parmesan cheese, grated
- 1/4 Cup mayonnaise
- 1/2 Teaspoon garlic salt
- your favorite hot sauce
- paprika

Directions:
1. Clean the mushrooms with a damp paper towel. Remove the stems and discard or save for another use.
2. Using a small spoon, scoop out the inside (gills, etc.). Combine the artichoke hearts, parmesan, mayonnaise, garlic salt, and hot sauce and mix well.
3. Mound the filling in the mushroom caps. Dust the tops with paprika.
4. Arrange the mushrooms in an oven-safe baking dish.

5. Supply your smoker with wood pellets and follow the start-up procedure. Preheat the grill, with the lid closed, to 350° F.
6. Bake the mushrooms (uncovered) until the filling is bubbling and just beginning to brown, about 25 to 30 minutes. Serve immediately. Grill: 350 °F
7. For a simple variation, stuff the mushrooms with your favorite bulk sausage and bake on your Traeger as directed above. Enjoy!

Grilled Broccoli Rabe

Servings: 4
Cooking Time: 10 Minutes

Ingredients:
- 4 Tablespoon extra-virgin olive oil
- 4 Bunch broccoli rabe or broccolini
- kosher salt
- 1 lemon, halved

Directions:
1. Supply your smoker with wood pellets and follow the start-up procedure. Preheat the grill, with the lid closed, to 450° F.
2. On a platter or in a mixing bowl, drizzle the olive oil over the broccoli rabe. Use your hands to mix thoroughly, coating the vegetables evenly with the oil. Season with sea salt.
3. Place the broccoli rabe in one layer directly on the lowest grill grate. Close the lid and cook for 5 to 10 minutes. You want there to be some color and slight char on the first side. Flip and cook for a few more minutes. Grill: 450 °F
4. Transfer the broccoli rabe to a serving platter and squeeze the juice of half a lemon evenly over the top.
5. Serve with more lemon wedges on the side. Enjoy!

Baked Sweet And Savory Yams By Bennie Kendrick

Servings: 6
Cooking Time: 60 Minutes

Ingredients:
- 3 Medium Yams
- 3 Tablespoon extra-virgin olive oil
- honey
- Goat Cheese
- 1/2 Cup brown sugar
- 1/2 Cup Pecans, pieces

Directions:
1. Supply your smoker with wood pellets and follow the start-up procedure. Preheat the grill, with the lid closed, to 350° F.
2. While Traeger comes to temperature, wash yams and poke a few holes all over. Wrap yams in foil.

3. Bake for 45-60 minutes or until knife tender. You don't want to overcook and get the yams too soft because you want to be able to cut each yam into rounds.

4. Once yams have cooled to the touch, cut each into 1/4" rounds. Lightly coat each round with oil olive and place on sheet tray.

5. Sprinkle each top with brown sugar. Using a teaspoon, place desired amount of goat cheese on each round. Next top with chopped pecans. Finally, drizzle Bee Local honey over each round.

6. Based on how sweet you like your yams, you can add more brown sugar and honey.

7. After complete, place your sheet tray back in the grill and cook, lid closed, for another 20 minutes. Enjoy!

Spicy Asian Brussels Sprouts

Servings: 4
Cooking Time: 10 Minutes

Ingredients:
- 2 Cup fresh Brussels sprouts
- 2 Tablespoon vegetable oil
- 1 Tablespoon Asian BBQ Rub
- 1/4 Cup Thai sweet chile sauce

Directions:
1. Supply your smoker with wood pellets and follow the start-up procedure. Preheat the grill, with the lid closed, to 350° F.
2. Spread the halved brussel sprouts in a single layer on a lined cookie sheet. Drizzle with the oil and toss to coat.
3. Sprinkle the brussel sprouts evenly with an Asian BBQ rub and put the cookie sheet on the grill. Close the lid and cook for 7-8 minutes. Grill: 350 °F
4. Toss the brussels sprouts in the Thai Chili Sauce and return to the grill for an additional 3-4 minutes, or until the sprouts are crisp-tender. Grill: 350 °F
5. Serve immediately. Enjoy!

Grilled Beer Cabbage

Servings: 4
Cooking Time: 50 Minutes

Ingredients:
- 2 Cabbage, head
- 1 Tablespoon extra-virgin olive oil
- 1 Teaspoon salt
- 1 Teaspoon freshly ground black pepper
- 14 Fluid Ounce Guinness Extra Stout

Directions:
1. Clean and core cabbages. Drizzle with olive oil and salt and pepper. Rub into the cabbage.

2. Supply your smoker with wood pellets and follow the start-up procedure. Preheat the grill, with the lid closed, to 180° F.
3. Place cabbages directly on grill grate; smoke for 15 to 20 minutes. Remove from grill and thickly slice cabbage. Grill: 180 °F
4. Place sliced cabbage in cast-iron skillet. Pour beer over cabbage and return to grill.
5. Increase temperature to 375°F and cook for 30 minutes, or until cabbage has reached desired softness. Grill: 375 °F
6. Serve with corned beef. Enjoy!

Baked Stuffed Avocados

Servings: 6
Cooking Time: 15 Minutes

Ingredients:
- 4 avocados, halved and pit removed
- 8 eggs
- 2 Cup shredded cheddar cheese
- 1/4 Cup cherry tomatoes, halved
- 4 Slices Bacon, cooked & chopped
- salt and pepper
- 1 scallion, thinly sliced

Directions:
1. Supply your smoker with wood pellets and follow the start-up procedure. Preheat the grill, with the lid closed, to 450° F.
2. After removing the pit from the avocado, scoop out a little of the flesh to make enough room to fit 1 egg per half.
3. Fill the bottom of a cast iron pan with kosher salt and nestle the avocado halves into the salt, cut side up. The salt helps to keep them in place while cooking, like ice with oysters.
4. Crack one egg into each half, top with shredded cheddar cheese, cherry tomatoes and bacon. Season with salt and pepper to taste.
5. Place the cast iron pan directly on the grill grate and bake the avocados for 12 to 15 minutes until the cheese is melted and the egg is just set. Grill: 450 °F
6. Remove from the grill and let rest 5 to 10 minutes. Top with sliced scallions and enjoy!

Roasted New Potatoes With Compound Butter

Servings: 4
Cooking Time: 45 Minutes

Ingredients:
- 2 Pound Small Red, White or Purple Potatoes (or Combination of All Three)
- 3 Tablespoon olive oil
- salt and pepper
- 2 Stick Butter, unsalted

- 1 Tablespoon shallot, minced
- 3 Tablespoon Finely Chopped Herbs, Such As Tarragon, Parsley, Basil or Combination
- 2 Teaspoon kosher salt

Directions:

1. Supply your smoker with wood pellets and follow the start-up procedure. Preheat the grill, with the lid closed, to 400° F. Cut the potatoes in half and place in a large mixing bowl. Cover with the olive oil, a teaspoon of salt and generous grinding of pepper.

2. Place on a large baking sheet so there is space between the potatoes. Place on the grill and roast for 45 minutes to 1 hour, until crispy skinned. Toss once during cooking. Grill: 400 °F

3. To make the butter: Place it in a medium sized shallow mixing bowl. Use a wooden spoon or strong spatula to break it up and soften it even more. Sprinkle the shallot, herbs, and salt over the butter, then use the spoon to combine the ingredients. Taste, adding more salt or herbs if necessary. Reserve a few tablespoons of the butter to serve on the potatoes.

4. To freeze the butter for future use, place a foot long piece of plastic wrap on the counter. Spread the butter out into a 6" log across the long direction of the plastic wrap towards the bottom. Begin to roll the plastic wrap away from you to roll it into a log, twisting the sides of the plastic wrap like a candy wrapper to secure.

5. Using your hands, shape the log into an even cylinder. Once it's wrapped tightly, place in the freezer. Then when more is needed, simply slice off coins of it to serve over grilled steak, chicken, veggies, or roasted potatoes. The butter holds well in the freezer for up to one month. Enjoy! *Cook times will vary depending on set and ambient temperatures.

Green Bean Casserole

Servings: 6
Cooking Time: 25 Minutes

Ingredients:

- 1/2 Stick butter
- 1 Small onion
- 1/2 Cup sliced button mushrooms
- 4 Can green beans, drained
- 2 Can cream of mushroom soup
- 1 Teaspoon Lawry's Seasoned Salt
- pepper
- 1 Can French's Original Crispy Fried Onions
- 1 Cup grated sharp cheddar cheese

Directions:

1. Supply your smoker with wood pellets and follow the start-up procedure. Preheat the grill, with the lid closed, to 375° F.

2. Melt butter in a cast iron skillet and add onions and mushrooms, stirring occasionally until softened.

3. Add drained green beans and cream of mushroom soup and stir gently to combine.

4. Season with seasoned salt and pepper and sprinkle the top with grated cheddar cheese and fried onions.

5. Bake for 25 minutes. Serve warm, enjoy! Grill: 375 °F

Sicilian Stuffed Mushrooms

Servings: 6
Cooking Time: 25 Minutes

Ingredients:

- 12 Medium Fresh Mushrooms, about 1-1/2 inches in diameter
- 4 Ounce cream cheese, room temperature
- 1/4 Cup Parmesan cheese, grated
- 1/4 Cup shredded mozzarella cheese
- 8 Whole Pimento Stuffed Green Olives, chopped
- 3 Tablespoon Pepperoni, finely diced
- 1 1/2 Tablespoon Sun Dried Tomatoes, drained & minced
- 1/4 Teaspoon freshly ground black pepper

Directions:

1. Dampen a paper towel and wipe the outside of the mushrooms clean. Remove the stem. Using a small spoon, scoop out the inside of the mushroom leaving a shell.

2. Filling: In a small mixing bowl, beat together the cream cheese, Parmesan, and mozzarella. Stir in olives, pepperoni, tomatoes, basil, and pepper.

3. Mound the filling in the mushroom caps. Set each filled cap into the well of a muffin tin.

4. Supply your smoker with wood pellets and follow the start-up procedure. Preheat the grill, with the lid closed, to 350° F.

5. Arrange the muffin tin on the grill grate and bake the mushrooms for 25 to 30 minutes, or until the mushrooms are tender and the filling is beginning to brown.

6. Transfer to a serving plate or platter. Enjoy!

Roasted Tomatoes With Hot Pepper Sauce

Servings: 4
Cooking Time: 60 Minutes

Ingredients:

- 2 Pound fresh Roma tomatoes
- 3 Tablespoon parsley, chopped
- 2 Tablespoon garlic, chopped
- salt and pepper
- 1/2 Cup extra-virgin olive oil
- 1 Pound Spaghetti
- Hot peppers

Directions:

1.   Supply your smoker with wood pellets and follow the start-up procedure. Preheat the grill, with the lid closed, to 400° F.
2.   Wash tomatoes and cut them in half, lengthwise. Place them in a baking dish cut side up.
3.   Sprinkle with chopped parsley, garlic, add salt and black pepper and pour 1/4 cup (100 mL)of olive oil over them.
4.   Place on pre-heated grill and bake for 1 1/2 hours. Tomatoes will shrink and the skins will be partly blackened. Grill: 400 °F
5.   Remove tomatoes from baking dish and place in a food processor leaving the cooked oil, and puree them.
6.   Drop pasta into boiling salted water and cook until tender. Drain and toss immediately with the pureed tomatoes.
7.   Add the remaining 1/4 cup (60mL) of raw olive oil and crumbled hot red pepper to taste. Toss and serve. Enjoy!

Christmas Brussel Sprouts

Servings: 6
Cooking Time: 50 Minutes

Ingredients:

- 1/2 Pound thick-cut bacon
- 1 Medium onion, diced
- 2 Pound fresh Brussels sprouts
- 2 Tablespoon olive oil
- salt and pepper

Directions:

1.   Supply your smoker with wood pellets and follow the start-up procedure. Preheat the grill, with the lid closed, to 350° F.
2.   Place bacon directly on grill grate and cook for 15-20 minutes, or until lightly browned. Remove from grill and set aside on paper towel lined plate.
3.   Slice onion in half and then slice into 1⁄4 inch moons and add to large mixing bowl. Slice brussels sprouts in half lengthwise and add to bowl.
4.   Cut reserved bacon into 1⁄2 inch pieces and add to bowl. Drizzle with olive oil and sprinkle with salt and pepper. Toss to coat and pour into baking pan.
5.   Turn the temperature on grill to 375 and place baking pan on grill. Roast for 30 minutes mixing halfway through cooking. Grill: 375 °F

Smoked Bbq Onion Brussels Sprout

Servings: 4
Cooking Time: 110 Minutes

Ingredients:

- 4 strip bacon
- 1 onion minced
- 2 cloves garlic minced
- 1 lb brussels sprouts stems trimmed and cut in half

- 1 tbsp BBQ Spice Blend
- 1/2 cup Apple Habanero Bar-B-Que Sauce (or other BBQ sauce)

Directions:

1.   Supply your smoker with wood pellets and follow the start-up procedure. Preheat the grill, with the lid closed, to High heat. Place a cast iron skillet over the highest heat spot and cook the bacon until crisp.
2.   Remove the bacon from pan and drain, reserving the bacon fat in the pan.
3.   Reduce the heat on your smoker to 250°F.
4.   Add the onions, garlic, and brussels to the pan and toss to coat in the bacon drippings. Sprinkle the BBQ spice blend over top.
5.   Cover the lid and allow to smoke for 1 to 1 1/2 hours, until the sprouts are fork tender.
6.   For the last 20 minutes of smoking, toss the brussels sprouts in half of the barbecue sauce.
7.   Remove the sprouts from the smoker.
8.   Chop the bacon and add it and the remaining barbecue sauce to the pan of sprouts, tossing to coat.
9.   Serve hot.

Grilled Cabbage Steaks With Warm Bacon Vinaigrette

Servings: 4
Cooking Time: 10 Minutes

Ingredients:

- 3 Strips thick-cut lean bacon, cut into 1/4 inch strips
- 1 Large shallot, minced
- 2 Tablespoon sherry vinegar
- 1 Tablespoon whole grain mustard
- 1 Teaspoon chopped thyme
- 2 Tablespoon olive oil, plus more as needed
- 1 Head green cabbage, cut into 3/4 inch thick slices (about 6 steaks)
- salt and pepper

Directions:

1.   Supply your smoker with wood pellets and follow the start-up procedure. Preheat the grill, with the lid closed, to 450° F.
2.   For the Vinaigrette: In a large skillet, cook the bacon in 2 tablespoons olive oil over medium-high heat until browned and crisp. Remove bacon from heat and stir in the shallot, vinegar, mustard and thyme then set aside.
3.   Brush cabbage steaks with olive oil and season with salt and pepper. Place cabbage steaks directly on grill grate and grill for 5 minutes per side. Grill: 450 °F
4.   Remove cabbage steaks from grill and drizzle with bacon vinaigrette. Enjoy!

Baked Kale Chips

Servings: 4
Cooking Time: 20 Minutes

Ingredients:
- 2 Bunch kale, leaves washed and stems removed
- 1 As Needed extra-virgin olive oil
- 1 To Taste sea salt

Directions:
1. Dry the kale leaves well and lay them out on a sheet tray. Drizzle lightly with olive oil and sprinkle with sea salt.
2. Supply your smoker with wood pellets and follow the start-up procedure. Preheat the grill, with the lid closed, to 250° F.
3. Place the sheet tray directly on the grill grate and cook until kale is lightly browned and crispy, about 20 minutes. Enjoy! Grill: 250 °F

Cast Iron Potatoes

Servings: 4
Cooking Time: 60 Minutes

Ingredients:
- 4 Tablespoon butter, cut into cubes
- 2 1/2 Pound potatoes, peeled and cut into 1/8 inch slices
- 1/2 Large sweet onion, thinly sliced
- salt
- black pepper
- 1 1/2 Cup grated mild cheddar or jack cheese
- 2 Cup milk
- paprika

Directions:
1. Butter the inside of a cast iron skillet and layer half the potato slices on the bottom. Top with half the onions. Season with salt and pepper.
2. Sprinkle 1 cup of the cheese over the potatoes and onions and dot with half the butter. Layer the remaining potatoes and onions on top. Dot with remaining butter.
3. Pour the milk into the skillet. Cover the skillet tightly with aluminum foil.
4. Supply your smoker with wood pellets and follow the start-up procedure. Preheat the grill, with the lid closed, to 350° F.
5. Bake for 1 hour, or until the potatoes are very tender. Grill: 350 °F
6. Remove the foil and top with the remaining 1/2 cup of cheese. Bake for 30 minutes more (uncovered) until the cheese is lightly browned. Dust the top with paprika and serve immediately.

Roasted Red Pepper White Bean Dip

Servings: 4

Cooking Time: 40 Minutes

Ingredients:
- 4 Whole garlic
- 4 Tablespoon extra-virgin olive oil
- 2 Bell Pepper, Red
- 3 Tablespoon Dill Weed, fresh
- 3 Tablespoon chopped flat-leaf parsley
- 2 Can cannellini beans, mashed
- 4 Teaspoon lemon juice
- 1 1/2 Teaspoon salt

Directions:
1. Roasting the garlic and red peppers:
2. Supply your smoker with wood pellets and follow the start-up procedure. Preheat the grill, with the lid closed, to 400° F.
3. Peel away the outside layers of the garlic husk. Cut off the top of the garlic bulb, exposing each of the individual cloves. Drizzle olive oil over the top of the head of garlic and rub it in. Wrap the garlic in foil, completely covering it. Put the head of garlic and the two red peppers (washed and dried) on the Traeger.
4. Roast the garlic for 25-30 minutes and the peppers for about 40 minutes. Rotate the peppers a quarter-turn every 10 minutes until the exterior is blistered and blackened. Grill: 400 °F
5. Pull the peppers off the grill and put them in a bowl. Cover the bowl with plastic wrap and leave them for 15 minutes. The steam will loosen the skins so that they slip off like a drumstick covered in barbecue sauce.
6. Peel off the pepper skin. Cut off the stems and scrape out the seeds and they're ready to use.
7. As for the garlic, let it cool and then pull out the individual cloves as needed.
8. The dip:
9. In a blender put the roasted red peppers, 4 cloves of roasted garlic, dill, parsley, drained and rinsed beans, olive oil, lemon juice and salt.
10. Blend until the dip is smooth and creamy. You may need to scrape down the sides of the blender a couple of times. If it's having difficulty blending or looks too thick add more olive oil or lemon juice. (Add more lemon juice if it tastes like it needs more acid or brightness.) Enjoy!

Roasted Do-ahead Mashed Potatoes

Servings: 6
Cooking Time: 50 Minutes

Ingredients:
- 5 Pound Yukon Gold or russet potatoes
- 9 Tablespoon butter
- 8 Ounce cream cheese
- 1/2 Cup milk
- salt and pepper

Directions:

1. Peel the potatoes and cut into chunks that are roughly the same size. Cover with cold water and add a teaspoon of salt. Bring to a boil over high heat, then reduce the heat to medium and simmer the potatoes until they are tender.

2. Drain the potatoes and return them to the pot. Stir over low heat for 2 to 3 minutes to evaporate any excess moisture.

3. Mash the potatoes with a hand-held potato masher. (Alternative, rice the potatoes using a ricer.) Incorporate 8 tbsp butter and cream cheese. Add milk until the potatoes are of a good consistency. Stir in salt and pepper to taste.

4. Butter the inside of a casserole dish. Spread the potatoes out in an even layer in the casserole dish, smoothing the top with a spatula. Cool, cover, and refrigerate if not cooking right away. Before cooking, let the potatoes warm to room temperature (about an hour).

5. Supply your smoker with wood pellets and follow the start-up procedure. Preheat the grill, with the lid closed, to 350° F.

6. Bake the potatoes for 45 to 50 minutes, or until hot through. Grill: 350 °F

BEEF LAMB AND GAME RECIPES

Lamb Chopswith Lemon Vinaigrette

Servings: 4
Cooking Time: 16 Minutes

Ingredients:

- 8 lamb rib chops, about 2lb (1kg) total and each about ¾ inch (2cm) thick
- 3 tbsp extra virgin olive oil
- coarse salt
- freshly ground black pepper
- for the vinaigrette
- 4 lemons, halved
- 1 tbsp plus 1 cup extra virgin olive oil, plus more
- 4 large basil leaves, coarsely chopped
- 1 garlic clove, peeled and coarsely chopped
- 1 tsp Dijon mustard
- 1 tsp honey
- 1 tsp coarse salt
- ½ tsp freshly ground black pepper, plus more

Directions:

1. Supply your smoker with wood pellets and follow the start-up procedure. Preheat the grill, with the lid closed, to 450° F.
2. Coat the lamb chops on each side with the olive oil. Season with salt and pepper. (For the best crust, do this 45 minutes before grilling.)
3. Begin making the vinaigrette by brushing the lemon halves with 1 tablespoon of olive oil. Place the halves cut sides down on the grate and grill until they exhibit some charring, about 6 to 8 minutes. Transfer the lemons to a bowl and let cool.
4. Juice 4 lemon halves through a strainer positioned over a blender. (Reserve the remaining lemon halves for garnishing.) Add the basil leaves, garlic, mustard, honey, and salt and pepper to the blender. Add ¼ cup of olive oil and blend until the garlic is minced and everything's well combined. While the machine's running, slowly add the remaining ¾ cup of olive oil. Taste for seasoning, adding more salt. (If the dressing is too tart, add a little more honey or olive oil—the latter 1 tablespoon at a time.) Transfer the vinaigrette to a pitcher or a cruet.
5. Place the lamb chops on the still-hot grate at an angle to the bars. Grill until the chops have grill marks and the internal temperature reaches 125 to 135°F (52 to 57°C), about 3 to 4 minutes per side.
6. Transfer the chops to a platter and let rest for 3 minutes. Drizzle the lemon vinaigrette over the top. Place 1 reserved lemon half on each plate before serving.

Smoked Cheese Beef Burgers

Servings: 4
Cooking Time: 66 Minutes

Ingredients:

- 1 ½ pounds ground beef chuck 80/20
- 4 slices cheddar cheese optional
- 4 burger buns
- Assorted burger toppings
- Smoked Burger Seasoning
- 1 Tablespoon Kosher salt
- 1 Tablespoon coarse ground black pepper
- 1 Tablespoon garlic powder

Directions:

1. Supply your smoker with wood pellets and follow the start-up procedure. Preheat the grill, with the lid closed, to 225 °F.
2. Shape your ground beef into 4 patties, about 1/2 inch larger in diameter than your burger buns.
3. In a small bowl combine the burger seasoning and sprinkle on both sides of your burger patties.
4. Place the seasoned patties on the grill and smoke for up to 1 hour, or until the internal temperature of your burgers reads 135 °F.
5. Increase the heat of your grill to the high setting (at least 400 °F). Sear the burger patties for about 2-3 minutes on both sides. Add cheese after the first flip, if desired.
6. Check the temperature of your burger patties for desired doneness. The FDA recommends 165 °F for a well done burger.
7. Remove the burger patties and toast the buns over high heat. Assemble your smoked burgers on your toasted buns with any desired toppings and serve immediately.

Reuben Sandwich

Servings: 4
Cooking Time: 10 Minutes

Ingredients:

- 2 Cup mayonnaise
- 1/2 Cup ketchup
- 1/4 Cup pickle relish
- 2 Tablespoon Chicken Rub
- 4 Pound leftover corned beef, thinly sliced
- 2 1/2 Cup sauerkraut
- 10 Slices Swiss cheese
- 10 Slices marble rye bread
- 6 Tablespoon butter, room temperature

Directions:

1. See Traeger Smoked Corned Beef Brisket recipe for corned beef instructions.
2. Supply your smoker with wood pellets and follow the start-up procedure. Preheat the grill, with the lid closed, to 350° F.
3. Place a large griddle directly on the grill grate to heat up while the sandwiches are being assembled.
4. Combine the mayonnaise, ketchup, relish and Traeger Chicken Rub in a bowl and stir until well mixed.
5. Butter the outsides of the bread (the side that goes on the grill). Place a layer of sauce on the other side of the bread and top with the corned beef, sauerkraut and 2 Swiss cheese slices. Top with another slice of sauced bread.
6. Place sandwiches on the hot griddle in the Traeger and cook for 5 minutes. Using a spatula, flip the sandwiches and cook for an additional 5 minutes, or until toasted with melty cheese and warm meat. Grill: 350 °F
7. Remove sandwiches from the Traeger. Enjoy!

Braised Onion Chuck Roast Beef Sandwiches

Servings: 4
Cooking Time: 540 Minutes

Ingredients:
- 3 cups beef stock, divided
- 2 lbs chuck roast
- 4 hoagie rolls, sliced lengthwise
- to taste, lone star brisket rub
- 1 yellow onion

Directions:
1. Place chuck roast in a glass baking dish. Season with Lone Star Brisket Rub, then cover with plastic wrap and refrigerate overnight.
2. The next day, remove chuck roast from the refrigerator. Supply your smoker with wood pellets and follow the start-up procedure. Preheat the grill, with the lid closed, to 225° F. If using a gas or charcoal grill, set it up for low, indirect heat.
3. Place chuck roast directly on the grill grate, then close the lid and smoke for 3 hours, spraying with 1 cup of beef stock every hour.
4. Slice the onion and place in a cast iron skillet, then pour the remaining cup of stock over the onions and set roast on top of onions.
5. Increase temperature to 275° F and cook an additional 2 ½ to 3 hours, or until internal temperature reaches 165° F.
6. Cover the roast with a cast iron lid or aluminum foil, and cook for another 2 ½ to 3 hours, or until the internal temperature reaches 200° F.

7. Remove chuck roast from the grill. Allow the roast to rest for 10 minutes, then remove from the skillet and shred.
8. Serve pulled roast beef in a hoagie roll with braised onions and pan jus.

Sirloin Steak

Servings: 2
Cooking Time: 45 Minutes

Ingredients:
- 2 Tablespoons Chili Pepper Flakes
- 1/2 Cup Extra-Virgin Olive Oil
- 1 Garlic, Cloves
- 2 Tbsp Oregano, Leaves
- 1/4 Teaspoon Paprika, Powder
- 2 Cups Lightly Packed Parsley, Leaves
- 1 Teaspoon Smoked Infused Classic Sea Salt
- 1/4 Cup Red Onion, Chopped
- 1 1/2 Lbs Steak, Sirloin
- 6 Tablespoon Vinegar, Red Wine

Directions:
1. Supply your smoker with wood pellets and follow the start-up procedure. Preheat the grill, with the lid closed, to 250° F.
2. Season both sides of your steaks with salt and pepper to your liking. Place on the grates of your preheated grill. You'll want to cook the steaks until the internal temperature reaches 130°F (for medium-rare). Follow these internal temperatures if you'd like to cook your steak more/less done:
3. Rare: 125°F
4. Medium Rare: 130°F
5. Medium: 140°F
6. Well Done: 160°F
7. If you're cooking your steaks medium rare, it will take around 45 minutes.
8. While the steaks are cooking, combine parsley, garlic, red onion, oregano, paprika, and chili pepper flakes in a food processor and pulse to combine. Add salt, vinegar, and oil and continue to pulse for another 20 seconds, or until mixture is chunky but combined.
9. When the steaks have reached your desired internal temperature, remove steaks from the grill and let them rest for 15 minutes. In the meantime, open your flame broiler and crank up the grill to HIGH. Sear each side of the steak for about 1 minutes each. Slice steak thinly and drizzle with chimichurri sauce.

Chuck Roast Burnt Ends

Servings: 4
Cooking Time: 480 Minutes

Ingredients:

- 1 chuck roast, about 3 to 4lb (1.4 to 1.8kg)
- 2 tbsp Worcestershire sauce, plus more
- coarse salt, plus more
- freshly ground black pepper, plus more
- granulated garlic, plus more
- 1 cup low-carb barbecue sauce
- ¼ cup sugar-free dark-colored soda, plus more

Directions:

1. Supply your smoker with wood pellets and follow the start-up procedure. Preheat the grill, with the lid closed, to 250° F.
2. Place the roast on a rimmed sheet pan and brush with the Worcestershire sauce. Lightly season with salt, pepper, and granulated garlic. Place the roast on the grate and smoke until the internal temperature reaches 170°F (77°C), about 5 to 6 hours.
3. Transfer the roast to a cutting board and let rest for 10 minutes. (Leave the grill going.) Use a sharp knife to slice the meat into bite-size cubes, trimming any excess fat if necessary. Place the meat in an aluminum foil roasting pan. Lightly season with more salt, pepper, and granulated garlic and toss the cubes with your hands to distribute the seasonings. Add the barbecue sauce and soda. Toss again to coat.
4. Place the pan on the grate and smoke until the meat is tender and somewhat sticky with sauce, about 1 to 2 hours, stirring occasionally. (Don't let the sauce scorch.) Add another splash of soda if needed.
5. Remove the pan from the grill and stir the meat again before serving.

Salt-crusted Prime Rib

Servings: 8
Cooking Time: 180 Minutes

Ingredients:

- 1 1/2 Cup Jacobsen Salt Co. Pure Kosher Sea Salt
- 3/4 Cup coarse ground black pepper
- 1 Head garlic, peeled
- 1/2 Cup rosemary
- 2 Tablespoon chile powder
- 3/4 Cup extra-virgin olive oil
- 1 (15-16 lb) 6-bone prime rib roast

Directions:

1. In a food processor, combine salt, pepper, garlic cloves, rosemary and chile powder and process until fine. Add the olive oil and pulse to form a paste.

2. Place the prime rib roast on a cutting board, bone-side up and rub with 1 tablespoon of the salt paste.
3. Transfer the meat to a large roasting pan and place bone-side down. Pack the salt paste all over the fatty surface, pressing to help it adhere. Let the prime rib stand at room temperature for 1 hour.
4. Supply your smoker with wood pellets and follow the start-up procedure. Preheat the grill, with the lid closed, to 450° F.
5. Roast the prime rib for 1 hour, or until the crust is slightly darkened. Lower the Traeger temperature to 300°F and roast for about 2 hours and 15 minutes longer, or until an instant-read thermometer inserted into the center of the roast (not touching the bone) registers 125°F for medium-rare. Grill: 450 °F
6. Transfer the roast to a large carving board and let the meat rest for 30 minutes. Grill: 300 °F Probe: 135 °F
7. Carefully lift the salt crust off the meat and transfer to a bowl. Brush away any excess salt.
8. To remove the roast in one piece while keeping the rib rack intact, run a long sharp carving knife along the bones, using them as your guide. Leave on 1/2 inch of meat, or more if reserving for leftovers.
9. Carve the prime rib roast 1/2 inch thick and serve, using some of the crumbled salt crust as a condiment.

Slow Smoked Rib-eye Roast

Servings: 6
Cooking Time: 240 Minutes

Ingredients:

- 1 (4-6 lb) rib-eye roast
- 4 Tablespoon yellow mustard
- 1 Tablespoon Worcestershire sauce
- 1 Clove garlic, minced
- Prime Rib Rub
- 4 Sprig fresh thyme

Directions:

1. Supply your smoker with wood pellets and follow the start-up procedure. Preheat the grill, with the lid closed, to 250° F.
2. While the Traeger is warming up, prepare roast. Trim excess fat from the top of the roast down to 1/4 inch thick.
3. In a small bowl, combine the mustard, Worcestershire sauce and garlic. Cover entire roast with the mustard mixture and season liberally with Traeger Prime Rib rub.
4. Lay the sprigs of fresh thyme on the top of the roast.
5. Place the roast directly on the grill grate and smoke until the internal temperature of the roast reaches 135°F for rare or 145°F for medium, about 3 to 4 hours. Grill: 250 °F Probe: 135 °F
6. Remove roast from grill. Tent with foil and rest for 20 minutes before carving. Enjoy!

Texas Hill Country Brisket With Mustard Barbecue Sauce

Servings: 10-12
Cooking Time: 660 Minutes

Ingredients:
- 1 whole packer brisket, about 12 to 14lb (5.4 to 6.4kg)
- for the sauce
- ½ cup yellow mustard
- ½ cup brown mustard
- ½ cup apple cider vinegar
- ¼ cup light brown sugar or low-carb substitute, plus more
- 1 tbsp ketchup
- 1 tbsp Worcestershire sauce
- 1 tbsp hot sauce
- 1 tsp beef bouillon granules
- 1 tsp granulated garlic
- 1 tsp coarse salt, plus more
- ½ tsp freshly ground black pepper
- for the rub
- ¼ cup coarse salt
- ¼ cup fresh coarsely ground black pepper
- 1 tbsp granulated garlic
- 1 tbsp chili powder

Directions:
1. Place a pan of water on the grate.Supply your smoker with wood pellets and follow the start-up procedure. Preheat the grill, with the lid closed, to 250° F.
2. In a medium saucepan on the stovetop over medium-low heat, make the sauce by whisking together the ingredients. Bring the mixture to a simmer, stirring occasionally. Simmer for 10 minutes. Taste, adding brown sugar or salt. Transfer the sauce to a covered jar and refrigerate until ready to use.
3. In a small bowl, make the rub by combining the ingredients. Trim some of the excess exterior fat off the brisket, leaving a cap of at least ¼ inch (.5cm). Place the brisket on a rimmed baking sheet. Evenly but conservatively season the meat on all sides with the rub.
4. Place the brisket fat side down on the grate and smoke until the internal temperature reaches 165°F (74°C), about 5 to 6 hours.
5. Remove the brisket from the grill and wrap it fat side up in unlined butcher paper, crimping the seams. (You can also use aluminum foil—many well-known Texas pitmasters do—but it's not as porous.) Return the brisket seam side up to the grate. Continue to cook until the internal temperature reaches 203°F (95°C), about 6 to 8 hours more. The meat should be very tender, with the melted collagen making it almost jiggly.
6. Transfer the brisket to an insulated cooler lined with clean towels or a thick layer of newspapers. Let the meat rest for 1 to 2 hours.
7. Place the brisket on a cutting board and unwrap it. Separate the point from the flat following the seam of fat that runs between them. Use a serrated knife to slice the meat against the grain into pencil-thick pieces. (The grain in the point runs perpendicular to the grain in the flat.)
8. Shingle the meat on a platter. Drizzle with any meat juices from the cutting board. Serve with the barbecue sauce.

Reverse-seared Elk Tenderloin With Green Peppercorn Sauce

Servings: 8
Cooking Time: 66 Minutes

Ingredients:
- 1 whole elk tenderloin, about 2½lb (1.2kg)
- extra virgin olive oil
- coarse salt
- fresh coarsely ground black pepper
- granulated garlic
- for the sauce
- 3 tbsp unsalted butter, divided
- 2 large shallots, peeled and finely diced
- 2 cups low-salt beef stock
- ½ cup Cognac or brandy
- 1 cup heavy whipping cream
- 1 tbsp Dijon mustard
- ¼ brined green peppercorns, drained
- 2 tbsp fresh coarsely ground dried green peppercorns
- coarse salt
- freshly ground black pepper

Directions:
1. Supply your smoker with wood pellets and follow the start-up procedure. Preheat the grill, with the lid closed, to 225° F.
2. Tie the tenderloin at 2-inch (5cm) intervals with butcher's twine. Tuck the tail under the thicker portion of the tenderloin and secure with twine. Trim any loose strings close to the knots. Place the tenderloin on a rimmed sheet pan and use your hands to coat all the sides with olive oil. Generously season with salt and pepper and granulated garlic.
3. In a skillet on the stovetop over medium heat, make the sauce by melting 2 tablespoons of butter. Add the shallots and cook until softened but not browned, about 2 to 3 minutes. Add the beef stock and raise the heat to medium high. Bring the mixture to a boil and reduce to ½ cup, about 10 minutes. Add the Cognac and cream and then whisk in the mustard.

4. Crush some of the brined peppercorns with the side of a knife. Stir all the brined and dried peppercorns into the sauce. Cook until the sauce is thick enough to coat a spoon, about 3 minutes. Whisk in the remaining 1 tablespoon of butter. Season with salt and pepper to taste. Keep warm.

5. Place the tenderloin on the grate at an angle to the bars. Smoke until the internal temperature in the thickest part of the meat reaches 110 to 115°F (43 to 46°C), about 1 hour. Transfer the tenderloin to a rimmed sheet pan lined with aluminum foil.

6. Raise the temperature to 500°F (260°C). Place the tenderloin on the grate at an angle to the bars. Sear until the internal temperature reaches 135°F (57°C), about 2 to 3 minutes per side.

7. Transfer the meat to a cutting board. Remove the butcher's twine and slice the tenderloin into steaks. Place the slices on a platter. Rewarm and rewhisk the sauce if necessary. Spoon over the steaks before serving.

Lime Carne Asada Tacos

Servings: 4
Cooking Time: 10 Minutes

Ingredients:
- 1/2 Tsp Black Pepper
- 1 Tsp Garlic Powder
- 2 Lime, Juiced
- 1 Tsp Salt
- 1 1/2 Lbs Steak, Skirt
- 8 Tortilla

Directions:
1. Supply your smoker with wood pellets and follow the start-up procedure. Preheat the grill, with the lid closed, to 400° F. Place the steaks on the grill, and grill them for 4-8 minutes, then flip the steaks and grill for an additional 4-8 minutes.

2. Remove steaks from the grill, loosely cover them with foil, and let them sit for 5-10 minutes. Next chop the steaks into pieces and serve with tortillas and any desired toppings.

Smoked Beef Back Ribs

Servings: 6
Cooking Time: 480 Minutes

Ingredients:
- 2 Rack beef back ribs
- 1/2 Cup Beef Rub

Directions:
1. If your butcher has not already done so, remove the thin papery membrane from the bone-side of the ribs by working the tip of a butter knife underneath the membrane over a middle bone. Use paper towels to get a firm grip, then tear the membrane off.

2. Season both sides of ribs with Traeger Beef Rub.

3. Supply your smoker with wood pellets and follow the start-up procedure. Preheat the grill, with the lid closed, to 225° F.

4. Arrange the ribs on the grill grate, bone side down. Cook for 8-10 hours, or until internal temperature reaches 205°F. Grill: 225 °F Probe: 205 °F

5. Remove ribs from grill and let rest, lightly covered for 20 minutes before slicing and serving. Enjoy!

Mesquite Smoked Brisket

Servings: 8-12
Cooking Time: 720 Minutes

Ingredients:
- 1 (12-pound) full packer brisket
- 2 tablespoons yellow mustard (you can also use soy sauce)
- Salt
- Freshly ground black pepper

Directions:
1. Supply your smoker with wood pellets and follow the start-up procedure. Preheat the grill, with the lid closed, to 225°F.

2. Using a boning knife, carefully remove all but about ½ inch of the large layer of fat covering one side of your brisket.

3. Coat the brisket all over with mustard and season it with salt and pepper.

4. Place the brisket directly on the grill grate and smoke until its internal temperature reaches 160°F and the brisket has formed a dark bark.

5. Pull the brisket from the grill and wrap it completely in aluminum foil or butcher paper.

6. Increase the grill's temperature to 350°F and return the wrapped brisket to it. Continue to cook until its internal temperature reaches 190°F.

7. Transfer the wrapped brisket to a cooler, cover the cooler, and let the brisket rest for 1 or 2 hours.

8. Remove the brisket from the cooler and unwrap it.

9. Separate the brisket point from the flat by cutting along the fat layer, and slice the flat. The point can be saved for burnt ends (see Sweet Heat Burnt Ends), or sliced and served as well.

Venison Steaks

Servings: 4
Cooking Time: 80 Minutes

Ingredients:
- 4 (8-ounce) venison steaks
- 2 tablespoons extra-virgin olive oil
- 4 garlic cloves, minced
- 1 tablespoon ground sage
- 2 teaspoons sea salt
- 2 teaspoons freshly ground black pepper

Directions:

1. Supply your smoker with wood pellets and follow the start-up procedure. Preheat, with the lid closed, to 225°F.
2. Rub the venison steaks well with the olive oil and season with the garlic, sage, salt, and pepper.
3. Arrange the venison steaks directly on the grill grate, close the lid, and smoke for 1 hour and 20 minutes, or until a meat thermometer inserted in the center reads 130°F to 140°F, depending on desired doneness. If you want a better sear, remove the steaks from the grill at an internal temperature of 125°F, crank up the heat to 450°F, or the "High" setting, and cook the steaks on each side for an additional 2 to 3 minutes.

Irish Pasties

Servings: 4
Cooking Time: 20 Minutes

Ingredients:

- 1 Pound Roast Beef, cubed & browned
- 4 Whole Potatoes, cooked & cut into 1/2" cubes
- salt and pepper
- 1 Piecrust
- milk
- 2 Cup Beef Gravy

Directions:

1. Supply your smoker with wood pellets and follow the start-up procedure. Preheat the grill, with the lid closed, to 425° F.
2. Mix the beef, potatoes, salt, and pepper in a large mixing bowl. Unroll the piecrust, and cut in half. Put a good amount of filling in each half, fold over, and seal shut. Brush with a little milk.
3. Place on a greased basking sheet, and poke a few holes in the top of each pasty. Bake for 16-20 minutes, or until the crust is golden brown. Grill: 425 °F
4. Remove from the Traeger, brush with butter, and serve with gravy. Enjoy!

Smoked Corned Beef & Cabbage

Servings: 6
Cooking Time: 300 Minutes

Ingredients:

- 1 (3-5 lb) corned beef brisket
- 1 Quart chicken stock
- 12 Ounce (12 oz) beer, preferably pilsner or lager
- 1/4 Teaspoon garlic salt
- 1/2 Cup (1 stick) butter, cut into slices
- 2 Cup baby carrots
- 1 Pound baby or fingerling potatoes
- 1 Head cabbage, cut into wedges

- 2 Tablespoon fresh chopped dill

Directions:

1. Soak the corned beef in water for about 8 hours, changing water every 2 hours.
2. Supply your smoker with wood pellets and follow the start-up procedure. Preheat the grill, with the lid closed, to 180° F.
3. Remove brisket from water and pat dry. Place directly on the grill grate and smoke for 2 hours. Grill: 180 °F
4. Transfer brisket from grill and place in a roasting pan. Increase grill temperature to 325°F and preheat, lid closed. Grill: 325 °F
5. Sprinkle seasoning packet on top of brisket and pour chicken stock and dark beer over the roast.
6. Cover roasting pan with foil and place on the grill. Cook for 2 hours or until beef is fork tender. Grill: 325 °F
7. Remove foil and add carrots and potatoes to the roasting pan. Cover meat and vegetables with garlic salt and butter slices. Grill: 325 °F
8. Recover with foil and cook for an additional hour or until carrots and potatoes are just tender. Add cabbage, cover and return to grill for 20 minutes more. Grill: 325 °F
9. Remove vegetables from the pan to a bowl or serving platter. Slice beef and serve with potatoes, cabbage and carrots. Garnish with fresh dill and thyme if desired. Enjoy!

Smoked Seed Pastrami

Servings: 16
Cooking Time: 480 Minutes

Ingredients:

- For the brisket and brine:
- 1 beef brisket flat with plenty of fat intact (6 to 8 pounds)
- 2 quarts hot water and 2 quarts ice water
- 2/3 cup coarse salt (sea or kosher)
- 2 teaspoons pink curing salt (Prague Powder No. 1 or Insta Cure No. 1)
- 1 small onion, peeled and cut in half widthwise
- 8 cloves garlic, peeled and cut in half widthwise
- For the spice rub:
- 1/2 cup cracked black peppercorns
- 1/2 cup coriander seeds
- 2 tablespoons mustard seeds
- 1 tablespoon light or dark brown sugar
- 1 teaspoon ground ginger
- Beer (optional)

Directions:

1. Trim the brisket, leaving a fat cap on top at least 1/4 inch thick.
2. Make the brine: Place the hot water, coarse salt, and pink salt in a large bowl or plastic tub and whisk until the salt crystals are

dissolved. Stir in the ice water, onion, and garlic. Place the brisket in a jumbo heavy-duty resealable plastic bag. Add the brine and seal the top, squeezing out the air as you go. Place in a second bag and seal, then place in an aluminum foil pan or roasting pan to contain any leaks. Brine the brisket in the refrigerator for 12 days, turning it over once a day.

3. Make the rub: Place the peppercorns, coriander seeds, mustard seeds, brown sugar, and ginger in a spice mill and grind to a coarse powder, running the machine in short bursts, working in batches as needed. The final rub should feel gritty like coarse sand.

4. Drain the brisket, rinse well under cold running water, and blot dry with paper towels. Place it on a rimmed baking sheet or in a roasting pan and thickly crust it on all sides with the rub.

5. Supply your smoker with wood pellets and follow the start-up procedure. Preheat the grill, with the lid closed, to 225 °F-250 °F. Fill an aluminum foil pan with water or beer to a depth of 3 inches and place it below the rack on which you'll be smoking the ribs.

6. Place the pastrami fat side up in the smoker, directly on the rack. Smoke the pastrami until crusty and black on the outside and cooked to 175 °F on an instant-read thermometer, 7 to 8 hours.

7. Wrap the pastrami in butcher paper. Return it to the smoker. Continue cooking until the internal temperature is 200 °F and the meat is tender enough to pierce with a gloved finger or wooden spoon handle, an additional 1 to 2 hours, or as needed. (You'll need to unwrap it to check it.)

8. Transfer the wrapped pastrami to an insulated cooler and let rest for 1 to 2 hours. Unwrap and slice crosswise (across the grain) for serving.

Bbq Sweet Pepper Meatloaf

Servings: 8
Cooking Time: 180 Minutes

Ingredients:

- 5 Pound ground beef, 80% lean
- 2 eggs
- 1 Cup plain panko breadcrumbs
- 1 Tablespoon kosher salt
- 1 Tablespoon black pepper
- 2 Tablespoon Rub
- 1 Cup diced sweet red peppers
- 1 Cup green onion, finely chopped
- 1 Cup ketchup

Directions:

1. Thoroughly mix together the ground beef, eggs, plain panko bread crumbs, kosher salt, black pepper, Traeger Rub, red sweet peppers and green onion.

2. Supply your smoker with wood pellets and follow the start-up procedure. Preheat the grill, with the lid closed, to 225° F.

3. Mold the meat mixture into a loaf and season exterior with the Traeger Rub.

4. Place meatloaf directly on the grill grate and cook for 2 hours and 15 minutes. Grill: 225 °F

5. Increase the grill temperature to 375°F and cook until an internal temperature of 155°F. Grill: 375 °F Probe: 155 °F

6. Glaze the meatloaf with ketchup and cook an additional 15 minutes. Grill: 375 °F

7. Allow to rest for 15 minutes before slicing. Enjoy!

Jalapeno Pepper Jack Cheese Bacon Burgers

Servings: 4
Cooking Time: 30 Minutes

Ingredients:

- 4 Slices, Raw Bacon
- 1/2 Cup Prepared Barbecue Sauce
- 1 Pound Ground Beef
- Hickory Bacon Seasoning, Plus More For Sprinkling
- 2 Thinly Sliced Jalapeno Peppers
- 1/2 Cup Olive Oil
- 4 Onion Burger Buns
- Onion, Crispy
- 4 Pepper Jack Cheese, Sliced

Directions:

1. Supply your smoker with wood pellets and follow the start-up procedure. Preheat the grill, with the lid closed, to 350° F. If using a gas or charcoal grill, set it up for medium high heat.

2. Make the burgers: in a large bowl, mix together the ground beef and Hickory Bacon seasoning until the seasoning is well incorporated. Use the Burger Press to make burger patties. Repeat until all the ground beef is gone.

3. In a small bowl, toss the sliced raw jalapenos with the olive oil and place them in the vegetable grill basket. Grill the jalapenos, stirring occasionally, until soft and charred in some spots. Remove from the grill and set aside.

4. Place the bacon on the vegetable grill basket and grill for 5-7 minutes, or until the bacon is crispy and brown. Remove from the grill and set aside.

5. Grill the burgers: place the burger patties on the grill and, if desired, sprinkle more Hickory Bacon seasoning on the patties. Grill the burgers for 5 minutes on one side, then flip and top with a slice of pepper jack cheese and grill for another 5-7 minutes, or until the internal temperature of the burgers is 135-140°F.

6. Remove the burgers from the grill and place on an onion bun. Top with the bacon, grilled jalapenos, crisped onions, and a spoonful of barbecue sauce.

Vietnamese Beef Jerky

Servings: 6
Cooking Time: 240 Minutes

Ingredients:

- 2 Pound lean bottom round, rump roast or sirloin
- 2 Large garlic, roughly chopped
- 1 Stalk fresh lemongrass, trimmed and white parts thinly sliced
- 1 1/2 inch fresh ginger, peeled and roughly chopped
- 1/2 Cup soy sauce or Bragg Liquid Aminos
- 3 Tablespoon water
- 3 Tablespoon sugar
- 2 Tablespoon fish sauce
- 2 Teaspoon red chile flakes, or more to taste
- 1/2 Teaspoon pink curing salt (optional)

Directions:

1. Remove any visible fat from the meat and slice it into thin strips against the grain with a sharp chef's knife. (This is easier if the meat is partially frozen.) Transfer to a large, sturdy resealable bag.

2. Make the Marinade: In a blender jar or food processor bowl, combine the garlic, lemongrass, ginger, soy sauce, water, sugar, fish sauce, chile flakes and pink curing salt, if using. Pulse until relatively smooth.

3. Pour over the meat and massage the bag so the meat strips are evenly coated with the marinade. Refrigerate for at least 8 hours, or overnight. Turn the bag once or twice to redistribute the juices.

4. Supply your smoker with wood pellets and follow the start-up procedure. Preheat the grill, with the lid closed, to 165° F.

5. Drain the meat (discard the marinade) and pat dry with paper towels. Arrange the meat strips directly on the grill grate, perpendicular to the bars in a single layer. If you like your jerky spicy, feel free to lightly sprinkle additional red chile flakes on the meat.

6. Smoke the jerky, turning once, until the jerky is dry, but still pliant, about 4 to 6 hours. Grill: 165 °F

7. Let cool completely, then transfer to a clean resealable bag. Store in the refrigerator for the longest shelf life. The jerky can also be frozen. Enjoy!

Garlic Beef Meatballs

Servings: 6
Cooking Time: 15 Minutes

Ingredients:

- 1 1/2 Pounds Beef, Ground Round
- 1/2 Cup Breadcrumb, Dry
- 2 Cloves Garlic, Crushed

- 3/4 Tsp Italian Seasoning, Dried
- 1 Tsp Mustard, Dry
- 1/4 Cup Parmesan Cheese, Shredded
- 1/3 Cup Parsley, Minced Fresh
- 1/4 Tsp Crushed Red Red Bell Peppers
- 1/4 Tsp Salt
- 1/4 Cup Tomato Sauce

Directions:

1. Start your Grill on "smoke" with the lid open until a fire is established in the burn pot (3-7 minutes).

2. Supply your smoker with wood pellets and follow the start-up procedure. Preheat the grill, with the lid closed, to 400° F.

3. Place all ingredients in a bowl, combine them and stir well. Shape the mixture into 30 meatballs (1 ½ inches in width).

4. Spray a broiler pan with cooking spray, place on the grill, and bake for 15 minutes until fully cooked and browned.

5. Remove from grill, cool for 5 minutes, and serve.

Texas Pepper Beef Ribs

Servings: 16
Cooking Time: 360 Minutes

Ingredients:

- 8 lbs beef ribs (two 4 bone racks of plate ribs)
- 8 tbsp salt, pepper, garlic
- 4 tbsp olive oil

Directions:

1. Supply your smoker with wood pellets and follow the start-up procedure. Preheat the grill, with the lid closed, to 250 °F.

2. Pour two tbsp of olive oil on each rack of ribs and rub into meat on all sides.

3. Season the ribs on all sides using the salt, pepper, and garlic seasoning.

4. Set ribs in the smoker and cook for 3 hours before checking for color. Insert a temperature probe into the thickest part of the ribs.

5. Continue cooking until it reaches an internal temperature of around 170 °F.

6. Wrap ribs tightly with two layers of Peach Butcher Paper. Replace the probe into the ribs.

7. Continue cooking until it reaches an internal temperature of 205 °F(usually takes about 2 hours). Use a toothpick or the probe to check for doneness. Meat should be tender like butter. If meat is still tough, continue to cook until it becomes tender.

8. Once meat is tender, leave ribs wrapped and rest until the temperature lowers to around 160-170 °F(about 1 hour).

9. Slice and serve.

Smoked Brisket With Traeger Coffee Rub

Servings: 8
Cooking Time: 540 Minutes

Ingredients:
- 1 (15 lb) beef brisket
- 1/4 Cup Coffee Rub, divided
- 15 Ounce beef broth
- 4 Tablespoon salt, divided

Directions:
1. Supply your smoker with wood pellets and follow the start-up procedure. Preheat the grill, with the lid closed, to 225° F.
2. Trim brisket of all excess fat.
3. To make the beef broth injection, combine 2 tablespoons Traeger Coffee Rub, beef broth and 2 tablespoons salt in a small bowl, stirring until the salt is dissolved. Inject the brisket by inserting the needle parallel to the grain about 1 inch apart in a checker pattern over the entire brisket. Pull it back out as you press the plunger. Inject in a high-sided aluminum pan or bus tub and hold your hand over where you are injecting to contain the mess.
4. Season the exterior of the brisket with remaining rub and remaining salt.
5. Place brisket directly on the grill grate and cook for about 6 hours or until the internal temperature reaches 160℉. Grill: 225 ℉ Probe: 160 ℉
6. Wrap the brisket tightly in two layers of foil or butcher paper. Return to grill.
7. Cook an additional 3 hours or until the internal temperature reaches 204℉. Remove brisket from the grill and make a small opening in the foil to let steam escape. Grill: 225 ℉ Probe: 204 ℉
8. Close the opening after 10 minutes and allow meat to rest 60 minutes before slicing. Slice and enjoy!

Spiced Leg Of Lamb Gyros

Servings: 8 – 10
Cooking Time: 180 Minutes

Ingredients:
- 1 Tbsp Black Pepper
- 4 Oz. Cremini Mushrooms
- ¼ Cup Dijon Mustard
- 8, Smashed Garlic Cloves
- 1 Cup + 1 Tbsp Grapeseed Oil, Divided
- 5 Lb, Bone-In Sirloin Leg Of Lamb
- ⅓ Cup Lemon Juice
- ½ Tbsp + 1 Tsp Dried, Divided Oregano
- 8-10 Pita
- Large Wedge Chop Red Onion
- 1 Tbsp Rosemary Leaves, Dried
- ⅔ Cup Scallions, Chopped
- 3 Tbsp, Coarse Sea Salt
- ½ Tbsp Thyme, Dried
- Tzatziki Sauce
- 1 Vine-Ripe Tomato, Chopped

Directions:
1. Fire up your grill and preheat to "Smoke" mode. If using a gas or charcoal grill, set it up for low, indirect heat.
2. In a food processor, combine grapeseed oil, lemon juice, mustard, scallions, garlic, rosemary, thyme, salt and pepper. Process until it forms a thick marinade.
3. Score the fat cap of the lamb, then truss with butcher's twine. Pour two-thirds of the marinade onto the leg of lamb to cover completely. Set remaining marinade aside for vegetables. Wrap the lamb in foil and marinate at room temperature for 1 hour.
4. Place the lamb in the smoking cabinet by hanging truss from S hooks. Insert temperature probe and smoke for 45 minutes. Increase the temperature to 400°F.
5. Supply your smoker with wood pellets and follow the start-up procedure. Preheat the grill, with the lid closed, to 225 to 250° F. (If you're using a grill or vertical smoker, set your temperature to 225°F). Once it has reached this temperature, make sure the upper chimney caps are fully open, and you can lower the grill temp to 300°F. As long as the cabinet doors remain closed this should maintain temperature in the upper cabinet.
6. Smoke the lamb until the internal temperature of the meat reaches 135°F, about 3 hours.
7. While the lamb is cooking, skewer together red onion and mushrooms. Brush with remaining marinade, then transfer to grill with sear slide open, 3 to 5 minutes. In a small bowl combine 1 tbsp of grape seed oil and 1 tsp of oregano and brush lightly over pita breads. Grill pita bread to warm while skewers are on the grill.
8. Remove the leg of lamb from the smoker and loosely cover with aluminum foil. Rest the meat for 30 minutes before slicing.
9. Thinly slice the lamb, and serve in warm pita with grilled mushrooms and onions, and chopped tomatoes, and tzatziki, if desired.

Italian Beef Pinwheels

Servings: 6
Cooking Time: 45 Minutes

Ingredients:
- 3 Pound skirt steak
- Prime Rib Rub
- 2 Cup spinach
- 4 Slices havarti cheese
- 4 Slices provolone cheese
- 1 Cup sun-dried tomatoes

Directions:

1. Supply your smoker with wood pellets and follow the start-up procedure. Preheat the grill, with the lid closed, to 375° F.

2. Season skirt steak generously with Traeger Prime Rib Rub. Lay your skirt steak flat and add a layer of spinach. Depending on the size of the steak, add up to the full 2 cups. Then add a layer of cheese and lastly the sun-dried tomatoes.

3. Tightly roll the meat up and insert toothpicks to hold it together.

4. Place meat roll directly on the grill grate and cook for 45 minutes. After 45 minutes, remove from the grill and let rest for 10 minutes before slicing. Grill: 375 °F

5. Serve with a large helping of mashed potatoes or your favorite side dish. Enjoy!

Fajita Style Mexican Hot Dogs

Servings: 4
Cooking Time: 10 Minutes

Ingredients:

- 1 Green Bell Pepper, Sliced
- 1 Package Hot Dog Bun(S)
- 1 Package High Quality Ballpark Hot Dog(S)
- 1 Tbsp Olive Oil
- 1 Tsp Beef And Brisket Rub
- 1 Yellow Bell Pepper, Sliced
- 1 Yellow Onion, Sliced

Directions:

1. Supply your smoker with wood pellets and follow the start-up procedure. Preheat the grill, with the lid closed, to 350° F.

2. In a large bowl, toss the peppers and onions with the olive oil and Beef and Brisket Rub. Place the vegetables on the mesh grilling basket.

3. Remove from the grill and assemble the hot dogs. Top the buns with a hot dog and a generous scoop of the onion and pepper mixture. Serve immediately.

Spicy Chopped Brisket Sandwich

Servings: 4
Cooking Time: 10 Minutes

Ingredients:

- 3 Cups Cooked And Chopped Brisket
- Dill Pickle, Slice
- Pickled Jalapeno, Sliced
- 4 Sandwich Buns
- 1 Cup Spicy Barbecue Sauce
- White Onion, Sliced

Directions:

1. Supply your smoker with wood pellets and follow the start-up procedure. Preheat the grill, with the lid closed, to 350° F. If you're using gas or charcoal, prep your grill to cook with medium indirect heat.

2. Add the chopped brisket and spicy barbecue sauce to the aluminum pan and mix well. The brisket should be fully coated with sauce. If 1 cup is not enough, feel free to more sauce ¼ cup at a time.

3. Cover the aluminum pan tightly with foil and place it in the center of the grill. Close the lid and cook the brisket for about 10 minutes or until it's heated all the way through.

4. Remove the brisket from the grill and pile the meat on top of the sandwich buns. Top the brisket sandwich with pickle slices, jalapeno slices, and sliced onions. Serve immediately.

Green Bell Pepper Cheese Steak Burger

Servings: 4
Cooking Time: 30 Minutes

Ingredients:

- 4 Burger Buns
- 1 Green Bell Pepper, Sliced
- 1 Pound Ground Beef
- 1 Tablespoon Olive Oil
- 1 Tablespoon Chop House Steak Seasoning
- 4 Provolone Cheese, Sliced

Directions:

1. In a large bowl, mix the ground beef and Chop House Steal seasoning together until well combined. Form into patties. Supply your smoker with wood pellets and follow the start-up procedure. Preheat the grill, with the lid closed, to 350° F and grill for 5-7 minutes, flipping halfway through. Once you flip the burgers, top with a slice of provolone cheese.

2. Once the burgers have cooked to your desired degree of doneness, remove from the grill and set aside.

3. For the pepper and onion: in a sauté pan over medium heat, heat the olive oil until it shimmers, then add the onion and pepper. Cook until the pepper and onion are soft and start to caramelize and develop a little char, about 15 minutes.

Brined Smoked Brisket

Servings: 4
Cooking Time: 420 Minutes

Ingredients:

- 1 (5-7 lb) flat cut brisket
- 1 Cup brown sugar
- 1/2 Cup kosher salt
- 1/4 Cup Beef Rub

Directions:

1. Dissolve salt and sugar in 6 quarts boiling water. Add 6 cups ice then let it cool. Place the brisket in the brine and cover. Leave brine in the refrigerator overnight.

2. Remove the brisket from the brine and pat it dry with a paper towel. Sprinkle evenly with Traeger Beef Rub.

3. Supply your smoker with wood pellets and follow the start-up procedure. Preheat the grill, with the lid closed, to 250° F.

4. Place the brisket on the Traeger, fat cap down and smoke for 3 hours. Grill: 250 °F

5. After 3 hours, double wrap the brisket in foil and turn the temperature up to 275°F. Cook meat until internal temperature reaches 204°F, about 3 to 4 hours. Grill: 275 °F Probe: 204 °F

6. Unwrap the brisket and place it unwrapped on the grill for 30 more minutes. Grill: 275 °F

7. Remove the brisket from the grill and let it rest for 15 minutes before slicing against the grain. Enjoy!

Peppered Beef Tenderloin

Servings: 6
Cooking Time: 75 Minutes

Ingredients:
- 2 1/2 lb center cut beef tenderloin, trimmed and tied if uneven
- 2 tbsp unsalted butter, room temperature
- 6 tbsp peppercorns, mixed colors
- 1 tbsp kosher salt
- 1 cup parsley, chopped
- Horseradish sauce, on the side
- 4 tbsp Dijon mustard

Directions:
1. Coarsely grind peppercorn mixture into a bowl. Add parsley, mustard, butter, and salt. Mix until thoroughly combined

2. Rub spiced butter mixture generously and thoroughly on all sides of the tenderloin. Coat completely and roll tenderloin in bowl if necessary to soak up as much seasoning as possible.

3. Preheat pellet grill to 450°F4. Place tenderloin on an elevated rack (important) and roast. Use a probe meat thermometer to measure internal temperature. Cook until the center of the tenderloin reaches a temperature of 130°F. This typically takes 30-45 minutes but could be more or less depending on the size of your tenderloin

4. Once tenderloin reaches desired doneness, remove from grill and allow to rest for at least 15 minutes6. Move tenderloin to a cutting board and slice. Try to catch as many juices as possible. Garnish with additional parsley

Smoked Sirloin Roast Beef

Servings: 2

Cooking Time: 10 Minutes

Ingredients:
- 1 top sirloin beef roast (5-6 pounds)
- 3 tbsp sea salt
- 1/4 cup Montreal steak spice

Directions:
1. Trim the roast of any excess fat. Tie the roast up with kitchen twine if desired.

2. Rub the roast down with the sea salt and then rub the roast with the Montreal steak spice.

3. Supply your smoker with wood pellets and follow the start-up procedure. Preheat the grill, with the lid closed, to 250 °F.

4. Lay the roast on the grill grate and smoke until 135 degrees F, or until the desired doneness.

5. Remove the roast from the pellet smoker and let rest for 10 minutes. Slice and serve.

Delicious Reverse Seared Picanha Steak

Servings: 4
Cooking Time: 120 Minutes

Ingredients:
- olive oil
- 3 lbs picanha steak, top sirloin cap, fat cap removed
- chop house steak rub

Directions:
1. Supply your smoker with wood pellets and follow the start-up procedure. Preheat the grill, with the lid closed, to 225° F. If using a gas or charcoal grill, set it up for low, indirect heat.

2. Generously season both sides of steak with Chop House, insert temperature probe, and place steak directly on the grill grate.

3. Cover grill and cook 1 ½ to 2 hours, or until internal temperature reads 125°F to 130°F.

4. Remove steak from grill, then preheat KC Combo griddle to medium-high flame. Heat olive oil on the griddle, then sear steak 2 minutes per side on all sides.

5. Remove steak from the griddle, and allow to rest on a cutting board for 10 minutes. Slice steak, against the grain, and serve warm.

Spiced Smoked Kielbasa Dogs

Servings: 12
Cooking Time: 300 Minutes

Ingredients:
- 1 tsp all spice, ground
- 2 tsp black peppercorns, ground
- 3 tbsp brown sugar
- 1 cup distilled ice water, divided
- 1 1/2 tsp garlic powder

- 1 1/2 lbs ground beef
- 5 lbs ground pork
- 32 - 35 hog casings
- 2 tbsp kosher salt
- 2 tsp marjoram, dried
- 1 1/2 tsp paprika
- 1 1/4 tsp speed cure, pink salt curing

Directions:

1. In a glass bowl or measuring cup, cover hog casings in warm water and let soak for 1 hour.
2. In a small bowl, whisk together brown sugar, salt, black pepper, marjoram, garlic powder, paprika, allspice, and speed cure.
3. In a large tub, combine ground pork and ground beef. Mix together by hand, then add seasoning and distilled ice water. Mix mixture by hand for 1 minute, until seasoning is incorporated throughout.
4. Prepare the sausage stuffer, and fit one hog casing over a 1 to 1 ¼ inch horn. Place a sheet tray, with a bit of water on it, underneath the nozzle of the stuffer and start filling the casings.
5. Once the casings are filled, twist off into desired lengths, and refrigerate overnight.
6. Hang the links with S-hooks from the top rack of your Grill or Smoker. Smoke on SMOKE mode for 3 hours. Supply your smoker with wood pellets and follow the start-up procedure. Preheat the grill, with the lid closed, to 300° F, which will raise the temperature of the smoking cabinet to 170°F. If using a vertical smoker, keep smoking on SMOKE mode. Continue smoking the sausage for another 1 to 2 hours, until the internal temperature of the sausage reaches 155° F.
7. Remove sausage from the smoking cabinet and either enjoy hot with your favorite toppings, or place in an ice water bath for 15 minutes, dry at room temperature and refrigerate or freeze for future use.

Teriyaki Bbq Beef Skewers

Servings: 8
Cooking Time: 8 Minutes

Ingredients:

- 2 Pound Top Round Steak, boneless, cut into 1/4" slices
- 3/4 Cup light brown sugar
- 1/2 Cup soy sauce
- 1/4 Cup Pineapple Juice (optional)
- 1/4 Cup water
- Cup vegetable oil
- 1 Clove Garlic (Large), finely chopped

Directions:

1. Slice the beef into 1-1/2 - 2" wide strips.
2. Whisk brown sugar, soy sauce, pineapple juice, water, vegetable oil, and garlic together.

3. Pour the marinade into a large zip-top bag and drop beef slices into the mixture. Marinate beef in refrigerator for 24 hours.
4. Remove beef from the marinade, shaking to remove any excess liquid. Discard marinade. Thread beef slices in a zig-zag onto the skewers.
5. Supply your smoker with wood pellets and follow the start-up procedure. Preheat the grill, with the lid closed, to 325° F.
6. Cook skewers on preheated grill until the beef is cooked through, about 3 minutes per side. Enjoy! Grill: 325 °F

Succulent Lamb Chops

Servings: 4-6
Cooking Time: 20 Minutes

Ingredients:

- ½ cup rice wine vinegar
- 1 teaspoon liquid smoke
- 2 tablespoons extra-virgin olive oil
- 2 tablespoons dried minced onion
- 1 tablespoon chopped fresh mint
- 8 (4-ounce) lamb chops
- ½ cup hot pepper jelly
- 1 tablespoon Sriracha
- 1 teaspoon salt
- 1 teaspoon freshly ground black pepper

Directions:

1. In a small bowl, whisk together the rice wine vinegar, liquid smoke, olive oil, minced onion, and mint. Place the lamb chops in an aluminum roasting pan. Pour the marinade over the meat, turning to coat thoroughly. Cover with plastic wrap and marinate in the refrigerator for 2 hours.
2. Supply your smoker with wood pellets and follow the start-up procedure. Preheat, with the lid closed, to 165°F, or the "Smoke" setting.
3. On the stove top, in a small saucepan over low heat, combine the hot pepper jelly and Sriracha and keep warm.
4. When ready to cook the chops, remove them from the marinade and pat dry. Discard the marinade.
5. Season the chops with the salt and pepper, then place them directly on the grill grate, close the lid, and smoke for 5 minutes to "breathe" some smoke into them.
6. Remove the chops from the grill. Increase the pellet cooker temperature to 450°F, or the "High" setting. Once the grill is up to temperature, place the chops on the grill and sear, cooking for 2 minutes per side to achieve medium-rare chops. A meat thermometer inserted in the thickest part of the meat should read 145°F. Continue grilling, if necessary, to your desired doneness.
7. Serve the chops with the warm Sriracha pepper jelly on the side.

Three Ingredient Pot Roast

Servings: 4
Cooking Time: 180 Minutes

Ingredients:

- 4 Pound chuck roast, cut into 4 inch chunks
- 2 yellow onions, finely sliced
- 2 Teaspoon kosher salt
- 1/4 Cup extra-virgin olive oil
- freshly ground black pepper

Directions:

1. Supply your smoker with wood pellets and follow the start-up procedure. Preheat the grill, with the lid closed, to 400° F.Place half of the chuck roast into a 3-to-4 quart Dutch oven. (Note: if using a roast that is smaller than 4 lbs, make sure to use a smaller Dutch oven as well.) Add half the onions, half the salt, pepper, and half the olive oil. Repeat with the remaining ingredients.

2. Place a tight-fitting lid on the Dutch oven and place on the grill. Cook for 2 to 3 hours, until the chuck roast can be easily shredded with a fork. Reduce the grill temperature to 350°F if the chuck roast is boiling and not simmering. Grill: 400 °F

3. Remove Dutch oven from the grill and remove the lid. Allow the meat to cool, then skim the fat off the top. Alternatively, allow the meat to cool, refrigerate overnight, then skim the fat cap off the meat before reheating the next day. It will keep for 2 days in the fridge.

4. When ready to serve, this pot roast can be topped with many things to make it your own, including my Preserved Lemon Gremolata, chimichurri, peperonata, horseradish cream (horseradish, sour cream and mayo) or a variety of salsas.

Traeger Smoked Salami

Servings: 8
Cooking Time: 480 Minutes

Ingredients:

- Pound Ground Sirloin
- 1 Tablespoon Morton Tender Quick Home Meat Cure
- Tablespoon Worcestershire sauce
- 1 Tablespoon ground black pepper
- 2 Teaspoon mustard seeds
- 1 Teaspoon red pepper flakes
- 1 Teaspoon black peppercorn
- Teaspoon honey

Directions:

1. Plan ahead! This recipe requires overnight time. In a large glass bowl combine the beef, curing salt, Worcestershire, pepper, mustard, red pepper flakes, and peppercorns. Gently distribute the ingredients through the meat.

2. Cover with plastic wrap and refrigerate for 1 day.

3. After the meat has cured for 1 day, lay two pieces of long plastic wrap on top of each other on your work surface. Overturn the meat directly into the middle of the plastic wrap. Form the meat into a long log shape.

4. Pull the plastic wrap around one side and smooth out the edges of the log. Use even pressure across the length to work out any bubbles. Pull the plastic wrap tightly around the other side and overlap the edges of the wrap to create a tight seal. Roll the sausage forward and back with both hands. Once you have the sausage fairly uniform in width, tightly twist the ends of the plastic wrap. Return to the refrigerator for 1 day.

5. Supply your smoker with wood pellets and follow the start-up procedure. Preheat the grill, with the lid closed, to 180° F.

6. Unwrap the sausage and drizzle with the honey. Place directly on the grill grate, close the lid and smoke for 6-8 hours or until the internal temperature of the sausage reads 170°F with a meat thermometer. Probe: 170 °F

7. Allow the sausage to cool completely before slicing and serving. Enjoy!

Flavour Texas Twinkies

Servings: 7-14
Cooking Time: 40 Minutes

Ingredients:

- 14, slices bacon
- ½ cup BBQ sauce
- 1 lb. brisket
- 8 oz. cream cheese
- 1 tsp cumin
- 14 large jalapeños
- ½ tsp pepper
- 1 cup pepper jack cheese, grated
- 2 tsp hickory bacon rub
- ½ tsp salt

Directions:

1. Supply your smoker with wood pellets and follow the start-up procedure. Preheat the grill, with the lid closed, to 400° F. If using a gas or charcoal grill, set it for medium-high heat.

2. In a food processor, combine the brisket, Hickory Bacon, cumin, salt, pepper, pepper jack and cream cheese. Pulse several times until well combined. Transfer to a bowl and place into refrigerator to chill while preparing jalapeños.

3. Place jalapeños on a sheet tray. Cut each in half lengthwise and remove the seeds and rib with a spoon or by hand, then discard. Note: we recommend using gloves when handling jalapenos, as the seeds can be very hot.

4. Fill each jalapeño half with cream cheese mixture until full, then place other jalapeño half on top. Wrap each jalapeño with a slice of bacon, then skewer crosswise with toothpicks.

5. Place a mesh, metal pan on grill grate and transfer jalapeños to pan. Cover grill and cook for 35 minutes.

6. Open grill and baste jalapeños generously with BBQ sauce, close grill and continue to cook another 5 minutes.

7. Remove from grill and serve hot.

Garlic Parmesan Grilled Filet Mignon

Servings: 2
Cooking Time: 10 Minutes

Ingredients:

- 4 filet mignon steaks
- 1 Teaspoon salt
- 1 Teaspoon black pepper
- 1 Teaspoon garlic salt
- 1 Cup Parmesan cheese
- 4 garlic
- 1 Tablespoon Dijon mustard

Directions:

1. Supply your smoker with wood pellets and follow the start-up procedure. Preheat the grill, with the lid closed, to High heat.

2. While the grill is heating up, season the filets with salt, pepper, and garlic salt. Also mince your garlic and chop your Parmesan so it's fine, and combine.

3. When the grill reaches temperature, place filets on the grill and cook for 4 minutes on each side. After 8 minutes total, spread the filets with the Dijon mustard and dip in the minced garlic and Parmesan cheese mixture and place back on the grill for another 1-2 minutes or until the cheese is melted.

4. Let rest for 5 minutes and serve. Enjoy!

Smoked Black Pepper Beef Cheeks

Servings: 6
Cooking Time: 240 Minutes

Ingredients:

- 4 beef cheeks, trimmed and with silver skin removed
- Beef Rub:
- 2 parts ground black pepper
- 1 part kosher salt
- 1 part brown sugar (optional)

Directions:

1. Supply your smoker with wood pellets and follow the start-up procedure. Preheat the grill, with the lid closed, to 275 °F.

2. Trim silver skin and excess fat from the beef cheeks.

3. In a bowl combine beef rub ingredients and apply generously to all sides of the beef, including crevices.

4. Transfer to grill grates. Leave to smoke for 4 hours, lid closed.

5. Remove from smoker and wrap in aluminum foil, or place in an aluminum tray and cover with foil.

6. Transfer back to the smoker and leave to smoke for one more hour.

7. Allow to cook until the internal temperature has reached 210 °F.

8. Remove from smoker and leave wrapped in foil. Let it rest for about 10 minutes.

9. Slice and serve, or pulled for beef cheek tacos or sandwiches.

Bbq Beef Sandwich

Servings: 4
Cooking Time: 360 Minutes

Ingredients:

- 1 (4-6 lb) chuck roast
- 1/4 Cup Coffee Rub
- 1 Cup beef broth
- 6 hamburger buns
- 1 white onion, sliced
- dill pickles
- 1/2 Cup Special Sauce
- Sweet & Heat BBQ Sauce

Directions:

1. Supply your smoker with wood pellets and follow the start-up procedure. Preheat the grill, with the lid closed, to 250° F.

2. Trim excess fat from chuck roast. Rub roast with Traeger Coffee Rub. Place roast on Traeger and cook for 3-1/2 hours or until roast reaches an internal temperature of 160°F. Grill: 250 °F Probe: 160 °F

3. Remove roast from grill and wrap in a double layer of aluminum foil, add beef broth and place roast back in grill. Continue to cook for 1-1/2 hours while checking the temperature. The roast is done when the internal temperature reaches 204°F. Check every 30 minutes if internal temperature has not been reached. Grill: 250 °F Probe: 204 °F

4. Remove roast from grill and pull or shred the meat. Add the drippings back into the meat to help keep it moist.

5. Serve pulled roast in buns and top with sliced onions, pickles Traeger Special Sauce and Traeger Sweet & Heat BBQ Sauce.

Savory Smoked Brisket

Servings: 10
Cooking Time: 600 Minutes

Ingredients:

- 4 Tbsp Apple Cider Vinegar
- 10Lb Trimmed Brisket
- 2 Cups Broth, Beef
- Sweet Heat Rub
- 2 Tbsp Worcestershire Sauce

Directions:

1. Trim the fat cap from your brisket, leaving enough fat to baste the meat during the smoke process.
2. Generously coat the brisket with Sweet Heat rub, and massage into the brisket.
3. In a bowl, whisk together the apple cider vinegar, Worcestershire sauce and beef broth, then pour into a clean spray bottle.
4. Supply your smoker with wood pellets and follow the start-up procedure. Preheat the grill, with the lid closed, to 225° F. Once the smoker is up to temperature, place the brisket inside and insert the temperature probe. Smoke for 10 to 12 hours, or until the internal temperature of the brisket reaches 200°F at the thickest part. Once an hour, spray the brisket with the mop sauce to baste it.
5. Once the brisket is done, remove from the smoker, allow to rest for 30 minutes under tin foil, then slice and enjoy!

Tater Tot Nachos With Brisket

Servings: 4
Cooking Time: 600 Minutes

Ingredients:
- Your Favorite BBQ Sauce
- 1 12 Lb Brisket
- 1, Skiced Jalapeno Pepper
- ¼ Cup Beef And Brisket Rub
- ¾ Cup Sharp Cheddar Cheese, Shredded
- ⅓ Cup Sour Cream
- 32 Oz. Tater Tots, Frozen

Directions:
1. Supply your smoker with wood pellets and follow the start-up procedure. Preheat the grill, with the lid closed, to 225° F. If using a gas or charcoal grill, set to medium-low heat.
2. While your grill is heating up, trim your brisket of excess fat (you'll want to leave about ¼ of an inch of fat so the meat stays moist during the long cooking process), and season generously with Beef and Brisket Rub. Place your brisket on the grates of the grill, fat side up. Let it smoke for about 8-10 hours, or until the internal temperature reaches 190°F.
3. Let it rest in the cooler for up to an hour so the juices can settle back into the meat. Shred with meat claws and reserve 1 lb.
4. Return grill to 325°F. Place tater tots on the bottom of a large cast-iron skillet and arrange in one layer. Place skillet on preheated grill and cook tater tots until crispy and golden.
5. Top tater tots with reserved brisket, BBQ sauce and cheddar cheese. Return to the grill for 15 minutes or until cheese has melted.
6. Remove from oven and top with sour cream and jalapenos. Serve immediately.

Smoked Bourbon Jerky

Servings: 6
Cooking Time: 360 Minutes

Ingredients:
- 3 Pound flank steak
- 1 Cup bourbon
- 1/2 Cup brown sugar
- 1/4 Cup Jerky Rub
- 1 Can chipotle peppers in adobo sauce
- 3 Tablespoon Worcestershire sauce
- 1/2 Cup apple cider vinegar

Directions:
1. Roll flank steak up parallel to the grain. Slice, with the grain, into 1/4 inch thick slices.
2. Combine all ingredients for marinade in a medium bowl and mix well. Place sliced flank steak in a large zip top bag and pour marinade over steak.
3. Place in refrigerator and marinate overnight.
4. Supply your smoker with wood pellets and follow the start-up procedure. Preheat the grill, with the lid closed, to 180° F.
5. Remove flank from the marinade, discard marinade and lay slices on a jerky rack or directly on the grill grate. Grill: 180 °F
6. Smoke for about 6 hours or until jerky has dried out but is still pliable. Grill: 180 °F
7. Remove from grill and let cool at room temperature, lightly covered for 1 hour.
8. Store in an airtight container or zip top bag in the refrigerator. Enjoy!

Smoked Corned Beef Brisket

Servings: 4
Cooking Time: 300 Minutes

Ingredients:
- 1 (3 lb) flat cut corned beef brisket, fat cap at least 1/4 inch thick
- 1 Bottle Apricot BBQ Sauce
- 1/4 Cup Dijon mustard

Directions:
1. Remove the corned beef brisket from its packaging and discard the spice packet, if any. Soak the corned beef in water for at least 8 hours changing the water every 2 hours.
2. Supply your smoker with wood pellets and follow the start-up procedure. Preheat the grill, with the lid closed, to 275° F.
3. Put the brisket directly on the grill grate, fat side up and cook for 2 hours. Grill: 275 °F
4. Meanwhile, combine the Traeger Apricot BBQ Sauce and the Dijon mustard in a medium bowl, whisking to mix.

5. Pour half of the BBQ sauce-mustard mixture in the bottom of a disposable aluminum foil pan. With tongs, transfer the brisket to the pan, fat-side up. Pour the remainder of the BBQ sauce-mustard mixture over the top of the brisket, using a spatula to spread the sauce evenly. Cover the pan tightly with aluminum foil.

6. Return the brisket to the grill and continue to cook for 2 to 3 hours, or until the brisket is tender. The internal temperature should be 203°F on an instant-read meat thermometer. Probe: 203°F

7. Remove from the grill and allow the meat to rest for 15 to 20 minutes at room temperature. Slice across the grain into 1/4 inch slices with a sharp knife and serve immediately. Enjoy!

Grilled Bell Pepper Flank Steak Fajitas

Servings: 1
Cooking Time: 30 Minutes

Ingredients:
- 1 Green Bell Pepper, Sliced
- 3 Tbsp Olive Oil
- 1 Onion, Diced
- Sweet Heat Rub
- 1 Red Bell Peppers, Sliced
- 1 -16Oz Steak, Flank
- 8 Tortilla, Corn
- 1 Yellow Bell Pepper, Sliced

Directions:
1. Rub flank steak with 1 tbsp olive oil and Sweet Heat Rub Grill seasoning. Cover and marinate in the refrigerator for 1 hour.
2. Lightly brush peppers and onion with olive oil.
3. Supply your smoker with wood pellets and follow the start-up procedure. Preheat the grill, with the lid closed, to 400° F. Place pepper and onion on grill and cook 5 minutes per side. Watch carefully to ensure the peppers and onion do not burn.
4. Remove peppers and onion from grill and toss lightly with remaining olive oil in a medium sized bowl. Transfer peppers and onions to a cutting board and slice into strips. Set aside.
5. Place flank steak directly on grill. Cook until medium rare (an internal temperature of 165°F).
6. Remove flank steak from the grill and transfer to cutting board. Let meat rest for 5 minutes, then slice against the grain into strips.
7. Place flank steak, peppers, and onions in a platter and serve immediately with warm tortillas, salsa, guacamole, sour cream, shredded cheese, thinly sliced iceberg lettuce, or your favorite fajita toppings.

Pulled Beef

Servings: 5-8

Cooking Time: 840 Minutes

Ingredients:
- 1 (4-pound) top round roast
- 2 tablespoons yellow mustard
- 1 batch Espresso Brisket Rub
- ½ cup beef broth

Directions:
1. Supply your smoker with wood pellets and follow the start-up procedure. Preheat the grill, with the lid closed, to 225°F.
2. Coat the top round roast all over with mustard and season it with the rub. Using your hands, work the rub into the meat.
3. Place the roast directly on the grill grate and smoke until its internal temperature reaches 160°F and a dark bark has formed.
4. Pull the roast from the grill and place it on enough aluminum foil to wrap it completely.
5. Increase the grill's temperature to 350°F.
6. Fold in three sides of the foil around the roast and add the beef broth. Fold in the last side, completely enclosing the roast and liquid. Return the wrapped roast to the grill and cook until its internal temperature reaches 195°F.
7. Pull the roast from the grill and place it in a cooler. Cover the cooler and let the roast rest for 1 or 2 hours.
8. Remove the roast from the cooler and unwrap it. Pull apart the beef using just your fingers. Serve immediately.

Traditional Tomahawk Steak

Servings: 4-6
Cooking Time: 120 Minutes

Ingredients:
- 1 tomahawk ribeye steak (2 1/2 to 3 1/2 lbs)
- 5 garlic cloves, minced
- 2 tbsp kosher salt
- 1 bundle fresh thyme
- 2 tbsp ground black pepper
- 8 oz butter stick
- 1 tbsp garlic powder
- 1/8 cup olive oil

Directions:
1. Mix rub ingredients (salt, black pepper, and garlic powder) in a small bowl. Use this mixture to season all sides of the ribeye steak generously. You can also substitute your favorite steak seasoning. After applying seasoning, let the steak rest at room temperature for at least 30 minutes.
2. While the steak rests, preheat your pellet grill to 450°F - 550°F for searing
3. Sear the steak for 5 minutes on each side. Halfway through each side (so after 2 1/2 minutes), rotate the steak 90° to form grill marks on the tomahawk

4. After the tomahawk steak has seared for 5 minutes on each side (10 minutes total), move the steak to a raised rack

5. Adjust your pellet grill's temperature to 250°F and turn up smoke setting if applicable. Leave the lid open for a moment to help allow some heat to escape

6. Stick your probe meat thermometer into the very center of the cut to measure internal temperature.

7. Place butter stick, garlic cloves, olive oil, and thyme in the aluminum pan. Then place the aluminum pan under the steak to catch drippings. After a few minutes, the steak drippings and ingredients will mix together

8. Baste the steak with the aluminum pan mixture every 10 minutes until the tomahawk steak reaches your desired doneness

9. Once the steak reaches its desired doneness, remove from the grill and place on a cutting board or serving dish. The steak should rest for 10-15 minutes before cutting/serving.

Salt & Pepper Dinosaur Bones

Servings: 3-4
Cooking Time: 480 Minutes

Ingredients:
- 1 rack of beef plate short ribs, about 4 to 5lb (1.8 to 2.3kg) total, or 3 bones
- coarse kosher salt
- freshly ground black pepper
- granulated garlic
- crushed red pepper flakes (optional)
- 1½ cups sugar-free dark-colored soda, sugar-free root beer, beef broth, or brewed coffee

Directions:
1. Supply your smoker with wood pellets and follow the start-up procedure. Preheat the grill, with the lid closed, to 250° F.

2. Place the ribs in an aluminum foil roasting pan. If the rack has a thick cap of fat on the meaty side, trim most of it off because that will impede the formation of a nice bark on the ribs.

3. Generously season the ribs on all sides with salt, pepper, garlic, and red pepper flakes (if using). Place the ribs bone side down on the grate and smoke for 3 hours.

4. Add the soda to a spray bottle and spritz the ribs. Continue to smoke the ribs until the internal temperature reaches 203°F (95°C), about 4 to 5 hours more, spritzing once an hour. (Insert the probe next to the middle rib, being careful not to touch the bone.) When the ribs are tender, the meat will feel gelatinous and springy and will have shrunk back from the ends of the bones by up to 2 inches (5cm).

5. Transfer the ribs to a clean sheet pan and wrap with heavy-duty aluminum foil. Let rest for 1 hour, preferably in an insulated cooler.

6. Slice the ribs apart or remove the meat from the bones and thinly slice before serving with additional salt and pepper.

The Perfect T-bones

Servings: 4
Cooking Time: 30 Minutes

Ingredients:
- 4 (1½- to 2-inch-thick) T-bone steaks
- 2 tablespoons olive oil
- 1 batch Espresso Brisket Rub or Chili-Coffee Rub

Directions:
1. Supply your smoker with wood pellets and follow the start-up procedure. Preheat the grill, with the lid closed, to 500°F.

2. Coat the steaks all over with olive oil and season both sides with the rub. Using your hands, work the rub into the meat.

3. Place the steaks directly on a grill grate and smoke until their internal temperature reaches 135°F for rare, 145°F for medium-rare, and 155°F for well-done. Remove the steaks from the grill and serve hot.

Slow Smoked And Roasted Prime Rib

Servings: 8
Cooking Time: 240 Minutes

Ingredients:
- 1 (8-10 lb) 4-bone prime rib roast
- 5 Tablespoon kosher salt
- 5 Tablespoon ground black pepper
- 3 Tablespoon fresh chopped thyme
- 3 Tablespoon fresh chopped rosemary

Directions:
1. Supply your smoker with wood pellets and follow the start-up procedure. Preheat the grill, with the lid closed, to 250° F.

2. While grill preheats, trim excess fat off roast. Combine remainder of ingredients and coat the entire roast with the mixture.

3. Place roast on grill and cook until the internal temperature reaches 120°F, about 4 hours. Begin checking the internal temperature every hour or so until it reaches 120°F. Pull roast off the grill and allow to rest for 20 minutes. Grill: 250 °F Probe: 120 °F

4. While roast rests, increase grill temperature to 450°F and preheat. Once the grill is hot, place the roast back on for 15 minutes, flipping halfway through or until the internal temperature registers 130°F for medium rare. Grill: 450 °F Probe: 130 °F

5. Remove roast from grill and allow to rest for 30 minutes before slicing. Enjoy!

Roasted Prime Rib With Mustard And Herbs De Provence

Servings: 8
Cooking Time: 180 Minutes

Ingredients:
- 1 Whole 7-bone prime rib roast
- extra-virgin olive oil
- kosher salt
- coarse ground black pepper
- 2 Cup Dijon mustard
- 2 Cup herbs de Provence

Directions:
1. Note: this recipe requires an overnight marinade, plan ahead. A day before you are ready to cook, prep your prime rib. Trim any excess fat.
2. Coat the prime rib evenly with olive oil to allow the seasoning to adhere. Season all sides of the roast generously with salt and pepper. Next, coat all sides evenly with a layer of Dijon mustard, and season liberally with the herbs de Provence. Let sit in the refrigerator for up to 24 hours, uncovered.
3. Supply your smoker with wood pellets and follow the start-up procedure. Preheat the grill, with the lid closed, to 325° F.
4. Place the prime rib fat side up, directly on the grill grate or on a sheet tray, and roast for 3 to 3 ½ hours, or until the internal temperature reaches 110℉.
5. Pull the prime rib off the grill and allow to rest for one hour. The internal temperature will continue to rise as it rests, you are looking for a finished temp of 130℉ for medium rare.
6. Carve the roast. First stand the prime rib upright, and using a sharp, thin-bladed carving knife, carve along the bones, following the curvature of the bones as closely as you can until you cut through the base. Next, slice the roast into even slices, about 1" thick. To carve the bones, stand it upright again and slice along the bones. Enjoy!

Bbq Beef Short Ribs With Traeger Prime Rib Rub

Servings: 6
Cooking Time: 480 Minutes

Ingredients:
- 2 (4 bone) beef short rib racks
- Prime Rib Rub
- 1 Cup beef broth

Directions:
1. Clean and trim beef short ribs. Season generously with Traeger Prime Rib Rub.

2. Supply your smoker with wood pellets and follow the start-up procedure. Preheat the grill, with the lid closed, to 225° F.
3. Place ribs directly on the grill grate and cook for 5 hours or until the internal temperature reaches 160℉. Grill: 250 ℉ Probe: 160 ℉
4. Stack two sheets of foil on a flat surface. Place 1 rack of ribs directly in the center of the foil sheets and wrap up like a packet leaving one end open. Pour in 1/2 cup beef broth and close packet. Repeat with remaining rack.
5. Place ribs back on grill, meat side down for 2-3 more hours or until the internal temperature reaches 204℉. Remove from grill and allow to rest 10 minutes before slicing. Grill: 250 ℉ Probe: 204 ℉
6. Cut into individual ribs and serve with your favorite sides. Enjoy!

Braised Mediterranean Beef Brisket

Servings: 8
Cooking Time: 720 Minutes

Ingredients:
- 3 Tablespoon dried rosemary
- 2 Tablespoon ground cumin seeds
- 2 Tablespoon Coriander, Dried
- 1 Tablespoon dried oregano
- 2 Teaspoon ground cinnamon
- 1/2 Teaspoon salt
- 8 Pound beef brisket
- 1 Cup beef stock

Directions:
1. For a 6 to 8 lb brisket, plan for 8 to 12 hours of cook time, roughly 90 minutes per pound. A remote probe thermometer is critical to use for brisket.
2. Mix all seasoning together and coat brisket liberally. Wrap in plastic wrap. Let the wrapped brisket sit 12 to 24 hours in the refrigerator. Allow plenty of time for cooking.
3. Supply your smoker with wood pellets and follow the start-up procedure. Preheat the grill, with the lid closed, to 180° F.
4. Place brisket fat side down on the grill grate, insert thermometer probe and smoke for 4 hours.
5. After 4 hours, turn grill up to 250℉ and preheat. Grill: 250 ℉ Probe: 250 ℉
6. When internal meat temperature reaches 160℉, remove brisket from the grill and wrap in foil along with beef stock - DO NOT remove thermometer probe.
7. Place foiled brisket back on grill and cook until internal temperature reaches 204℉. Grill: 250 ℉ Probe: 204 ℉
8. Remove brisket and allow it to rest in the foil for at least 30 minutes before slicing. Enjoy!

Roasted Duck

Servings: 4
Cooking Time: 180 Minutes

Ingredients:

- 1 (5-6 lb) duck, defrosted
- Pork & Poultry Rub
- 1 Small onion, peeled and quartered
- 1 orange, quartered
- fresh herbs, such as parsley, sage or rosemary

Directions:

1. Remove the giblets and discard or save for another use. Trim any loose skin at the neck and remove excess fat from around the main cavity. Remove the wing tips if desired.
2. Rinse the duck under cold running water, inside and out, and dry with paper towels.
3. Prick the skin all over with the tip of a knife or the tines of a fork; do not pierce the meat. This helps to render the fat and crisp the skin.
4. Season the bird, inside and out, with Traeger Pork and Poultry Rub. Tuck the onion, orange, and fresh herbs into the cavity.
5. Tie the legs together with butcher's string.
6. Supply your smoker with wood pellets and follow the start-up procedure. Preheat the grill, with the lid closed, to 225° F.
7. Place the duck directly on the grill grate. Roast for 2-1/2 to 3 hours, or until the skin is brown and crisp. The internal temperature should register 160°F in the thigh (be sure to avoid the bone as this will give you an inaccurate reading). Grill: 225 °F Probe: 160 °F
8. If the duck is not browned to your liking, increase the grill temperature to 375°F and roast for several minutes at the higher temperature. Grill: 375 °F
9. Tent the duck loosely with foil and allow it to rest for 30 minutes.
10. Remove the butcher's twine and carve. Enjoy!

Smoked Spiced Beef Pot Roast

Servings: 8
Cooking Time: 30 Minutes

Ingredients:

- roast
- 2 tbsp sugar
- 1 tbsp kosher salt
- 1 tbsp ground black pepper
- 1 tbsp garlic powder
- 1 tbsp smoked paprika
- 1 tsp cayenne pepper

Directions:

1. Drizzle roast with maple syrup and apply rub.
2. Randomly insert garlic chunks into roast approximately 1-2" deep.
3. Supply your smoker with wood pellets and follow the start-up procedure. Preheat the grill, with the lid closed, to 450 °F.
4. Set roast on grate in roast pan and fill bottom 1/2" with beef broth and red wine.
5. Roast at 450 °F for about 30 minutes.
6. Remove roast.
7. Drop cooking temp to 225°F.
8. Replace the roast and cook your desired temp. 130°F for med rare.
9. Tent for 5-10 minutes and slice away.

Smoked Duck Breast Bacon

Servings: 6
Cooking Time: 30 Minutes

Ingredients:

- 4 Cup water
- 2 Cup freshly brewed strong coffee
- 1 Cup kosher salt
- 1/2 Cup dark brown sugar
- 2 1/2 Tablespoon curing salt
- 1/4 Cup molasses
- 3 Cup ice
- 3 Pound skin-on duck breasts

Directions:

1. Stir together 4 cups water with coffee, kosher salt, brown sugar, and curing salt in a container with a lid. Mix until solids are dissolved. Add the molasses and stir until completely dissolved. Add 3 cups ice and stir until cure is cold. (It's ok if all the ice doesn't melt completely.)
2. Add duck breasts to cure and weigh them down with a large plate to keep submerged. Place covered container in refrigerator for a minimum of 6 hours.
3. Remove from refrigerator, take breasts out of brine and discard brine. Rinse duck breasts under cold running water and pat dry.
4. Supply your smoker with wood pellets and follow the start-up procedure. Preheat the grill, with the lid closed, to 165° F.
5. Place duck breasts on grill grate and smoke for 2 hours. Grill: 165 °F
6. Cool duck completely, wrap in plastic wrap and place in refrigerator until ready to use.
7. To cook, slice breast thinly and fry in a pan just like you would pork bacon. Or slice breast thinly, place on Traeger set to 350°F and cook for 10 minutes per side. Enjoy! Grill: 350 °F

Grilled Lemon Skirt Steak

Servings: 1-2
Cooking Time: 5 Minutes

Ingredients:
- 2 Cloves Garlic, Chopped
- 1 Lemon, Juice
- 2 Tablespoons Mustard, Grainy
- 1/4 Cup Olive Oil
- 2 Tablespoons Java Chophouse Seasoning
- 2 Pounds Skirt Steak, Trimmed
- 1 Tablespoon Worcestershire Sauce

Directions:
1. In a small bowl, mix together the Java Chophouse Seasoning, oil, garlic, lemon juice, and Worcestershire. Generously rub the mixture all over the skirt steak and allow to marinate for 45 minutes.
2. Supply your smoker with wood pellets and follow the start-up procedure. Preheat the grill, with the lid closed, to 400° F.
3. Grill the skirt steaks for 3-5 minutes on each side or until the steak is done to the desired degree of doneness.
4. Remove the steaks from the grill and allow to rest for 5 minutes before slicing and serving.

Bbq Brisket Breakfast Tacos

Servings: 6
Cooking Time: 30 Minutes

Ingredients:
- 4 Pound leftover beef brisket
- 1/2 Teaspoon extra-virgin olive oil
- 1 green bell pepper, diced
- 1 Yellow Bell Pepper, diced
- 10 eggs
- 1/2 Cup milk
- salt and pepper
- 2 Cup shredded cheddar cheese
- flour tortillas

Directions:
1. Supply your smoker with wood pellets and follow the start-up procedure. Preheat the grill, with the lid closed, to 375° F.
2. Place leftover brisket in a double layer of foil and warm in grill. Grill: 375 °F
3. Coat the inside of a cast iron skillet with oil and preheat the skillet in the grill for 10 minutes. When skillet is hot, sauté diced peppers, stirring every few minutes until desired doneness.
4. While peppers are cooking, whisk together the eggs, milk, salt and pepper to taste. Add the beaten eggs to the skillet and scramble. Add cheese to the skillet when the eggs are almost done.

5. Remove eggs and heated brisket from grill. Serve eggs in a tortilla topped with brisket. Top with salsa or guacamole if desired. Enjoy!

Bbq Elk Shoulder

Servings: 4
Cooking Time: 240 Minutes

Ingredients:
- 6 Pound Elk, shoulder
- 12 Fluid Ounce beef broth
- 1 Whole meat injector
- 1 Tablespoon kosher salt
- 1 Tablespoon ground black pepper

Directions:
1. Take elk roast out of the fridge and allow to sit on counter for 30-60 minutes before cooking.
2. Supply your smoker with wood pellets and follow the start-up procedure. Preheat the grill, with the lid closed, to 225° F.
3. Inject the elk all over with beef broth. Combine salt and pepper and rub over entire roast.
4. Place on preheated grill and cook for 4 to 5 hours or until an instant read thermometer inserted in the thickest part of the meat registers 145°F. Remove from grill and allow to rest for 30 minutes before slicing. Grill: 225 °F Probe: 145 °F
5. Serve with baked beans, potato salad, coleslaw, white bread, Traeger BBQ sauce or your favorite BBQ sides and sauces. Enjoy!

Asian Steak Skewers

Servings: 6
Cooking Time: 80 Minutes

Ingredients:
- 1 1/2 lbs top sirloin steak
- 6 garlic cloves, minced
- 1 red onion
- 1/3 cup sugar
- 3/4 cup soy sauce
- 1 tbsp ground ginger
- 1/4 cup sesame oil
- 3 tbsp sesame seeds
- 1/4 cup vegetable oil
- Bamboo skewers

Directions:
1. Cut sirloin steak into cubes, about 1 inch.
2. Cut red onion into chunks similar in size to the sirloin steak cubes.
3. In a bowl, combine and whisk soy sauce, sesame oil, vegetable oil, minced garlic, sugar, ginger, and sesame seeds.

4. Add steak to sauce bowl and toss to coat until steak is covered in the sauce.

5. Marinate for at least 1 hour in a refrigerator (if you are in a rush it's ok to skip this part, but you'll sacrifice a little bit of flavor).

6. Preheat pellet grill to 350°F.

7. Thread marinated beef and red onion pieces onto bamboo skewers.

8. Grill the skewers, turning after about 4 minutes. Cook for 8 minutes total or until meat reaches your desired doneness.

Reverse Sear Tomahawk Chop

Servings: 4
Cooking Time: 60 Minutes

Ingredients:
- 2 Tbsp Coarsely Ground Black Peppercorns
- 1 Melted Stick Butter, Salted
- 2 Tablespoons Chophouse Steak Seasoning
- 2 Tbsp Sea Salt
- 2 Tsp Sprigs Fresh Thyme, Minced
- 2 Steaks, Tomahawk

Directions:
1. In a small mixing bowl, add the black peppercorns, sea salt, Chophouse Seasoning, and fresh thyme. Mix together and reserve half the seasoning.

2. Place your Tomahawk Steaks onto a sheet pan covered with butcher paper, foil, or parchment paper. Generously season the steaks with the seasoning mixture and rub it into the steaks. Let steaks sit for 1-2 hours if you would like the seasoning to penetrate the meat.

3. Supply your smoker with wood pellets and follow the start-up procedure. Preheat the grill, with the lid closed, to 225° F. If you're using a gas or charcoal grill, set it up for low, indirect heat. Insert a temperature probe into the thickest part of one of the tomahawk chops and place them in the center of the grill. If you have 2 temperature probes insert another into the other steak. Grill until the internal temperature of the steaks reaches 110°F, about 30-40 minutes.

4. Once the steaks reach their internal temperature, remove them from the grill and set aside. Increase the grill temperature to 450-500°F. While the grill is heating up melt one stick of butter and add the reserved seasoning to the melted butter. Mix together and brush the steaks with the butter making sure to evenly coat both sides of the steaks.

5. Place the steaks back on the grill over an open flame and sear for 3-5 min per side to reach 130°F-140°F. Remove the steaks from the grill, let them rest for 5 minutes and slice and serve immediately.

Garlic Standing Rib Roast

Servings: 4
Cooking Time: 240 Minutes

Ingredients:
- 1 tbsp cracked black pepper
- 1/2 tbsp granulated garlic
- 1/2 tbsp granulated onion
- 2 tbsp kosher salt
- 1 tbsp olive oil
- 2 tsp oregano, dried
- 1/2 tbsp parsley, dried
- 5 1/2 lbs prime rib roast, bone-in
- 2 tsp smoked paprika

Directions:
1. Place the roast in a glass baking dish. In a small mixing bowl, combine the salt, pepper, granulated garlic, granulated onion, parsley, oregano and smoked paprika. Season the entire roast with the spice blend, then cover and refrigerate overnight.

2. One hour prior to cooking, remove roast from the refrigerator, uncover, and let it sit out at room temperature.

3. Supply your smoker with wood pellets and follow the start-up procedure. Preheat the grill, with the lid closed, to 225° F. If using a gas or charcoal grill, set it up for low, indirect heat.

4. Place seasoned roast on a cast iron skillet, drizzle with olive oil, and transfer to the grill. Smoke the roast for 1 hour 45 minutes, or until internal temperature reaches 120° F. Remove from the grill and allow roast to rest for 15 minutes.

5. Increase the grill temperature to 450 F, then return roast to grill for an additional 10 to 15 minutes. Allow roast to rest for 15 minutes, slice and serve warm.

Braised Short Ribs

Servings: 2-4
Cooking Time: 240 Minutes

Ingredients:
- 4 beef short ribs
- Salt
- Freshly ground black pepper
- ½ cup beef broth

Directions:
1. Supply your smoker with wood pellets and follow the start-up procedure. Preheat the grill, with the lid closed, to 180°F.

2. Season the ribs on both sides with salt and pepper.

3. Place the ribs directly on the grill grate and smoke for 3 hours.

4. Pull the ribs from the grill and place them on enough aluminum foil to wrap them completely.

5. Increase the grill's temperature to 375°F.

6. Fold in three sides of the foil around the ribs and add the beef broth. Fold in the last side, completely enclosing the ribs and liquid. Return the wrapped ribs to the grill and cook for 45 minutes more. Remove the short ribs from the grill, unwrap them, and serve immediately.

Smoked Peppered Beef Tenderloin

Servings: 4
Cooking Time: 60 Minutes

Ingredients:
- 1 (2 to 2-1/2 lb) Snake River Farms Beef Tenderloin Roast, trimmed
- 1/2 Cup Dijon mustard
- 2 Clove garlic, minced to a paste
- 2 Tablespoon bourbon or strong cold coffee
- Jacobsen Salt Co. Pure Kosher Sea Salt
- coarse ground black and green peppercorns

Directions:
1. Lay the tenderloin on a large piece of plastic wrap.
2. Combine the mustard, garlic and bourbon in a small bowl. Slather the mixture evenly all over the tenderloin. Wrap in plastic and allow to sit at room temperature for 1 hour.
3. Unwrap the plastic wrap and generously season the tenderloin on all sides with the salt and ground black and green peppercorns.
4. Supply your smoker with wood pellets and follow the start-up procedure. Preheat the grill, with the lid closed, to 180° F.
5. Place the tenderloin directly on the grill grate and smoke for 60 minutes. Grill: 180 ˚F
6. Remove the tenderloin from the grill and set aside. Increase the grill temperature to 400˚F. Once the grill is hot, place the tenderloin back on the grill. Roast until the internal temperature reaches 130˚F, about 20 to 30 minutes depending on the thickness of the tenderloin. Do not overcook. Grill: 400 ˚F Probe: 130 ˚F
7. Let rest for 10 minutes before slicing. Enjoy!

Grilled Dill Pickle Tri Tip Steak

Servings: 4
Cooking Time: 300 Minutes

Ingredients:
- BBQ sauce
- dill pickles
- jalapeño
- to taste, java chophouse seasoning
- 2 tbsp mustard
- onion, sliced & minced
- 2 lbs tri tip steak

Directions:

1. Supply your smoker with wood pellets and follow the start-up procedure. Preheat the grill, with the lid closed, to 225° F. If using a gas or charcoal grill, set it up for low, indirect heat.
2. Rub the mustard all over the tri tip, then season with Java Chophouse.
3. Place the tri tip directly on the grill grates and smoke until the internal temperature reaches 165° F (about 2 1/2 hours).
4. Remove the tri tip from the grill and wrap it in butcher paper. Return the tri tip to the grill and continue to smoke until the internal temperature reaches 200° F (an additional 2 ½ to 3 hours).
5. Remove the tri tip from the grill, and rest for 30 minutes. Slice thin and serve with pickles, jalapeño, onion, and BBQ sauce, if desired.

Herb Chipotle Lamb

Servings: 6
Cooking Time: 120 Minutes

Ingredients:
- Black Pepper
- 1 Tbsp Chipotle Peppers, Crushed
- 3/4 Cup Extra-Virgin Olive Oil
- 3 Garlic, Cloves
- 2 Tbsp Italian Parsley
- 1 Rack Lamb Ribs
- ¼ Cup Applewood Bacon Rub
- 2 Tbsp Rosemary, Fresh
- 2 Tbsp Sage, Fresh
- 2 Tbsp Thyme, Fresh Sprigs

Directions:

1. For the dry rub: baste the lamb ribs with olive oil and season with the chipotle powder and black pepper. Let the lamb ribs rest for at least 15 minutes in the refrigerator.
2. Supply your smoker with wood pellets and follow the start-up procedure. Preheat the grill, with the lid closed, to 275° F.
3. For the wet rub: Blend rosemary, cilantro, Italian parsley, sage, thyme, and oregano with ¼ cup Extra Virgin Olive Oil, ¼ cup of Smoke Infused Applewood Bacon and 2-3 garlic cloves.
4. Apply the wet rub all over the lamb ribs.
5. Lay your lamb ribs bone side down on the grill and smoke until they reach an internal temp of 120-125°F.
6. Turn your grill temp up to 425°F and sear until it of 135-145°F.
7. Rest 10-15 minutes. Carve and enjoy!

Citrus Grilled Lamb Chops

Servings: 4 - 6
Cooking Time: 15 Minutes

Ingredients:

- 2 Tablespoons Chophouse Steak Seasoning
- 4 Finely Garlic Clove, Minced
- 2 Pounds Thick Cut Rib Chops Or Lamb Loin
- Juice From 1/2 Lemon
- Juice From 1/2 Lime
- ¼ Cup Olive Oil
- 3 Tablespoons Orange Juice
- ¼ Cup Red Wine Vinegar

Directions:

1. In a mixing bowl, whisk together all the ingredients and 2 tbsp Chophouse Steak. Place the lamb chops in a glass baking pan and pour the marinade over the top. Flip the chops over a few times to make sure that they are completely coated.
2. Cover the glass pan in aluminum foil and allow the lamb chops to marinade for 4-12 hours. Once the meat has finished marinating, drain off the excess marinade and discard.
3. Supply your smoker with wood pellets and follow the start-up procedure. Preheat the grill, with the lid closed, to 400° F. If you're using a gas or charcoal grill, set it up for medium high heat. Grill the chops for 5-7 minutes per side, then lower the temperature to 350°F or medium heat, and flip and grill for another 5-7 minutes.
4. Remove the lamb chops from the grill, cover in foil, and allow to rest for 5 minutes before serving.

Smoked Meatball Egg Sandwiches

Servings: 4
Cooking Time: 25 Minutes

Ingredients:

- 3/4 Cup Breadcrumbs
- 2 Cloves Garlic, Minced
- 1 & 1/2 Lb. Ground Chuck
- 1 Jar Of Your Favorite Marinara Sauce
- 1 Large Eggs
- ¼ Cup Onion
- ¼ Cup Parsley, Minced Fresh
- ½ Tsp Pepper
- 1 Tbsp Chop House Steak Seasoning
- Provolone Cheese, Sliced
- ½ Tsp Salt
- Shredded Mozzarella Cheese
- 4 Sub Rolls Or Baguettes (6"), Sliced
- 2 Tbsp Worcestershire

Directions:

1. In a larger mixing bowl, combine the ground chuck, onions, garlic, Chop House Steak seasoning, salt, pepper, fresh parsley, Worcestershire, and egg. Add the breadcrumb mixture and parmesan cheese to the bowl and fold it into meat until well combined.
2. Supply your smoker with wood pellets and follow the start-up procedure. Preheat the grill, with the lid closed, to 400° F. If you're using a gas or charcoal grill, set it up for medium high heat and add your cast iron pan to the grill to warm up.
3. Roll the meat mixture into balls about 1 ½ inches wide, roughly the size of golf balls. Place meatballs into the cast iron skillet. Cook for 15 minutes or until meatballs are fully cooked and beginning to brown.
4. Pour full jar of marinara into the cast iron pan and gently stir to coat meatballs. Let simmer for 10-15 minutes.
5. Tear off four sheets of aluminum foil and place a sliced bun in the center of each. Divide the meatballs with sauce among the rolls. Top each roll with provolone cheese slices and mozzarella, and wrap entire sandwich tightly in foil. Return to the grill and cook an additional 10 minutes or until cheese is melty and bread has toasted. Serve immediately and enjoy!

Diva Q's Herb-crusted Prime Rib

Servings: 4
Cooking Time: 300 Minutes

Ingredients:

- 1/4 Cup fresh rosemary leaves
- 1/4 Cup fresh flat-leaf parsley leaves
- 1/4 Cup minced garlic
- 1/4 Cup canola oil
- 3 Tablespoon Dijon mustard
- 2 Tablespoon finely ground black pepper
- 2 Tablespoon kosher salt
- 1 (5-7 lb) bone-in prime rib roast

Directions:

1. Combine rosemary, parsley, garlic, canola oil, mustard, salt and pepper in a food processor. Pulse until the herbs are finely chopped and the ingredients are combined.
2. Coat the entire prime rib with the herb mixture. Refrigerate prime rib uncovered, for 4 hours.
3. Supply your smoker with wood pellets and follow the start-up procedure. Preheat the grill, with the lid closed, to 250° F.
4. Place the prime rib bone side down on the grill. Roast meat (allowing 12 to 15 minutes per pound) until the internal temperature in the thickest part of the prime rib reaches 120°F-130°F for rare to medium-rare, about 5 hours. Begin taking the internal temperature every 45 minutes after the 2 hour mark. Grill: 250 °F Probe: 120 °F
5. Remove the prime rib from the grill, tent loosely with foil and let rest for 15 minutes before slicing. Enjoy!

Baked Venison Tater Tot Casserole

Servings: 4
Cooking Time: 40 Minutes

Ingredients:

- 2 Pound Venison, ground
- 2 Can Peas, canned
- 2 Can cream of mushroom soup
- 28 Ounce frozen tater tots

Directions:

1. Cook ground venison in a medium sauté pan over medium high until browned. Drain off excess fat and set venison aside.
2. In a 13x9 pan, combine venison, peas and soup. Top with tater tots.
3. Supply your smoker with wood pellets and follow the start-up procedure. Preheat the grill, with the lid closed, to 350° F.
4. Place casserole dish directly on grill grate and cook for 30 minutes. Serve hot, enjoy!

Roasted Venison Steaks By The Bowmars

Servings: 4
Cooking Time: 25 Minutes

Ingredients:

- 10 Whole Venison Steaks, 6oz
- 1 L Diet Sprite
- 6 Ounce Big Game Rub
- 2 Pound asparagus
- 3 Tablespoon Rub

Directions:

1. The night before, marinade the steaks with sprite and big game rub.
2. Supply your smoker with wood pellets and follow the start-up procedure. Preheat the grill, with the lid closed, to 350° F.
3. Remove steaks from marinade and pat dry. Place steaks directly on the grill grate and cook 10-15 minutes flipping once until the internal temperature reaches 125 degrees for medium rare. Grill: 350 °F
4. Sprinkle asparagus with Traeger Rub and add to Traeger. Cook for 10 minutes turning once.
5. Let steaks rest ten minutes before serving. Enjoy!

Marinated Flank Steak

Servings: 6
Cooking Time: 10 Minutes

Ingredients:

- 2lb (1kg) flank steak
- coarse salt
- freshly ground black pepper

- for the marinade
- ¼ cup red wine vinegar
- 2 tbsp Worcestershire sauce
- 1½ tsp coarse salt
- ½ cup extra virgin olive oil
- 2 garlic cloves, peeled and smashed with a chef's knife
- 1 small white onion, coarsely chopped
- 2 tbsp finely chopped fresh rosemary leaves
- sprigs of fresh rosemary

Directions:

1. In a jar with a tight-fitting lid, make the marinade by combining the vinegar, Worcestershire sauce, salt, and olive oil. Shake vigorously. Stir in the garlic, onion, and rosemary leaves.
2. Place the flank steak in a resealable plastic bag and pour the marinade over it. Turn the steak to thoroughly coat. Refrigerate for 8 to 24 hours, turning the bag periodically to thoroughly marinate the steak.
3. Supply your smoker with wood pellets and follow the start-up procedure. Preheat the grill, with the lid closed, to 232° F.
4. Remove the steak from the marinade and pat dry with paper towels. (Discard the marinade.) Season on both sides with salt and pepper.
5. Place the steak on the grate and grill until the internal temperature reaches 125 to 135°F (52 to 54°C), about 4 to 5 minutes per side.
6. Remove the steak from the grill and let rest for 5 minutes. Slice thinly against the grain with a knife held on a sharp diagonal. Transfer the slices to a platter and scatter rosemary sprigs over the top before serving.

Roasted Elk Jalapeno Poppers

Servings: 10
Cooking Time: 15 Minutes

Ingredients:

- 4 elk steaks
- 1 Cup Worcestershire sauce
- 1 Cup lime juice
- 1 Cup soy sauce
- 20 jalapeño peppers
- 10 Pieces bacon
- 12 Ounce herb & garlic flavored cream cheese, room temp
- Raw Honey

Directions:

1. Mix the lime juice, Worcestershire, and soy sauce together in a large bowl. Alternatively you can pour the ingredients directly into a large ziplock bag. Add sliced steak, cover and let sit for 4-6 hours to overnight.
2. Supply your smoker with wood pellets and follow the start-up procedure. Preheat the grill, with the lid closed, to 350° F.

3. Remove the steak from the marinade and thinly slice into bite-sized pieces so they are approximately the same width and length as the jalapeños.

4. Cut the jalapeños in half lengthwise; remove seeds and center membrane and set aside.

5. Cut the bacon in half crosswise. Set aside.

6. Spoon cream cheese equally into all jalapeño halves.

7. Lay one slice of marinated elk on top of each jalapeño. Wrap each jalapeño popper with one piece of bacon and secure with a toothpick if needed.

8. Place on grill, cut side up for 10-15 minutes or until elk is cooked and jalapeños are tender and lightly charred.

9. Remove from the grill and optionally drizzle with honey before serving. Enjoy!

Pastrami

Servings: 6-8
Cooking Time: 960 Minutes

Ingredients:
- 1 (8-pound) corned beef brisket
- 2 tablespoons yellow mustard
- 1 batch Espresso Brisket Rub
- Worcestershire Mop and Spritz, for spritzing

Directions:
1. Supply your smoker with wood pellets and follow the start-up procedure. Preheat the grill, with the lid closed, to 225°F.

2. Coat the brisket all over with mustard and season it with the rub. Using your hands, work the rub into the meat. Pour the mop into a spray bottle.

3. Place the brisket directly on the grill grate and smoke until its internal temperature reaches 195°F, spritzing it every hour with the mop.

4. Pull the corned beef brisket from the grill and wrap it completely in aluminum foil or butcher paper. Place the wrapped brisket in a cooler, cover the cooler, and let it rest for 1 or 2 hours.

5. Remove the corned beef from the cooler and unwrap it. Slice the corned beef and serve.

Texas Smoked Brisket

Servings: 12-15
Cooking Time: 960 Minutes

Ingredients:
- 1 (12-pound) full packer brisket
- 2 tablespoons yellow mustard
- 1 batch Espresso Brisket Rub
- Worcestershire Mop and Spritz, for spritzing

Directions:

1. Supply your smoker with wood pellets and follow the start-up procedure. Preheat the grill, with the lid closed, to 225°F.

2. Using a boning knife, carefully remove all but about ½ inch of the large layer of fat covering one side of your brisket.

3. Coat the brisket all over with mustard and season it with the rub. Using your hands, work the rub into the meat. Pour the mop into a spray bottle.

4. Place the brisket directly on the grill grate and smoke until its internal temperature reaches 195°F, spritzing it every hour with the mop.

5. Pull the brisket from the grill and wrap it completely in aluminum foil or butcher paper. Place the wrapped brisket in a cooler, cover the cooler, and let it rest for 1 or 2 hours.

6. Remove the brisket from the cooler and unwrap it.

7. Separate the brisket point from the flat by cutting along the fat layer and slice the flat. The point can be saved for burnt ends (see Sweet Heat Burnt Ends), or sliced and served as well.

Korean Style Bbq Prime Ribs

Servings: 5
Cooking Time: 480 Minutes

Ingredients:
- 3 lbs beef short ribs
- 2 tbsp sugar
- 3/4 cup water
- 1 tbsp ground black pepper
- 3 tbsp white vinegar
- 2 tbsp sesame oil
- 3 tbsp soy sauce
- 6 cloves garlic, minced
- 1/3 cup light brown sugar
- 1/2 yellow onion, finely chopped

Directions:
1. Combine soy sauce, water, and vinegar in a bowl. Mix and whisk in brown sugar, white sugar, pepper, sesame oil, garlic, and onion. Whisk until the sugars have completely dissolved

2. Pour marinade into large bowl or baking pan with high sides. Dunk the short ribs in the marinade, coating completely. Cover marinaded short ribs with plastic wrap and refrigerate for 6 to 12 hours3. Preheat pellet grill to 225°F.

3. Remove plastic wrap from ribs and pull ribs out of marinade. Shake off any excess marinade and dispose of the contents left in the bowl.

4. Place ribs on grill and cook for about 6-8 hours, until ribs reach an internal temperature of 203°F. Measure using a probe meat thermometer

5. Once ribs reach temperature, remove from grill and allow to rest for about 20 minutes. Slice, serve, and enjoy!

Bbq Burnt End Sandwich

Servings: 2

Cooking Time: 480 Minutes

Ingredients:

- 1 point cut brisket
- Beef Rub
- 1/2 Cup beef broth
- 1 Cup Texas Spicy BBQ Sauce
- 4 Slices Monterey Jack cheese
- 4 burger buns

Directions:

1. Supply your smoker with wood pellets and follow the start-up procedure. Preheat the grill, with the lid closed, to 250° F.

2. Trim excess fat off brisket point. Season brisket point liberally with Traeger Beef rub.

3. Place brisket point directly on the grill grate. Cook until it reaches an internal temperature of 170°F, approximately 4 to 5 hours. Grill: 250 °F

4. Remove brisket from grill and cut into 1-inch cubes. Add the beef broth to the pan with the cubed brisket. Cover pan with aluminum foil.

5. Place pan in grill and cook for 90 minutes. Grill: 250 °F

6. Remove the foil and add Traeger Texas Spicy BBQ sauce. Stir and put back on the grill, uncovered, for an additional 45 minutes. Remove from grill. Grill: 250 °F

7. Top each bun with the burnt ends, cheese, and additional BBQ sauce. Enjoy!

Smoked Black Pepper Beef Ribs

Servings: 4-6

Cooking Time: 330 Minutes

Ingredients:

- 1/4 Cup Hot Sauce
- Kosher Salt
- Coarse Black Pepper
- Your Favorite Beef Rib Rub Or Sweet Heat Rub
- 4 Pound Rib(S)

Directions:

1. Supply your smoker with wood pellets and follow the start-up procedure. Preheat the grill, with the lid closed, to 250° F.

2. Peel the membrane off the bone side and remove excess fat.

3. Rub the ribs down with hot sauce and season generously with Sweet Heat, salt, and pepper.

4. Place the ribs on the grill. Then, insert your meat probe before closing the lid to cook.

5. Check on your ribs after 3-4 hours. If one side is cooking faster than the other, rotate them.

6. Once the beef reaches 195°F, start probe testing the ribs for doneness. Because the finished temperature can vary, do a check with each time the temperature increases by 3°F.

7. To probe test: insert the meat probe vertically in between the bones to push through the second membrane on the bottom. The meat should have a consistent butter like tenderness throughout the rack with a final internal temp ranging from 200°F – 205°F.

8. Once the ribs finish cooking, remove from the grill to let them rest.

9. To let the ribs rest: wrap them tightly in foil. Then, wrap in a towel and place in a dry, empty cooler for 1 hour.

10. Slice between the bones to serve and enjoy!

Herb Grilled Venison Stew

Servings: 4 - 6

Cooking Time: 210 Minutes

Ingredients:

- 2 Bay Leaves
- 2 Cups Beef Stock
- 3 Carrots, Chopped
- 2 Cups Cauliflower Florets
- ¼ Tsp Cayenne Pepper
- 2 Celery Stalks, Chopped
- 4 Garlic Cloves, Minced
- 1 Tbsp Italian Parsley
- ¼ Tsp Marjoram, Dried
- 2 Tbsp Olive Oil
- 1 Onion, Chopped
- 1 Tsp Pulled Pork Rub
- 1 Cup Red Wine
- 1 Tsp Chopped Rosemary, Fresh
- (To Taste) Salt And Pepper
- 2 Cups Chopped Spinach
- 2 Sweet Potatoes, Diced
- 2 Tbs Tomato Paste
- ½ Cup Tomatoes, Canned And Diced
- 2 Lbs. Venison Stew Meat, Cut Into 1" Cubes
- 1 Cup Zucchini, Largely Diced

Directions:

1. Supply your smoker with wood pellets and follow the start-up procedure. Preheat the grill, with the lid open, to 400° F. If using a gas or charcoal grill, set heat to medium-high heat.

2. Place cast iron Dutch oven directly on grill grates and heat olive oil until shimmering. Add onion, celery, carrot, and garlic and cook, stirring constantly, for about 5-10 minutes or until onion is translucent.

3. Increase heat on the grill to 500° F. Add venison to the pot and cook until browned on all sides. Add the red wine and allow to simmer for 2 minutes.

4. Add tomato paste, beef stock, mushrooms, sweet potato, tomatoes, rosemary, Pulled Pork Rub, sage, marjoram, cayenne, salt, pepper and bay leaves and mix well to combine. Cover pot,

reduce temperature to 300° F and let the stew simmer for at least 2.5 to 3 hours.

5. Remove lid and stir in the cauliflower, spinach, and zucchini. Return cover to pot and simmer an additional 15 minutes. Stir in parsley and serve hot.

Grass-fed Beef Burgers

Servings: 4
Cooking Time: 30 Minutes

Ingredients:
- 2 Pound grass-fed ground beef
- 4 Teaspoon kosher salt
- 4 Slices provolone cheese
- 4 brioche burger buns
- 4 Slices Tomato
- Burger Toppings Of Your Choice

Directions:
1. Divide grassfed beef into four portions. To not overwork the meat, remove from the package and directly shape into burger patties about 5" (12cm) across- do not knead the meat. Sprinkle each burger with one teaspoon Kosher salt divided one half on each side.
2. Supply your smoker with wood pellets and follow the start-up procedure. Preheat the grill, with the lid closed, to 415° F.
3. Lay the hamburgers on the grill grate. Cook for 12 minutes for medium rarer- the exterior should be nicely browned. Thermometer should be placed into the center of the burger and should register 130°F(55 C). Grill: 415 °F Probe: 130 °F
4. During the last few minutes of cooking, add provolone slices to burgers and place buns on the grill to toast. Serve with condiments. Enjoy!

London Broil

Servings: 4
Cooking Time: 16 Minutes

Ingredients:
- 1 (1½- to 2-pound) London broil or top round steak
- ¼ cup soy sauce
- 2 tablespoons white wine
- 2 tablespoons extra-virgin olive oil
- ¼ cup chopped scallions
- 2 tablespoons packed brown sugar
- 2 garlic cloves, minced
- 2 teaspoons red pepper flakes
- 1 teaspoon freshly ground black pepper

Directions:
1. Using a meat mallet, pound the steak lightly all over on both sides to break down its fibers and tenderize. You are not trying to pound down the thickness

2. In a medium bowl, make the marinade by combining the soy sauce, white wine, olive oil, scallions, brown sugar, garlic, red pepper flakes, and black pepper
3. Put the steak in a shallow plastic container with a lid and pour the marinade over the meat. Cover and refrigerate for at least 4 hours.
4. Remove the steak from the marinade, shaking off any excess, and discard the marinade
5. Supply your smoker with wood pellets and follow the start-up procedure. Preheat, with the lid closed, to 350°F6. Place the steak directly on the grill, close the lid, and smoke for 6 minutes. Flip, then smoke with the lid closed for 6 to 10 minutes more, or until a meat thermometer inserted in the meat reads 130°F for medium-rare
6. Let the steak rest for about 10 minutes before slicing and serving. The meat's temperature will rise by about 5 degrees while it rests

New York Strip Steaks With Blue Cheese Butter

Servings: 4
Cooking Time: 8 Minutes

Ingredients:
- 4 boneless New York strip steaks, each about 12oz (340g) and 1 inch (2.5cm) thick
- coarse salt
- freshly ground black pepper
- for the butter
- 8 tbsp unsalted butter, at room temperature
- 1 garlic clove, peeled and finely minced
- ⅓ cup crumbled blue cheese, mashed with a fork
- 1 tbsp minced chives
- 1 tsp Worcestershire sauce
- ½ tsp fresh coarsely ground black pepper

Directions:
1. Approximately 45 minutes before you're ready to cook, lightly season the steaks on both sides with salt and pepper. Place the steaks on a wire rack on a rimmed sheet pan.
2. Supply your smoker with wood pellets and follow the start-up procedure. Preheat the grill, with the lid closed, to 450° F.
3. In a small bowl, make the blue cheese butter by combining the ingredients. Mix thoroughly. Set aside.
4. Place the steaks on the grate at an angle to the bars. Sear until the internal temperature reaches 130°F (54°C), about 3 to 4 minutes per side, turning once.
5. Transfer the steaks to a platter and immediately top with a spoonful of room temperature blue cheese butter. Tent the steaks with aluminum foil for 2 to 3 minutes to encourage the butter to melt before serving.

RECIPE INDEX

Cold-smoked Salmon Gravlax 63
Cornbread Chicken Stuffing 21
Cornish Game Hen 147
County Fair Turkey Legs 139
Cran-apple Tequila Punch With Smoked Oranges 88
Cranberry Turkey Breast 151
Crème Brûlée 33
Crispy Chicken Quarters 143
Crispy Spiced Chicken Wings 129
Crown Roast Of Pork 117
Crust Chicken Pizza 150
Cuban Onion Pork Sandwich 99
Cured Cold-smoked Lox 69

D
Dark Chocolate Brownies With Bacon-salted Caramel 17
Delicious Asian Bbq Wings 149
Delicious Deviled Crab Appetizer 80
Delicious Peanut Butter Cookies 29
Delicious Pellet Grill Cornbread 18
Delicious Reverse Seared Picanha Steak 192
Delicious Smoked Bone-in Pork Chops 100
Delicious Smoked Candied Pecan Pie 35
Delicious Smoked Trout 50
Deviled Eggs With Smoked Paprika 77
Diva Q's Herb-crusted Prime Rib 204
Double Chocolate Chip Brownie Pie 15
Double Vanilla Chocolate Cake 28
Double-smoked Cheese Potatoes 169
Dry Brine Traeger Turkey 140
Dublin Delight Cocktail 90
Duck Breast With Pomegranate Sauce 150

E
Eggs Ham Benedict 27
Eyeball Cookies 22

F
Fajita Style Mexican Hot Dogs 191
Fig Glazed Chicken Stuffed Cornbread 143
Fig Slider Cocktail 87
First-timer's Pulled Pork 96
Flavour Fire Spiced Shrimp 66
Flavour Texas Twinkies 194

Flavoured Hibachi Chicken 129
Florentine Shrimp Al Cartoccio 69
Fried Chicken Sliders 133

G
Garden Gimlet Cocktail 85
Garlic Beef Meatballs 189
Garlic Blackened Catfish 59
Garlic Blackened Salmon 48
Garlic Grilled Shrimp Skewers 63
Garlic Lemon Pepper Chicken Wings 18
Garlic Parmesan Grilled Filet Mignon 195
Garlic Sriracha Buffalo Chicken Wings 128
Garlic Standing Rib Roast 202
Grass-fed Beef Burgers 208
Green Bean Casserole 178
Green Bean Casserole Circa 1955 29
Green Bell Pepper Cheese Steak Burger 191
Green Chile Chicken Enchiladas 130
Green Goddess Chicken Legs 135
Grilled Albacore Tuna With Potato-tomato Casserole 58
Grilled Apple Pie 18
Grilled Asparagus & Honey-glazed Carrots 167
Grilled Asparagus And Hollandaise Sauce 158
Grilled Asparagus And Spinach Salad 161
Grilled Bacon Dog 116
Grilled Bbq Pork Chops 102
Grilled Beer Cabbage 177
Grilled Beer Cheese Dip 16
Grilled Bell Pepper Flank Steak Fajitas 197
Grilled Blackened Saskatchewan Salmon 72
Grilled Blood Orange Mimosa 83
Grilled Bourbon Pecan Pie 32
Grilled Broccoli Rabe 176
Grilled Cabbage Steaks With Warm Bacon Vinaigrette 179
Grilled Chicken Wings 144
Grilled Chili-lime Corn 174
Grilled Chipotle Chicken Skewers 155
Grilled Corn On The Cob With Parmesan And Garlic 159
Grilled Crab Legs With Herb Butter 53

London Broil 208

M

Mandarin Chicken Breast 131

Mango Rice Wine Thai Shrimp 60

Maple Syrup Bacon Wrapped Tenderloin 114

Maple Syrup Pancake Casserole 42

Marbled Brownies With Amaretto & Ricotta 39

Marinated Flank Steak 205

Mashed Red Potatoes 168

Mesquite Smoked Brisket 186

Mexican Black Bean Cornbread Casserole 32

Mexican Mahi Mahi With Baja Cabbage Slaw 61

Mezcal Shrimp With Salsa De Molcajete 47

Mini Sausage Rolls 109

Mint Butter Chocolate Chip Cookies 37

Moules Marinières With Garlic Butter Sauce 66

N

New York Strip Steaks With Blue Cheese Butter 208

O

Onion Cheese Nachos 15

Onion Pork Shoulder 119

Onion Turkey Burger Sliders 143

Orange & Maple Baked Ham 111

Oysters In The Shell 49

P

Pacific Northwest Salmon 63

Parmesan Roasted Cauliflower 162

Pastrami 206

Peanut Butter Chicken Wings 141

Peper Fish Tacos 71

Peppered Beef Tenderloin 192

Pickled-pepper Pork Chops 110

Pig Pops (sweet-hot Bacon On A Stick) 78

Pigs In A Blanket 77

Pineapple Cake 43

Pineapple-pepper Pork Kebabs 113

Pizza Bites 43

Pork & Pepperoni Burgers 104

Pork Tenderloin 118

Portobello Marinated Mushroom 168

Potluck Salad With Smoked Cornbread 165

Pound Cake 36

Pretzel Rolls 42

Prosciutto-wrapped Scallops 56

Pull-apart Dinner Rolls 45

Pulled Beef 197

Pulled Pork Loaded Nachos 75

Pulled Pork Shoulder And Chicken 98

Pulled Pork Taquitos With Sour Cream 115

Pumpkin Bread 26

Q

Quick Baked Dinner Rolls 28

R

Red Potato Grilled Lollipops 161

Reuben Sandwich 182

Reverse Sear Tomahawk Chop 202

Reverse-seared Elk Tenderloin With Green Peppercorn Sauce 185

Roasted Artichokes With Garlic Butter 163

Roasted Asparagus 157

Roasted Bacon Weave Holiday Ham 96

Roasted Beer Can Chicken 137

Roasted Beet & Bacon Salad 170

Roasted Chicken With Wild Rice & Mushrooms 148

Roasted Do-ahead Mashed Potatoes 180

Roasted Duck 200

Roasted Duck With Cherry Salsa 147

Roasted Elk Jalapeno Poppers 205

Roasted Fall Vegetables 175

Roasted Garlic Herb Fries 164

Roasted Green Beans With Bacon 169

Roasted Halibut With Spring Vegetables 64

Roasted Hasselback Potatoes By Doug Scheiding 156

Roasted Jalapeno Cheddar Deviled Eggs 170

Roasted Jalapeño Poppers 169

Roasted Mashed Potatoes 156

Roasted New Potatoes 167

Roasted New Potatoes With Compound Butter 177

Roasted Olives 161

Roasted Pickled Beets 171

Roasted Pork With Balsamic Strawberry Sauce 125

Roasted Potato Poutine 156

Roasted Prime Rib With Mustard And Herbs De Provence 199
Roasted Prosciutto Stuffed Chicken 145
Roasted Pumpkin Seeds 160
Roasted Red Pepper Dip 79
Roasted Red Pepper White Bean Dip 180
Roasted Sheet Pan Vegetables 166
Roasted Stuffed Turkey Breast 141
Roasted Sweet Potato Steak Fries 166
Roasted Tin Foil Dinners 127
Roasted Tomatoes 173
Roasted Tomatoes With Hot Pepper Sauce 178
Roasted Vegetable Napoleon 168
Roasted Venison Steaks By The Bowmars 205
Roasted Whole Chicken 131
Rosemary Cranberry Apple Sage Stuffing 16
Rub-injected Pork Shoulder 103
Ryes And Shine Cocktail 83

S

Salt & Pepper Dinosaur Bones 198
Salt Crusted Baked Potatoes 157
Salt-crusted Prime Rib 184
Savory Beaver Tails 26
Savory Cheesecake With Bourbon Pecan Topping 22
Savory Jerk Chicken Wings 134
Savory Smoked Brisket 195
Savory Smoked Chicken Breasts 128
Savory Smoked Turkey Legs 131
Savory-sweet Turkey Legs 136
Seared Ahi Tuna Steak With Soy Sauce 71
Seared Bluefin Tuna Steaks 49
Shrimp Cabbage Tacos With Lime Cream 51
Sicilian Stuffed Mushrooms 178
Simple Cream Cheese Sausage Balls 77
Simple Smoked Baby Backs 102
Sirloin Steak 183
Skillet Buttermilk Cornbread 24
Skillet Potato Cake 176
Skinny Smoked Chicken Breasts 145
Slow Smoked And Roasted Prime Rib 198
Slow Smoked Rib-eye Roast 184
Smoke And Bubz Cocktail 94

Smoked & Loaded Baked Potato 173
Smoked Apple Cider 83
Smoked Asparagus Soup 159
Smoked Bacon Roses 106
Smoked Barnburner Cocktail 90
Smoked Bbq Onion Brussels Sprout 179
Smoked Beef Back Ribs 186
Smoked Beer Garlic Chicken 149
Smoked Beet-pickled Eggs 174
Smoked Berry Cocktail 82
Smoked Black Pepper Beef Cheeks 195
Smoked Black Pepper Beef Ribs 207
Smoked Blackberry Pie 44
Smoked Blt Sandwich 98
Smoked Bourbon Jerky 196
Smoked Brisket With Traeger Coffee Rub 190
Smoked Cashews 78
Smoked Cedar Plank Salmon 50
Smoked Cheese 79
Smoked Cheese Beef Burgers 182
Smoked Chicken Fajita Quesadillas 140
Smoked Chicken Leg & Thigh Quarters 139
Smoked Chili Con Queso By Doug Scheiding 109
Smoked Cold Brew Coffee 89
Smoked Corned Beef & Cabbage 187
Smoked Corned Beef Brisket 196
Smoked Crab Legs 57
Smoked Deviled Eggs 139
Smoked Ditch Chicken 137
Smoked Drumsticks 139
Smoked Duck Breast Bacon 200
Smoked Eggnog 94
Smoked Fish Chowder 55
Smoked Grape Lime Rickey 92
Smoked Hibiscus Sparkler 89
Smoked Honey Chicken Drumsticks 127
Smoked Hot Buttered Rum 84
Smoked Ice Mojito Slurpee 86
Smoked Irish Coffee 91
Smoked Jacobsen Salt Margarita 89
Smoked Jalapeño Poppers 168
Smoked Lemon Cheesecake 25
Smoked Macaroni Salad 160

Smoked Mango Shrimp 56
Smoked Mashed Potatoes 174
Smoked Meatball Egg Sandwiches 204
Smoked Mulled Wine 85
Smoked Mushrooms 167
Smoked Parmesan Herb Popcorn 163
Smoked Peppered Beef Tenderloin 203
Smoked Pickled Green Beans 165
Smoked Pico De Gallo 159
Smoked Pineapple Hotel Nacional Cocktail 90
Smoked Plum And Thyme Fizz Cocktail 93
Smoked Pomegranate Lemonade Cocktail 85
Smoked Pork Tomato Tamales 124
Smoked Pulled Chicken 152
Smoked Pumpkin Spice Latte 87
Smoked Quarters 154
Smoked Raspberry Bubbler Cocktail 94
Smoked Rendezvous Ribs 101
Smoked Ribs 119
Smoked Salmon Candy 61
Smoked Salt Cured Lox 50
Smoked Salted Caramel White Russian 88
Smoked Sangria 86
Smoked Seed Pastrami 187
Smoked Sirloin Roast Beef 192
Smoked Spiced Beef Pot Roast 200
Smoked Sugar Halibut 48
Smoked Texas Ranch Water 91
Smoked Texas Spicy Drumsticks 155
Smoked Trout 70
Smoked Turkey Jerky 134
Smoked Turkey Sandwich 80
Smoked Whole Chicken 143
Smoked Wings 145
Smoked, Salted Caramel Apple Pie 39
Smoker Wheat Bread 17
Smoke-roasted Halibut With Mixed Herb Vinaigrette 72
Smokin' Lemon Bars 44
Smoking Gun Cocktail 82
Smoky Apple Crepes 45
Smoky Crab Dip 56
Smoky Mountain Bramble Cocktail 95

Smoky Pork Tenderloin 120
Smoky Scotch & Ginger Cocktail 88
Sopapilla Cheesecake By Doug Scheiding 41
Sourdough Pizza 16
Spatchcocked Chicken With Toasted Fennel & Garlic 145
Spiced Carrot Cake 29
Spiced Coffee-rubbed Ribs 117
Spiced Cornish Hens With Cilantro Chutney 148
Spiced Leg Of Lamb Gyros 190
Spiced Lemon Cherry Pie 37
Spiced Orange Ribs 121
Spiced Pork Belly 112
Spiced Pulled Pork Nachos 118
Spiced Pulled Pork Shoulder 99
Spiced Smoked Kielbasa Dogs 192
Spiced Smoked Swordfish 61
Spicy Asian Brussels Sprouts 177
Spicy Chopped Brisket Sandwich 191
Spicy Crab Poppers 56
Spicy Lime Shrimp 58
Spicy Shrimp Skewers 70
Sriracha & Maple Cashews 80
St Louis Style Bbq Ribs With Texas Spicy Bbq Sauce 115
St. Louis Bbq Ribs 111
Steak Fries With Horseradish Creme 162
Strawberry Basil Daiquiri 20
Strawberry Mule Cocktail 84
Stuffed Jalapenos 160
Stuffed Pork Crown Roast 122
Succulent Lamb Chops 193
Summer Paella 67
Sunset Margarita 83
Sweet And Spicy Baked Pork Beans 35
Sweet And Spicy Pork Roast 98
Sweet And Spicy Smoked Wings 154
Sweet Cajun Wings 140
Sweet Cheese Muffins 26
Sweet Mandarin Salmon 62
Sweet Potato Marshmallow Casserole 165
Sweet Smoked Salmon Jerky 62
Swordfish With Sicilian Olive Oil Sauce 72

Printed in the USA
CPSIA information can be obtained
at www.ICGtesting.com
LVHW071635020224
770787LV00003B/372